Studien zu Recht und Rechtskultur Chinas

Edited by
Björn Ahl, Universität zu Köln

Volume 9

Jasper Habicht

The Role of Campaigns in Law Enforcement

The Example of Sanfei Campaigns in Chinese Immigration Law

Nomos

The publication of this work was supported by the German Research Foundation (Deutsche Forschungsgemeinschaft, DFG) under grant AH 210/1-1 and the German–Chinese Jurists' Association (Deutsch-Chinesische Juristenvereinigung e.V., DCJV).

The Deutsche Nationalbibliothek lists this publication in the Deutsche Nationalbibliografie; detailed bibliographic data are available on the Internet at http://dnb.d-nb.de

a.t.: Köln, Univ., Diss., 2020

ISBN 978-3-8487-6670-3 (Print)
978-3-7489-0781-7 (ePDF)

British Library Cataloguing-in-Publication Data
A catalogue record for this book is available from the British Library.

ISBN 978-3-8487-6670-3 (Print)
978-3-7489-0781-7 (ePDF)

Library of Congress Cataloging-in-Publication Data
Habicht, Jasper
The Role of Campaigns in Law Enforcement
The Example of Sanfei Campaigns in Chinese Immigration Law
Jasper Habicht
362 pp.

ISBN 978-3-8487-6670-3 (Print)
978-3-7489-0781-7 (ePDF)

Onlineversion
Nomos eLibrary

D 38

1st Edition 2020

Acknowledgements

This work could not have been accomplished without the help of many people. First of all I would also like to thank Prof. Dr. Björn Ahl for generously including this work in the publication series "Studies on Chinese Law and Legal Culture". Above all, I thank him the great support and freedom he gave me as my doctoral supervisor during the drafting process, but also for the comments and criticism with which he accompanied the progress of the work. Furthermore, I am grateful for the opportunity to work and teach at the Chair of Chinese Legal Culture at the University of Cologne. However, I would also like to thank my other supervisors, Prof. Dr. Felix Wemheuer and Prof. Dr. Michaela Pelican, as well as Prof. Dr. Weiping Huang who chaired the examination committee. Many thanks go to my colleagues at the Institute of East Asian Studies at the University of Cologne, without whose support and help this work could not have been completed. Special thanks at this point go to Dr. Daniel Sprick, Rita Chan, Eva-Lena Richter and Pilar-Paz Czoske, who have discussed some challenging questions with me and who have helped me considerably in my research. I also would like to thank the many researchers around the world who have given me valuable information and advice on my research project. Last but not least, of course, my thanks also go to my family, who have supported and driven me forward over the many years.

This thesis was accepted by the Faculty of Arts and Humanities at University of Cologne in the winter semester of 2019/20 as an inaugural thesis for the award of a doctorate.

The research this book is based on and its publication have been made possible by a grant from the German Research Foundation (DFG) for a research project entitled "Chinese immigration law and policy: perspectives of lawmakers, administrators and immigrants". The publication of this work was also supported by a funding from the German–Chinese Jurists' Association (DCJV).

Cologne, January 2020 Jasper Habicht

Contents

List of Tables and Figures

List of Tables

List of Figures

Chapter 1: Introduction

A. *Subject Matter*

> Along with the continuous expansion of China's rapid socio-economic development and opening up to the outside, international contacts are more and more frequent, the number of Chinese nationals exiting and foreign nationals entering China is increasing rapidly, and exit–entry administration work has experienced a number of new situations and problems: first, the large number of foreign nationals who come to China for travel, for visit, or to conduct business activities provide opportunities for China's socio-economic development, but also raises still higher challenges for national security and social management; second, the visa system and residence management system as regulated by current laws and regulations are still not perfect and loopholes exist in the administration; third, the problem of 'illegal entry, illegal stay and illegal employment' of foreign nationals (abbreviated as 'sanfei') has emerged in recent years, and the relevant [administrative] system has to be further improved by adopting focused measures.[1]

With this justification, the first draft for a revised *Exit–Entry Administration Law* was presented to the Standing Committee of the National People's Congress[2] in October 2011, emphasising that, albeit being in principle beneficial for the Chinese economy, the increasing influx of foreign nationals poses a potential threat to national security and the increasing problem of foreign nationals engaging in illegal activities in the context of immigration law calls for a revision of the current legal provisions. In Chinese literature, the protection of China's national security and public order are frequently highlighted as major aims of immigration legislation.[3] How are we to make sense of this statement that foreign nationals are beneficial for the Chinese economy on the one hand, but pose a threat to national security on the other? In the People's Republic of China, regulations on immigration issues were

---

1 *Guide to Interpretation and Application of the 'Exit–Entry Administration Law of the People's Republic of China'* (《中华人民共和国出境入境管理法》释义及实用指南) (2012), p. 230.

2 The National People's Congress is abbreviated with 'NPC' in certain titles of publications cited in this study.

3 E.g. SUN Zhihui (2013), p. 13. Indeed, the Chinese *Exit–Entry Administration Law* (2012) defines its aims by focusing on the interests of the state and only in its third article refers to the protection of rights of foreign nationals; Art. 3 *Exit–Entry Administration Law* (2012).

first codified in the 1960s, but laws to codify exit–entry administration were only promulgated in 1985, shortly after the introduction of the Chinese economic reform. The 1985 laws aimed to balance control of exit and entry and promotion of the economy. However, as almost 20 years had passed, other general legislation in the field of administrative law had been established and the old legal framework on exit–entry administration conflicted with the newer provisions. As a result, the hitherto existing provisions could no longer serve as a legal foundation for the enforcement of exit–entry administration law.

The above justification refers to increasing numbers of foreign nationals who have visited China in recent years, which pose a problem for exit–entry administration. Although, in the past, Chinese citizens mainly emigrated to Western countries, China's accession to the World Trade Organisation marked a shift in migration flows and China indeed has gradually become a destination country for international migrants from developed and developing countries. As can be seen from figure 1.1, immigration to China was very limited until 1980 when the reform and opening policy was initiated under DENG Xiaoping.[4] In 1978, only 229 600 entries of foreign nationals to China were reported.[5] But after 1980, the increase in entries of foreign nationals to mainland China accelerated until the 2000s. After China's accession to the World Trade Organisation in 2001, entries to China increased sharply until 2007 where, after a small drop around 2009, the figures seem to level at somewhat over 2.5 million entries per year. Only very recently, i. e. in 2016 and 2017, are figures again on the rise. While the increase of entries of foreign nationals to mainland China is remarkable, the figure is still relatively small when compared to the total Chinese population.[6] Even in 2016, when the number of foreign entries to China reached a maximum of around 2.8 million, this figure only amounts to 2.04 percent of the population of mainland China. In comparison, the ratio of foreign entries to the

4 Chinese: 邓小平.

5 Guofu LIU (2011), p. 3. Entries are measured in person-times, i. e. each entry of each person is counted.

6 As I want to compare the number of entries to mainland China to that of other countries, I calculated the migration ratio to account for the different size of these countries' population. The migration ratio is calculated by dividing the migrating population (i. e. entries of non-nationals in the present case) by the total population to the country of immigration. Note that the figures on population represent the amount of individuals in a certain area at a certain time, while the figures on entries may include multiple entries of the same person.

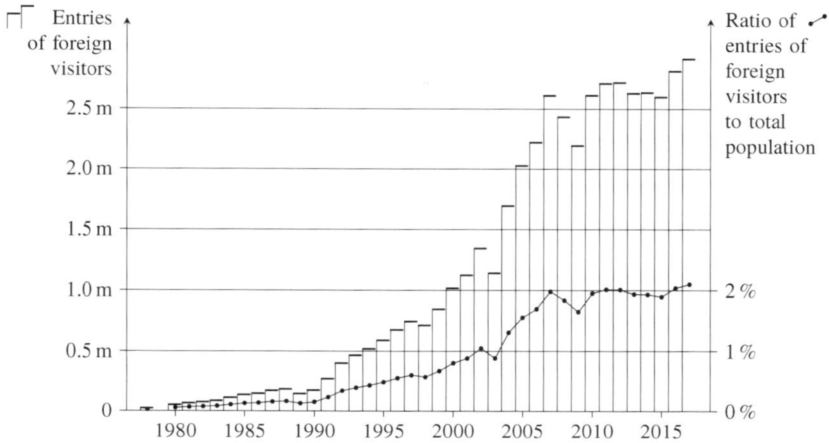

Figure 1.1: Immigration to China over time [11]

total population for the U. S. in 2016 is 23.40 percent;[7] for Germany, the ratio amounts to 43.01 percent for the same year.[8] Certainly there is a concentration of foreign nationals in the large cities and in the coastal areas of China: Beijing reports 3 548 000 entries of foreign visitors in 2016, yielding a ratio of foreign entries to the total population of 16.33 percent,[9] Guangzhou reports 3 296 800 entries, yielding a ratio of 37.87 percent.[10] Still, the ratios of Beijing and Guangzhou are comparatively low when compared internationally as the concentration of foreign nationals in big cities is not an exclusively Chinese phenomenon. Further, as figure 1.2 shows, net immigration is relatively low and declining, suggesting that more Chinese are exiting the country than foreign nationals are entering. Taking these numbers, immigration should be seen as a much less severe problem than emigration.

7 That is 75 608 000 arrivals on a population of 323 127 513; data taken from statistics of The World Bank.

8 35 555 000 arrivals on a population of 82 667 685; data taken from statistics of The World Bank.

9 Based on a population of 21 729 000; Tables 3-2, 17-3 *Beijing Statistical Yearbook* (北京统计年鉴) (2017).

10 Based on a population of 8 704 901; Tables 2-1, 15-20 *Guangzhou Statistical Yearbook* (广州统计年鉴) (2017).

11 Figures are taken from on-line statistics (China Statistical Yearbook) issued by the National Bureau of Statistics of China; *China Statistical Yearbook* (中国统计年鉴) (n. d.). No figures available for 1979. Figures only consider entries of foreign

However, major cities like Beijing and Shanghai recorded sharply increasing numbers of foreign visitors,[12] while cities in the Pearl River Delta like Guangzhou became centres of attraction for international migrants, especially for African traders.[13] The difficulties of the local police in Guangzhou to properly enforce immigration law attracted international media coverage, especially in 2009, when a Nigerian died after trying to escape a police raid, which resulted in protests by the local African community against the police,[14] and in 2012, when another Nigerian died while being held in police custody.[15] *Inter alia* to address such enforcement problems, a revision of the framework of immigration law was initiated in 2003. In the context of this revision process, experimental local regulations were promulgated especially in Guangdong province where the concentration of foreign nationals was particularly high.[16]

The problems in exit–entry administration were, however, not only tackled by revising the law: In parallel to the revision process of the *Exit–Entry Administration Law*, different regional specialised actions—so called *sanfei* campaigns—were deployed that aimed at thoroughly enforcing legal provisions and especially targeted illegal immigration. Such campaigns were deployed in particular between late 2003 to early 2004, around 2007 in the province of Guangdong and finally in Beijing where in 2012 a major *sanfei* campaign was given large-scale media coverage.[18] Most campaigns

---

visitors to mainland China; figures on population do not include Hong Kong, Macau or Taiwan. Figures of entries represent person-times (*renci*; Chinese: 人次).

12 Fulong Wu / Webber (2004); Jun Wang / Lau (2008).

13 Zhigang Li / Lyons / Brown (2012); Lyons / Brown / Zhigang Li (2012); Lan (2015).

14 Branigan (2009).

15 Branigan (2012).

16 According to data from the relevant statistical yearbooks, the ratio of entries of foreign nationals in comparison to the total population in Beijing amounts to 16.33 percent, while the ratio amounts to 37.87 percent in Guangzhou; Tables 3-2, 17-3 *Beijing Statistical Yearbook* (北京统计年鉴) (2017); Tables 2-1, 15-20 *Guangzhou Statistical Yearbook* (广州统计年鉴) (2017).

17 Figures are taken from on-line statistics (China Statistical Yearbook) issued by the National Bureau of Statistics of China; *China Statistical Yearbook* (中国统计年鉴) (n. d.). Figures do not consider visitors to or tourists from Hong Kong, Macau or Taiwan. Figures of entries and exits represent person-times (*renci*; Chinese: 人次).

18 E. g. Pan Xiaotian (2012), Cao (2012), or *Mid of May to End of August: Beijing Joins Forces to Clean Up 'Sanfei' Foreigners. Almost 200 000 Foreign Nationals Each Day* (5月中旬至8月底　北京集中清理'三非'外国人　每日实有近20万外国人) (2012).

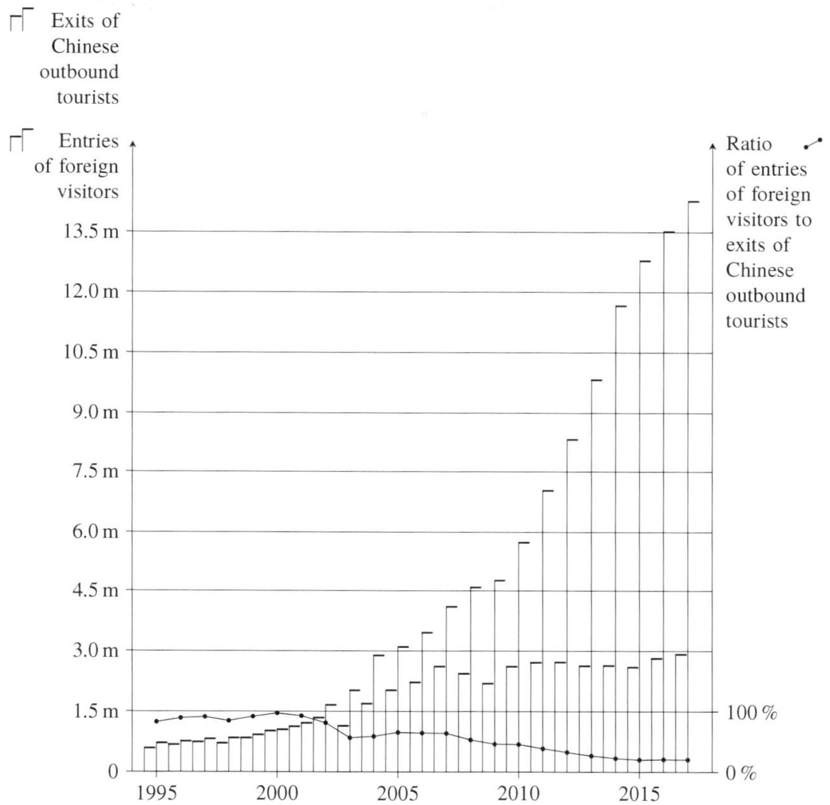

Figure 1.2: Immigration to China compared to emigration from China [17]

were accompanied by newspaper announcements that introduced to the public the aims of these campaigns and explained the subject of *sanfei* foreign nationals. Furthermore, in the context of several *sanfei* campaigns, the public was requested to report suspicious foreign nationals to the police. The campaigns did not cease with the promulgation of the new *Exit-Entry Administration Law* (2012), which suggests that they are an inherent part of the enforcement and implementation of Chinese immigration law.

The revised *Exit-Entry Administration Law* entered into force as of January 2013. It replaced the 1985 *Foreign Nationals Exit–Entry Administration Law* and 1985 *Citizens Exit–Entry Administration Law*. The new law features harsher penalties for the illegal employment of foreign nationals, for illegal entry and for illegal stay. It also announces the establishment of a platform that shall serve to share information between different authorities in charge of exit–entry administration. The new law further introduces a whistle-blower provision that asks Chinese nationals to report illegal activities of foreign nationals to the police. This new provision has obviously been taken from the experimental local regulations in Guangdong and apparently also stands in relation to mechanisms of reporting of suspicious foreign nationals in the context of campaigns.

Apart from focusing on illegal immigration, the new law on exit–entry administration also aims to promote the controlled attraction of foreign experts to China. The *Exit–Entry Administration Law* (2012) introduces a new visa category for foreign experts and incorporates and enhances the existing framework on permanent residence. In 2008, China launched the Thousand Talent Plan aiming to attract foreign talent and to strengthen China's innovative competitiveness in the world, and in 2017, a points system grading foreign nationals according to their salary, education, age, experience and language proficiency was introduced nationwide. The increased focus on selective immigration, i. e. the attraction of highly educated foreign talent while at the same time blocking low-skilled foreign nationals, in combination with tighter governance of illegal immigration, reflects a current trend of stronger control of the Chinese government in the area of immigration.[19] This tendency to combine increased control with selectively allowing for immigration in order to stablise the domestic economy is in line with policies in most developed countries, where such a trend possibly but not necessarily is a reaction to public hostility against immigrants, as findings in international comparative literature on immigration policies suggest.[20]

The focus of this study is exactly on this tightened control of immigration by the Chinese government, which becomes manifest in efforts to abolish regulatory failure in the context of immigration law. This study primarily looks at policies and regulations regarding illegal immigration and the prevention and prosecution thereof. In the context of the reform of Chinese immigration law between 2003 and 2012, the following aspects emerge to which special attention will be devoted throughout this study. First, the revision process of the law made use of local experimentation and took into consideration local implementation and experiences. Second, the institutional structure was supplemented by establishing entities with the aim of

19 Bork-Hüffer / Yuan-Ihle (2014), p. 592.
20 Hollifield / Martin / Orrenius (2014), p. 5, 26.

enhancing co-ordination and communication between different authorities that are responsible for the management of foreign nationals. Third, the campaigns targeting foreign nationals who illegally entered China, illegally stayed in China or were illegally employed in China stand in connection with the law-making process, as the new law introduces a reporting system that was previously applied during the campaigns. Fourth, the campaigns also stand in connection with the new establishment of entities to enhance co-ordination and communication between different responsible administrative organs. This study hypothesises that the revision process of the law and the deployment of campaigns were mainly driven by the perception of regulatory failure in the context of exit–entry administration and the resulting aim to increase control of the government over immigration.

B. State of Research

Guofu Liu analysed the legal framework shortly before the new unified *Exit–Entry Administration Law* came into force. He concludes that immigration legislation has developed from "restriction" until 1978 when the reform and opening policy was initiated to "relaxation" around 2000 with the accession of China to the World Trade Organisation.[21] The revision process of the current *Exit–Entry Administration Law* started in 2003, which demands an analysis of the genesis of the 2012 law. Chinese literature analyses shortcomings of the legal framework before 2013 by highlighting contradictions between the 1985 immigration framework and other laws, especially in the field of administrative law.[22] While these investigations contribute to an understanding of the problems that led to the revision of immigration law, there is no similar analysis of the current legal framework regarding exit-entry administration that focusses on the subject of illegal immigration. A comprehensive body of literature exists on international standards regarding national migration law that is of relevance also in the context of Chinese immigration law[23] and which can help us to assess the Chinese legal framework on immigration matters in comparison with international practice and standards.

---

21 Liu Xunzhi (2009).
22 E. g. Jiang Jianyun (2013).
23 E. g. Opeskin / Perruchoud / Redpath-Cross (2012), Chetail (2013), and Vohra (2007).

On the current immigration law, aspects like attraction of foreign talents and employment of foreign nationals have been the focus of recent research. Björn AHL and Pilar CZOSKE traced the legal framework regarding the employment of foreign nationals, especially foreign experts, in the context of the current 'Belt and Road' initiative that aims to foster China's economic relations with its neighbouring states.[24] Mimi ZOU highlights the precarious legal status of foreign nationals in China, with the focus on employment relations.[25] For the period prior to the promulgation of the revised law in 2012, Shanshan LAN analysed the influence of experimental local legislation on the legislation process of national law by focusing on undocumented Africans in China.[26] Experimentation in the context of law making has always been an important aspect of Chinese governance, as Sebastian HEILMANN analysed in detail for law-making processes after the era of MAO Zedong.[27]

In the field of migration, Zhigang LI, Michal LYONS and Alison BROWN conducted one of the first studies on foreign nationals in contemporary China with the focus on migrants from Africa living in so-called "ethnic enclaves" in Guangdong.[28] The subject of foreign nationals in Guangzhou has been studied extensively, but mostly from an anthropological point of view that does not take into consideration political and legal causes and implications in more detail.[29] Heidi Ø. HAUGEN and Shanshan LAN analyse the situation of Africans in China, especially Nigerians in Guangzhou;[30] other analyses focus on Koreans living in Beijing.[31] These investigations show the local implementation of immigration law and its implications for the local foreign population. They also highlight that the national legal framework often fails in its application to the very diverse and specific local situations. While most investigations focus on certain groups of foreign nationals in distinct geographical areas, only a few studies more generally analyse politics and regulations concerning foreign nationals in China.[32]

---

24 AHL / CZOSKE (2016).
25 ZOU (2016).
26 LAN (2015).
27 Chinese: 毛泽东. HEILMANN (2008).
28 Zhigang LI / LYONS / BROWN (2012).
29 One exception is probably BORK-HÜFFER / YUAN-IHLE (2014).
30 HAUGEN (2012); LAN (2017 a).
31 E. g. KIM (2003).
32 E. g. BORK-HÜFFER / YUAN-IHLE (2014) and a range of Chinese papers like WEI / ZHU Xudong (2009), HU Zhangwei / ZHAO Wei / CHEN Wanning (2011), ZHOU Xueguang (2012), or ZHANG Huide / LIU Hongbin / ZENG Fanjing (2014).

Most research conducted on political campaigns concentrates on the analysis of political campaigns before the economic reforms started in 1978. In his book *Yundong: Mass Campaigns in Chinese Communist Leadership*, Gordon A. BENNETT discusses the typologies of campaigns established by Frederick T. C. YU, Charles P. CELL and Alan P. L. LIU.[33] While LIU arranges campaigns chronologically into seven consecutive stages and classifies their function as specific or diffuse, BENNETT identifies seven concrete goals campaigns may aim for. Newer research, e. g. by Børge BAKKEN, Susan TREVASKES, and Murray S. TANNER, focuses on the *yanda* campaigns in 1983, 1996 and 2001, which had the goal to prosecute serious criminal acts severely and swiftly.[34] These studies mainly concentrate on the question of compliance with procedural standards and human rights. In the context of the *yanda* campaigns, the use of campaigns as a means of law enforcement is criticised by the authors, as legal provisions were often disregarded during such politically motivated campaigns. TREVASKES in contrast reaches the conclusion that campaigns in the post-MAO era seem to be affected by the developing institutionalisation and thus more and more abide by legal norms and adhere to legal proceedings.[35] Furthermore, literature debates whether campaigns after the initiation of the economic reforms are comparable to the political campaigns of the MAO era. HEILMANN e. g. rather refers to a "crisis mode" where an *ad-hoc* centralisation is temporarily established in order to swiftly enforce political decisions and which is regarded as counterpart to a "routine mode".[36] Sarah BIDDULPH states, as does Michael DUTTON, that campaigns in the post-MAO era were of a more punitive nature rather than revolutionary, and campaigns today have largely set aside the ideological character inherent to the early campaigns.[37] Although campaigns today may be less political in nature, their deployment as a political means to enforce directives or legal norms remains unchanged in the post-MAO era.[38]

After 2000, literature investigated campaigns as a means of law enforcement in areas other than criminal law. Sarah BIDDULPH and Benjamin VAN ROOIJ analysed the use of law-enforcement campaigns in the area of labour law and environment protection law respectively. Sarah BIDDULPH argues

33 Frederick T. C. YU (1967); CELL (1981); Alan P. L. LIU (1971).
34 BAKKEN (1993); TREVASKES (2002); TREVASKES (2003); Murray S. TANNER (2000).
35 See TREVASKES (2003) where the author shows that later *yanda* campaigns stricter adhered to legal provisions than earlier campaigns; see especially p. 275.
36 HEILMANN (2016), p. 150.
37 BIDDULPH (2017), p. 340; DUTTON (1995), p. 437.
38 See e. g. the concept of "managed campaigns" by PERRY (2011).

that policy and law in China influence each other and campaigns play an important role in lawmaking.[39] Benjamin VAN ROOIJ states that campaigns are increasingly used for law enforcement and denies the latent Maoist tendency of campaigns upheld by other academics like Donald CLARKE.[40] VAN ROOIJ still claims that campaigns exhibit certain elements that point to their political heritage. Finally, Xin Frank HE conducted an analysis of law-enforcement campaigns in the context of internal migration.[41] Substantial research of law-enforcement campaigns in the field of immigration law has, however, not been carried out. Furthermore, actions of public authorities against foreign nationals conducting illegal activities have been considered as campaigns or even as law-enforcement campaigns only by a few authors.

While literature often questioned the efficiency of campaign-style policing or rather looked at the history of campaigning and experimentation as means of government that stem from a revolutionary past,[42] recent research by Alex L. WANG interprets as symbolic legitimation the use of certain government measures, such as the issuance of programmatic norms, target setting merely to signal efforts, and campaign-style governance.[43] WANG argues that the public perceives the very action of the government as a proxy for performance outcomes when the said governance measures are applied and the actual efficiency of these measures is no more important. The more obscure and immeasurable performance outputs are, the more likely it is that government action is perceived as proxy for actual outcomes[44] and hence the more likely it is that performance-based legitimacy is achieved. In this context, uncertainty and populist notions can support symbolic legitimation.[45]

C. *Research Objectives and Methodology*

This study asks how the law-making process of the revised *Exit-Entry Administration Law* and the deployment of *sanfei* campaigns interact. As the *sanfei* campaigns refer to concepts laid out in legal norms, a relation between the law-making process and campaigns targeting illegal immigration is evid-

39 BIDDULPH / COONEY / Ying ZHU (2012).
40 See e. g. VAN ROOIJ (2002); CLARKE (1985).
41 Xin Frank HE (2003).
42 HEILMANN / PERRY (2011).
43 Alex L. WANG (2018), especially p. 717–721.
44 Alex L. WANG (2018), p. 724.
45 Alex L. WANG (2018), p. 724.

ent. Was the law-making process a major driver for campaign deployment, or was the law amended in a certain way to facilitate campaigns? I assume the existence of an overarching political aim to increase control over immigration issues that served as a common driver and resulted in both the deployment of *sanfei* campaigns and the revision of exit–entry administration law. This study analyses how the aim to strengthen control in the area of immigration administration has resulted in the use of different means to abolish or limit the extent of regulatory failure in exit–entry administration. I argue that parallel use of campaigns and institutional reforms including law revisions is a characteristic mode of governance in China that incorporates means stemming from the revolutionary past into contemporary administration and law enforcement and combines factual with symbolic governance.

By analysing these different means to target regulatory failure, this study contributes to and advances the above outlined research. First, it extends the research of LIU about the legal framework of exit–entry administration by adding information about the law-making processes of the 1985 and the 2012 laws. As the research of LIU focuses on the framework of immigration law prior to the revised *Exit–Entry Administration Law*, this study aims to analyse the current legal framework by locating the 2012 *Exit–Entry Administration Law* and its implementation regulations within the framework of administrative law. The analysis of legal rights and remedies that a foreign national may use against administrative punishment or compulsory enforcement measures, especially detention and deportation, will be supplemented by evaluating the Chinese legal norms against international standards. In order to be able to locate the law-making process of the 2012 *Exit–Entry Administration Law* in the overall development of immigration law in China, this study aims to carve out the drivers that led to the revision of the law. I argue that institutional reforms in the context of the reform and opening policy were the underlying driver of the revision process of the *Exit–Entry Administration Law*.

Second, this study aims to contribute to research on campaigns in the post-MAO era by elaborating on the most recent research on law-enforcement campaigns, especially developing the concepts coined by VAN ROOIJ and BIDDULPH, COONEY and ZHU. This study aims to identify the main drivers and targets of campaigns in the context of immigration law. I assume that these so-called *sanfei* campaigns not only target foreign nationals engaging in illegal activities, but also target regulatory failure of local-level authorities, and that the campaigns are interlinked with the law-making process of the *Exit–Entry Administration Law*. In this context, the campaigns against *sanfei* foreign nationals not only aim to directly enforce legal norms, but also address shortcomings that hamper the enforcement of national law at the local level. Furthermore, the campaigns as means of enforcement and the law as the legitimation of the campaigns are interlinked insofar as the law makes provisions that facilitate or even promote campaign-style enforcement. The findings of this study can finally serve a better understanding of the use of campaigns in the context of current Chinese politics and law.

This study is divided into five chapters, the first being this introduction. Chapter 2 analyses the historical foundations of current exit–entry administration law and traces the making of current legislation by focusing on the 1985 laws, experimental local legislation as well as on the current *Exit–Entry Administration Law* of 2012. Using mainly a historic approach, this chapter aims to shed light on the continuities and relations of the first exit–entry administration rules of 1964, the first legal framework in immigration law in 1985 and the current legislation on nationality and exit–entry administration by embedding the development of the legal framework into the context of institutional reform. It highlights the experimental approach applied in the revision process of immigration legislation. Finally, the chapter analyses the structure of different authorities responsible for exit–entry administration—especially the exit–entry administration offices in local police bureaus, the border control authorities, as well as the embassies and consulates abroad. It outlines persisting problems like insufficient flows of information or contradicting enforcement aims that result from the lack of co-operation between these authorities and focuses on the establishment of inter-administrative structures on different administrative levels that aim to tackle these problems.

Chapter 3 carves out the main aims and drivers of *sanfei* campaigns by applying the concept of regulatory failure campaigns. Information collection is conducted through a textual analysis of legal and political documents as well as newspaper articles. The temporal and geographical distribution of *sanfei* campaigns is used to analyse to what extent major political events and legislation in the context of immigration law triggered the deployment of campaigns. By analysing newspaper reports, announcements and internal documents, the organisation structure of *sanfei* campaigns is carved out, which is established in parallel to the administrative structure of relevant authorities and establishes inter-administrative structures that aim for the co-ordination of different relevant authorities. The third chapter further assesses the targets of *sanfei* campaigns, which not only address foreign nationals conducting illegal activities, but also local officials who are reluctant in enforcing legal provisions or engaging in collusion with each other, the local public or foreign nationals.

Chapter 4 embeds the current *Exit–Entry Administration Law* (2012) in the context of administrative law by applying a mainly teleological analysis of legal norms. This chapter explains administrative punishment and administrative compulsion in the field of exit–entry administration against the background of other relevant norms in administrative law as well as international standards. By carving out the legal definitions, legal consequences and legal remedies of illegal entry, illegal stay and illegal employment, this chapter analyses the legal concepts that underlie *sanfei* campaigns. This chapter also assesses the legal position of the foreign national towards the Chinese state and Chinese employers. Problems such as unclear definitions of the offences of illegal entry, illegal stay and illegal employment are pointed out as well as restricted access to judicial review especially in the context of detention and deportation. However, the role of courts in the context of employment of foreign nationals as well as enhanced legal remedies also suggest that the legal position of foreign nationals has improved in comparison with the old legal framework.

The final concluding chapter sums up the findings and answers the initial research question by taking into account the concept of symbolic legitimation.

D. Remarks Regarding Terminology

Certain fundamental terms that are used throughout this study need to be explained beforehand, because they are used in different ways throughout the literature or in different contexts.

I. 'Nationality' and 'Foreign Nationals'

The Chinese term *guoji*[46] literally means '(registered) membership to the state'. The second character *ji* refers to the book of ancestral records and is

46 Chinese: 国籍; note that this study is not talking about *minzu* (民族) which would be translated as 'ethnic minority' or 'nation' (in the sense of the 'people') rather than 'nationality'.

also used in the national household registration system called *huji*[47] which underlines the nature of a system of enrolment. Traditionally, state membership in ancient China was linked to descent regardless of the place of birth,[48] thus following primarily the principle of *ius sanguinis*. This principle was codified in the first Chinese law on nationality in 1909[49] and since then has been kept as a basic legal principle until today.[50]

The terms 'nationality' and 'citizenship' are often used interchangeably, even in legal literature and laws.[51] Chinese law does not differentiate between separate concepts of 'citizens' and 'nationals', in contrast to, e. g., U. S. law.[52] The official English version of the *Nationality Law of the People's Republic of China* (1980) translates *guoji*[53] with the term 'nationality'[54] to depict the legal concept of an individual being member of the state with full political rights.[55] Following the official use in this and other legal documents of the People's Republic of China, the term 'nationality' is preferred over 'citizenship' in this study. The Chinese term *guoji* is always translated with 'nationality'. According to its use in international law, 'nationality' describes the legal bond between an individual and the state

---

47 Chinese: 户籍.

48 Sainson / Cluzel (1910), p. 411.

49 Art. 1 *Nationality Ordinance* (1909) stated that, regardless of the place of birth, a child born to Chinese parents would have Chinese nationality. Only in cases where both parents were unknown or stateless, the place of birth determined the child's nationality according to Art. 2 *Nationality Ordinance* (1909).

50 See e. g. Art. 4 *Nationality Law* (1980) that states that a child shall have Chinese nationality if its parents are Chinese. Art. 5 *Nationality Law* (1980) further states that the child shall also have Chinese nationality if its parents are Chinese and it is born outside of China, unless its parents are settled abroad and the child acquires the foreign nationality due to the relevant laws of that state.

51 Shearer / Opeskin (2012), p. 95 f.

52 Hong Kong and Macau residents are considered Chinese nationals with a special status; *Nationality Law Implementation Explanations* (1996) and *Nationality Law Implementation Explanations* (1998). However, the *Nationality Law* (1980) and the *Exit–Entry Administration Law* (2012) apply equally to mainland residents as they apply to Hong Kong or Macau residents.

53 Chinese: 国籍.

54 Legislative Affairs Commission of the Standing Committee of the National People's Congress of the People's Republic of China (1987), p. 182; see as well the use in Hong Kong legislation as in Art. 24(1) *Hong Kong Basic Law* (1990).

55 According to the *Constitution*, "any individual holding the nationality of the People's Republic of China is a citizen of the People's Republic of China." Art. 33 *Constitution* (1982).

which defines a person as a member of this state.[56] Hence, 'nationality' is understood in this study as a legal concept emphasising its international aspect and without including cultural, ethnic, religious, or racial connotations, unless otherwise noted.

The terms 'foreign national' or 'foreigner' and 'alien' are interchangeably used in the literature to depict an individual who does not hold the nationality of the state in question, i. e. a person who is not a national of this state. Some official translations of the term *waiguoren*[57] use the term 'alien' while others use 'foreign national' or 'foreigner'. While 'alien' is sometimes defined as comprising foreign nationals and the stateless, such differentiation cannot be found in the Chinese sources. In Chinese law, the term *waiguoren* does not include the stateless as the provisions e. g. in the current *Nationality Law* suggest.[58] However, foreign nationals and the stateless are typically treated the same in Chinese law, except in some cases where a different treatment is technically necessary.[59] In this study, the term 'foreign national' will be preferably used as long as the term 'alien' is not used in more recent official translations.[60] Although, strictly speaking, the term 'foreign national' as translation of *waiguoren* should only depict foreign nationals, because of the equal treatment of the stateless in most legal provisions, the term 'foreign national' also refers to the stateless throughout this study unless separately discussed or explicitly defined otherwise.

Similarly, the term 'national' is used in this study in general to denote an individual who holds the nationality of a state. With the term 'Chinese national', a person holding the nationality of the People's Republic of China (or one of its predecessors) is meant unless otherwise noted. While Hong Kong Chinese and inhabitants of Macau are also considered nationals of the People's Republic of China legally, different regulations apply regarding travel to and from mainland China or other countries which are not covered

---

56 See the definition of the International Court of Justice in the *Nottebohm Case* (1955), p. 23.

57 Chinese: 外国人.

58 Art. 7 *Nationality Law* (1980) e. g. lists the preconditions for naturalisation of "foreign nationals or the stateless" (*waiguoren huo wuguojiren*; Chinese: 外国人或无国籍人).

59 E. g. Art. 7 *Nationality Law* (1980), Art. 89 *Exit–Entry Administration Law* (2012), Art. 41 *Administrative Reconsideration Law* (2009), or Art. 100 *Administrative Litigation Law* (2014). Art. 6 *Nationality Law* (1980), however, provides for regulations specific to stateless individuals.

60 The official translation of the 2012 *Exit–Entry Administration Law* only refers to 'foreign nationals'.

in this study. Thus, if not stated otherwise, a 'Chinese national' in this study is considered a national of the People's Republic of China who is not subject to the jurisdiction of Hong Kong or Macao. Finally, inhabitants of Taiwan who do not hold a passport issued by the government of the People's Republic of China are not considered nationals of the People's Republic of China throughout this study.

Throughout this study, the use of the term 'immigration legislation' depicts legislation regulating migration of foreign nationals or stateless into a state. Immigration legislation comprises norms that formally regulate the exit and entry of foreign nationals or stateless as well as norms meant to support the integration of foreign nationals into a state. Further, border control related to immigration or emigration and visa issuance are considered part of 'immigration legislation'. Chinese immigration legislation mainly consists of the 1985 *Foreign Nationals Exit–Entry Administration Law* or its successor the 2012 *Exit–Entry Administration Law* as well as related implementation provisions. The exit and entry of Chinese nationals from or into China is per definition not part of 'immigration legislation'. However, the exit and entry of Chinese nationals will be covered in part in this study inasmuch as it is necessary for analysing immigration legislation. The exit and entry to mainland China of Chinese nationals who are residents of Hong Kong or Macau or of inhabitants of Taiwan is not the primary subject of this study.

II. 'Sanfei' as Political and Legal Concept

The term 'sanfei'[61] as used in the context of *sanfei* campaigns but also in the context of the revision of exit–entry administration law denotes 'three illegalities', i. e. 'illegal entry',[62] 'illegal stay'[63] and 'illegal employment'.[64] Some sources on *sanfei* campaigns denote 'illegal stay' also as 'illegal sojourn',[65] and 'illegal employment' is sometimes also called 'illegal work'[66]

61 Chinese: 三非.
62 Chinese: 非法入境.
63 Chinese: 非法居留.
64 Chinese: 非法就业.
65 Chinese: 非法滞留. Mao (2004).
66 Chinese: 非法工作.

or 'illegal labour'[67]. While the term 'sanfei' in the campaign context is hence not too distinct in its definition, it still refers to the legal concepts of 'illegal entry', 'illegal stay' and 'illegal employment'.[68] As this study focuses on international migration that conflicts with legal provisions and because *sanfei* campaigns also refer to these legal provisions regarding immigration, I use the term 'illegal immigration' instead of terms that cover wider concepts such as 'irregular immigration' or 'undocumented immigrants'. Apart from where I need to directly translate the Chinese term *sanfei waiguoren* as ' "sanfei" foreigner', I avoid using the somewhat unsuitable term 'illegal foreign national' but rather refer to foreign nationals who commit offences or crimes according to immigration law.

While based on the three legal concepts of 'illegal entry', 'illegal stay' and 'illegal employment', the term 'sanfei' as it is used in campaigns partly expands these legal definitions. From a purely legal point of view, 'illegal stay' would only cover the stay without a valid visa or residence permit including the overstay of one's visa. The legal framework, i. e. the 1985 *Foreign Nationals Exit–Entry Administration Law* together with its *Foreign Nationals Exit–Entry Administration Law Implementation Rules*, codifies different registration requirements, of which only one is included in the definition of 'illegal stay'. Holders of D, Z, X or J-1 visas and individuals who do not need to apply for a visa to enter China need to apply for a residence permit and register their residence. According to Article 42 *Foreign Nationals Exit–Entry Administration Law Implementation Rules* (2010), 'illegal stay' comprises the failure to register residence. Apart from that, foreign nationals need to register their temporary stay (*zhusu dengji*[69]). While the failure to register one's residence is defined as illegal stay according to the 1985 legal framework, the failure to register a merely temporary stay is defined as a separate administrative offence and would hence not count as 'illegal stay' in the purely legal sense. The 2012 legal framework does not clearly define the failure to register residence as 'illegal stay', but the registration of temporary stay is defined as a separate administrative offence in the 2012 law as well.

A definition used in several newspaper reports refers to the underlying legal concepts that can be deduced from the provisions laid out in the 1985

67 Chinese: 非法务工. *Action Plan of the Town of Qingxi on the Launch of the Campaign to Clear Up and Correctively Punish 'Sanfei' Foreigners* (2014).

68 See chapter 4 on the legal definitions. See as well Guobin Zhu / Price (2013), p. 11.

69 Chinese: 住宿登记.

Foreign Nationals Exit–Entry Administration Law, the *Foreign Nationals Exit–Entry Administration Law Implementation Rules* as well as relevant other detailed provisions like the 1996 *Foreign Nationals Employment Regulations*. According to this definition, the failed registration of temporary stay is not referred to as 'illegal stay', which is in line with the findings above:

> 1) Illegally entering foreign nationals: Foreign nationals like those who do not hold a valid passport or travel documents upon entry, who enter without a valid entry visa or other valid document issued by a competent Chinese authority, who do not enter via a port designated by the visa authorities, or who entered the country without passing trough a control conducted by border inspection authorities.
> 2) Illegally staying foreign nationals: Foreign nationals like those who stay in China without a valid Chinese visa or documents, who did not apply for a residence permit within 30 days after having entered holding a D, Z, X, or J-1 visa, or who did not apply for a residence permit within 30 days or exceeded the limit of stay as indicated on the visa or document after having entered without a visa according to an agreement with the country concerned.
> 3) Illegally employed foreign nationals: Foreign nationals like those who are employed or hold an office without holding a residence permit or a temporary residence permit and a Z visa (excluding foreign nationals from visa-free countries), a work permit, an expert certificate, a permit for foreign nationals to engage in offshore oil operations or a permit for temporary performances with commercial objectives.[70]

As several newspaper reports suggest, however, a number of *sanfei* campaigns, especially those launched in Guangdong province, also persecuted failed registrations of temporary stay, although such administrative offences are not part of the legal definition of 'illegal entry', 'illegal stay' and 'illegal employment'.[71] Further, although *sanfei* campaigns directed at illegal immigration typically always target 'illegal entry', 'illegal stay' and 'illegal employment', certain local differences and different foci can be determined. Local *sanfei* campaigns may, for example, primarily be targeted at illegal employment in the context of education.[72] Other *sanfei* campaigns, however, also target associated aspects like illegal drug trade or human trafficking.[73] In the following research, I consider all campaigns as relevant that use the

70 TAN / WEN (2006).

71 *As 'Two Sessions' Come Closer: 'Sanfei' Foreigners Extensively Searched* (兩會期近 深搜「三非」外國人) (2007); CHEN Xiang (2009).

72 *Action Plan of the Education Bureau of the City of Changsha on the Launch of the Campaign to Clear Up and Correctively Punish 'Sanfei' Foreigners* (2013).

73 *Implementation Plan of the City of Fangchenggang for the Launch of the Campaign to Strike on 'Sanfei Individuals'* (2011). Human traffickers are often referred to as 'snake heads' (Chinese: 蛇头).

term 'sanfei' to refer to illegal immigrants according to the legal definition, as long as illegal immigration is the primary target of the campaigns.

The term 'sanfei' has been used at least since 1995 to denote immigrants who illegally crossed the border, illegally stayed or were illegally employed in China, while the focus of the 'sanfei' problem first emerged in border regions especially in the southern part of the Chinese border with Myanmar, Laos, and Vietnam,[74] but also at the Chinese border to North Korea.[75] Only as from around 2003, the focus of *sanfei* campaigns shifted to illegal immigration to cities like Beijing, Shanghai or Guangzhou, while campaigns in the border regions persisted. Apart from denoting illegal immigration, the term 'sanfei' may also denote other illegal actions targeted by campaigns, such as illegal religious activities, illegal dissemination of religious articles, and illegal religious communication on the internet. Although campaigns targeted against illegal religious activities sometimes also targeted illegal immigration, I decided not to take into account campaigns that aim at illegal immigration only as a secondary target. The term 'sanfei' has further to be separated from similar terms like 'sanwu'.[76] 'Sanwu' denotes individuals who do not have a regular income and thus depend on social support by the government, who don't have the ability to work, or who don't have a legally appointed financial supporter. Although foreign nationals may belong to this group of individuals as well,[77] I did not cover campaigns targeted against 'sanwu' individuals in this study.

To sum up, the term 'sanfei' as it is used in the context of *sanfei* campaigns that focus on foreign nationals almost always denotes a combination of the legal concepts of 'illegal entry', 'illegal stay' and 'illegal employment' as defined in the legal framework consisting of the 1985 *Foreign Nationals Exit–Entry Administration Law*, the *Foreign Nationals Exit–Entry Administration Law Implementation Rules* as well as other relevant provisions. After the 2012 revision of exit–entry administration law, the term accordingly refers to the revised legal framework.[78] While the legal definition of this term can be regarded as uncontroversial, *sanfei* campaigns may still narrow or extend their target focus depending on the administrative and geographical area of deployment. *Sanfei* campaigns may for example focus

74 See e. g. Wang Yanbin (2011) and Wu Xi (2013).
75 Wu Xingchun (2013), p. 47.
76 Chinese: 三无.
77 Chen Ji / Li Shu / Ji (2008), p. 61.
78 See e. g. Cheng Xianshu (2013) referring to the provision on 'illegal employment' introduced in the *Exit–Entry Administration Law* (2012).

on a particular application of these legal concepts, like the application only in the education sector, but *sanfei* campaigns may as well comprise related aspects like human trafficking that are equally targeted apart from 'illegal entry', 'illegal stay' and 'illegal employment'.

Chapter 2: Framework of Chinese Immigration Legislation

A. *Introduction*

To clarify the relation between law-making processes and campaigns in the context of immigration law, which is the aim of this study, it is necessary to assess the drivers for the revision of exit–entry administration law. Knowing the drivers for the revision process helps to understand why the law was revised and whether or not the deployment of campaigns was a direct result of the revision process. The making of the current *Exit–Entry Administration Law* of 2012 and the enforcement of its provisions via campaigns cannot be understood without taking into consideration the development of immigration law in China. For the analysis of the deployment of campaigns, on the other hand, it is beneficial to identify the communication structure of relevant authorities. This chapter aims to carve out the drivers for the revision process of exit–entry administration law as well as the influences of administrative structures and organisation on the implementation of legal provisions.

The revision process of the current *Exit–Entry Administration Law* as well as the current structure of responsible agencies must be viewed against the background of economic reforms since 1978. The transition to a market economy, which has been official policy in China since 1993,[1] called for a reliable legal framework not only in the area of civil law, but also in administrative law. In the context of a market economy, the state should refrain from interfering in economic transactions and the government must be held accountable for its actions.[2] The revision of the *Exit–Entry Administration Law* (2012) has thus to be evaluated in the context of the comprehensive administrative legal framework that has been set up since 1989 with the promulgation of the *Administrative Litigation Law*. With growing numbers of foreign nationals entering China, not only the control of exit, entry and stay, but also of aspects like employment, permanent residence, attraction of foreign experts, or the use of biometric data became more important and eventually found their way into the revised *Exit–Entry Administration Law*. I argue that the economic reforms not only manifested in the applica-

1 Long (2010), p. 352.
2 Weijiu Zhu (2010), p. 111 f.

tion of experimental provisions in the context of immigration law, but also influenced the revision process in exit–entry administration law indirectly through the harmonisation of administrative legislation.

Economic reforms not only led to the revision of exit–entry administration law, but also resulted in institutional reforms. Administrative structures were first subject to organisational streamlining and centralisation, for example with the establishment of the Bureau of Exit–Entry Administration in 1983.[3] After China's accession to the World Trade Organisation in 2001, the structural optimisation and the improvement of police work came into focus.[4] Before I analyse the deployment of campaigns and the enforcement of exit–entry administration law in the next chapter, I will assess how the relevant agencies communicate and instruct each other. I assume that a vertical incentive system is implemented in exit–entry administration, as it is commonplace in the Chinese administrative system in general,[5] and that this system results in transgressions of power at the local level due to pressure from higher-level authorities.

This chapter lays out the basic framework for a deeper analysis of campaigns and the law that is conducted in the following chapters. It analyses the development of regulations in the field of immigration administration and the genesis of the current law on exit–entry administration against the background of economic reforms. This chapter carves out how economic reform influenced the making and the revision of laws and the organisation of administrative structures in the field of exit–entry administration. In order to explain the effects of economic reforms on exit–entry legislation, I give a concise presentation of the legal norms on immigration of the first years of the People's Republic that formed the basis for the first laws on exit–entry administration in the 1980s, before elaborating on the making of the 1985 and the 2012 law. Further, I analyse the organisational structures of government agencies in charge of the enforcement of immigration law against the background of institutional reforms that are again a manifestation of ongoing economic reforms. In order to understand vertical and horizontal communication between competent administrative agencies, I analyse hierarchical and organisational structures between relevant administrative organs.

3 Guofu Liu (2011), p. 9.
4 Wong (2012), p. 228 f.
5 See e. g. Edin (2003), p. 7–8.

B. Early Normative Framework of Exit and Entry Administration

Before analysing the making of the first laws in exit–entry administration that were promulgated in 1985,[6] the aim of this section is to assess the state of regulation in the field of immigration law before and in the course of the initiation of the economic reforms. As researchers state, the development of exit–entry administration in the People's Republic of China from the foundation of the People's Republic until the accession of China to the World Trade Organisation (WTO) can be described as a development "[f]rom prohibition policy to relaxation policy".[7] In the first years of the People's Republic until 1957, a restrictive migration framework was established and in the following years until 1978 further developed. However, from 1979 onwards, this framework underwent a reform process that peaked in 2001 resulting in several new laws and regulations issued in the years to follow.[8] In order to provide a basic context of the research topic of this study, i. e. Chinese immigration law, this section aims to locate exit–entry administration law within its historical, political and legal context.

The first part of this section reviews the early development of regulations on exit–entry administration in order to assess how economic reforms led to the establishment of a new framework of immigration law and why the former framework had to be replaced. This section then looks into the making of laws and regulations in the context of exit–entry administration in the early years of economic reforms and especially into the provisions of the final 1985 law in comparison to its draft and analyses the changes made by several amendments of the relevant implementation rules. By doing this, this section also aims to locate exit–entry administration law within Chinese law in general and to outline the relation of exit–entry administration law with the frameworks of administrative law, nationality law in particular, as well as of criminal law. This section finally outlines the shortcomings of the legal framework of exit–entry administration law that made it necessary to revise it.

---

6 *Foreign Nationals Exit–Entry Administration Law* (1985); *Citizens Exit–Entry Administration Law* (1985).
7 Guofu Liu (2009), p. 312.
8 Guofu Liu (2009).

I. Foundations of the Current Legal Framework on Immigration

Until 1951, the basis for the treatment of foreign nationals[9] in China were the *Instructions of the Central Authorities on the Policy Regarding the Treatment of Foreign Nationals in China*[10], a policy guideline issued by the new government in 1948 that implicitly required the establishment of concrete measures regarding foreign nationals in China.[11] This policy called for the protection of foreign nationals, regardless of their political attitude or affiliation, as long as they abode by the regulations and decrees issued by the government and the People's Liberation Army.[12]

First regulations concerning exit and entry administration of overseas Chinese, of passengers travelling to and from Hong Kong and Macau, as well as of foreign nationals in the People's Republic of China, all of which were issued by the Ministry of Public Security, came into being in 1951.[13] The *Provisional Measures on the Exit and Entry of Overseas Chinese*[14] entered into force on 2 August 1951 as the first legal document in the People's Republic to codify migration across the national borders.[15] The regulations required Chinese who travelled via Hong Kong or Macau to hold a passport issued by the public security authorities. The *Provisional Regulations on the Exit, Entry, and Stay of Foreign Nationals* that came into effect on 28 November 1951[16] were the first legal basis concerning the administration of foreign nationals in the People's Republic, featuring a strict policy that required foreign nationals to hold a valid passport and a valid visa issued by the Ministry of Foreign Affairs or equivalent institutions, to register their residence at the local police department, and to abide by Chinese legal provisions and the household registration system.[17] Foreign

9 Until 1964, foreign nationals were called *waiguo qiaomin* (外国侨民) or *waiqiao* (外侨), possibly in reference to the term *huaqiao* (华侨) that designates overseas Chinese.

10 *Foreign Nationals Treatment Instructions* (1948).

11 Guofu Liu (2011), p. 5.

12 *Foreign Nationals Treatment Instructions* (1948), p. 35, 38.

13 Guofu Liu (2011), p. 5 f.

14 *Overseas Chinese Exit and Entry Provisional Regulations* (1951).

15 Guofu Liu (2011), p. 5.

16 *Foreign Nationals Exit, Entry, and Stay Provisional Regulations* (1951).

17 Art. 2–5 *Foreign Nationals Exit, Entry, and Stay Provisional Regulations* (1951).

nationals had to conduct formalities for travel or exit at the local police departments.[18] Without a valid certificate, exit could be denied.[19]

In 1954, the first *Constitution* of the People's Republic of China replaced the hitherto existing *Common Program*[20], indicating the aim to further develop a comprehensive legal framework. However, a policy to strengthen efforts in preventing foreign nationals "from spying on, destroying and interfering with Chinese internal affairs"[21] was pursued. This aim is also reflected in the implementation of three subordinate rules on the exit from China, on residence registration, and on travel within China that entered into force in 1954[22] and developed the relevant provisions of the 1951 *Provisional Regulations on the Exit, Entry, and Stay of Foreign Nationals*.[23] The new framework required every individual—Chinese nationals as well as overseas Chinese and other foreign nationals—to apply for an exit visa to leave the People's Republic.[24] Moreover, Chinese nationals had to apply for a passport in order to leave the country, which in turn required a proper *hukou* (i. e. household) registration as from 1958.[25]

According to the *Provisional Measures on the Exit of Foreign Nationals* (1954), prior to the exit of the country, foreign nationals had to apply for emigration at the local police department,[26] hand in their passport and relevant documents, fill out an application form in duplicate with three photographs attached, hand in proofs to declare that there are no current liability disputes, outstanding taxes, or unsettled civil or criminal lawsuits, and pay an administrative fee.[27] Provisions for payment of administrative fees could also be found in the *Provisional Measures on the Travel of Foreign Nationals* (1954) and the *Provisional Measures on Residence Registration of and Issuance of Residence Certificates for Foreign Nationals* (1954). Both

18 Art. 6, 7 *Foreign Nationals Exit, Entry, and Stay Provisional Regulations* (1951).
19 Art. 8 *Foreign Nationals Exit, Entry, and Stay Provisional Regulations* (1951).
20 *Common Program* (1948).
21 *Foreign Nationals Treatment Instructions* (1948), p. 38, as translated in Guofu Liu (2011), p. 5.
22 *Foreign Nationals Exit Provisional Regulations* (1954); *Foreign Nationals Residence Registration Provisional Regulations* (1954); *Foreign Nationals Travel Provisional Regulations* (1954).
23 Guofu Liu (2011), p. 6.
24 Guofu Liu (2007), p. 135 f.
25 Guofu Liu (2007), p. 138. The *Hukou Regulations* (1958) were promulgated by the State Council on 9 January 1958.
26 Art. 2 *Foreign Nationals Exit Provisional Regulations* (1954).
27 Art. 3 *Foreign Nationals Exit Provisional Regulations* (1954).

measures, too, featured very strict provisions that constrained the freedom of movement within China. According to the *Provisional Measures on Residence Registration of and Issuance of Residence Certificates for Foreign Nationals*, foreign nationals had to register at the local police department at their designated place of residence within three days of their arrival.[28] According to the *Provisional Measures on the Travel of Foreign Nationals*, foreign nationals had to apply for a permit at the local police departments if they wanted to leave the city or the county or village[29] of their residence.[30] They then had to conduct their travel according to this permit in terms of destination, route, means of transportation, and time span; changes in the original plans required reapplication with the relevant police department.[31] It was not even allowed to stop at any other place than designated in the permit.[32] These strict provisions also applied when moving house.[33] Until 1964, this bundle of regulations formed the legal basis for exit–entry and foreign national administration. While the Ministry of Foreign Affairs had initially been responsible for the administration of exit and entry of foreign nationals, this task has been assigned to the Ministry of Public Security as from 1959.[34]

With the *Regulations on the Entry, Exit, Transit, Residence and Travel Administration of Foreign Nationals in China* of 1964[35] the basic structure of a comprehensive exit–entry administration was eventually outlined, which is in part effective until today. The three provisional measures on travel, residence, and exit of foreign nationals issued by the Ministry of Public Security in 1954[36] that were based on the provisional rules on exit–entry administration promulgated by the Government Administration Council in 1951[37] were replaced by these new regulations promulgated by the State Council and approved by the Standing Committee of the National People's Congress. The main provisions of this basic system required foreign nationals to apply for

28 Art. 2 *Foreign Nationals Residence Registration Provisional Regulations* (1954).
29 Chinese: 县镇或乡村.
30 Art. 2 *Foreign Nationals Travel Provisional Regulations* (1954).
31 Art. 5 *Foreign Nationals Travel Provisional Regulations* (1954).
32 Art. 7 *Foreign Nationals Travel Provisional Regulations* (1954).
33 Art. 6 *Foreign Nationals Residence Registration Provisional Regulations* (1954).
34 Guofu Liu (2011), p. 6.
35 *Exit and Entry Administration Regulations* (1964).
36 These are the *Foreign Nationals Travel Provisional Regulations* (1954), the *Foreign Nationals Residence Registration Provisional Regulations* (1954) and the *Foreign Nationals Exit Provisional Regulations* (1954).
37 I. e. the *Foreign Nationals Exit, Entry, and Stay Provisional Regulations* (1951).

a permit before being able to enter, exit, transit or settle in China,[38] they assigned the responsibility for the exit–entry administration within the country to the Ministry of Public Security and the administration abroad, like issuance of visas etc., to the Ministry of Foreign Affairs.[39] The regulations required foreign nationals to abide by the household registration system,[40] underlined the sovereignty of the People's Republic of China with regard to immigration matters, and finally bound foreign nationals to the legal system of the People's Republic including the right of the authorities to punish foreign nationals who did not adhere to legal regulations.[41]

The 1964 regulations can be seen as the first comprehensive normative framework to regulate the exit and entry of foreign nationals. Although a definition of the term 'foreign national' or 'foreigner' was missing and the regulations only comprised of seventeen articles, the basic structure of these regulations was adopted into the legal norms issued in 1985 and can even partly be found in current laws. Examples for continuous norms are the shared responsibility of the Ministry of Public Security and the Ministry of Foreign Affairs or the requirement for foreign nationals to abide by the household registration system. While the exit–entry administration system was set up quite thoroughly in 1964, it was not of practical use most of the time. During the Cultural Revolution between 1966 and 1976, the exit and entry system virtually came to a halt, as any individual who tried to leave the country was considered to be part of the opposing forces leading to a rapid decrease of regular emigration, while irregular emigration increased due to political instability within the country.[42] Only after 1978 was a comprehensive legal framework on exit–entry administration finally set up.

II. Immigration Legislation in the Context of Economic Reforms

As from 1978, Chinese economic reform established a new orientation in the economic system and an opening of China towards the outside world. The stronger focus on economic development also required increased institutionalisation in order to provide a stable and reliable basis for economics and business. As Deng proclaimed, "Democracy has to be institutionalised

38 Art. 2, 7 *Exit and Entry Administration Regulations* (1964).
39 Art. 4 *Exit and Entry Administration Regulations* (1964).
40 Art. 10 *Exit and Entry Administration Regulations* (1964).
41 Guofu Liu (2011), p. 7.
42 Guofu Liu (2007), p. 139.

and written into law, so as to make sure that institutions and laws do not change whenever the leadership change their views or shift their focus of attention."[43] With the perceived need to open up the country and promote trade especially with Western countries, a reform of the existing exit–entry system was inevitable. Not only would the restrictive provisions hinder increased economic exchange with other countries, but it was also necessary to build up an exit–entry administration framework that was based on laws rather than on regulations issued by the State Council or ministries.

With new regulations regarding nationality, passports and visas around 1980, the exit–entry administration system was slowly rebuilt after its collapse during the Cultural Revolution. The foundation of this new system was laid with the promulgation of the *Nationality Law* (1980), the *Law on the Administration of the Exit and Entry of Citizens* (1985) and the *Law on the Administration of the Exit and Entry of Foreign Nationals* (1985). These three legal documents constituted the legal basis for exit–entry administration until 2013, when the revised *Exit–Entry Administration Law* entered into force.

The 1980 *Nationality Law*,[44] which is still in force today and has remained unaltered over time, offers the basis for immigration legislation by codifying acquisition and loss of the nationality of the People's Republic of China as well as naturalisation. This way, it not only clarifies the pathways for the acquisition of Chinese nationality, but also defines who is a Chinese national and who is not, a distinction of great relevance when it comes to exit–entry administration. Along with the foundation of the People's Republic of China, different jurisdictions emerged on the geographic area of what historically has been defined as 'China'. Aside from the island of Taiwan that has been governed by the Republic of China since 1945 and does not belong to the jurisdiction of the People's Republic, the territories of Hong Kong and Macau also have their own jurisdictions, despite formally belonging to the territory People's Republic of China as from 1997 and 1999. The complexity in defining Chinese nationality is reflected in several provisions of the *Nationality Law* (1980) that refer to 'China' and not explicitly to the People's Republic. One precondition for naturalisation e. g. is that the individual has "Chinese relatives,"[45] an alternative requirement is that he or she has "settled in China."[46] While some English translations interpret 'China'

43 Harold M. Tanner (1999), p. 5; Chinese original in Deng Xiaoping (1994 a), p. 146.
44 *Nationality Law* (1980).
45 Chinese: 中国人的近亲属. Art. 7(1)i *Nationality Law* (1980).
46 Chinese: 定居在中国的. Art. 7(1)ii *Nationality Law* (1980).

as 'People's Republic of China' and 'Chinese relatives' as relatives holding the nationality of the People's Republic of China, literally speaking no such restriction is made in the original Chinese legal text. After the transfer of sovereignty over Hong Kong and Macau to the People's Republic of China in 1997 and 1999 respectively, the *Nationality Law* (1980) also applies to these two territories, albeit with some distinct amendments.

The 1980 *Nationality Law* was promulgated on 10 September 1980 and defines the Ministry of Public Security and its local bureaus as responsible authorities for the application of Chinese nationality law.[47] The law is primarily based on the principle of *ius sanguinis* by assigning Chinese nationality to individuals whose father or mother (or both) is of Chinese nationality in its Article 4.[48] Apart from this, according to Article 5, Chinese nationality can not be obtained via birth if the individual has already obtained another nationality e. g. when born abroad.[49] Naturalisation is only possible if near relatives of the applicant hold Chinese nationality or if the applicant has settled in China or has "other legitimate reasons"[50]. Article 3 rejects the recognition of dual nationality, and, accordingly, a foreign national who applies for Chinese nationality is required to give up his or her former nationality.[51] According to Article 9, a Chinese national who resides abroad and acquires a foreign nationality automatically loses his or her former Chinese nationality.[52] Court rulings have shown that settlement abroad is an important requirement for the application of Article 9 and the mere appropriation of a foreign passport does not suffice.[53] For the automatic loss of Chinese nationality it is irrelevant whether the individual applied for the renunciation of Chinese nationality or whether this application has been approved.[54] However, in order to give up Chinese nationality in accordance with Article 10 *Nationality Law* (1980), an official approval of the renunciation application is needed.[55]

Further clarification of the status of foreign nationals would only later be given by the *Foreign Nationals Exit–Entry Administration Law* (1985),

47 Art. 15, 16 *Nationality Law* (1980).
48 Art. 4 *Nationality Law* (1980).
49 Art. 5 *Nationality Law* (1980).
50 Art. 7 *Nationality Law* (1980).
51 Art. 8, 13 *Nationality Law* (1980).
52 Art. 9 *Nationality Law* (1980).
53 *Fraudulent Appropriation of Exit Documents Case* (1999); *Contract Dispute Jurisdiction Case* (2017).
54 *Funds Missappropriation Case* (2012).
55 *Fraudulent Appropriation of Exit Documents Case* (1999).

which defined that individuals without the nationality of the People's Republic of China as defined in the *Nationality Law* are to be regarded as foreign nationals.[56] This includes nationals of the Republic of China as well as—at least until 1997 and 1999—nationals of Hong Kong and Macau. After the transfer of sovereignty to the People's Republic of China, nationals of Hong Kong and Macau automatically received the nationality of the People's Republic of China as from 1 July 1997 or 20 December 1999 respectively if they met certain conditions laid down in the *Nationality Law Implementation Explanations* regarding the Hong Kong Special Administrative Region and the Macau Special Administrative Region.[57] In the example of Hong Kong, each individual "of Chinese descent and born in the Chinese territories (including Hong Kong)" who complies with the requirements as stated in the *Nationality Law* (1980), is recognised as a Chinese national.[58] However, holding the nationality of the People's Republic of China does not entitle Hong Kong and Macau residents to travel freely to and from mainland China or both Special Administrative Regions as they have to apply for a Mainland Travel Permit for Hong Kong and Macau Residents[59] issued by the Ministry of Public Security. The *Foreign Nationals Exit–Entry Administration Law* (1985), as well as its implementation measures, did not provide any concrete provisions regarding travel from mainland China to Hong Kong or Macau. However, as it defines a foreign national as individual without Chinese nationality, residents of Hong Kong or Macau are not considered as foreign nationals according to this law.

Apart from these regulations concerning nationality, provisions regarding travel documents were issued shortly after the initiation of the economic reforms. On 13 May 1980, *Regulations on Passports and Visas* were promulgated that regulated the types of passports and visas to be issued to Chinese and foreign nationals.[60] The provisional regulations of 1975 were repealed. The 1980 regulations constitute the basic administrative framework for the issuance of passports and visas to Chinese and foreign nationals until today. While new regulations concerning passports and visas have been issued

---

56 Art. 31 *Foreign Nationals Exit–Entry Administration Law* (1985).

57 *Nationality Law Implementation Explanations* (1996); *Nationality Law Implementation Explanations* (1998).

58 Art. 1 *Nationality Law Implementation Explanations* (1996).

59 Chinese: 港澳居民来往内地通行证; also shortened 'Home Return Permit' (*huixiangzheng*, Chinese: 回乡证).

60 Although these regulations are still valid, they have never been published in any official gazette.

since then, it is not explicitly stated that the 1980 regulations ceased to apply. According to the 1980 *Regulations on Passports and Visas*, a passport (*huzhao*)[61] is an identification document abroad that is issued to Chinese nationals who exit or enter the country, while visas (*qianzheng*)[62] are permits used within the country (or at its borders) for exit, entry, and transit and issued to Chinese and foreign nationals.[63] These legal documents are further classified into diplomatic passports and visas, duty passports and visas, and regular passports and visas.[64] Regular passports are further classified into business and personal passports (*yingong putong huzhao*[65] and *yinsi putong huzhao*[66]). The different kinds of passports are issued only to holders of specific positions listed in Articles 6, 7, and 8 respectively.[67] The 1980 *Regulations on Passports and Visas* state that forging, fraudulent appropriation, alteration, disclosure, and lending of Chinese passports or visas shall be punished in severe circumstances without, however, defining concrete sanctions.[68]

In 1984, a *Notification about the Conscientious Implementation of Document Gongfa (Jing) 59 to Further Relax the Restrictions on Exiting the Country for Private Affairs*[69] was published by the Ministry of Public Security that stressed the obligation of administrative organs to safeguard the right to exit of Chinese nationals. While the issuance of this document illustrates the stated objective to facilitate exit and entry in order to support economic exchange with foreign countries, it did not imply the immediate abolishment of exit visas. In fact, only in 1980 did the *Regulations on Passports and Visas* codify exit visas as an instrument to regulate emigration on a national level[70]

With regard to travel of foreign nationals within the country, a new framework that partly abolished the requirement to apply for visas was established. The *Regulations on the Administration of Foreign Nationals Travelling in*

61 Chinese: 护照.
62 Chinese: 签证.
63 Art. 1, 2 *Passport and Visa Regulations* (1980).
64 Chinese law differentiates between diplomatic passports (*waijiao huzhao*, Chinese: 外交护照), official passports (*gongwu huzhao*, Chinese: 公务护照), and regular passports (*putong huzhao*, Chinese: 普通护照).
65 Chinese: 因公普通护照.
66 Chinese: 因私普通护照.
67 Art. 6, 7, 8 *Passport and Visa Regulations* (1980).
68 Art. 17 *Passport and Visa Regulations* (1980).
69 *Exit Restrictions Relaxing Notification* (1984).
70 Art. 2 *Passport and Visa Regulations* (1980); Guofu Liu (2007), p. 142.

China (1982) divided the Chinese territory into districts that are assigned the classes A to D. This system is still in force today. While class-A districts are free for travel for foreign nationals without prior permit. For class-B districts, as before, a travel permit is needed. Class-C and class-D districts are closed for regular foreign visits.[71] Although this system still recognises the existence of certain regions to which entry by foreign nationals is forbidden, it considerably facilitates travel of foreign nationals throughout most parts of China by establishing regions that are accessible without prior approval.

The promulgation of the *Nationality Law* (1980) and the *Regulations on Passports and Visas* (1980) were important steps towards the establishment of a new framework on immigration law, as both legal documents contained important provisions that form the foundation for exit–entry administration. Legal documents like the cited *Exit Restrictions Relaxing Notification* (1984) or the *Regulations on the Administration of Foreign Nationals Travelling in China* (1982) illustrate the aim to facilitate exit and entry as well as travel within the country for both Chinese citizens and foreign nationals.

III. First Immigration Legislation in the Context of Economic Reforms

The *Foreign Nationals Exit–Entry Administration Law* (1985) was promulgated on 22 November 1985 and entered into force on 1 February 1986. A prior draft, written in September 1979 and presumably supervised by the Ministry of Public Security,[72] was discussed in the 12th Session of the Standing Committee of the 6th National People's Congress between 26 August and 6 September 1985[73] and then submitted to the Law Committee of the National People's Congress which, in three readings on 26 and 28 October and 7 November 1985, collected the proposals and suggestions of other committees and relevant authorities at the national as well as at the provincial

71 Art. 3 *Foreign Nationals Travel Administration Regulations* (1982).

72 *Explanations Regarding the 'Law of the People's Republic of China on the Administration of the Exit and Entry of Foreign Nationals (Draft)'* (关于《中华人民共和国外国人入出境管理法（草案）》的说明), *NPC Press Release* (1985).

73 *Briefing of the 12th Session of the Standing Committee of the 6th National People's Congress* (第六届全国人民代表大会常务委员会第十二次会议简况), *NPC Law Committee Press Release* (2000).

level.[74] Unlike the draft bill eventually submitted to the Standing Committee of the National People's Congress, this original draft has never been openly published and is hence not available for deeper analysis. However, in the explanations of the draft, presented to the Standing Committee of the National People's Congress, TAO Siju,[75] then Vice-Minister of the Ministry of Public Security, stated that although national and public security had to be safeguarded, the hitherto regulations had to be amended in order to allow for intensified foreign exchange and the establishment of the 'Four Modernisations' in line with the new opening policy.[76]

According to the explanations of TAO, the original draft aimed at better protecting the legal rights of foreign nationals, introduced different types of visas for different purposes of stay and allowed for denying foreign nationals entry to China in Article 13 if they were suspected of being harmful to the national security or public order.[77] The draft allowed foreign nationals who invested in China or who came to China to engage in business or scientific activities to apply for long-term or even permanent residence in Article 16, but also excluded certain groups like students, travellers or foreign nationals only staying temporarily from working in China in Article 23. TAO stated that this rule was relatively strict compared with international practice, but it was still deemed suitable for the establishment of the 'Four Modernisations'.[78] The draft further aimed at facilitating travel and exit from the country by abolishing the hitherto classification of districts and the need to apply for exit visas in Articles 26 and 30 respectively. It further allowed for legal remedies against administrative punishment imposed on foreign nationals

74 *Report of the Law Committee of the National People's Congress on the Consultation Results on the 'Law of the People's Republic of China on the Administration of the Exit and Entry of Foreign Nationals (Draft)'* (全国人民代表大会法律委员会对《中华人民共和国外国人入出境管理法（草案）》审议结果的报告), *NPC Law Committee Press Release* (1985).

75 Chinese: 陶驷驹

76 *Explanations Regarding the 'Law of the People's Republic of China on the Administration of the Exit and Entry of Foreign Nationals (Draft)'* (关于《中华人民共和国外国人入出境管理法（草案）》的说明), *NPC Press Release* (1985).

77 *Explanations Regarding the 'Law of the People's Republic of China on the Administration of the Exit and Entry of Foreign Nationals (Draft)'* (关于《中华人民共和国外国人入出境管理法（草案）》的说明), *NPC Press Release* (1985).

78 *Explanations Regarding the 'Law of the People's Republic of China on the Administration of the Exit and Entry of Foreign Nationals (Draft)'* (关于《中华人民共和国外国人入出境管理法（草案）》的说明), *NPC Press Release* (1985).

in Article 40.[79] According to the explanations of the Law Committee, some provisions of the original draft were removed since they had already been codified in other provisions or were considered to be of minor importance and thus rather to be codified in the corresponding *Implementation Measures*.[80]

The draft stated that foreign nationals had "to respect the public ethics and the customs and habits of Chinese society",[81] which, adopting the general statement that foreign nationals should abide by Chinese law, was eventually modified to state that foreign nationals "may not endanger the national security of China, harm public interests or disrupt the public order."[82] Further, the draft originally stated that "the exit–entry administration departments of public security organs of every level can dispatch foreign affairs police officers to investigate the compliance of foreign nationals and foreign organisation with this law" and that "during this investigation, the relevant organisations or individuals have the duty to provide assistance."[83] The suggested amendment later included in the law limited the scope of authorised officers to those of district level and above and specified that they had the right to check passports or other travel documents of foreign nationals. Further, the amended provision prescribed that these officers should show their official identification papers.[84] Because the draft was considered to be too general in terms of assigning sanctions to offences, Articles 29 and 30 were added to the final legal text that defines the scope of offences punishable

79 *Explanations Regarding the 'Law of the People's Republic of China on the Administration of the Exit and Entry of Foreign Nationals (Draft)'* (关于《中华人民共和国外国人入出境管理法（草案）》的说明), *NPC Press Release* (1985).

80 *Report of the Law Committee of the National People's Congress on the Consultation Results on the 'Law of the People's Republic of China on the Administration of the Exit and Entry of Foreign Nationals (Draft)'* (全国人民代表大会法律委员会对《中华人民共和国外国人入出境管理法（草案）》审议结果的报告), *NPC Law Committee Press Release* (1985).

81 Chinese: 尊重中国的社会公德和风俗习惯. *Report of the Law Committee of the National People's Congress on the Consultation Results on the 'Law of the People's Republic of China on the Administration of the Exit and Entry of Foreign Nationals (Draft)'* (全国人民代表大会法律委员会对《中华人民共和国外国人入出境管理法（草案）》审议结果的报告), *NPC Law Committee Press Release* (1985).

82 Art. 5 *Foreign Nationals Exit–Entry Administration Law* (1985).

83 *Report of the Law Committee of the National People's Congress on the Consultation Results on the 'Law of the People's Republic of China on the Administration of the Exit and Entry of Foreign Nationals (Draft)'* (全国人民代表大会法律委员会对《中华人民共和国外国人入出境管理法（草案）》审议结果的报告), *NPC Law Committee Press Release* (1985).

84 Art. 28 *Foreign Nationals Exit–Entry Administration Law* (1985).

with a warning, a fine, with detention of not more than ten days, with deportation if the circumstances are serious, or according to the *Criminal Law* if applicable. Article 29 further provided for administrative complaint and lawsuit.[85] The amended draft was discussed again in the 13th Session of the Standing Committee between 8 and 22 November 1985 and promulgated as law apparently without further amendments.[86]

The main aim of the 1985 *Foreign Nationals Exit–Entry Administration Law* was to structure the process of immigration of foreign nationals to China, as can already be seen by its composition. In its first part with general provisions, the law emphasised the personal freedom of foreign nationals, and that detention could only be imposed by the public or national security organs.[87] Chinese embassies and consulates in foreign countries were designated responsible for issuing visas abroad,[88] while the border control authorities were assigned the task of verifying legal documents of immigrants at the immigration ports to China.[89] The local public security offices handled applications for entry, transit, stay, travel, permanent residence and other domestic issues as well as persecution of offences concerning exit–entry administration.[90] In this regard, the law remained loyal to the tradition of shared responsibility between the Ministry of Foreign Affairs and the Ministry of Public Security and their subordinate organs, which had already been implemented in previous frameworks.

After having set out responsibilities and other general provisions, the law defined the procedures of entry, stay, travel and exit. In the second part, the law stated that foreign nationals first, i. e. before their entry to China, had to apply for a visa at the consulates or the embassies of the People's Republic of China in the relevant country.[91] It required individuals applying for a job or already being hired within China as well as people planning to settle in China to hand in the relevant documents to obtain an appropriate visa.[92] In the third part, the law regulated the stay in China. It required foreign nationals who planned to stay longer in China to apply for an identity card or

85 Art. 29, 30 *Foreign Nationals Exit–Entry Administration Law* (1985).
86 *Briefing of the 13th Session of the Standing Committee of the 6th National People's Congress* (第六届全国人民代表大会常务委员会第十三次会议简况), *NPC Law Committee Press Release* (2000).
87 Art. 4 *Foreign Nationals Exit–Entry Administration Law* (1985).
88 Art. 25 *Foreign Nationals Exit–Entry Administration Law* (1985).
89 Art. 3, 6 *Foreign Nationals Exit–Entry Administration Law* (1985).
90 Art. 9, 25, 29 *Foreign Nationals Exit–Entry Administration Law* (1985).
91 Art. 6 *Foreign Nationals Exit–Entry Administration Law* (1985).
92 Art. 8, 9 *Foreign Nationals Exit–Entry Administration Law* (1985).

a residence permit and abide by the Chinese household registration system.[93] In its fourth part, the law prohibited foreign nationals to travel to areas not open to foreign travellers except with special permission.[94] In this regard, the categorisation of districts of limited access was not fully abolished as the draft suggested. The fifth part of the law regulated emigration, which was not permitted if the foreign national was involved in a pending legal procedure or held no valid travel documents.[95]

While the 1985 *Foreign Nationals Exit–Entry Administration Law* provided for special sanctions that the public security organs at county level or above could impose on foreign nationals, it did not define the scope of the fines or the exact period of detention for different offences. The law only very generally provided in two articles for the possibility of the public security authorities at or above county level to impose a warning, a fine or a detention up to ten days for offences like illegal entry or exit, illegal residence, travelling in areas prohibited to foreign nationals without permission, or forging, modifying, using under false pretences, or transferring visa or residence permits.[96] In serious circumstances, the Ministry of Public Security could decide upon an order to leave or the deportation of the foreign national.[97] The law also provided only one provision regarding legal remedies, stating that a foreign national subject to fine or detention may use administrative reconsideration or administrative litigation to challenge the decision of the public security organ.[98] Although the provisions in the final law were more precise than those of the draft law, they still lacked a detailed assignment of offences and penalties and did not clarify which legal remedies existed against administrative actions such as denial of entry, detention for examination, residential surveillance or detention for deportation.

Concrete scopes of punishment for different offences, different visa types as well as other detailed measures were, however, defined in the *Foreign Nationals Exit–Entry Administration Law Implementation Rules* (1986) that served as implementation provisions to the law. As the law did not define

93 Art. 13, 17 *Foreign Nationals Exit–Entry Administration Law* (1985). The *Foreign Nationals Exit–Entry Administration Law Implementation Rules* (1986) more concretely codify the registration procedures for foreign nationals; Art. 29–33 *Foreign Nationals Exit–Entry Administration Law Implementation Rules* (1986).

94 Art. 20, 21 *Foreign Nationals Exit–Entry Administration Law* (1985).

95 Art. 23, 24 *Foreign Nationals Exit–Entry Administration Law* (1985).

96 Art. 29 *Foreign Nationals Exit–Entry Administration Law* (1985).

97 Art. 30 *Foreign Nationals Exit–Entry Administration Law* (1985).

98 Art. 29 *Foreign Nationals Exit–Entry Administration Law* (1985).

concrete situations in which a foreign national could be denied entry to the country, apart from a situation where he or she was suspected of harming national security or disrupting public order, the *Foreign Nationals Exit–Entry Administration Law Implementation Rules* provided for certain categories of foreign nationals who should not be permitted to enter: According to the *Implementation Rules*, a denial of entry would apply to foreign nationals who had been deported and were hence subject to a re-entry ban, to foreign nationals who were suspected of conducting terrorist, violent, subversive activities or who were suspected of conducting smuggle, drugs trade, or prostitution in China.[99] Finally, foreign nationals with serious transmissible diseases or who were unable to finance their stay could be denied entry.[100] Further, foreign nationals without a valid passport or exit–entry documents or foreign nationals who refused border inspection could be denied entry to the country, as well as foreign nationals whom the Ministry of Public Security or the Ministry of State Security prohibited entry to China.[101]

According to the 1986 *Foreign Nationals Exit–Entry Administration Law Implementation Rules*, illegal entry to China was sanctioned with a fine between RMB 500 and 2 000 or detention between three or ten days; illegal stay was sanctioned with a fine between RMB 100 and 500 or detention between one to three days; illegal work, i. e. working without permission from the Ministry of Labour, was punishable with the termination of the employment relationship and a fine between RMB 200 and 1 000.[102] The *Foreign Nationals Exit–Entry Administration Law Implementation Rules* (1986) further provided detailed sanctions for not adhering to the provisions concerning foreign aircraft or vessels, not carrying a valid passport and exit–entry documents or failing to present them upon examination, failing to register with the local authorities, entering areas not open to foreign nationals without permission, and forging or carrying forged exit–entry documents.[103] In addition to fines and detention, foreign nationals illegally entering China or those who forged or carried forged exit–entry documents

99 Art. 7(1)i–iii, vi *Foreign Nationals Exit–Entry Administration Law Implementation Rules* (2010).

100 Art. 7(1)iv–v *Foreign Nationals Exit–Entry Administration Law Implementation Rules* (2010).

101 Art. 12(1)i–iv *Foreign Nationals Exit–Entry Administration Law Implementation Rules* (2010).

102 Art. 40, 42, 44 *Foreign Nationals Exit–Entry Administration Law Implementation Rules* (1986).

103 Art. 41, 43, 45, 46, 47 *Foreign Nationals Exit–Entry Administration Law Implementation Rules* (1986).

could be ordered to leave the country within a certain period of time or be repatriated.[104] Foreign nationals illegally staying or working in China, those without proper exit–entry documents or those entering areas not open to foreign nationals without permission could be ordered to leave only in severe circumstances.[105]

Apart from detailed sanctions, the *Foreign Nationals Exit–Entry Administration Law Implementation Rules* defined different visa types for foreign nationals to enter China with the aim of permanent residence (D), employment (Z), study or fieldwork (X), travelling (L), transit (G), as a crew member (C), as correspondent (J),[106] or for scientific, technical, cultural, or business exchange (F).[107] For each of these different types of visas, the application procedures were defined.[108] It was not explicitly stated in the *Foreign Nationals Exit–Entry Administration Law Implementation Rules* that behaviour different from the purpose of stay as indicated on the visa was not permitted. However, to be able to get required permits for permanent residence, employment, or study, a visa of the appropriate visa type was needed.

The *Foreign Nationals Exit–Entry Administration Law Implementation Rules* were revised twice in 1994 and 2010. While in 2010 only item 4 of Article 7 was amended to extend the scope of diseases due to which entry was denied,[109] the revision of 1994 was of considerably larger scope. Besides the introduction of another visa category for foreign correspondents (J-1 and J-2)[110] and a new provision stating that tourists had to hold a ticket for their return trip when necessary,[111] the 1994 revision especially concerned tightening of sanctions. Illegal stay of foreign nationals, e. g., could now be punished with a fine of RMB 500 per day not exceeding RMB 5 000 or

104 Art. 40, 47 *Foreign Nationals Exit–Entry Administration Law Implementation Rules* (1986).

105 Art. 42, 43, 44, 46 *Foreign Nationals Exit–Entry Administration Law Implementation Rules* (1986).

106 Visa types J-1 and J-2 for correspondents were introduced in 1994.

107 Art. 4(1)i–viii *Foreign Nationals Exit–Entry Administration Law Implementation Rules* (2010).

108 Art. 5(1)i–viii *Foreign Nationals Exit–Entry Administration Law Implementation Rules* (2010).

109 Art. 7(4) *Foreign Nationals Exit–Entry Administration Law Implementation Rules* (1994); Art. 7(4) *Foreign Nationals Exit–Entry Administration Law Implementation Rules* (2010).

110 Art. 4(8) *Foreign Nationals Exit–Entry Administration Law Implementation Rules* (1994).

111 Art. 7(4) *Foreign Nationals Exit–Entry Administration Law Implementation Rules* (1994).

with detention of three to ten days, while the old rules provided for a single charge of RMB 100 to 500 or detention of one to three days.[112] Foreign nationals who ignored decisions of the public security organs could be charged RMB 1 000 to 10 000 instead of formerly only RMB 100 to 500; when foreign nationals were not able or not willing to present their legal documents for examination they could be fined RMB 500 instead of formerly RMB 20 to 50.[113] A new provision codified the punishment of illegally employing foreign nationals with a fine of RMB 5 000 to 50 000 that was added to the expenses for repatriation of the foreign national.[114]

Summing up, the first law on exit–entry administration of foreign nationals was obviously designed as a mere framework that the legislators planned to fill with more specific regulations over time. The fact that the law only contained one general provision concerning punishment and legal remedies clearly underlines this assumption. Detailed provisions concerning specific sanctions, as well as concerning specific kinds of legal documents needed for the entry to China, along with the relevant procedures for application were codified in separate regulations jointly issued by the Ministry of Public Security and the Ministry of Foreign Affairs. Being implementation provisions issued by the executive, by their very nature such provisions can be amended easier and quicker in comparison to a law. Amendments to the implementation provisions indeed were made several times, which again suggests that the law was intended to serve as a rough framework. Certain other aspects of exit–entry administration, however, such as procedures of employment of foreign nationals or permanent residence, were neither covered in detail by the law nor in the implementation provisions and only over time became codified in separate regulations, resulting in an increasingly complex legal framework.

---

112 Art. 42 *Foreign Nationals Exit–Entry Administration Law Implementation Rules* (1986); Art. 42(1) *Foreign Nationals Exit–Entry Administration Law Implementation Rules* (1994).

113 Art. 42, 43 *Foreign Nationals Exit–Entry Administration Law Implementation Rules* (1986); Art. 42(3), 43 *Foreign Nationals Exit–Entry Administration Law Implementation Rules* (1994).

114 Art. 44(2) *Foreign Nationals Exit–Entry Administration Law Implementation Rules* (1994).

IV. Provisions on Exit–Entry Administration in Other Laws

One result of economic reforms that opened up China to foreign investment and gradually allowed for privatisation was an increase of foreign nationals entering China. As migration into the country increased, new challenges to the legal framework emerged. How should employment of foreign nationals in China be regulated? How should permanent residence of foreign nationals in China be managed? How could those foreign nationals be attracted who could contribute to economic growth in order to support the domestic economy? The cursory legal framework promulgated in 1985 did not address these questions and several supplemental regulations were therefore codified. The process "[f]rom prohibition policy to relaxation policy,"[115] that began with a comparatively restrictive migration framework in the 1950s and evolved to a more relaxed framework until China's accession to the World Trade Organisation (WTO)[116] continued after 2001. Jia Chunwang[117], Minister of Public Security, announced in 2001 several important reforms in the area of immigration legislation, such as the introduction of a 'green card' system, without, however, mentioning any wider law reform plans.[118] Furthermore, with the accession to the WTO, the system that allowed foreign visitors to stay only at authorised hotels was repealed in several cities.[119]

Until 2013, regulations concerning exit, entry, and stay of foreign nationals were spread over a multitude of legal norms mainly promulgated by the Ministry of Public Security.[120] Liu cites an astonishing number of not less than 24 different rules and regulations related to entry to China that were applicable until 2013.[121] In addition to subordinate regulations to codify specific areas of exit–entry administration, a framework of administrative law was established gradually. The regulations of the 1985 laws on exit–entry administration became hence embedded in a complex framework of superordinate and subordinate norms.

---

115 Guofu Liu (2009), p. 312.
116 Guofu Liu (2009).
117 Chinese: 贾春旺.
118 Mao (2001).
119 See e. g. *Beijing People's Government: Foreigners Free to Choose Hotels* (2003).
120 Guofu Liu (2007), p. 143.
121 Guofu Liu (2011), p. 11 f.

1. Establishment of Administrative Law

The ongoing institutional reforms placed their focus on accountability to the central authorities and control of local authorities, which is reflected in the promulgation of the 1989 *Administrative Litigation Law* and the 1999 *Administrative Reconsideration Law*. On the 3rd Plenary Session of the 16th Congress of the Communist Party of China in October 2003, it was highlighted that the "government's role in managing the economy should shift to providing market services",[122] and in December 2004, WEN Jiabao[123] made clear that a service-oriented governance[124] in the context of the long-term goal of a "harmonious society"[125] was the aim of administrative reform.[126] HU Jintao[127] further stressed that reform of the administrative system was the precondition for the development of a service-oriented government[128] and in the *Outline to Promote Measures for Administration According to Law*,[129] the State Council on 22 March 2004 stated that the objective of the reforms was administration on the basis of law.[130] As a result of this new policy to promote administrative reform, a set of legal norms was promulgated in the area of administrative law in the years to follow.

At the time of the promulgation of the 1985 *Foreign Nationals Exit–Entry Administration Law* and the 1985 *Citizen Exit–Entry Administration Law*, the framework of administrative law was only in the making. The *Administrative Litigation Law* entered into force in 1990, followed by the *Administrative Penalty Law* and the *Administrative Reconsideration Law*. In the 2003, the *Administrative Licence Law* was promulgated, in 2005, the *Regulations on Administrative Penalties for Public Security* became codified as *Public Security Administration Punishments Law*, and in 2012, the *Administrative Compulsion Law* entered into force. In 2009, the *Administrative Reconsideration Law* and the *Administrative Penalty Law* were amended. Apart from the establishment of an administrative law framework, the *Legislation Law* was promulgated in 2000, which determines a hierarchy of norms and clarifies that newer laws supersede older norms and more specific norms

122 Cited in Guanghui ZHOU (2010), p. 149.
123 Chinese: 温家宝.
124 Chinese: 服务型政府.
125 Chinese: 和谐社会.
126 Guanghui ZHOU (2010), p. 149 f.
127 Chinese: 胡锦涛.
128 Guanghui ZHOU (2010), p. 151.
129 *Outline to Promote Measures for Administration According to Law* (2004).
130 Guanghui ZHOU (2010), p. 162.

supersede general norms. In 1995, the *Regulations on Exit and Entry Border Inspection* were promulgated in order to regulate border control procedures. Finally, the handling of criminal litigation, administrative litigation, and administrative reconsideration cases became codified in the relevant *Procedural Provisions of the Handling by Public Security Organs*.[131]

2. Relevant Provisions in Criminal Law

Sanctions for illegal behaviour in the context of exit–entry administration were not only codified in the *Foreign Nationals Exit–Entry Administration Law* and the *Citizen Exit–Entry Administration Law* as well as in the *Administrative Penalty Law* and the *Public Security Administration Punishments Law*, but the *Criminal Law* made and still makes certain provisions that define crimes against border control administration, too. Detailed definitions of crimes against border control administration were promulgated in 2000.[132] The 1979 *Criminal Law* already provided for the independent or supplemental penalty of expelling foreign nationals from the territory[133] and defined the crimes of crossing the national frontier in violation of exit–entry administration regulations[134] as well as of organising or transporting others in order to illegally cross the border for profit.[135] These provisions were revised in 1997 when they obtained their present shape. After 1997, only Article 322 *Criminal Law* was amended once in 2015 to also cover the offence of illegally crossing the border with the aim of organising or participating in the training or actual execution of terrorist activities. In 1997, the *Criminal Law* was restructured and in its second part entitled "Special Provisions", Section 3 concerning "Crimes of Disrupting Border Administration" was added to Chapter VI on "Crimes of Disrupting the Order of Social Administration". In this section, Article 318 now covers the crime of organising people to secretly cross the border, Articles 319 and 320 define the crimes of defrauding exit–entry documents and providing falsified or forged exit–entry documents, Article 321 incriminates the secret transport-

131 *Provisions on Handling Criminal Cases* (2012); *Provisions on Handling Administrative Cases* (2012); *Provisions on Handling Administrative Reconsideration Cases* (2002).
132 *Border Administration Crimes Note* (2000).
133 Art. 30 *Criminal Law* (1979).
134 Art. 176 *Criminal Law* (1979).
135 Art. 177 *Criminal Law* (1979).

ation of others across the border while Article 322 covers secretly crossing the border in general. Finally, Article 323 defines the crime of intentional sabotage of boundary markers. As most part of the underlying legal framework still applies today, a detailed analysis of administrative as well as of criminal sanctions concerning illegal entry, illegal stay, and illegal employment as well as offences against border control administration on the basis of current exit–entry legislation will be conducted in chapter 4. As for now, it should be sufficient to refer to these different legal provisions to illustrate the legal framework in which the legal provisions on exit–entry administration are embedded.

3. Administration of the Employment of Foreign Nationals

In 1996, the *Rules for the Administration of Employment of Foreign Nationals in China* were issued jointly by the Ministry of Labour, the Ministry of Public Security, the Ministry of Foreign Affairs and the Ministry of Foreign Trade and Economic Cooperation. These rules are still in force today, albeit amended in 2017, and their current application will be discussed in more detail in chapter 4. The *Rules for the Administration of Employment of Foreign Nationals in China* regulate the procedures foreign nationals have to pass through in order to be employed in China and replaced the previous rules of 1987. According to their own definition, the rules only apply to foreign nationals without permanent residence status engaging in remunerative work.[136]

According to the 1996 version of the rules, the Chinese employer first had to apply for a foreign nationals employment licence[137] in order to be able to employ a foreign national. In order to apply for such a permit, the employer had to hand in a *curriculum vitae* and health certificate of the foreign national, a letter of intention and a report of reasons for employment and other required documents to his or her competent trade authority.[138] After approval by this authority, the responsible labour authority subordinate to the Ministry of Labour would issue the foreign nationals employment licence together with a letter of visa notification directly to the foreign national who

136 Art. 2(2) *Foreign Nationals Employment Regulations* (1996).
137 Chinese: 外国人就业许可证书. Art. 5 *Foreign Nationals Employment Regulations* (1996).
138 Art. 11 *Foreign Nationals Employment Regulations* (1996).

was to be employed.[139] The foreign national then had to go through the general visa application procedures with the Chinese consulate or embassy in order to be issued a visa for work purposes (Z visa).[140] After the entry of the foreign national to China, the employer had to sign an employment contract with the foreign employee and, within 15 days apply for a work permit[141] for this foreign national. In order to apply for the work permit, the signed employment contract, the employment licence, as well as the exit–entry documents of the foreign nationals had to be handed in with the labour authority that issued the employment licence.[142] Finally the foreign national had to, within 30 days after entry, apply for a residence permit with the responsible public security organ by handing in his or her exit–entry documents and the work permit,[143] as well as a health certificate.[144]

4. Administration of Permanent Residence of Foreign Nationals

Codification also developed in the areas of permanent residence and attraction of foreign talent. In the original legal framework of 1985, permanent residence and attraction of foreign talent were codified only basically. The 1985 *Foreign Nationals Exit–Entry Administration Law* provided merely one general provision stating that foreign nationals "for the purpose of investing in China or engaging in cooperative projects with Chinese enterprises or institutions in the economic, scientific, technological and cultural fields, or for other purposes" could apply for permanent residence with the competent authorities.[145] The *Foreign Nationals Exit–Entry Administration Law Implementation Rules* added that foreign nationals who meet the requirements of Article 14 of the *Foreign Nationals Exit–Entry Administration Law* (1985)

139 Art. 12, 14 *Foreign Nationals Employment Regulations* (1996).

140 Art. 15 *Foreign Nationals Employment Regulations* (1996). Before 1996, foreign nationals holding visas other than Z could, in certain cases also apply for employment; *Foreign Nationals Employment Regulations* (1987).

141 Chinese: 就业证.

142 Art. 16 *Foreign Nationals Employment Regulations* (1996).

143 Art. 17 *Foreign Nationals Employment Regulations* (1996).

144 Art. 17(1)iii *Foreign Nationals Exit–Entry Administration Law Implementation Rules* (1986) or *Foreign Nationals Exit–Entry Administration Law Implementation Rules* (2010).

145 Art. 14 *Foreign Nationals Exit–Entry Administration Law* (1985).

and who obtained "outstanding achievements"[146] may qualify for permanent residence.[147]

In 2004, the *Measures for the Administration of Examination and Approval of Foreign Nationals' Permanent Residence in China* were issued jointly by the Ministry of Public Security and the Ministry of Foreign Affairs introducing a permanent residence scheme for foreign nationals, also known as 'green card' system, which is still in force today. According to these measures, certain foreign nationals are granted an ID certificate that enables them to exit and enter China together with their passport.[148] Such an ID certificate is only issued to foreign nationals who have made direct investments of a certain amount in China, who hold certain high-ranking posts or "who have made outstanding contributions to China and who are of special need for the country"[149], as well as to those who are the spouse or children of another foreign national already holding permanent residence status, or who have reached the age of 60 years or more without direct relatives abroad.[150] The measures further specify the concrete amount of direct investment and the scope of high-ranking posts that enable application for permanent residence.

After 2000, the attraction of foreign talent, an item on the political agenda since the early 1980s,[151] became a focus of legislation.[152] In 2002, *Provisions on Providing Entry and Residence Conveniences to Foreign Highly Skilled Persons and Investors*[153] were issued; in 2008, the Central Committee Working Group of the Communist Party on the Coordination of Talent Work issued *Opinions on Foreign Talent Regarding the Implementation of the Plan of Attracting Foreign Highly Skilled Talent*[154], the *Provisions on Special Benefits for Foreign Highly Skilled Talent*[155] as well as the *Trial*

146 Chinese: 显著成效.

147 Art. 18 *Foreign Nationals Exit–Entry Administration Law Implementation Rules* (2010).

148 Art. 3, 4 *Permanent Residence Measures* (2004).

149 Chinese: 对中国有重大、突出贡献以及国家特别需要的. Art. 6(3) *Permanent Residence Measures* (2004).

150 Art. 6 *Permanent Residence Measures* (2004).

151 *Provisional Rules on Introducing Overseas Talented People* (1983).

152 Ahl / Czoske (2016).

153 *Provisions on Providing Entry and Residence Conveniences to Foreign Highly Skilled Persons and Investors* (2002).

154 *Opinions on Foreign Talent Regarding the Implementation of the Plan of Attracting Foreign Highly Skilled Talent* (2008).

155 Chinese: 关于海外高层次引进人才享受特定生活待遇的若干规定.

Measures on Attracting Highly Skilled Foreign Talent[156] were promulgated. The 'green card' system codified with the *Permanent Residence Measures* (2004) also, at least partly, can be traced back to this policy line aiming at strengthening the attraction of foreign talent. Finally, in 2011, the Ministry of Human Resources and Social Security issued a *Notice Regarding Questions of the Proper Participation of Foreign Workers in the Social Insurance System*[157] that provided a detailed legal framework for the participation of foreign nationals in the Chinese social security scheme according to the provisions of the *Social Insurance Law* (2010).

V. Shortcomings of the 1985 Legal Framework

The legal framework of exit–entry administration based on the laws of 1985 could no longer meet the requirements demanded by the development of immigration issues and thus needed to be revised. One problem already tackled by the 1994 amendment of the *Foreign Nationals Exit–Entry Administration Law Implementation Rules* was the claimed inability of the sanctions to unfurl a deterrent effect on offenders. A much more significant problem, however, was identified in the emerging conflicts of the legal provisions of the 1985 laws with newer or higher-ranking legislation that were reported not only officially but also by academics.[158] A framework on administrative law has been established since the late 1980s in the context of which new laws on administrative reconsideration, administrative litigation, administrative licences, administrative penalties, administrative compulsion as well as on public security administrative punishments have been promulgated.[159] Certain regulations codified in the 1985 exit–entry administration laws were not in line with these new provisions.

The underlying problem for certain legal conflicts between provisions of the *Foreign Nationals Exit–Entry Administration Law* (1985) and of other, newer national laws is the fact that according to the *Legislation Law* (2000)

156 Chinese: 引进海外高层次人才暂行办法.
157 *Notice Regarding Questions of the Proper Participation of Foreign Workers in the Social Insurance System* (2011).
158 See e. g. Jiang Jianyun (2013).
159 *Administrative Litigation Law* (1989); *Administrative Penalty Law* (1996); *Administrative Licence Law* (2003); *Public Security Administration Punishments Law* (2005); *Administrative Reconsideration Law* (2009); *Administrative Compulsion Law* (2011).

newer laws or regulations shall supersede older laws or regulations, but specific laws or regulations again shall prevail over general laws or regulations.[160] In case of conflicts between the special but older norms of the *Foreign Nationals Exit–Entry Administration Law* and newer but more general norms of higher-ranking laws, such as the *Administrative Penalty Law* or the *Administrative Litigation Law*, the correct implementation of immigration legislation could be difficult. Although the Standing Committee of the National People's Congress or, if only provisions promulgated by a body of the executive branch are concerned, the State Council may issue rulings to clarify such conflicts,[161] no such clarification was made concerning contradictory provisions such as penalties and legal remedies in the context of exit–entry administration. Due to that omission and because the new legal framework established rules whose implementation in the context of exit–entry administration law was not specified, in practice there was often no other way than to stick to the old, albeit outdated rules of the *Foreign Nationals Exit–Entry Administration Law*.[162]

The incompatibility of the old exit–entry administration legislation with this new administrative legislation framework is best illustrated by Article 29 *Foreign Nationals Exit–Entry Administration Law*, that consisted of a general provision regarding penalties and legal remedies and only explicitly provided for access to legal remedies in cases where the foreign national was fined or detained. This regulation became incompatible in many ways with relevant provisions of the current framework of administrative law. While the *Public Security Administrative Punishment Law* e. g. clarifies that officials of local police stations (*paichusuo*[163]) below county level are entitled to impose warnings of fines up to RMB 500,[164] it is questionable whether this rule also applies in the area of immigration law, as the more specific regulation of the *Foreign Nationals Exit–Entry Administration Law* stated that any punishment should be imposed by police authorities at county level or above.[165]

The *Administrative Reconsideration Law* and the *Administrative Litigation Law* grant legal remedies against administrative acts such as revocation

160 Art. 83 *Legislation Law* (2000).
161 Art. 85 *Legislation Law* (2000).
162 Jiang Jianyun (2013), p. 72.
163 Chinese: 派出所.
164 Art. 91 *Public Security Administration Punishments Law* (2005).
165 Art. 29 *Foreign Nationals Exit–Entry Administration Law* (1985); Jiang Jianyun (2013), p. 73.

or non-issuance of licences or compulsory measures and in general allow for administrative reconsideration or litigation against infringements of personal or property rights resulting from an administrative act.[166] The *Foreign Nationals Exit–Entry Administration Law,* however, only explicitly recognised administrative reconsideration against fines or detention and remained silent with regard to other administrative acts.[167] As the *Foreign Nationals Exit–Entry Administration Law* does not explicitly exclude certain administrative acts from administrative reconsideration or litigation, it would be possible to apply administrative litigation or reconsideration against repatriation measures, which is, however, difficult to apply in practice. Further, the *Foreign Nationals Exit–Entry Administration Law* required applications for administrative reconsideration or administrative litigation to be handed in within 15 days, while the *Administrative Reconsideration Law* and the *Administrative Litigation Law* define a time limit of 60 days and three months respectively.[168] This makes it unclear whether the shorter time limit as defined in the more specific *Foreign Nationals Exit–Entry Administration Law* or the longer time limit as defined in the *Administrative Reconsideration Law* and the *Administrative Litigation Law* should apply in the context of exit–entry administration law.

Certain contradictions also appear between newer laws and regulations on immigration administration. Newer regulations on the same normative level supersede older regulations. However, the provisions defined in a law should always supersede those of lower-level legal norms.[169] Article 48 *Foreign Nationals Exit–Entry Administration Law Implementation Rules* (2010), e. g., allowed for detention as alternative sentence if a fine could not be paid, but neither the *Administrative Penalty Law* nor the *Public Security Administration Punishments Law* provide for the conversion of a fine into detention.[170] The 1995 *Exit–Entry Border Inspection Regulations* provide for measures that restrict the personal freedom as well as certain coercive

166 Art. 6(1)i,ii,viii,ix *Administrative Reconsideration Law* (2009); Art. 11(1)i,ii,iv,viii *Administrative Litigation Law* (1989).

167 Art. 29 *Foreign Nationals Exit–Entry Administration Law* (1985); see as well Jiang Jianyun (2013), p. 75.

168 Art. 29 *Foreign Nationals Exit–Entry Administration Law* (1985); Art. 9 *Administrative Reconsideration Law* (2009); Art. 39 *Administrative Litigation Law* (1989); see as well Jiang Jianyun (2013), p. 75.

169 Art. 83 *Legislation Law* (2000).

170 Art. 48 *Foreign Nationals Exit–Entry Administration Law Implementation Rules* (2010); see as well Jiang Jianyun (2013), p. 73 f.

measures,[171] but according to the *Legislation Law*, the *Administrative Penalty Law* and the *Administrative Compulsion Law*, regulations restricting the personal freedom and coercive measures may only be defined by formal law adopted by the National People's Congress or its Standing Committee.[172] The 1995 *Exit–Entry Border Inspection Regulations* further require administrative reconsideration before filing an administrative litigation lawsuit,[173] while the *Foreign Nationals Exit–Entry Administration Law* did not stipulate such an requirement.[174]

Apart from contradictory or unclear provisions, swift enforcement of legal norms was hampered because of too cumbersome procedures. According to the *Provisions on Handling Administrative Cases* (2003) and the *Provisions on Handling Administrative Cases* (2006), deportations or orders to leave of foreign nationals had to be decided by the Ministry of Public Security.[175] According to the *Provisions on Handling Criminal Cases* (1998), compulsory measures imposed on foreign nationals like detention, residential confinement or bail pending trial had to be reported to the Ministry of Public Security and to the foreign affairs authority at the same administrative level.[176] Although, in 2008, the authority of approval concerning orders to leave were shifted downwards to the public security authorities on provincial level,[177] these provisions rendered it difficult for police authorities at lower levels to impose a deportation or an order to leave or to implement compulsory measures on foreign nationals in a timely manner. In addition to the inefficiency of enforcement there is also the problem of decentralised administration and a lack of cooperation between the authorities, which will be discussed in the last section of this part.

VI. Summary

This section outlines the historical development of Chinese exit–entry administration law and concludes that its latest development was influenced

171 Art. 32, 33 *Exit–Entry Border Inspection Regulations* (1995).

172 Art. 8(1)v *Legislation Law* (2000).

173 Art. 42 *Exit–Entry Border Inspection Regulations* (1995).

174 JIANG Jianyun (2013), p. 79; Art. 44 *Administrative Litigation Law* (2014) explicitly allows for administrative litigation without prior administrative reconsideration.

175 Art. 187 *Provisions on Handling Administrative Cases* (2003); Art. 195 *Provisions on Handling Administrative Cases* (2006).

176 Art. 331 *Provisions on Handling Criminal Cases* (1998).

177 Art. 1 *Notice on Approval Authority for Orders to Leave* (2008).

by the economic reforms. This section further illustrates how Chinese exit–entry administration law is embedded into Chinese law as well as its relation to administrative law and criminal law. Finally, an analysis is made of the provisions of Chinese nationality law that primarily apply the principle of *ius sanguinis* and constitute the legal foundation for immigration law. The findings of this section regarding the relationship of exit–entry administration law with the overall framework of administrative and criminal law will be taken up again in chapter 4 where the current legal framework of exit–entry administration law is analysed in depth.

Summing up the above findings, exit–entry administration before 1985 was merely based on rules or regulations or provisional measures issued by the State Council, which could not serve as the stable and predictive normative framework needed for economic reforms. The increased exchange with foreign countries, especially economically, resulted in the need for a reliable legal framework that facilitated exit and entry. The promulgation of the *Nationality Law* or the *Regulations on Passports and Visas* in the early years of economic reform illustrate the aim to establish a comprehensive legal framework. The issuance of legal documents like the *Notification about the Conscientious Implementation of Document Gongfa (Jing) 59 to Further Relax the Restrictions on Exiting the Country for Private Affairs* or the *Regulations on the Administration of Foreign Nationals Travelling in China* illustrates the aim to facilitate exit and entry.

While the 1985 laws surely represented a milestone in immigration law, constituting the first comprehensive legal framework to codify exit–entry administration, they were not able to keep up with the overall legal development in consequence of economic and institutional reforms. Especially the framework of administrative law, which has gradually been established as a result of ongoing institutionalisation driven by economic reforms, led to the factual invalidity of certain provision of the 1985 laws. However, in practice, the 1985 regulations could not easily be ignored due to the lack of other legal norms on the subject. Especially the phenomenon of newer, but more general provisions that stood in conflict with older, but more specific provisions emerged. The 1985 laws only cursorily regulated exit–entry administration and did not cover aspects like employment or permanent residence, which became ever more important with the growing number of foreign nationals entering the country. In the context of attracting foreign talent, permanent residence and procedures for the employment of foreign nationals, new policies and regulations were promulgated, to which the 1985 law could no longer serve as an appropriate legal basis.

The 1985 laws on exit–entry administration were clearly formulated to be in line with economic reforms and the overall opening policy when they aimed at intensifying foreign exchange and supporting the establishment of the 'Four Modernisations' as it was officially claimed. In the course of intensified institutional reform, however, several shortcomings of the old legal framework became visible. First, with the overall increasing influx of foreign nationals, the old framework proved to be insufficient in providing for dissuasive penalties and efficient enforcement measures. Furthermore, normative conflicts with other legal provisions, especially with higher-ranking laws, became a problem for the enforcement of legal provisions. I conclude that economic reforms served as a direct driver to the revision of exit–entry administration law, because increasing exchange with foreign countries necessarily resulted in challenges to the legal framework. But economic reforms also indirectly drove the revision of exit–entry administration law, as an increased institutionalisation led to the codification of a new legal framework of administration law that again made a revision of exit–entry administration law necessary.

C. Revision of Immigration Legislation and the Making of the Current Law

Although experimentation decreased after China's accession to the World Trade Organisation in 2001, which led to a harmonisation of Chinese laws with international standards,[178] experimentation as an essential part of Chinese law making did not cease to be deployed. Rooted in the revolutionary years of the Communist Party of China,[179] experimentation has been an important element of economic and institutional reforms. HEILMANN identifies the distinct style of Chinese experimental governance as "experimentation under hierarchy".[180] Experimentation in this sense does not mean that certain local units have unlimited leeway in establishing experimental rules or structures. Rather, the scope of action is strictly controlled and the area of governance as well as the intended objectives are clearly defined. After initial input, which may stem from local initiatives but has to be supported and approved by central-level organs, the central

178 See HEILMANN (2008) who finds an overall decrease of regulations with experimental status especially between 1997 and 2001; HEILMANN (2008), p. 6.
179 HEILMANN (2011), p. 64.
180 HEILMANN (2008), p. 2.

government typically authorises a certain administrative unit to deploy experimental policies by assigning a certain scope of discretionary power to this unit. During the implementation of experimental policies, feedback through inspection work groups dispatched by the central government and reporting schemes is collected. On the basis of positive feedback, national regulations are drafted and, if no objections are raised, finally enacted.[181] As immigration law does not primarily cover economic aspects of policing, I assume that experimentation also played an important role in the reform of exit–entry administration.

This section focuses on the revision process in exit–entry administration legislation that resulted in the 2012 law. In order to carve out the major aims of the revision process of exit–entry administration law, which will serve as a basis for the deeper analysis conducted in chapter 4, this section analyses the drafting process of the *Exit–Entry Administration Law* at the national level as well as the implementation of legal provisions established in Guangdong province, where immigration legislation was enacted earlier on a local level. This section analyses the role of experimentation in the context of the revision of exit–entry law, by assessing in which way local provisions were adopted by national legislation.

The previous section pointed to the development of administrative law that made a revision of exit–entry administration law necessary. In 2003, the Central Committee of the Communist Party of China issued a *Decision to Further Strengthen and Improve Public Security Work*[182] that underlines the need to reform administrative processes. The revision process and the institutional reforms in the context of exit–entry administration, however, were both initiated around 2003. I hence assume that the process of the revision of immigration law was a result of a larger political aim to enhance the improvement of foreign nationals management work as an important part of public security work.

---

181 See Heilmann (2008) who analyses the underlying structure of the experimentation process in detail.

182 *Decision by the CPC Central Committee to Further Strengthen and Improve Public Security Work* (2003).

I. Consideration of Local Implementation During National Legislation

At the 1st Session of the 10th National People's Congress, a proposal submitted by Zulpiye ABDUQADIR[183] and 23 other deputies to the Foreign Affairs Committee of the National People's Congress to revise the *Foreign Nationals Exit–Entry Administration Law* was discussed.[184] The Foreign Affairs Committee requested the Ministry of Public Security and the Ministry of Foreign Affairs to submit their opinions on this legislation initiative and organised working groups to be dispatched to Jilin, Guangxi, Guangdong, Shanghai, Zhejiang, Fujian and other places to examine the local implementation of the law.[185] The Ministry of Public Security, in response to the request of the Foreign Affairs Committee, submitted an proposal to draft[186] a new law in October 2003 which was then approved by the Committee.[187]

The Foreign Affairs Committee recognised the need to revise the two existing laws on exit–entry administration as they were regarded as no longer able to keep up with social development and not in line with more recent

183 Uyghur: زۇلپىيە ئابدۇقادىر; Chinese: 祖丽菲娅·阿不都卡德尔. Zulpiye ABDUQADIR was Chief Economist at the Xinjiang Uyghur Autonomous Region Road Transport Administration at that time; TRANSPORT DEPARTMENT OF XINJIANG UYGUR AUTONOMOUS REGION (新疆维吾尔自治区交通运输厅) (2014).

184 *Report of the Foreign Affairs Committee of the National People's Congress on the Results of the Consideration of the Proposal Handed over at the 1st Session of the 10th National People's Congress* (全国人大外事委员会关于第十届全国人民代表大会第一次会议主席团交付审议的代表提出的议案审议结果的报告), *NPC Foreign Affairs Committee Press Release* (2003). The exact date of the submission of this proposal has not been published, but it is already mentioned in a press release of the National People's Congress that covers all submissions until March 2003; *Report on Opinions to Handle Proposals Submitted by Deputies of the 1st Session of the 10th National People's Congress* (关于第十届全国人民代表大会第一次会议代表提出议案处理意见的报告), *NPC Foreign Affairs Committee Press Release* (2003).

185 *Report of the Foreign Affairs Committee of the National People's Congress on the Results of the Consideration of the Proposal Handed over at the 1st Session of the 10th National People's Congress* (全国人大外事委员会关于第十届全国人民代表大会第一次会议主席团交付审议的代表提出的议案审议结果的报告), *NPC Foreign Affairs Committee Press Release* (2003).

186 Chinese: 制定.

187 *Answers by Officials of the Ministry of Public Security to Journalists on the Implementation of the 'Exit–Entry Administration Law of the People's Republic of China'* (公安部负责人就贯彻执行《中华人民共和国出境入境管理法》答记者问), *NPC Standing Committee Press Release* (2012).

legislation. Starting from December 2004, the Ministry of Public Security began working on a draft of a revised law by establishing a working group.[188] The resulting draft was finalised by October 2007 according to a report of the Foreign Affairs Committee succeeding the 5th Plenary Session of the 10th National People's Congress.[189] In January 2008, the Ministry of Public Security laid out a draft for examination[190] to the State Council.[191]

Apart from the assessment of local practice, international practice and legal frameworks of exit–entry administration in other countries were also examined. One of these activities was the attendance of Chinese public security officials in the E. U.-funded project "Capacity Building for Migration Management in China", implemented by the International Organization of Migration and the International Labour Organization, which took place from 2008 to 2010 and again from 2012 to 2013, and during which legal provisions in the area immigration law of China and different E. U. countries were analysed.[192]

In May 2011, discussions were held by the Foreign Affairs Committee of the National People's Congress to amend the current exit–entry legislation, as the 11th National People's Congress had put the revision of the *Exit–Entry Administration Law* on its legislative agenda.[193] On 8 October

---

188 *Answers by Officials of the Ministry of Public Security to Journalists on the Implementation of the 'Exit–Entry Administration Law of the People's Republic of China'* (公安部负责人就贯彻执行《中华人民共和国出境入境管理法》答记者问), *NPC Standing Committee Press Release* (2012).

189 *Report of the Foreign Affairs Committee of the National People's Congress on the Results of the Consideration of the Proposal Handed over at the 5st Session of the 10th National People's Congress* (全国人大外事委员会关于第十届全国人民代表大会第五次会议主席团交付审议的代表提出的议案审议结果的报告), *NPC Foreign Affairs Committee Press Release* (2007); *Answers by Officials of the Ministry of Public Security to Journalists on the Implementation of the 'Exit–Entry Administration Law of the People's Republic of China'* (公安部负责人就贯彻执行《中华人民共和国出境入境管理法》答记者问), *NPC Standing Committee Press Release* (2012).

190 Chinese: 送审稿.

191 *Answers by Officials of the Ministry of Public Security to Journalists on the Implementation of the 'Exit–Entry Administration Law of the People's Republic of China'* (公安部负责人就贯彻执行《中华人民共和国出境入境管理法》答记者问), *NPC Standing Committee Press Release* (2012).

192 *Capacity Building For Migration Management in China* (2008); *Capacity Building For Migration Management in China Project Phase II* (2012).

193 *Foreign Affairs Committee of the National People's Congress Launches Investigation in Qingdao on the Amendment of the Exit–Entry Administration Law* (外事委

2011, the State Council passed a draft law and on 16 October forwarded it to the National People's Congress for consideration.[194] On 8 December 2011, a research group went to Zhuhai to gather suggestions on the draft of the amended *Exit–Entry Administration Law*.[195] The draft law was discussed in three sessions by the Standing Committee of the National People's Congress on 26 December 2011, 26 April 2012, and 26 June 2012.

On 31 December 2011, a first draft for the revised *Exit–Entry Administration Law* with explanations about the main aims of the new law was published by the Standing Committee of the National People's Congress for public consultation.[196] It contained eight sections with 90 articles in all, combining provisions on the administration of exit and entry of foreign as well as of Chinese nationals. The objectives of the new law were to tackle the problems of increased requirements for national safety and public administration, the existing loopholes in the visa and registration systems, as well as the increase of 'sanfei' incidents that had already been reported at least as from 2002. The main issue to be addressed as stated by Vice Minister of Public Security YANG Huanning[197] was the containment of illegal entry, stay, and employment (*sanfei*), which had to be brought into line with the need to amend and harmonise the old laws concerning exit and entry administration and to facilitate the visa administration processes to attract foreign experts.[198] To achieve this aim, the procedures for the employment

---

在青岛开展出境入境管理法修改立法调研), *NPC Standing Committee Press Release* (2011).

194 *Answers by Officials of the Ministry of Public Security to Journalists on the Implementation of the 'Exit–Entry Administration Law of the People's Republic of China'* (公安部负责人就贯彻执行《中华人民共和国出境入境管理法》答记者问), *NPC Standing Committee Press Release* (2012).

195 *Research Group of the National People's Congress Launches Investigation in Zhuhai on the Amendment of the Exit–Entry Administration Law* (全国人大调研组到珠海开展出入境管理法修改立法调研), *NPC Standing Committee Press Release* (2011).

196 *Clauses of the Exit–Entry Administration Law (Draft) and Explanations* (出境入境管理法（草案）条文及草案说明), *NPC Press Release* (2011); *Exit–Entry Administration Law (Draft)* (2011). The prior drafts are not publicly available.

197 Chinese: 杨焕宁.

198 Attraction of foreign talent has been on the political agenda at least since 1983 when relevant regulations were issued; *Provisional Rules on Introducing Overseas Talented People* (1983). However, detailed regulations have never been codified in a law since then.

of foreign nationals as well as administrative means to tackle the problem of illegal entry, stay, and employment were thoroughly amended.[199]

The draft improved several provisions of the old legal framework. For example, it defined a basic framework for the employment of foreign nationals in China. The task of directing the preparation of a foreign national employment catalogue was assigned to the Ministry of Human Resources and the task of issuing provisions on the administration of employment of foreign nationals to the State Council.[200] Foreign nationals to be employed as well as employers were required to apply for working permits and employment certificates respectively.[201] These requirements were in line with the existing framework on the employment of foreign nationals laid out in the *Foreign Nationals Employment Regulations* (1996). The draft further defined the scope of actions deemed as illegal employment, which had not been codified in the old law,[202] and imposed penalties for illegal employment of foreign nationals on the employee, the employer and also on intermediaries.[203]

Certain provisions of the old framework were defined in more detail. According to the draft, foreign nationals were not allowed to pursue activities inconsistent with the cause of stay indicated on their visa and had to leave the country within the allowed period of time.[204] They needed to register through the hotel or themselves within 24 hours after arrival[205] and to carry their legal documents with them and allow for inspection by the police at all times.[206] The draft also defined the length of stay without having to apply for a residence permit as 180 days.[207] Foreign nationals were not allowed to enter areas of prohibited entry without permission.[208]

The draft further described in more detail the provisions on expulsion of foreign nationals and on permanent residence. It contained detailed provisions for the detention by the police of foreign nationals suspected of having

199 *China to Enact Law to Solve the Problem of Foreign Nationals Illegally Entering, Residing, and Being Employed in China* (中国将立法解决外国人非法入境非法居留非法就业问题), *NPC Standing Committee Press Release* (2011).
200 Art. 41(1) *Exit–Entry Administration Law (Draft)* (2011).
201 Art. 30 *Exit–Entry Administration Law (Draft)* (2011).
202 Art. 42(1) *Exit–Entry Administration Law (Draft)* (2011).
203 Art. 78 *Exit–Entry Administration Law (Draft)* (2011).
204 Art. 36 *Exit–Entry Administration Law (Draft)* (2011).
205 Art. 38(1) *Exit–Entry Administration Law (Draft)* (2011).
206 Art. 37 *Exit–Entry Administration Law (Draft)* (2011).
207 Art. 28 *Exit–Entry Administration Law (Draft)* (2011).
208 Art. 43(2) *Exit–Entry Administration Law (Draft)* (2011).

entered, of staying, or of being employed illegally[209] as well as for the expulsion of foreign nationals who illegally entered or illegally stayed in China by the competent authorities.[210] The former law only contained one general provision that allows the Ministry of Public Security to order a foreign national to leave or to expel him or her.[211] The draft also contained detailed provisions regarding the administration of permanent residence permits—aiming to establish a legal basis for the framework codified in the *Permanent Residence Measures* (2004)—, regarding visa issuance,[212] as well as regarding the issuance of invitations by enterprises or organisations.[213] The draft further addressed the legal status of refugees[214] in order to "comply with China's international obligations."[215] Finally, the draft clarified the circumstances in which the competent authorities could deny the issuance of a visa.[216]

The draft law was based on an amended version of the 1985 *Foreign Nationals Exit–Entry Administration Law*, its 1986 *Implementation Rules* as well as the 1995 *Regulations on Border Inspection*. In comparison to the 1985 law, it codified several new aspects, like the notion to combine service and administration or the exchange of data between different authorities.[217] It also put more emphasis on the collection of data, biometric data in particular,[218] regarding the exit and entry of individuals as well as on investigation procedures and legal remedies, and it took into account special requirements of districts in the border regions.[219]

Most importantly, the draft law abolished a range of problematic regulations of the old legal framework. For example, the contradictory provisions

---

209 Art. 58 *Exit–Entry Administration Law (Draft)* (2011).
210 Art. 61 *Exit–Entry Administration Law (Draft)* (2011).
211 Art. 29 *Foreign Nationals Exit–Entry Administration Law* (1985).
212 Art. 46–48 *Exit–Entry Administration Law (Draft)* (2011).
213 Art. 18 *Exit–Entry Administration Law (Draft)* (2011).
214 Art. 85 *Exit–Entry Administration Law (Draft)* (2011).
215 *China to Enact Law to Solve the Problem of Foreign Nationals Illegally Entering, Residing, and Being Employed in China* (中国将立法解决外国人非法入境非法居留非法就业问题), *NPC Standing Committee Press Release* (2011).
216 Art. 20 *Exit–Entry Administration Law (Draft)* (2011).
217 *Exit–Entry Administration Law Draft: Establishing a Unified Data Administration Platform to Enable Data Sharing* (出入境管理法草案: 建立统一管理信息平台实现信息共享), *NPC Standing Committee Press Release* (2012).
218 Art. 7 *Exit–Entry Administration Law (Draft)* (2011); *China's Projected Regulations to Introduce the Collection of Fingerprints in Exit–Entry Administration* (我国拟立法规定将指纹采集引入出境入境管理), *NPC Standing Committee Press Release* (2011).
219 Art. 87 *Exit–Entry Administration Law (Draft)* (2011).

regarding the time limit for administrative reconsideration and administrative litigation that was only 15 days according to the *Foreign Nationals Exit–Entry Administration Law* (1985) but 60 days or three months respectively according to the *Administrative Reconsideration Law* and the *Administrative Litigation Law* were abolished. Moreover, while the old legal framework defined the applicability of legal remedies only for certain sanctions, the draft law, following an opposing logic, provided for the exclusion of certain legal remedies only in certain cases,[220] which is in line with the provisions of the legal framework on administrative reconsideration and administrative litigation.

After its first issuance, the draft was discussed three times, the first two times at the 24th Session of the Standing Committee of the 11th National People's Congress on 26 December 2011, and at its 26th Session on 24 April 2012. In February and March 2012, the National People's Congress conducted inspections in Guangdong, Hainan, Guangxi and Beijing to collect information about exit–entry administration and service to foreign nationals, finding that the current provisions still could not meet the requirements of every-day application, especially regarding visa issuance and employment. Thus, it was considered necessary to enhance the sharing of information and, to this end, establish a data exchange platform.[221] At the 27th Session of the Standing Committee of the 11th National People's Congress on 26 June 2012, at the third reading, the revised law was finally promulgated and entered into force on 1 January 2013. Together with the new law, the relevant implementation regulations were revised. The *Regulations on the Administration of the Exit and Entry of Foreign Nationals* promulgated on 3 July 2013 replaced the *Foreign Nationals Exit–Entry Administration Law Implementation Rules* (2010) and entered into force on 1 September 2013. The *Citizens Exit–Entry Administration Law Implementation Rules*, however, remained in force unaltered. The *Exit–Entry Administration Regulations* (2013) comprise detailed provisions regarding the different visa and resident permit types, a detailed definition of 'illegal stay' as well as implementation provisions regarding the administration of stay and residence, police inspections and repatriations. In contrast to the old implementation

220 See e. g. Art. 25, 63, 79(2) *Exit–Entry Administration Law (Draft)* (2011).

221 *China Promotes Opening Up and Foreign Relations by Enacting Norms on Exit–Entry Administration* (中国立法规范出入境管理促进对外开放和交往), *NPC Press Release* (2012).

provisions, the *Exit–Entry Administration Regulations* (2013) refrain from codifying specific sanctions.

II. Guangdong Province as Experimental Region for Immigration Legislation

The local regulations on administration of foreign nationals introduced in 2011 in Guangdong province can be regarded as experimental provisions that largely contributed to the revised *Exit–Entry Administration Law*. In this section, I look into the legal provisions that were promulgated in Guangdong, which served as an experimental region in the field of immigration legislation.

Prior to the promulgation of the revised *Exit–Entry Administration Law*, in May 2011, *Interim Provisions of Guangdong Province on Administration of and Services to Foreign Nationals*, promulgated by the Provincial Government,[222] entered into force. The declared objective of these provisions was the "standardisation of foreign nationals management, the improvement of service to foreign nationals and the promotion of the development of a harmonious society".[223] The *Guangdong Interim Provisions* explicitly targeted the problem of 'sanfei' population in the province by codifying a report and reward system in the field of immigration law.[224] According to the provisions, every natural and legal person as well as every organisation could be granted a reward for reporting foreign nationals who were illegally employed, who illegally entered or stayed in China, who conducted businesses without proper licenses, or who committed any crime or action causing harm to the national safety.[225] Additionally, high penalties were imposed on organisations or legal persons involved—but not on individuals—when they ignored their obligation to report such incidents to the relevant authorities, within the scope of their responsibility.[226]

A report and reward system in the area of immigration law, in fact, already existed in Guangdong at least since 2004, when the Provincial Public Secur-

222 Chinese: 广东省外国人管理服务暂行规定; *Guangdong Interim Provisions on Foreign Nationals Administration* (2011).

223 Art. 1 *Guangdong Interim Provisions on Foreign Nationals Administration* (2011).

224 Lan (2015), p. 296 f.

225 Art. 10 *Guangdong Interim Provisions on Foreign Nationals Administration* (2011).

226 Art. 44–66 *Guangdong Interim Provisions on Foreign Nationals Administration* (2011).

ity Department[227] introduced the *Measures on Rewarding of People Contributing to the Reporting of 'Sanfei' Foreigners*.[228] These measures were promulgated shortly before several campaigns against 'sanfei' foreigners were launched in the region.[229] According to these measures, each report of a 'sanfei' foreigner would be rewarded RMB 100.[230] The 2011 *Guangdong Interim Provisions* obviously adopted this report and reward system. The report and reward system administrated by the local Public Security Bureaus throughout Guangdong province was intensely promoted in newspapers and on-line media, aiming at persuading Chinese nationals to report foreign nationals who have entered illegally to, who stay illegally in or who are illegally employed in China.[231]

During certain campaigns tackling deviant behaviour in China in the past, legal provisions were amended or new regulations were issued to support campaign work.[232] This phenomenon obviously also occurred in the context of campaigns against illegal immigration, where the *Guangdong Measures on Rewarding Reports of 'Sanfei' Foreigners* (2004) allowed local public security organs to promote though media channels the possibility of reporting suspicious illegal activities of foreign nationals. Since their introduction, the *Guangdong Measures on Rewarding Reports of 'Sanfei' Foreigners* (2004) were often referred to, even before campaigns against illegal immigration were launched on a large scale in Guangdong province. In 2006, when campaign work in the area of illegal immigration had not yet reached its highest level, newspapers reported on the recently established report and reward system in Guangdong province and on campaigns targeting *sanfei* foreigners that were soon to be launched.[233] During a campaign in Foshan launched in June 2006, a report and reward system was implemented accordingly and promoted in the media.[234] Besides the telephone number of the local public security bureau, the newspaper articles regularly pointed out to the rewards to be gained for contributing reports.

227 Chinese: 省公安厅.

228 *Guangdong Measures on Rewarding Reports of 'Sanfei' Foreigners* (2004).

229 See the chapter 3 regarding detailed information on the deployment of *sanfei* campaigns.

230 *Guangdong Measures on Rewarding Reports of 'Sanfei' Foreigners* (2004).

231 See chapter 3 of this study.

232 During the *yanda* campaigns, laws were amended to facilitate campaign work and new legal documents were issued; Biddulph / Cooney / Ying Zhu (2012), p. 378.

233 E. g. Feng (2006).

234 Tan / Wen (2006).

Until 2015, no comparable reward systems existed in other parts of China except for Yanbian, where a similar system was introduced in 2014. On 28 March 2014, the People's Congress of Yanbian Korean Autonomous Prefecture issued *Regulations on the Administration of Foreign Nationals*[235], which introduced a reward system for contributions to police work in the area of the administration of foreign nationals. In contrast to the *Guangdong Measures*, no concrete amount was stated as reward in the *Yanbian Regulations*. The *Yanbian Regulations* rather explained that they would "honour and reward" helpful contributions.[236] After 2015, however, report and reward systems were established in other regions as well, some with much higher rewards.[237]

A number of local governments implemented report systems in the context of their campaign work. Not always, however, were explicit statements given about a possible reward. When, e. g., campaigns were launched in Xi'an from March 2006 onwards and first achievements were published, the public was requested to report to the police by phone in case of any suspicious activities of foreign nationals.[238] The phone number of the local public security bureau was given next to the number for emergency calls. Wuhan, Beijing, Yanbian,[239] Changsha, and the border region of Guangxi province are other examples of regions where reports encouraged the public to report *sanfei* foreigners by spreading the contact information of the local authorities through the media.[240]

---

235 *Yanbian Foreign Nationals Administration Regulations* (2014).

236 Chinese: 表彰和奖励. Art. 22 *Yanbian Foreign Nationals Administration Regulations* (2014).

237 The city of Jinhua established a reward system that grants RMB 500 for each reported suspect in the context of illegal exit or entry, illegal stay or illegal employment; Nantou, a town that belongs to the city of Zhongshan in Guangdong province, established a system with a reward of RMB 5 000 per reported suspect. Public Security Bureau of the City of Jinhua (金华市公安局) (2015); Nantou Office of the Public Security Bureau of the City of Zhongshan (中山市公安局南头分局) (2017).

238 Lu Hua / Li Conghua / Zhao Han (2006).

239 When the campaign was launched in 2012, the *Yanbian Regulations* had not yet come into force.

240 Luo Bin / Xu Rui / Wu Hao (2007); Pan Xiaotian (2012); *Problem of Sanfei Foreigners Emerges in Yanbian, Taking into Custody Those Who Cover up Their Real Identify* (延边三非外国人问题突出 隐瞒真实身份逃避监管) (2012); *Changsha Says No to 'Black Foreign Teachers', Clears Up 'Sanfei' For 50 Days* (长沙对 '黑外教' 说 No 为期 50 天的清理 '三非') (2013); Li Ping / Lei (2010).

The early implementation of a report system, which was later included in national law, suggests that the *Guangdong Interim Provisions on Foreign Nationals Administration* (2011) served as experimental rules to the revised *Exit–Entry Administration Law* to be promulgated 2012.[241] This view is supported by the fact that the Reform and Development Framework for the Pearl River Delta Region (2008–2020),[242] issued by the National Development and Reform Commission[243], explicitly defines this area as a field of experimental reform and development.[244] Furthermore, in 2009 and 2010, high-ranking officials like Zhou Yongkang,[245] head of the Central Political and Legislative Committee, and Meng Jianzhu,[246] Minister of Public Security, visited Jinlu Villa,[247] a neighbourhood in Xiaobei selected by the Guangzhou police as a model community for foreign housing managment.[248] Such visits from officials of national authorities to Guangdong province underline the status of the province as an experimental region for immigration policy and legislation. Despite the fact that the *Guangdong Interim Provisions* are called 'interim provisions', there is no date of expiration given. As in part referred to in the relevant literature,[249] the *Guangdong Interim Provisions* served as a predecessor to the national law in several aspects, which I will elaborate on in the following.

First, the *Guangdong Interim Provisions* expressly aimed at the problem of 'sanfei' population in the province by institutionalising the report and reward system.[250] The revised *Exit–Entry Administration Law* 2012 adopts the report system of the Guangdong provisions in part. In Article 45, and indeed already in Article 44 of the 2011 draft, the law encourages Chinese nationals and legal persons to report illegal activities involving foreign na-

241 See Heilmann (2011) on experimentation as a distinct feature of Chinese policy making.
242 Chinese: 珠江三角洲地区改革发展规划纲要（2008–2020年）; *PRD Reform and Development Framework* (2008).
243 Chinese: 国家发展和改革委员会.
244 *PRD Reform and Development Framework* (2008), p. 9, 40, 50 f.; Lan (2015), p. 296 f.
245 Chinese: 周永康.
246 Chinese: 孟建柱.
247 Chinese: 金麓山庄.
248 Lan (2017 a), p. 102; Pan Xianglong / Qin (2011), p. 87.
249 Primarily Lan (2015).
250 Art. 10 *Guangdong Interim Provisions on Foreign Nationals Administration* (2011); Lan (2015), p. 295.

tionals.[251] However, according to the provisions of the *Exit–Entry Administration Law*, there is no legal consequence tied to such a report. No sanction is defined if a Chinese national fails to report a foreign national, but the law also remains silent on rewarding helpful reports about *sanfei* foreigners. This is likely because the *Exit–Entry Administration Law* is a national law with more general provisions that may be further specified by regional norms. The official commentary by the Office of Administrative Law of the Commission of Legislative Affairs of the National People's Congress to Article 45 of the 2012 *Exit–Entry Administration Law* refers to the positive results such reporting schemes achieved during previous crackdowns such as in Beijing and other cities.[252] Interestingly, the interpretation does not expressly mention the *Guangdong Interim Provisions* (2011) nor draws on experiences from Guangzhou. While foreign nationals may in general also report illegal activities of other foreign nationals, the provisions of Article 45 *Exit–Entry Administration Law* (2012) only refer to "citizens, legal persons or other organisations" and there is no provision that encourages reporting by foreign nationals in a similar way.[253]

---

251 Art. 45 *Exit–Entry Administration Law* (2012). The explanations on the draft remain silent about the reasons why this provision has been codified. It has to be noted that this whistle-blower rule is different from other reporting obligations in the context of immigration law that exist for hotels or owners of rented houses or flats, as it addresses third persons not having any legal relation to the foreign national in question. The formulation of the whistle-blower rule, "shall report" (*yingdang baogao*, Chinese: 应当报告), is comparatively strong in comparison to similar provisions in other laws like the *Environmental Protection Law* (2016) or the *Circular Economy Promotion Law* (2008) that state that Chinese citizens "have the right to report" (*you quan jubao*, Chinese: 有权举报) illegal actions of others; Art. 57 *Environmental Protection Law* (2016), Art. 10(3) *Circular Economy Promotion Law* (2008). It is rather comparable to provisions in the *Counterterrorism Law* (2015) or the *Counterespionage Law* (2014) that also use the formulation "shall report" (*yingdang baogao*, Chinese: 应当报告); Art. 9, 23, 28 *Counterterrorism Law* (2015), Art. 21 *Counterespionage Law* (2014).

252 *Guide to Interpretation and Application of the 'Exit–Entry Administration Law of the People's Republic of China'* (《中华人民共和国出境入境管理法》释义及实用指南) (2012), p. 123. Another official interpretation of the State Council refers to the duty of Chinese nationals to safeguard public order and safety according to the constitution. *Interpretation of the 'Exit–Entry Administration Law of the People's Republic of China'* (《中华人民共和国出境入境管理法》释义) (2012), p. 137 f.

253 Art. 45 *Exit–Entry Administration Law* (2012). As the *Exit–Entry Administration Law* (2012), unlike other laws such as the *Administrative Litigation Law* (2014), does not contain a provision stating that the provisions of this law are in general

Second, the *Guangdong Interim Provisions* (2011) expanded the authority of the police.[254] The 1985 *Foreign Nationals Exit–Entry Administration Law* explicitly assigned the power to conduct investigations of foreign nationals and verifications of passports only to foreign affairs police officers, a division of the people's police of the relevant authority.[255] Article 48 of the *Guangdong Interim Provisions* (2011) allows any police official to perform such investigations.[256] It has to be noted that the 1957 *Police Regulations* had already assigned the people's police the general task of administrating the stay and travel of foreign nationals.[257] The *Police Law* (1995) stated in more detail that the task of the people's police is to administrate the entry, exit, stay and travel of foreign nationals.[258] However, as the foreign affairs police is a division of the people's police, the regulations of the *Foreign Nationals Exit–Entry Administration Law* do not contradict the provisions of the *People's Police Regulations* or the *People's Police Law*. In the same sense, the provision of the 2011 *Guangdong Interim Provisions* does not directly contradict other legal provisions although it expands the relevant provision of the 1985 *Foreign Nationals Exit–Entry Administration Law*.

In any case, the 2012 *Exit–Entry Administration Law* has adopted the approach of granting police officials greater authority in the context of exit–entry administration. The 2012 law omits the specification that only officials of the foreign affairs police of the public security organs at or above the county level have the authority to carry out examinations of passports, and states that the public security organs at or above county level as well as the relevant exit–entry administrations are in charge of administering the stay of foreign nationals, while the border control authorities are responsible for exit and entry inspections at the border.[259] The law further states that public security organs at and above county level have the authority to conduct

also applicable to foreign nationals, the provisions of Art. 45 should not be applied to foreign nationals.

254 Lan (2015), p. 295.

255 Art. 28 *Foreign Nationals Exit–Entry Administration Law* (1985). The 1985 law states that the foreign affairs police "have the authority" (*you quan*, Chinese: 有权) to conduct investigations.

256 The interim provisions also use the term 'authority'.

257 Art. 5(1)vii *Police Regulations* (1957).

258 Art. 6(1)ix *Police Law* (1995). The *People's Police Regulations* and the *People's Police Law* talk of the "duty" (*zhize*, Chinese: 职责) of administration of foreign nationals.

259 *Exit–Entry Administration Law* (2012), Art. 4.

on-the-spot or continued interrogations.[260] This implies that passport or visa checks may be conducted by officials of the public security organs in general and not only by officials of the foreign affairs police. Moreover, the 2012 *Exit–Entry Administration Law* states that no detailed reason has to be provided if a visa is not issued[261] or if an individual is not allowed to enter the country,[262] which also extends the power of decision of the relevant authorities. The 2012 *Exit–Entry Administration Law* even goes a step further by granting public security organs at or above county level the power to decide on an order to leave. Such a decision had to be approved by the Ministry of Public Security under the old law[263] or, after 2008 where the approval authority was delegated, by the public security authorities at the provincial levels.[264]

Third, the *Guangdong Interim Provisions* (2011) focused on increased sanctions on offences of foreign nationals regarding exit–entry administration, which is also an important aspect of the revised *Exit–Entry Administration Law*. While fines were raised considerably in the 2011 draft compared to the 1985 law, most penalties have been increased again in the final law of 2012. Examples of harsher punishments are the sanctions against hotels or employers. The *Foreign Nationals Exit–Entry Administration Law Implementation Rules* (2010) only provided for a general fine of RMB 50 to 500 for anyone who failed to properly implement the required registration procedures.[265] Employers who illegally employed foreign nationals could be fined RMB 5 000 to 50 000.[266] The *Guangdong Interim Provisions* (2011) introduced sanctions against hotels and employers that failed to verify the travel documents of foreign nationals. Failing to verify passports and visas in order to make sure that the foreign national was allowed to stay or to be employed should be fined between RMB 5 000 and RMB 10 000 according to the *Guangdong Interim Provisions*.[267] The revised *Exit–Entry Adminis-*

260 *Exit–Entry Administration Law* (2012), Art. 58.
261 *Exit–Entry Administration Law* (2012), Art. 21.
262 *Exit–Entry Administration Law* (2012), Art. 25.
263 Art. 30 *Foreign Nationals Exit–Entry Administration Law* (1985).
264 Art. 1 *Notice on Approval Authority for Orders to Leave* (2008).
265 Art. 45 *Foreign Nationals Exit–Entry Administration Law Implementation Rules* (2010). This sanction was already increased in 1994 from the original amount of RMB 10 to 50.
266 Art. 44(2) *Foreign Nationals Exit–Entry Administration Law Implementation Rules* (2010).
267 Art. 55, 62(1)i *Guangdong Interim Provisions on Foreign Nationals Administration* (2011).

tration Law (2012) does not codify sanctions for the failure to verify travel documents, but it increases the fine for hotels that fail to register their foreign guests properly to an amount between RMB 1 000 and 5 000 in serious circumstances.[268] Illegally employing a foreign national is now fined RMB 10 000 for each individual, up to RMB 100 000 in total.[269] The revised *Exit–Entry Administration Law* in general increases sanctions on illegal entry, exit, and stay both in scope and in severity in comparison with the 1985 law, especially with regard to offences of assisting others to commit illegal actions.[270]

Finally, the 2012 *Exit–Entry Administration Law* adopts the idea of establishing a data exchange platform for the involved authorities at the relevant administrative level from the *Guangdong Interim Provisions*.[271] The next sections looks into the 2012 law in more detail.

III. The Revised Law on Exit–Entry Administration

This section examines the provisions of the 2012 *Exit–Entry Administration Law* in detail by focusing on the changes that have been made in comparison to the 2011 draft law. The 2012 *Exit–Entry Administration Law* has taken over most provisions of the draft law. It integrates both previous laws on exit–entry administration and serves as a framework for several more detailed regulations such as, e. g., the *Permanent Residence Measures* (2004). It consists of eight sections with 93 articles in total. The law clarifies that foreign nationals enjoy legal protection within the Chinese territory, which was formulated differently in the draft law, which stated that the Chinese government is in charge of protecting the legal interests of foreign nationals.[272] Article 5 of the law explicitly states that the state will establish a platform to coordinate data exchange between different authorities in charge of exit–entry administration which was not stated so clearly in the draft law.[273] The collection of biometric data in the area of immigration administration by the

268 Art. 76(2) *Exit–Entry Administration Law* (2012).

269 Art. 80(3) *Exit–Entry Administration Law* (2012).

270 See e. g. Art. 72 and 79 *Exit–Entry Administration Law* (2012).

271 Art. 4 *Guangdong Interim Provisions on Foreign Nationals Administration* (2011), referred to as "coordination system" (*xietiao jizhi*, Chinese: 协调机制), and Art. 5 *Exit–Entry Administration Law* (2012).

272 Art. 3(2) *Exit–Entry Administration Law (Draft)* (2011); Art. 3(2) *Exit–Entry Administration Law* (2012).

273 Art. 5 *Exit–Entry Administration Law* (2012).

Ministry of Public Security or the Ministry of Foreign Affairs, however, has to be approved by the State Council.[274] The law also states that the relevant authorities entrusted with the task of immigration administration should coordinate and work together and enhance the immigration system.[275]

At immigration ports, the border inspection authorities shall take measures to facilitate the entry and exit of Chinese nationals.[276] In contrast to the draft law, the law makes clear that Chinese as well as foreign nationals who do not hold a valid exit or entry document or who "refuse or evade"[277] inspection at the border will be denied entry.[278] Article 16(3) extends the list of regular visa types codified in the draft law and already known from the 1985 legal framework by adding an R visa for "talent introduction".[279] Apart from the place of issuance, the date of issuance has to be stated on a visa or a residence permit as well.[280] The law states that authorities do not have to explain the reason for the denial of entry to a foreign national, which was not codified in the draft law.[281] As for the length of minimum validity of visas, the law, in contrast to the draft law, differentiates between working visas and non-working visas. While non-working visas may be valid from 180 days until five years, working visas may be valid from 90 days until five years.[282] The amount of time within which foreign nationals have to report modifications of the data of their residence permit (e. g. the place of residence) is defined as ten days in the law, while the draft law did not state any concrete time span.[283]

The provisions regarding registration and employment of foreign nationals have been reordered and modified considerably in comparison to the 2011 draft law and also in comparison to the 1985 law. However, there are no substantial semantic differences. The draft law required employers to check the working permit as well as the residence permit of the foreign

274 Art. 7 *Exit–Entry Administration Law* (2012). An exception to this general provision is the collection of biometric data when foreign nationals apply for residence permits as stated in Art. 30(2) *Exit–Entry Administration Law* (2012).
275 Art. 8 *Exit–Entry Administration Law* (2012).
276 Art. 11(2) *Exit–Entry Administration Law* (2012).
277 Chinese: 拒绝、逃避.
278 Art. 12(1)i, 25(1)i *Exit–Entry Administration Law* (2012).
279 Chinese: 人才引进. Art. 16(3) *Exit–Entry Administration Law* (2012).
280 Art. 17, 33(1) *Exit–Entry Administration Law* (2012).
281 Art. 25(2) *Exit–Entry Administration Law* (2012).
282 Art. 29(3) *Exit–Entry Administration Law (Draft)* (2011); Art. 30(3) *Exit–Entry Administration Law* (2012).
283 Art. 33(2) *Exit–Entry Administration Law* (2012).

national before hiring him or her, which has been deleted from the law.[284] Also, a draft provision was removed stating that in controversial cases the decision whether an activity counts as illegal employment lies with the public security authorities at provincial level in cooperation with the relevant authorities under the direction of the Ministries of Human Resources, Education, Commerce, and Foreign Affairs at the same level.[285] This suggests that the public security authorities may decide on their own without any consultation with other authorities whether an activity counts as illegal employment according to the law. The draft law originally defined as illegal employment "being hired by an employing unit or pursuing other activities that generate labour reward without a working permit and a residence permit that allows for work"[286], which has been simplified in the law to "work within the Chinese territory without a working permit and a residence permit that allows for work".[287] Obviously, whether or not the activities are rewarded does not count as prerequisite for illegal work according to the law, as will be discussed in chapter 4. Apart from the authorities under the direction of the Ministry of Human Resources, the State Administration of Foreign Experts Affairs, a body on sub-ministerial level in charge of the administration of foreign talent that was merged with the Ministry of Industry and Information Technology in 2018,[288] is as well assigned the task of directing the preparation of a foreign national employment catalogue together with the State Council.[289] Finally, as for the deprivation of permanent residence status, the wording has been slightly amended to limit the authority to decide whether to cancel the permanent residence status or not to the Ministry of Public Security.[290] With its special section dedicated to permanent residence, the new law establishes a basic legal framework for the already existing *Permanent Residence Measures* (2004). The provisions of the law concerning permanent residence, however, remain very general and rely on corresponding implementation regulations.

As for the inspection of means of transportation, the law specifies that between the time of crossing the border and the time of inspection, no person

284 Art. 40(2) *Exit–Entry Administration Law (Draft)* (2011).
285 Art. 42(2) *Exit–Entry Administration Law (Draft)* (2011).
286 Art. 42(1)i *Exit–Entry Administration Law (Draft)* (2011).
287 Art. 43(1)i *Exit–Entry Administration Law* (2012).
288 See a more detailed description of the structure and functions of relevant authorities below on page 97.
289 Art. 42(1) *Exit–Entry Administration Law* (2012).
290 Art. 48(1) *Exit–Entry Administration Law (Draft)* (2011); Art. 49(1) *Exit–Entry Administration Law* (2012).

may exit the means of transportation and no commodities or goods may be discharged without permission.[291] Article 52(2) is simplified, stating generally that the person responsible for the means of transportation is responsible for the depart of the passengers if they entered illegally.[292] The provision of the draft law that the person in charge of the means of transportation has to bear the cost for the departure has been removed.[293] Articles 52(1)i and ii of the draft law have been combined and formulated in accordance with Article 50(2) of the law stating that between the time of crossing the border and the time of inspection the border inspection authorities shall supervise the procedure according to the relevant rules.[294] Finally, the law adds a provision stating that the means of transportation has to be allowed to pass when the reason to call it back vanished after the transportation had already departed.[295]

The section on expulsion and repatriation has been amended significantly. The new law extends the possibility for repatriation of foreign nationals to those who are illegally employed in China.[296] The law keeps the provision of the draft law, specifying that on-site interrogations, continued interrogations, detentions for investigation, movement restrictions, and deportations are to be carried out by police authorities at or above district level or by border inspection authorities at or above district level. However, it places this provision at the very beginning of the section.[297] As for interrogations, the provisions of the *Police Law* have to be followed and the serving of subpoenas has to be carried out according to the *Public Security Administration Punishments Law*.[298] The provisions specifying the reasons for deportation as well as the provisions that allow for administrative reconsideration by foreign nationals are, according to the law, also applicable to other *"jingwai renyuan"*,[299] which presumably includes individuals from Taiwan, Hong Kong, and Macau.[300] The law also states that physical inspections have to be

291 Art. 50(2) *Exit–Entry Administration Law* (2012).
292 Art. 52(2) *Exit–Entry Administration Law* (2012).
293 Art. 52(2) *Exit–Entry Administration Law (Draft)* (2011).
294 Art. 53(1)i *Exit–Entry Administration Law* (2012).
295 Art. 56(2) *Exit–Entry Administration Law* (2012).
296 Art. 62(1)iii *Exit–Entry Administration Law* (2012).
297 Art. 58 *Exit–Entry Administration Law* (2012); Art. 62(1) *Exit–Entry Administration Law (Draft)* (2011).
298 Art. 59(2, 3) *Exit–Entry Administration Law* (2012).
299 Chinese: 境外人员.
300 Art. 62(2) *Exit–Entry Administration Law* (2012).

carried out by two people of the same sex as the individual to be checked.[301] In the event of loss or theft of a visa or residence permit, when a visa or residence permit is destroyed, or when it is discovered that the individual is not entitled to hold a visa or residence permit after its issuance, the issuing authority may nullify the document.[302] Further, the public security authorities also may declare invalid, cancel or seize forged, modified, fraudulent, as well as nullified visas or residence permits or visas or residence permits unjustly used by a third person.[303] Finally, the law states that the validity of exit and entry documents is decided upon by the issuing authority, by the border inspection authorities, or by the exit–entry administration sections of the public security authorities.[304]

Table 2.1: Penalties as defined by the *Exit–Entry Administration Law* (2012)

Offence	**Fine**	**Detention**	**Other penalty**
Illegal entry into or exit from China (Art. 71)	RMB 1 000–5 000, RMB 2 000–10 000 when serious	5–10 days when serious	
Assistance in illegal entry or exit (Art. 72)	RMB 2 000–10 000, RMB 5 000–20 000 when serious	10–15 days when serious	
Fraudulent appropriation of residence or exit–entry documents (Art. 73)	RMB 2 000–5 000, RMB 5 000–20 000 when serious	10–15 days when serious	
Illegal issuance of application material (Art. 74)	RMB 5 000–10 000		
Refusal of verification of residence or exit–entry documents (Art. 76(1)i, ii)	up to RMB 2 000		warning
Neglect of registration provisions (Art. 76(1)iii, iv, vi)	up to RMB 2 000		

301 Art. 66 *Exit–Entry Administration Law* (2012).
302 Art. 67(1) *Exit–Entry Administration Law* (2012).
303 Art. 67(3) *Exit–Entry Administration Law* (2012).
304 Art. 69 *Exit–Entry Administration Law* (2012).

Table 2.1: Penalties as defined by the *Exit–Entry Administration Law* (2012) (continued)

Offence	**Fine**	**Detention**	**Other penalty**
Fraudulent use of exit–entry documents of others (Art. 76(1)v)	up to RMB 2 000		
Entry to restricted areas (Art. 77(1))		5–10 days when serious	order to move
Refusal to adhere to order to move (Art. 77(2))		5–10 days when serious	warning
Illegal residence (Art. 78)	RMB 500–10 000	5-10 days when serious [a]	warning
Accommodation of foreign nationals illegally in China (Art. 79)	RMB 2 000–10 000, RMB 5 000–20 000 when serious	5–15 days when serious	
Assistance of foreign nationals in evading inspection (Art. 79)	RMB 2 000–10 000, RMB 5 000–20 000 when serious	5–15 days when serious	
Issuance of residence or exit–entry documents to foreign nationals illegally in China (Art. 79)	RMB 2 000–10 000, RMB 5 000–20 000 when serious	5–15 days when serious	
Illegal employment (employee) (Art. 80(1))	RMB 5 000–20 000	5–15 days when serious	
Provision of reference for illegal employment (Art. 80(2))	RMB 5 000–50 000		
Illegal employment (employer) (Art. 80(3))	RMB 10 000–100 000		
Conducting activities inconsistent with cause of stay (Art. 81)			order to leave, deportation when serious

Table 2.1: Penalties as defined by the *Exit–Entry Administration Law* (2012) (continued)

Offence	**Fine**	**Detention**	**Other penalty**
Disruption of the administration order in restricted areas in ports (Art. 82(1)i)	up to RMB 2 000	5–10 days when serious	warning
Illegal embarkation to or disembarkation from a foreign vessel (Art. 82(1)ii, iii)	up to RMB 2 000		warning
Neglect of border inspection provisions of conveyance (Art. 83(1))	RMB 5 000–50 000		
Transport of individuals prohibited from entering or exiting China (Art. 83(2))	RMB 5 000–10 000		
Illegal operations between Chinese and foreign vessels (Art. 84(1)i)	RMB 2 000–20 000		
Illegal navigation of foreign vessels (Art. 84(1)ii, iii)	RMB 2 000–20 000		

a Alternative punishment.

The *Exit–Entry Administration Law* (2012) in general establishes more severe punishments and also provides for the punishment of legal persons.[305] The new law imposes fines up to RMB 100 000 on different offences as shown in table 2.1. Higher fines in comparison to the draft law can be found in the provisions on providing assistance for illegal exit or entry,[306] on illegally issuing an invitation or other application documents to foreign nationals,[307] and on sheltering or hiding foreign nationals having illegally entered into or illegally staying in China or helping them to escape

305 Art. 72(2), 74(2), 79(2) *Exit–Entry Administration Law* (2012).

306 Art. 72(1) *Exit–Entry Administration Law* (2012); Art. 69(2) *Exit–Entry Administration Law (Draft)* (2011).

307 Art. 74(1) *Exit–Entry Administration Law* (2012); Art. 71 *Exit–Entry Administration Law (Draft)* (2011).

inspection.[308] Also, the law provides for a higher punishment on disturbing the administrative order of restricted zones in ports when the circumstances are serious.[309] The law does not take over from the draft law provisions on the forging or altering, the illegal sale, and the renting, lending, or conveyancing of visas and residence permits.[310] However, illegally issuing exit–entry documents to foreign nationals illegally staying in China is punished along with sheltering or hiding foreign nationals or helping them to escape inspection according to the law.[311] As for illegal stay of minors, the punishment for the parent or legal guardian is decreased in the law in comparison to the draft law.[312]

If a hotel fails to follow the registration process of foreign nationals, it shall be fined according to the relevant provisions of the *Public Security Administration Punishments Law*.[313] The *Public Security Administration Punishments Law* (2012) states that a hotel worker shall be fined between RMB 200 and 500 if he or she "fails to register the name, type and number of the identity certificate of a customer."[314] Apart from "text records, audio-visual data, and other articles" illegally obtained by the foreign nationals who have entered a forbidden area, also illegally obtained electronic data as well as the tools used to obtain these articles shall be confiscated.[315] Whereas the draft law only states that foreign nationals who or foreign entities which do not adhere to the decision of the public security authorities to change residence within a specified period of time can be given a warning or, in serious circumstances, may be subject to detention of five to fifteen

308 Art. 79 *Exit–Entry Administration Law* (2012); Art. 77 *Exit–Entry Administration Law (Draft)* (2011).
309 Art. 82(2) *Exit–Entry Administration Law* (2012).
310 Art. 72 *Exit–Entry Administration Law (Draft)* (2011).
311 Art. 79 *Exit–Entry Administration Law* (2012).
312 Art. 78(2) *Exit–Entry Administration Law* (2012).
313 Art. 76(2) *Exit–Entry Administration Law* (2012).
314 Art. 56(1) *Public Security Administration Punishments Law* (2012). The same fine applies to any landlord who rents a house to an individual without identity certificate or who does not register this individual; Art. 57(1) *Public Security Administration Punishments Law* (2012). Again, a fine between RMB 200 and 500, or detention of five days or more and an optional fine of RMB 500 or more in severe cases, applies to hotel workers and lessors who know (*mingzhi*, Chinese: 明知) that the customer or lessee is a criminal suspect and do not report to the public security organ; Art. 56(2), 57(2) *Public Security Administration Punishments Law* (2012). These rules were introduced with the first promulgation of the *Public Security Administration Punishments Law* in 2005.
315 Art. 77(1) *Exit–Entry Administration Law* (2012).

days,[316] the law assigns the power of decision also to the national security authorities and provides for the option of compulsory relocation.[317] The law introduces punishments to agents who introduce foreign nationals to illegal employment.[318] Also, provisions for the illegal hiring of foreign nationals, which are not to be found in the draft, are introduced in the law.[319]

Finally, as for the protection of legal rights and access to legal remedies, the 1985 *Foreign Nationals Exit–Entry Administration Law* stated that "[n]o foreign national may be arrested except with the approval or by decision of a people's procuratorate or by decision of a people's court, and arrest must be made by a public security organ or state security organ",[320] which is no longer to be found in the 2011 draft law nor in the 2012 *Exit–Entry Administration Law*. Still, in the final law (but not in the draft law) it is stated that "[t]he legitimate rights and interests of foreign nationals in China shall be protected by laws",[321] which implies that foreign nationals enjoy the same rights regarding the legal or administrative procedures as Chinese nationals. A thorough analysis on legal provisions concerning illegal entry, stay and employment, as well as relevant legal remedies of the 2012 *Exit–Entry Administration Law* is provided in chapter 4.

IV. Summary

The current *Exit–Entry Administration Law* promulgated in 2012 is the result of a long revision process that started in 2003 and in the context of which experimentation plays an important role. Although the WTO accession of China in 2001 may have curbed experimentation in the field of law making in general, the revision process of exit–entry administration law clearly utilised the experiences and suggestions of local jurisdictions and made use of experimentation by implementing local-level regulations prior to the promulgation of the final law. Local regulations implemented e. g. in Guangdong province served as experimental provisions in the context of the revision process and were partly included in the final law. One example of this is

316 Art. 77(2) *Exit–Entry Administration Law* (2012).
317 Art. 76(2) *Exit–Entry Administration Law* (2012); Art. 75(2) *Exit–Entry Administration Law (Draft)* (2011).
318 Art. 80(2) *Exit–Entry Administration Law* (2012).
319 Art. 80(3) *Exit–Entry Administration Law* (2012).
320 Art. 4 *Foreign Nationals Exit–Entry Administration Law* (1985).
321 Art. 3(2) *Exit–Entry Administration Law* (2012).

the extension of police power in the context of investigations of foreign nationals and verifications of passports, as the 2012 law abolishes a provision that limited the power of examining passports to foreign affairs police at or above county level. Another example is the codification of a whistle-blower rule that requests the Chinese public to report illegal activities of foreign nationals to the police. Input from local jurisdictions was not only collected in the beginning of the revision process by dispatching work groups to inspect local level enforcement practice, but again shortly before the final law was passed.

The legislators of the revised law not only made use of experimentation within the country, but also acknowledged international law and legal practice of other countries in the context of exit–entry administration. With a provision regarding applications for refugee status, the law takes into account China's obligations according to relevant international standards such as the *Convention Relating to the Status of Refugees* (1951). It further calls for a better integration of control of and services to foreign nationals and for the development of digitisation by calling for the use of biometric data as well as for improved data sharing between different authorities. In this regard the revised law responds to the international requirement to implement the use of biometric data in the context of exit–entry administration[322] and to the need for increased sharing of data between responsible authorities. Enhanced processing and sharing of data as well as the harmonisation of the provisions of exit–entry administration law within the existing framework of administration law respond to the aim to strengthen control over exit–entry administration.

D. Structure of Immigration Authorities

In order to understand the enforcement of legal provisions in practice and especially during campaigns, this section analyses how communication works between lower-level administration and superordinate authorities and to this end looks into the organisational structure of relevant authorities in the field of immigration administration. Economic reforms not only resulted in the establishment and later revision of the legal framework of exit–entry administration, but also in institutional reforms with the aim of optimising govern-

322 After the attacks on 11 September 2001, biometric passports have been successively introduced internationally; Perruchoud (2012), p. 135 f.

ment structures, especially in the context of China's accession to the World Trade Organisation in 2001. This section focuses on the structures of exit–entry administration, and begins its analysis with a short introduction to the development in the context of economic reforms. In the sections above, I found that the development of legal norms was shaped by requirements that originated in reform activities. Hence, I assume that administrative structures also evolved according to these changing requirements and that the communication structures and processes today are designed according to these developments.

In the first part of this section, I analyse the current structure of administrative authorities in the area of exit–entry administration as well as its latest developments. I will also look into the historical developments that led to the current structure where doing so is necessary to understand the organisation structures today, while taking into consideration the effects of institutional reforms in the context of economic reforms. After having set out the basic structure of the relevant administrative authorities and the assignment of tasks associated with exit–entry administration, I will then analyse processes within this structure, namely vertical incentive systems and horizontal co-operation structures to assess communication structures within and between administrative authorities.

This section further embeds the developments of administrative structures in the wider context of the recent reforms in exit–entry administration. It aims to show that the enhancement of administrative processes is one of the main objectives of these reforms, which is not only pursued by amending legal norms on the local or national level, but also, as will be shown in the next chapter, with campaign policing in the area of immigration legislation.

I. Development of Structures in Exit–Entry Administration

On 14 November 1956, a circular on the sole responsibility of the Ministry of Public Security regarding the exit of Chinese nationals for private purposes was issued by the State Council.[323] The administration of the exit and entry of foreign nationals was shifted from the Ministry of Foreign Affairs to the

323 *Notification to Pool Administration of the Exit of Chinese Citizens for Private Purposes at the Ministry Public Security* (1956).

Ministry of Public Security in 1959.[324] As of 1959 exit–entry administration has mainly been a task assigned to the public security organs.

In the area of immigration administration, the responsibilities stayed relatively stable after 1959, as the Ministry of Public Security remained in charge of enforcing immigration provisions within and at the borders of the People's Republic of China while the Ministry of Foreign Affairs remained in charge of issuing visas abroad. Within the public security administration apparatus, responsibility for exit–entry administration became pooled at the Bureau of Exit and Entry Administration[325] that was established in 1983, which allowed a comprehensive and centralised administration of immigration matters.[326] With the promulgation of the *Administrative Penalty Law* in 1996, the competence to detain individuals in the context of administrative punishment was limited to public security organs.[327]

Around 2003, a stronger focus was laid on the improvement of police work in general and foreign nationals management work in particular, when the Central Committee of the Communist Party of China issued the *Decision to Further Strengthen and Improve Public Security Work* and the Ministry of Public Security published the *Regulations on the Coordination Mechanism of Public Security Organs in Foreign Nationals Management Work*.[328] Already in late 2001, the then Minister of Public Security JIA Chunwang announced reforms in population management as well as further reforms in exit–entry administration such as the introduction of a 'green card' system.[329]

II. Current Structure of Competent Authorities in Exit–Entry Administration

According to the *Police Law* (1995), the "tasks of the people's police are safeguarding national security, maintaining public order, protecting the personal safety and freedom of citizens and their legal property, protecting pub-

324 Guofu LIU (2011), p. 6. "The [Ministry of Justice] was dismantled in 1959; the procuracy was downgraded, with much of the work for law enforcement turned over to the Public Security." PEERENBOOM (2002), p. 45.
325 Chinese: 公安部出入境管理局.
326 Guofu LIU (2011), p. 9.
327 Art. 16 *Administrative Penalty Law* (1996).
328 WONG (2012), p. 228 f.
329 SUN Chunying (2001); MAO (2001).

lic property, and preventing, stopping and punishing illegal and criminal activities."[330] The law further states that "the people's police comprises of police officials of the public security organs, the national security organs, prisons and authorities administrating re-education through labour, as well as judicial police officials in the people's courts and the people's procuratorates."[331]

While in the context of criminal law, Article 8 *Criminal Litigation Law* (2012) enumerates the powers of the police and assigns the supervision of police work to the People's Procuratorate, in the context of administrative law the police forces may exercise their power more or less independently, however being subject to legal provisions.[332] The *Administrative Penalty Law* states that

> [t]he State Council or the people's government of a province, autonomous region or municipality directly under the Central Government that is empowered by the State Council may decide to have an administrative organ exercise other administrative organs' power of administrative penalty. However, the power of administrative penalty involving restriction of freedom of person shall only be exercised by the public security organs.[333]

The *Police Law* (1995) assigns the officials of the people's police the tasks of household registration and exit–entry administration as well as the administration of the stay and travel of foreign nationals and of nationality issues.[334] Further, the maintenance of public order in border areas is defined as a task of the people's police.[335] As for exit–entry administration, the *Exit–Entry Administration Law* (2012) elaborates the general provisions of the *Police Law* by defining the public security authorities on county level or above as competent to impose punishments or compulsory measures according to this law.

The current basic administrative structure of exit–entry authorities can be depicted as in figure 2.1. As defined in Article 4 of the *Exit–Entry Administration Law* (2012), the Ministry of Public Security and the Ministry of Foreign Affairs are the responsible authorities for the main aspects of the administration of exit and entry of foreign nationals, while the Ministry of Public Security is responsible for all aspects concerning foreign nationals

330 Art. 2(1) *Police Law* (1995).
331 Art. 2(2) *Police Law* (1995).
332 Biddulph (2007), p. 8.
333 Art. 16 *Administrative Penalty Law* (2009).
334 Art. 6(1)ix *Police Law* (1995).
335 Art. 6(1)x *Police Law* (1995).

within China. The law also requires other ministerial bodies to work closely together with these two ministries,[336] while the corresponding implementation regulations require the Ministry of Public Security to implement a platform to share data with other ministries and set up a coordination mechanism for foreign nationals management work at the national as well as on the provincial level.[337]

According to the 1980 *Regulations on Passports and Visas*, the Ministry of Public Security and the Ministry of Foreign Affairs as well as their subordinate authorities are responsible for issuing passports and visas and may also refuse issuance or declare an issued document invalid.[339] The issuance of passports abroad, the handling of official passports, and the administration of foreign embassies and consulates within the Chinese territory are assigned to the Ministry of Foreign Affairs and its subordinate bodies. The handling of visa applications of Chinese and foreign nationals abroad is assigned to the Chinese consulates in the relevant country—being subordinate authorities of the Ministry of Foreign Affairs. The handling of other visa applications is assigned to the Ministry of Public Security and its subordinate bodies, while visas for diplomatic or official passports may also be handled by the Ministry of Foreign Affairs and its subordinate bodies.[340]

In practice, the Department of Diplomatic Affairs of the Ministry of Foreign Affairs is responsible for the issuance of visas to foreign nationals as well as to Chinese nationals who want to exit the country, a task that is implemented by the general consulates or the embassies in the relevant countries. The Bureau of Exit and Entry Administration of the Ministry of Public Security is in charge of issuing legal documents to foreign nationals who have already entered the country. This task is assigned to the exit-entry administration offices at the relevant local level that are part of the public security departments of the same administrative level.[341] In Beijing for example, the

336 Art. 4(4) *Exit–Entry Administration Law* (2012).

337 Art. 2, 3 *Exit–Entry Administration Regulations* (2013).

338 Among other sources see Border Control Department of the Ministry of Public Security (公安部边防管理局) (2016 a), Border Control Department of the Ministry of Public Security (公安部边防管理局) (2016 b), and Border Control Department of the Ministry of Public Security (公安部边防管理局) (2008 a).

339 Art. 4 *Passport and Visa Regulations* (1980).

340 Art. 3 *Passport and Visa Regulations* (1980).

341 Apart from exit–entry administration, there are other police branches in charge of handling crimes, public order, traffic, fire fighting, population management etc.

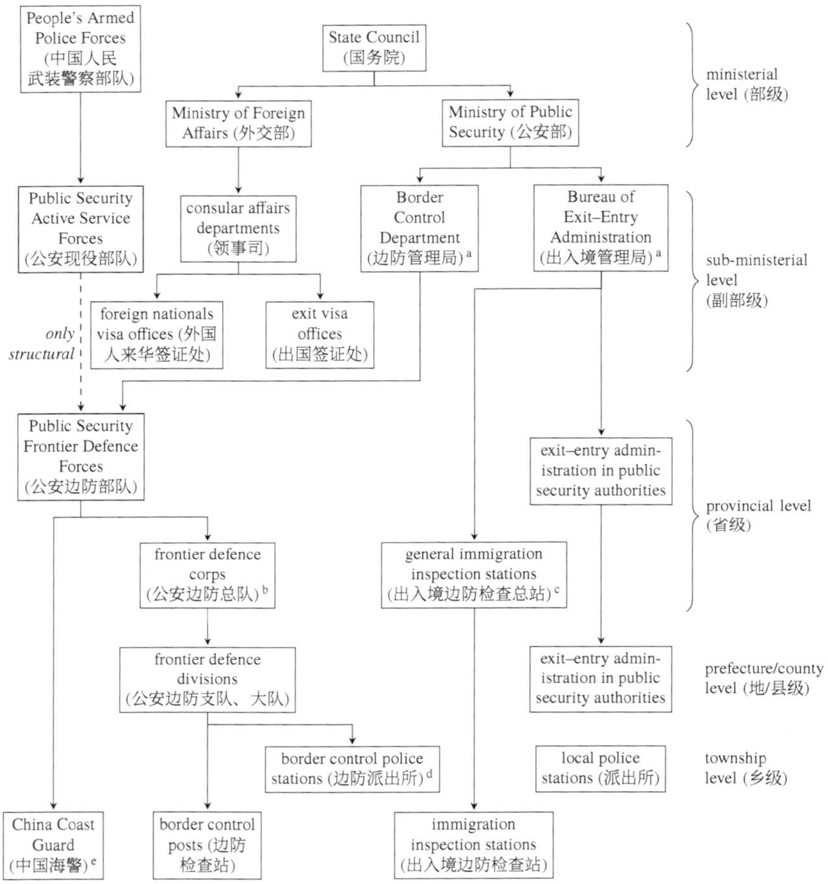

a Both departments have been joined to the newly established National Immigration Administration Bureau (国家移民管理局) in 2018.

b Also called Border Control Departments (边防局).

c Branch only exists in major cities, i. e. in Beijing, Tianjin, Shanghai, Guangzhou, Shenzhen, Zhuhai, Xiamen, Haikou, and Shantou.

d Only in districts at the border or at the coast.

e Structural administration shifted to the State Oceanic Administration (国家海洋局) under the Ministry of Land and Resources as from 2013.

Figure 2.1: Administrative structure of competent authorities in exit–entry administration.[338]

Port Visa Office of the Exit–Entry Administration Office[342] operates three posts[343] that are in charge of issuing on-arrival visas in case of emergency or, in special circumstances, for Taiwan, Hong Kong, and Macao residents.[344]

Under the supervision of the Ministry of Public Security, the Public Security Frontier Defence Forces[345] as part of the People's Armed Police, and hence structurally subject to the Central Military Commission, are responsible for law enforcement at the frontiers, for the prevention of illegal border crossing, smuggling, and human trafficking, and for the implementation of border traffic control.[346] Apart from the Public Security Frontier Defence Forces that were formed in 1982, the People's Liberation Army is responsible for border security as well, especially since 2003 at the border with the Democratic People's Republic of Korea and along the Yunnanese part of the border with the Republic of the Union of Myanmar.[347] The Public Security Frontier Defence Forces are organised in provincial-level frontier defence corps[348]. These corps are identical with the border control departments[349] at provincial level and govern frontier defence divisions with border control posts and border control police stations in border and coastal regions at lower levels.[350] In 1998, general immigration inspection stations[351] have taken over the task of border control at airports, seaports, and land border stations from the frontier defence corps in nine major cities,[352] which established lower-level immigration inspection stations. Hence, while in general immigration control checkpoints are subject to the authorities on the relevant administrative or military level, the checkpoints in Beijing, Tianjin, Shanghai, Guangzhou, Shenzhen, Zhuhai, Xiamen, Haikou, and Shantou

342 Chinese: 出入境管理处口岸签证处.
343 Chinese: 口岸签证办公场所.
344 Sun Zhihui (2013), p. 46.
345 Chinese: 公安边防部队.
346 Guofu Liu (2011), p. 17 f.
347 Guofu Liu (2011), p. 18 f.
348 Chinese: 公安边防总队.
349 Chinese: 边防局.
350 Border Control Department of the Ministry of Public Security (公安部边防管理局) (2008 b).
351 Chinese: 出入境边防检查总站.
352 These are Beijing, Tianjin, Shanghai, Guangzhou, Shenzhen, Zhuhai, Xiamen, Haikou, and Shantou. Guofu Liu (2011), p. 18; Border Control Department of the Ministry of Public Security (公安部边防管理局) (2008 a).

are directly governed by the Bureau of Exit and Entry Administration of the Ministry of Public Security.[353]

The task of the exit–entry administration authorities on the prefecture or county level is to handle, examine and approve applications for exit–entry documents as well as to investigate criminal cases or administrative offences. They are also assigned the task of operational guidance of lower-level exit–entry administration authorities. The exit–entry administration authorities at provincial level are responsible for organising, guiding and supervising the exit–entry administration work and its enforcement within the relevant administrative unit.[354] The border control authorities on the other hand are responsible for border defence and patrol, inspection of exit and entry of individuals and means of transportation, as well as for the investigation of criminal activities or administrative offences, especially in the context of exit–entry administration and crimes related to border-crossing.[355]

As of 2018, the Border Control Department and the Bureau of Exit–Entry Administration of the Ministry of Public Security have been merged into the newly established National Immigration Administration Bureau.[356] This way, the responsibilities of border protection and exit–entry administration have been integrated.[357] The tasks of the new authority at sub-ministerial level led by the Ministry of Public Security[358] basically combine the tasks originally assigned to the two authorities that were part of the Ministry of Public Security and comprise of administration of exit and entry, inspection of visa at ports, administration of stay and residence of foreign nationals, administration of asylum seekers and nationality issues.[359] The National Immigration Administration Bureau shall further take the lead in harmonising the handling and repatriation of *sanfei* foreigners and govern the administration of and service to Chinese nationals who travel abroad for private

353 *Interpretation of the 'Exit–Entry Administration Law of the People's Republic of China'* (《中华人民共和国出境入境管理法》释义) (2012), p. 171 f.

354 Border Control Department of the Ministry of Public Security (公安部边防管理局) (2016 b).

355 Border Control Department of the Ministry of Public Security (公安部边防管理局) (2008 b).

356 Chinese: 国家移民管理局.

357 *Structural Reforms Explanations* (2018).

358 The new authority has the rank of a *fubuji guojiaju* (Chinese: 副部级国家局), while the former authorities were classified as *buneishe zhinengju* (Chinese: 部内设职能局).

359 *Structural Reforms Explanations* (2018).

purposes as well as international cooperation in the field of migration.[360] Although one of the proclaimed aims of the overall reform processes in immigration law and administration is to establish a harmonised visa administration system, the relevant authorities of the Ministry of Foreign Affairs will, at least at first, not be included in the new National Immigration Administration Bureau.[361]

While the Ministry of Public Security and the Ministry of Foreign Affairs are assigned the fundamental tasks of exit–entry administration, the *Exit–Entry Administration Law* (2012) assigns the Ministry of Human Resources and Social Security as well as the State Administration of Foreign Experts Affairs the task of drawing up a "guiding catalogue for foreign nationals working in China".[362] It further assigns the Ministry of Education the task of establishing a system to administer foreign students who work in China.[363]

The administration of application for work permits for foreign nationals is today handled by the State Administration of Foreign Experts Affairs (SAFEA). This agency was established as administrative organ at subministerial level when it assimilated the Central Office of the Small Leading Group for Introduction of Foreign Talent[364] in 1988.[365] SAFEA was first under the leadership of the General Office of the State Council until 1993, when the Ministry of Personnel assumed control. As the Ministry of Personnel and the Ministry of Labour and Social Security were merged into the Ministry of Human Resources and Social Security in 2008, the newly founded ministry took over the lead.[366] As from 1996, the *Foreign Nationals Employment Regulations* (1996) assigned the human resources and social security departments the task of handling applications of regular work permits while the authorities for foreign experts affairs were to handle applications for foreign expert certificates.[367] In 2017, the application procedure

360 *Structural Reforms Explanations* (2018).
361 *Structural Reforms Explanations* (2018).
362 Art. 42(1) *Exit–Entry Administration Law* (2012).
363 Art. 42(2) *Exit–Entry Administration Law* (2012).
364 Chinese: 中央引进国外智力领导小组办公室.
365 Zhang Jianguo (2008), p. 34.
366 Zhang Jianguo (2008), p. 34.
367 The provisions assign the Ministry of Labour, of which the successor is the Ministry of Human Resources and Social Security, the task of preparing foreign nationals employment licenses and foreign nationals employment permits and allow the relevant authorities to exempt foreign nationals holding a foreign expert certificate issued by the Bureau of Foreign Expert Affairs, the successor of which is the State Administration of Foreign Experts Affairs, from the need to apply for an employment

for regular work permits and expert work permits was unified and is now handled by SAFEA via an on-line platform. The task of generally managing the employment of foreign nationals in China, however, remains with the human resource and social security authorities at the provincial and prefecture level.[368] As from 2018, SAFEA has become integrated into the Ministry of Science and Technology.[369]

As of today, exit–entry administration is spread over different authorities. While the Ministry of Public Security and the Ministry of Foreign Affairs share the main tasks of exit–entry administration, certain matters like the employment of foreign nationals in China rest with other authorities like the State Administration of Foreign Experts Affairs, which has become integrated into the Ministry of Science and Technology, or the Ministry of Human Resources and Social Security. Communications and cooperation between these different authorities, and in particular between different departments or subordinate organs, is hence important in order to implement smooth processes in exit–entry administration. In the next sections, I analyse vertical as well as horizontal communication and control structures within exit–entry administration.

1. Vertical Incentive Systems

A persisting problem in Chinese administration is rooted in the use of incentive structures that are frequently implemented to produce a certain behaviour at lower administrative levels, but which also sometimes lead to overstepping of the original aims or the transgression of legal norms. Another problem, which will be discussed in the following section, lies in the inertia of administrative authorities to communicate with other authorities of the same level.

Central–local control structures have first mainly been analysed in the area of economics.[370] However, as Tanner and Green show, law enforcement is affected by inefficient central–local control structures, too.[371] One major problem in the context of vertical control structures is the fact that

---

licence and employment permit; Art. 8(3), 9(1)i *Foreign Nationals Employment Regulations* (1996).

368 Art. 4 *Foreign Nationals Employment Regulations* (1996).

369 Para 1(8) *State Council Institutional Reform Decision* (2018).

370 See the findings of Chung (2001), p. 52.

371 Murray S. Tanner / Green (2007).

multiple principals have discretionary power over one single agent, in the context of exit–entry administration a local public security office, for example. While local public security offices are formally subject to superior public security departments and, eventually, to the Ministry of Public Security, local committees of the Chinese Communist Party as well exert control over local public security offices.[372] For example, local Party committees have the power to settle disagreements among different local political-legal departments, decide "important policy questions,"[373] draft public security legislation, and manage local security incidents.[374]

Different normative systems regulate behaviour within the administrative system and provide for control exercise. On the one hand, there are norms laid down in laws and regulations, and on the other hand, there are different responsibility systems that are mostly based on performance targets often defined numerically and to be achieved within a certain period of time.[375] While laws and regulations are issued by the National People's Congress or its Standing Committee or government authorities, certain normative documents may also be issued by Party organs. Similarly, responsibility systems may be imposed by both the Party and the government. Although the governmental supervision authorities effectively joined forces with the Party's disciplinary organs at the relevant administrative level when conducting investigations at least since 1994,[376] the Party's disciplinary system and the government's administrative disciplinary system in general could be applied in parallel.[377] In 2018, the Ministry of Supervision was dissolved and succeeded by the newly founded National Supervisory Commission that has the same administrative rank as the State Council or the Supreme People's Court[378] and integrates the operations of the Central Commission for Discipline Inspection.[379] Still, the disciplinary systems of the Party and of the gov-

372 Murray S. Tanner / Green (2007), p. 645 f.
373 Murray S. Tanner / Green (2007), p. 653.
374 Murray S. Tanner / Green (2007), p. 653 f.
375 Minzner (2009), p. 67 f.
376 Wedeman (2004), p. 901. At the national level the Ministry of Supervision share the same organisational structure with the Party's Central Commission for Discipline Inspection, while both institutions are authorised by different normative documents.
377 Yongshun Cai (2014), p. 63 f.
378 The Supreme People's Court is abbreviated to 'SPC' in certain titles of publications cited in this study.
379 *Central Committee Issues 'Plan to Deepen the Reform of the Party and State Institutions'* (中共中央印发《深化党和国家机构改革方案》) (2018).

ernment administration are based on different normative documents. While the disciplinary system of the Party adheres to Party rules and eventually to the *Constitution of the Communist Party of the China*, the government's administrative disciplinary system is codified in laws and regulations, such as the *Supervisory Law* (2010).

The above mentioned normative structures, be they established by the government or by the Party, be they based on normative rules or on incentive systems, may be imposed on the national level as well as locally. Often, local rules are more concrete in terms of targets to be met, while more general legal norms are more frequent at the national level. As local norms often have the aim to implement more abstract norms defined in higher-ranking normative documents,[380] responsibility systems with concrete performance targets are applied more often at a local level. Local norms and national norms may contradict each other, especially when performance targets are defined in a way that induces a certain behaviour which is prohibited according to other regulations. Since local norms are more concrete and often have direct influence on the career of individuals, cadres and officials are prone to fulfil locally set targets even if these targets contradict national law.[381] This effect can also be found in the context of exit–entry administration, as will be discussed in the following.

In 2001, the Ministry of Public Security issued *Regulations Concerning the Examination and Appraisal of the Quality of Law Enforcement by Public Security Organs*.[382] According to these regulations, annual examinations shall ensure a high quality of law enforcement by auditing the work of public security organs by the relevant superordinate authority. Law enforcement in criminal cases, public security administration cases as well as in administrative work is subject to such an audit, which is based on a points system. In 2016, the Ministry of Public Security issued a revision of the said regulations which state in Article 14 that certain items shall no longer be taken as a basis of the evaluation. Namely, "unscientific and unreasonable" items, such as the amount of collected fines, the number of criminal or administrative detainees, the number of cases, the rate of cases sent back by the procuratorate to the investigating public security organ or the rate of solved cases, shall not be used as audit indices.[383] The fact that this provision was introduced in the 2016 revision of the regulations indicates that such numbers had been used

380 Minzner (2009), p. 77 f.
381 Minzner (2009), p. 94.
382 Chinese: 公安机关执法质量考核评议规定.
383 Art. 14(2) *Quality Examination and Appraisal Regulations* (2016).

before by public security organs to assess their law enforcement quality. As an official statement by the Ministry of Public Security explains, the use of such indicators may easily result in situations where police officials impose fines or detain individuals just in order to increase the relevant figures.[384]

In the context of exit–entry administration, the use of point-system based quality assessment has been documented by different scholars. LAN points to certain quotas when she cites one of her interviewees who assumes that local police officials sometimes just arrest foreign nationals in order to be able to report satisfactory results of their work to their superiors.[385] HUANG cites officials of local public security bureaus who told the author that they were urged to submit positive statistics in their annual reporting.[386] Higher-level authorities assessed the number of arrests and penalties or conducted spot-checks to assess the number of foreign nationals without proper travel documents.[387] These assessments were then used to rank the relevant local public security office, and a low ranking would often lead to more inspections, clean-ups and monitoring by higher-ranking authorities.[388] In order to avoid being ranked low, officers of local public security offices hence tried to score points for example by apprehending 'sanfei' foreigners or in general punish more strictly.[389]

The revision of the *Regulations Concerning Examination and Appraisal of the Quality of Law Enforcement by Public Security Organs* (2001) illustrates the fact that the central level felt the need to regulate the quality of law enforcement but also had to rely on the further use of an examination and appraisal system exercised by subordinate levels which the central level has only indirect control over. The revision also illustrates the inability of the central level to exert sufficient control over local level authorities, which made it necessary to adjust the examination and appraisal system in order to prevent its implementation in an arbitrary way contrary to the original objectives. The most important finding here is that vertical incentive structures are firmly embedded in the administrative processes of exit–entry administration. At least before 2016, which is the period of main interest in this study as it covers the revision process of exit–entry legislation, local public security offices were assessed by higher-ranking authorities using a

384 MIN (2011).
385 LAN (2017 b), p. 56.
386 HUANG (2018).
387 HUANG (2018), p. 15.
388 HUANG (2018), p. 15.
389 HUANG (2018), p. 15.

point system that also included items like the number of arrests. Such assessments reportedly increased the pressure exerted on local public security offices, who responded by increasingly targeting illegal immigration.

2. Horizontal Co-operation Structures

A major point of criticism of exit–entry administration concerns a lack of communication between different authorities.[390] As interviews and talks with experts showed, cooperation between ministerial bodies is particularly inadequate, but also within the different departments under the Ministry of Public Security information flows are insufficient.[391] Communication between the Ministry of Public Security and the Ministry of Foreign Affairs is primarily implemented via the international departments of the Ministry of Public Security, which however have no decision-making power. Consulates often issue visas without prior consultation of data of the Ministry of Public Security, presumably because this data is not provided to them since the Ministry of Public Security is only involved in the visa issuing process in certain cases. This again leads to reluctance of officials of the Border Inspection Authorities to enforce their authority to return individuals at the border.[392] In the reading of a draft of the amended *Exit–Entry Administration Law*, Jin Shuoren,[393] representative of the Standing Committee of the National People's Congress, pointed to the problem that applications of individuals handed over to Chinese consulates to renounce Chinese nationality because of naturalisation frequently would not be forwarded to the local police offices, which would hence continue to regard the relevant household registrations as valid and assume that the individual still holds Chinese nationality.[394]

Coordination of administrative processes is further complicated by the fact that enforcement of legal provisions in certain cases is not only a task

390 E. g. Haugen (2012), p. 75.

391 The author of this study conducted open qualitative interviews with experts in international migration law in Beijing in April 2015 and in March 2017.

392 Information was gathered in qualitative interviews with staff of the Beijing Office of the International Organisation of Migration (IOM).

393 Chinese: 金硕仁.

394 *Delegates of the Standing Committee of the National People's Congress Propose the Elimination of 'Dual Nationality'* (全国人大常委会委员建言消除'双重国籍'), *NPC Press Release* (2012).

of the public security authorities. Practice in Guangzhou shows—and this practice is likely to be the case in other big cities as well—that the enforcement of exit–entry administration regarding the punishment of offences is frequently conducted by officials from the Urban Administrative and Law Enforcement Bureau (*chengguan*[395]),[396] local government authorities typically subordinate to the relevant local Urban Management Bureau and hence separate from the regular police forces. The authorities responsible for foreign nationals management, however, are still the local exit–entry administration offices.[397]

The call for a platform to share information about exit–entry administration[398] suggests that different ministries, at least around the time the new law entered into force, ran different databases autonomously, which are neither connected nor compatible with each other. The police in Beijing set up an information system only in 2016, which eventually allowed different authorities to access health data of foreign nationals who no longer need to submit different copies of their health certificates.[399] A smooth information flow would not only benefit the foreign national, but also improve the enforcement of legal provisions. If a foreign national, e. g., has been repatriated and he or she has been issued with a ban on re-entry, the consulates should know about this and refuse a visa to this person as long as the ban on re-entry is in effect. Employment of foreign nationals is another example where communication would certainly improve the application and handling processes, as many different authorities are involved. The local bureau of the Ministry of Human Resources and Social Security or, as from 2017, the State Agency of Foreign Experts Affairs issues an employment licence to the employer after approval by a competent trade authority, the consulate will issue the visa to the foreign national, the local bureau of the Ministry of Human Resources and Social Security or, again as from 2017, the State Agency of Foreign Experts Affairs will then issue the work permit, and the local bureaus of the

---

395 Chinese: 城管.

396 The main task of *chengguan* is not to handle crime, but to enforce local regulations, e. g. by taking action against illegal street vendors. According to Art. 16 *Administrative Penalty Law* (2009), they are not allowed to restrict the freedom of individuals.

397 Lan (2017 a), p. 104 f.

398 *China Promotes Opening Up and Foreign Relations by Enacting Norms on Exit–Entry Administration* (中国立法规范出入境管理促进对外开放和交往), *NPC Press Release* (2012).

399 Yi Zhang (2016).

Ministry of Public Security will finally issue the residence permit. At least three authorities subordinate to different ministries are involved in this process, apart from other authorities in charge of employment in general like tax authorities. The harmonisation of data and improvement of information flow would make it easier to enforce legal provisions and prosecute illegal behaviour.

The problem of insufficient communication and co-ordination structures between different authorities of the same level in exit–entry administration is also illustrated by the so-called *xiao waiguan*[400] and *da waiguan*[401] systems. These two different co-ordination systems were established initially in order to enhance communication between relevant authorities in the context of foreign nationals management work. While the *xiao waiguan* system depicts the co-ordination of foreign national administration by different police branches, the *da waiguan* system depicts the co-ordination of administration of foreign nationals between the Ministry of Public Security, the Ministry of Foreign Affairs and other ministerial bodies involved by setting up a small working group under the lead of the Ministry of Public Security. While both systems are necessary to establish inter-organisational co-operation, to create synergies and harmonisation and hence to reduce regulatory failure, they also have particular inherent shortcomings.

The system of *xiao waiguan* was established in 1959, when administration concerning foreign nationals, i. e. foreign nationals management work, was re-assigned from the Ministry and Foreign Affairs to the Ministry of Public Security and its subordinate authorities. The Ministry of Public Security established an Exit–Entry Administration Bureau in 1983, concentrating the tasks of foreign national administration within the public security apparatus.[402] However, as from 1996, the administration of foreign nationals management work, which had previously been conducted solely by the exit–entry administration branch of the Ministry of Public Security, was partly given to the public security authorities at the different lower administrative levels, and special branches concerning criminal investigation, communications, public order, household registration and exit–entry administration

400 Chinese: 小外管. Also called *zhong tizhi* (Chinese: 中体制) by Wei / Zhu Xudong (2009) who distinguishes between a co-ordination system between different branches within the public security apparatus and another co-ordination system, called *xiao tizhi* (Chinese: 小体), with an even more narrow scope, only within the exit–entry administration branch.

401 Chinese: 大外管. Called *da tizhi* (Chinese: 大体制) by Wei / Zhu Xudong (2009).

402 Wei / Zhu Xudong (2009), p. 32.

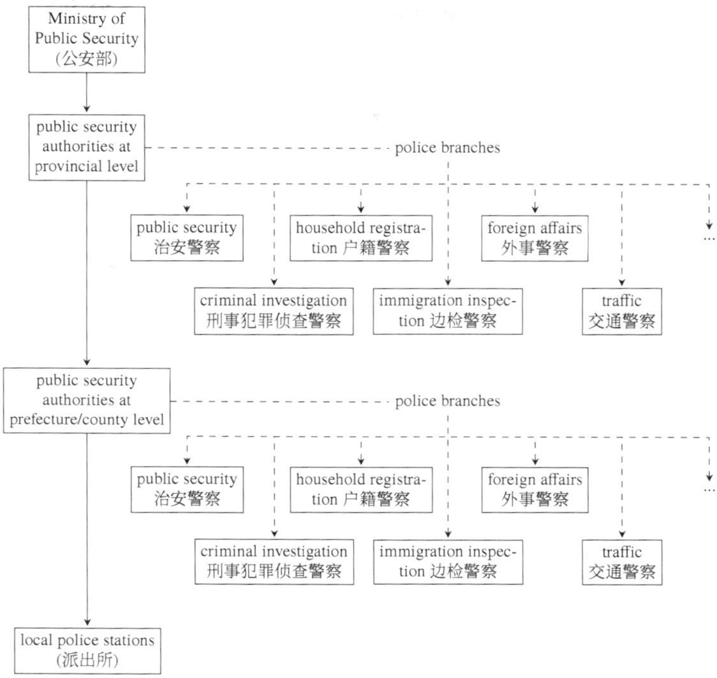

Figure 2.2: Structure of the *xiao waiguan* system.

were set up.[403] With the *Foreign Nationals Management Work Coordination Regulations* (2003), which required the different authorities to work together under the lead of the exit–entry administration authorities, the structure of the *xiao waiguan* system was eventually codified. All police branches concerned would meet regularly and report to the exit–entry authorities but also would have the possibility to voice suggestions on current policies set up by the exit–entry authorities.[404]

While the *xiao waiguan* system covers the administration of foreign nationals management work under the lead of the Ministry of Public Security and its subordinate lower-level authorities, the *da waiguan* system denotes the cooperation of the Ministry of Public Security and the Ministry of Foreign Affairs, both assigned the task of foreign national administration by the *Foreign Nationals Exit–Entry Administration Law* (1985) and the *Exit–*

403 Zhang Huide / Liu Hongbin / Zeng Fanjing (2014), p. 106.
404 Zhang Huide / Liu Hongbin / Zeng Fanjing (2014), p. 106.

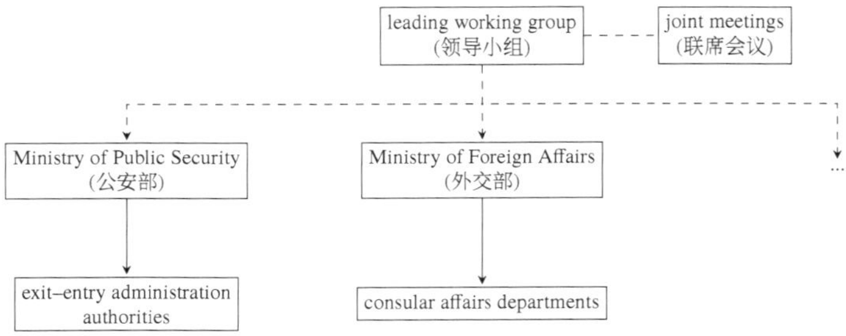

Figure 2.3: Structure of the *da waiguan* system.

Entry Administration Law (2012), as well as their respective subordinated authorities at different administrative levels.[405] As foreign nationals management work became more and more complex over time, other administrative bodies like those concerning education, human resources and social security, commerce, industry, justice, civil affairs, tourism, and hygiene, also became part of this system.[406] The origins of the *da waiguan* date back to the late 1960s. In order to coordinate administrative processes between the different ministerial bodies, the Working Group for Handling Foreign Nationals in China[407] was set up in 1968.[408] After the promulgation of the *Foreign Nationals Exit–Entry Administration Law* in 1985, a range of different legal regulations was set up to codify different aspects of foreign nationals management work that would affect the responsibility of different ministries. Coordination mechanisms between different ministries were set up especially in the context of a national conference on foreign nationals management work in 2007 in order to enhance cooperation between different authorities in charge of foreign nationals management work,[409] which also included the establishment of a Working Group for Cooperation between

405 Examples of local *da waiguan* systems are reported for Beijing by Lu Jing / Zhang Chi (2013), especially p. 147–149, for Guangdong Province by Wang Afang / Zhang Yuguang / Li Zhe (2010), and for Guangzhou in Task Group to the 'Research Report on Foreign Nationals Management Services of the City of Guangzhou' (《广州市外国人管理服务研究报告》课题组) (2014).

406 Wei / Zhu Xudong (2009), p. 32

407 Chinese: 在华外国人研究处理小组. Originally called Working Group for Handling Foreign Criminals (Chinese: 对外国犯人研究处理小组), but renamed in 1969; Wei / Zhu Xudong (2009), p. 32.

408 Zhang Huide / Liu Hongbin / Zeng Fanjing (2014), p. 106.

409 *Foreign Nationals Report* (2012), p. 424 f.; Liu Guofu (2015), p. 50.

Ministries in Foreign Nationals Management Work.[410] In 2011, coordination mechanisms were set up in order to regulate the administration of foreign exchange students[411] as well as to establish a service infrastructure for foreign nationals.[412] Apart from the leading working groups on foreign nationals,[413] joint meetings on foreign nationals management[414] have regularly been held in different provinces and cities as well as at the central level.[415] Finally, different specialised working groups have been established, such as "integrated forces for the enforcement of law concerning foreign affairs",[416] "mobile forces for the investigation of *sanfei* foreigners",[417] and "specialised working groups to crack down *sanfei* foreigners".[418]

Shortcomings within the *xiao waiguan* system are the poor sharing of information between the different authorities, overlapping administrative competencies as well as a lack of a system of enforcement of legal responsibilities. One example of insufficient information sharing exists in the context of foreign national registration implemented at the local police offices (*paichusuo*). While registration is handled at the very local level, the policy making concerning exit–entry administration that utilises the data collected by the local police offices is typically the task of the exit–entry administration organs at province level. Data has to be processed across several levels leading to long feedback cycles and lost information, which results in slow and inappropriate policy decisions.[419] Overlapping competencies exist e. g. in the area of criminal prosecution in the context of border control, where both the criminal investigation organs as well as the exit–entry administration organs are given shared power to conduct investigation of crimes.[420] Because there is no legal basis for the authority of exit–entry administration

410 Chinese: 外国人管理工作部际协调小组.

411 Zhang Huide / Liu Hongbin / Zeng Fanjing (2014), p. 106 f.; Liu Guofu (2015), p. 50.

412 *Foreign Nationals Report* (2012), p. 425; Liu Guofu (2015), p. 50.

413 Chinese: 外国人领导小组.

414 Chinese: 外管联席会议.

415 Zhang Huide / Liu Hongbin / Zeng Fanjing (2014), p. 107.

416 Chinese: 涉外综合执法队.

417 Chinese: 查处三非机动队.

418 Chinese: 打击三非专项工作组; Wei / Zhu Xudong (2009), p. 32.

419 Zhang Huide (2011), p. 105.

420 According to the *Note Concerning Adjustments of Task Sharing in the Administration of Cases Involving Crimes of Disrupting the Administration of the Border*, Gong Tong Zi (2002) 7 Hao (Chinese: 关于调整部分妨害国（边）境管理犯罪案件管辖分工的通知; 公通字〔2002〕7号). This note is not publicly accessible and was not available to the author of this study, but cited in Sun Zhihui (2013),

organs to conduct criminal investigations, the exit–entry administration organs still have to hand over the case to the criminal investigation branch for further processing. Moreover, no clear procedures concerning the handing over of cases and no legal responsibilities exist, which in the end often results in negligence of the exit–entry administration organs to criminally investigate a case after having handled it according to administrative law.[421]

Within the *da waiguan* system, information sharing and overlapping administrative competencies also are major shortcomings. Overlapping competencies especially exist for tasks shared by the Ministry of Public Security and the Ministry of Foreign Affairs. While ordinary passports are e. g. issued by consulates or embassies of the People's Republic of China subordinated to the Ministry of Foreign Affairs or by the public security organs, passports for public affairs, i. e. diplomatic passports or service passports for employees of the Chinese government or international organisations and their family members, are issued only by the foreign affairs authorities. Also, while visas for foreign nationals are typically issued by the visa offices of consulates or embassies abroad, visas can also be issued by the port visa offices[422] that are subordinated to the public security authorities on the same administrative level. Despite the multitude of working groups and joint meetings, both the *xiao waiguan* as well as the *da waiguan* system are rather weak instruments to enforce action of administrative bodies, as there is no legal basis to codify legal responsibilities.[423] Thus, adherence to the policies laid down by the working groups or in the joint meetings relies mainly on the voluntary participation of the authorities.

III. Summary

Immigration administration has traditionally been a task of the public security organs. Already the first regulations concerning exit–entry administration of 1951 assigned the task of the administration of registration, stay and travel of foreign nationals to the public security authorities.[424] Exit–entry administration within China today, covering the administration of foreign

p. 214. See as well the reference in *Current Summary of Work Sharing of Public Security Organs in the Administration of Criminal Cases* (n. d.).

421 Sun Zhihui (2013), p. 214.

422 Chinese: 口岸签证处.

423 Zhang Huide / Liu Hongbin / Zeng Fanjing (2014), p. 107.

424 Art. 3, 6 *Foreign Nationals Exit, Entry, and Stay Provisional Regulations* (1951).

nationals or the exit of Chinese nationals, is the responsibility of the Ministry of Public Security. The Ministry of Public Security also supervises the border control authorities, which are structurally organised as part of the People's Armed Police. However, while tasks are bundled at the Ministry of Public Security with regard to the administration of exit and entry within the country, the task of issuing passports and visa outside of China is assigned to the consular affairs departments, which are governed by the Ministry of Foreign Affairs. The fact that the Ministry of Public Security and the Ministry of Foreign Affairs share similar tasks is reflected in the legal framework, which in general assigns the task of exit–entry administration to both ministries. In any case, since border inspection and foreign nationals registration issues are the task of the public security authorities, the public security authorities factually have the power to finally decide who may enter the country even when a permission has been issued by the authorities of foreign affairs. This, and the responsibility for the revision process of the law on exit–entry administration, illustrates the primary authority of the Ministry of Public Security in the area of exit–entry administration.

Vertical incentive systems are not uncommon in Chinese administration. As shown in this part, incentive systems have also been established in the context of exit–entry administration. Higher-ranking authorities evaluate local public security offices and rank them according to a points system. Lower ranked public security entities are more likely to become subject to stricter monitoring, or clean-up activities may be increased in the relevant jurisdiction. At least until 2016, items like the number of arrests were used to assess the work of local level police offices. The use of such items in combination with the requirement to deliver positive statistics resulted in harsher punishments and increased detention numbers. However as reports suggest, such increased enforcement activities of local public security offices were not necessarily legitimate and primarily served the purpose of reporting positive numbers to higher-ranking authorities.

In the course of economic reforms, employment of foreign nationals in China became an ever more important issue. In 1996, a basic framework for the administration of foreign nationals was established. With the codification of provisions concerning the employment of foreign nationals, other authorities alongside those in charge of public security and foreign affairs became incorporated in the field of immigration administration. In charge of administrating the employment of foreign nationals are primarily the Ministry of Human Resources and Social Security (and its predecessor the Ministry of Labour) and the State Administration for Foreign Experts Affairs, an administrative entity on sub-ministerial level that was merged with the Ministry of Science and Technology in 2018. The increasing scope of responsible administrative organs in the field of immigration administration made it necessary to expand horizontal communication structures between the different authorities. Within the public security organs, communication between the different branches also became crucial for the effective enforcement of legal norms.

The so called *da waiguan* system depicts the establishment of entities, e. g. small leading groups or working groups, that comprise of deputies of different administrative branches at the relevant administrative level. The aim of this structure is the enhancement of intra-administrative communication and eventually effective and efficient enforcement of laws and regulations. In contrast, the so called *xiao waiguan* system depicts a similar superordinate organisation structure within the public security administration. It aims accordingly to enhance communication between the different branches in the public security sector. While intra-administrative communication may be enhanced using such structures, the problem of overlapping administrative competencies cannot be solved this way. As will be shown in the next section of this chapter, organisational structures like the *da waiguan* system are deployed also in the context of campaigns in order to increase effectiveness and efficiency.

This section illustrated several shortcomings in the administrative structure and processes that will help us understand the deployment of campaigns but also the enforcement of law in practice. First, although the public security organs are the main authorities in charge of exit–entry administration, other authorities, especially those entrusted with foreign affairs, human resources and social security as well as foreign experts affairs, have important decision power within the structure of exit–entry administration. For this reason, communication and information sharing is needed between the different authorities, which, however, is insufficient. Despite the fact that certain structures have been established that aim to enhance communication between different administrative branches, the flow of data is often slow and information is not shared or processed in an efficient way, which poses a problem to the effective enforcement of legal norms. Furthermore, vertical control structures create incentives resulting in higher punishment rates that do not necessarily map the actual number of administrative or criminal offences. Finally, vertical incentive structures are obviously more effective in influencing the behaviour of local-level officials than horizontal communication structures.

E. Conclusion

While the first rules to codify exit–entry administration in the People's Republic of China date back to 1951, a comprehensive legal framework on immigration only entered into force in 1986 in the context of the onset of the economic reforms. In 1980, in the first years of the reform and opening policy under DENG Xiaoping, nationality and exit–entry administration were eventually codified by laws. The *Nationality Law* still exists today in its first version of 1980, the *Foreign Nationals Entry–Exit Administration Law* and the *Citizen Exit–Entry Administration Law* were both promulgated in 1985. The reform and opening policy also meant an increasing institutionalisation with decreasing focus on political measures and strong emphasis on rule of law.[425] Economic reforms influenced the making of nationality and immigration legislation, as economic exchange with the outside demanded a reliable legal framework. The revision process of the *Exit–Entry Administration Law* that started around 2003, however, was also indirectly influenced by economic reforms, as a general reform of administrative law made it necessary to revise the law in the area of exit–entry administration. While the first laws on exit–entry administration aimed to facilitate exit and entry in line with the opening policy, inconsistencies and contradictions between the legal framework of exit–entry administration and administrative law in general became visible during the almost 20 years these laws were in force. During the revision process that spanned almost ten years, experimental provisions at local levels were introduced and local enforcement was assessed. The goal of this revision process was to merge different legal objectives, such as the deterrence of illegal immigration as well as the attraction of foreign talent, in one law that should cover exit–entry administration of both foreign and Chinese nationals. Of the experimental provisions, the local regulations in Guangdong are of particular interest, as the region of the Pearl River Delta served as an experimental region for immigration legislation, which eventually influenced different aspects of the final *Exit–Entry Administration Law* of 2012. I hence conclude that although research has shown that economic reforms in general reduced the application of experimentation in the context of law making in China due to increasing institutionalisation and increasing alignment of norms with international standards caused by China's accession to the WTO,[426] experimentation still continued to play

425 Murray S. TANNER (1994).
426 HEILMANN (2008), p. 6.

an important role in law making in the context of exit–entry administration, where legal norms were implemented in a local context first, in order to assess the possibility to apply them nation-wide.

The revision process of exit–entry legislation was driven by the increasing occurrence of overlapping or contradicting legal provisions that rendered enforcement of legal norms difficult. The revision of the law hence aimed to harmonise its provisions with the existing framework of administration law as well as with existing provisions in the field of immigration law. The insufficiency of exit–entry administration, however, was not only rooted in the outdatedness of certain provisions of the 1985 *Foreign Nationals Entry–Exit Administration Law*. Another important reason for unsatisfactory enforcement of exit–entry administration lay, and probably still lies, in the structure of the authorities in charge. Although institutional reforms led to certain optimisation of the administration as well as to the establishment of horizontal cooperation structures, major problems remain the insufficient flow of information, overlapping responsibilities and contradicting aims of normative documents regulating enforcement. While several authorities subordinated to different ministries are in charge of related tasks in exit–entry administration, it is very likely that, to the time of this writing, there is still no unified information sharing system regarding the administration of foreign nationals that all relevant authorities have access to. In addition to that, the assessment of local public security offices by higher-ranking authorities generates pressure on the local authorities to provide positive statistics on punishments and arrests, which are often achieved by excessive enforcement of norms. Vertical incentive structures seem to have much more effect on the behaviour of local-level authorities than horizontal communication structures, resulting in excessive punishment rather than in efficient prosecution. I conclude that economic reforms not only influenced the law-making processes in the field of immigration law, but also pushed institutional reform leading to the aim of optimisation of government structures especially after 2001. Although the number of governmental agents in the context of exit–entry administration did not decrease, certain intra- and inter-organisational co-operation systems have been established over time that aim to enhance communication between different administrative bodies in the context of exit–entry administration, however with only moderate success. The process from a restrictive to a more and more relaxed legal framework came to a halt with the revision of exit–entry administration law. Rather, the revised law of 2012 laid the foundation for a stricter but also more differentiated control of immigration that aims to curb illegal immigration on the one hand and to attract highly educated foreign experts on the other.

The next chapter analyses campaigns as means of enforcement in the area of exit–entry administration, where certain shortcomings of the administrative structures outlined in this section also apply. A similar implementation of co-ordination structure exists in the context of campaigns as well, but vertical incentive structures are related to the implementation of campaigns, too. The chapter after the following will then assess the successes and shortcomings of the revision of the *Exit–Entry Administration Law* by analysing the relevant legal framework of administrative law, as well as the relevant legal definitions, legal consequences and legal remedies concerning illegal entry, illegal stay and illegal employment.

Chapter 3: Targeting Regulatory Failure with *Sanfei* Campaigns

A. *Introduction*

The objective of this chapter is to identify the role of campaigns in the context of the law-making process in the field of exit–entry administration. In order to achieve this objective, this chapter aims to analyse and to classify campaigns that target foreign nationals who illegally enter, illegally stay or are illegally employed in China. So-called *sanfei* campaigns have been deployed at least since 2003 on a larger scale. Especially Guangdong province can be identified as a focus region. Furthermore, shortly before the revised *Exit–Entry Administration Law* was promulgated, Beijing also hosted a *sanfei* campaign with large media coverage.

In this chapter, I apply the concept of regulatory failure campaigns coined by Biddulph, Cooney, and Zhu to these *sanfei* campaigns. I assume that an important aim of *sanfei* campaigns is not only to directly target illegal activities of foreign nationals, but also to target administrative failure. As official statements frequently stated that one of the main problems of exit–entry administration was poor enforcement of legal norms due to bad communication between responsible authorities and contradicting provisions in different legal documents, I hypothesise that an important aim of *sanfei* campaigns was to tackle administrative failure and to enhance local structures to enforce legal norms in the context of exit–entry administration. I argue that *sanfei* campaigns can be classified as regulatory failure campaigns that however also target illegal behaviour.

In order to answer the question whether *sanfei* campaigns can be classified as regulatory failure campaigns, I will first clarify the concept of regulatory failure campaigns. To identify the strikes against illegal immigration as campaigns in general, I carve out the main aspects that characterise a campaign in the context of Chinese law and politics. After a literature review on the general topic of campaigns and their historical development in China and the clarification of the underlying terms and concepts, I will set out the conceptual framework of regulatory failure campaigns on which the following analysis of the deployment of *sanfei* campaigns builds. I will then explain how I collected data on the campaigns and which information collected this way I used for my analysis.

To identify *sanfei* campaigns as regulatory failure campaigns, I further assess the underlying drivers and aims of these campaigns. To this end, I analyse the temporal and geographic distribution of *sanfei* campaigns based on the collected information. I also analyse important structural aspects of *sanfei* campaigns like triggering events, addressees of *sanfei* campaigns, and their inner organisational structure. The application of the conceptual framework of regulatory failure campaigns on the *sanfei* campaigns helps to understand the role *sanfei* campaigns play in the context of the revision process of the *Exit–Entry Administration Law*.

I assume that the concept of regulatory failure campaigns is confined too tightly to a strict hierarchy from top to bottom in order to fit to *sanfei* campaigns. Campaigns may not always necessarily be the direct result of a central plan, but they may also result from central directions to solve problems using an experimental approach that allows institutions on the local level to apply governance mechanisms they consider to fit the respective problem best. Furthermore, pressure exerted by higher-ranking on lower-ranking authorities to achieve a certain outcome may result in the deployment of campaigns or raids initiated by the lower-ranking authorities in order to swiftly achieve the required outcome. I also argue that the interplay of campaigns and the law-making process may be much more differentiated than suggested by BIDDULPH, COONEY, and ZHU. Not only will laws be modified, unclear terminology interpreted according to the campaign, or existing gaps be filled with local administrative norms, but even new legal concepts will be introduced into the legal framework, which originate in campaign-style policing itself and thus interlace both means of governance, that of campaigns and that of legal norms.

I. Development of Research on Campaigns in China

Before explaining the conceptual framework of regulatory failure campaigns, I briefly review the development of research on campaigns in China in the following section. Some scholars focus on the deployment and inner structure of campaigns during the MAO era in which mainly political aims were pursued via campaigns.[1] Other research analyses law-enforcement campaigns in the late 20th and early 21st century that targeted mainly crim-

1 E.g. Frederick T. C. YU (1967), Alan P. L. LIU (1971), GREENBLATT (1977), or BENNETT (1976) and CELL (1981).

inal behaviour.[2] Finally, there is literature focusing on campaigns that are directed towards internal processes of the government or the Party targeting political deviation among officials and cadres.[3] Some recent research builds upon findings of earlier research to analyse law-enforcement campaigns in the area of environmental protection law,[4] migration law[5] and labour law.[6] In comparison with other research, however, the number of analyses on campaigns as a means of law enforcement in the area of administrative law is relatively small.

Apart from literature on campaigns and their structure and functions in general, there is extensive literature on the subject of foreign immigration to China, especially with a focus on African immigrants to Guangzhou.[7] The problem of illegal border crossing at the Yunnanese part of the Chinese border is the focus of a range of Chinese researchers.[8] Most of the Western literature uses anthropological approaches like qualitative interviews and participant observation to analyse new social dynamics of migration to China as an emerging immigration country. Within this body of literature, the subject of illegal migration and government reactions to this phenomenon is also discussed, which provides important insights into the application of legal norms as well as the enforcement of campaigns.[9] Finally, a larger body of Chinese literature covers the topic of illegal migration which is, however, rather technical in nature and analyses the reasons for illegal migration as well as possible countermeasures.[10]

The first comprehensive research on campaigns was conducted by Gordon A. Bennett. His research focuses on the deployment of campaigns before the era of reform and opening, where campaigns were mainly used for purely political aims. In his book *Yundong: Mass Campaigns in Chinese*

2 Especially Harold M. Tanner (1999), but also e. g. Murray S. Tanner (2005) and Trevaskes (2003).
3 E. g. Manion (2004).
4 See as main source van Rooij (2006 a).
5 Xin Frank He (2003).
6 Biddulph / Cooney / Ying Zhu (2012).
7 E. g. Bodomo (2010), Bredeloup (2012), Kim (2003), Zhigang Li / Lyons / Brown (2012), Pieke (2012), Li Zhang (2008), Guobin Zhu / Price (2013), or Zhang Moning (2012).
8 E. g. Wang Yanbin (2011) and Wu Xi (2013).
9 See especially Lan (2015), Haugen (2012) and Huang (2018).
10 E. g. Chen Ji / Li Shu / Ji (2008), Wu Guangzhen / Zhang Jian / Yan (2008), Wu Xingchun (2013), Ding Rui / Jiang Boren (2013), Du Wanbian (2013), Li Wei (2013), Xu Min (2008), and Wu Guangzhen / Yang (2011).

Communist Leadership, BENNETT gives a comprehensive model on mass campaigns in China.[11] I will give a short summary of his description of the typical structure of a campaign, because several aspects are still valid in today's campaign work. In his study, BENNETT concludes that campaigns offer Chinese nationals a means for political participation, that campaigns do contribute to economic growth, despite a range of contemporaneous scholars' doubts about this, and that campaigns will continue to be used even after the MAO era.[12] BENNETT gives an overview about how the campaigns he analysed are organised. The first step of a campaign is the establishment of key points for deployment of the campaign which takes place after the assignment of different tasks to activists. BENNETT has to admit that the process of underlying policy making is not accessible to him and he only can say with some certainty that policies and slogans are formed based on previous experiments and may also be subject to future change. This first step of assigning tasks aims at making the new policy popular and at the same time at training personnel. Representative entities are chosen as key-point units where the campaign shall take place first in an experimental manner. The selection of key-point units starts at the central level and reaches down to the local levels. In each selected key-point unit, cadres are chosen to organise the campaign at their level by first training a local group of activists—sometimes supported by work teams delegated by the party—before choosing another key point to spread the movement.[13] Within a local key-point unit, BENNETT points out, the campaign's general tasks have to be popularised among the Chinese nationals by means of publications in different media, activists and supporters have to be recruited, and data relevant to the campaign's aims has to be collected to find out how to best reach the campaign's targets.[14] After the first implementation stage, the next stage of the campaign typically gives rise to public criticism and denunciation and culminates in the final stage of struggle against previously identified culpable individuals.[15] While similar public criticism and denunciation patterns cannot be found in campaigns today, the basic structure of different stages of deployment, the top–down hierarchy as well as the experimental aspect are still important aspects in campaign work.

---

11 BENNETT (1976).
12 BENNETT (1976), p. 15.
13 BENNETT (1976), p. 39 f.
14 BENNETT (1976), p. 41 f.
15 BENNETT (1976), p. 43 f.

BENNETT also proposes his own typology of campaigns which differs from categorisations of previous studies, like those by YU, CELL, or LIU, insofar as he suggests a non-exclusive scheme of different tasks campaigns may follow. The aims which—according to BENNETT—campaigns pursue are "introducing and popularizing [new policies]" and "implementing existing polic[ies]", "correcting deviations from [...] public norms" and "rectifying malpractices among responsible cadres", the elimination of opponents, "emulating advanced experience" where the achievement of higher targets are stimulated by referring to ideals, and the production of "enduring changes in individual attitudes and social institutions" by consolidating a "collective spirit".[16] BENNETT admits that most of these aims, especially the last one, will not typically be the sole campaign target but rather a campaign would feature several of the tasks he proposes.[17]

With the reform and opening policy declared by DENG Xiaoping in 1978, the Chinese leadership strove for the institutionalisation of the political system. With the stronger focus on law, the aims of campaigns also shifted away from political notions towards law enforcement. While a new *Criminal Law* and *Criminal Litigation Law* were promulgated in 1979 indicating a shift from the "*ad hoc* nature of criminal justice"[18] to a basic legal framework that served as major step in institutionalising criminal legislation, the laws in the beginning still left much room for judicial interpretation and flexibility in administrative application,[19] which facilitated the use of campaign-style enforcement. Apart from pushing institutionalisation, the leadership urged the people to "unite in the struggle to modernize their poor and backward country" in terms of material as well as spiritual accomplishments.[20] This struggle—by the use of the very term already—also meant the resumption of the idea of campaign-policing especially in the field of criminal law. In his speech on *Crack down on Crime* in 1983, DENG Xiaoping pointed out that it was necessary to "mobilise the masses" to strike hard against criminals.[21] Similarly, a 1983 decision of the Central Committee of the Communist Party of China stated that the experiences of the years before had shown that only a range of organised campaigns in the spirit of "swift and hard elimination

16 BENNETT (1976), p. 46.
17 BENNETT (1976), p. 46 f.
18 Harold M. TANNER (1999), p. 5.
19 Harold M. TANNER (1999), p. 21.
20 Harold M. TANNER (1999), p. 1.
21 DENG Xiaoping (1994 b), p. 33.

at one stroke"[22] would be able to lastingly deter criminal elements, educate the youth, and restore the vigour of the public security organs.[23]

In his book *Strike Hard!*, Harold M. TANNER analyses the deployment and context of anti-crime campaigns—called *yanda* or 'strike hard' campaigns—during the mid-1980s and later in the early 2000s, which are infamous for their high death toll through executions.[24] To achieve a thorough implementation of the campaigns, public security offices, the procuratorate, as well as courts—especially, but not only, during the campaigns treated as regular administrative entities—were coordinated by so called "commando posts",[25] organising the "joint handling of cases" to swiftly adjudicate a high number of criminal cases.[26] After experimental deployment in some areas, the first *yanda* campaign was officially announced and elucidated to the public and party members on 25 August 1983[27] before the concrete basic principles were published in an official decision of the Central Committee of the Chinese Communist Party.[28] By clearly targeting deviant behaviour of individuals, the campaign was directed against individuals accused of a range of criminal actions as well as against "hooligans",[29] active members of reactionary secret societies, active counter-revolutionary elements and active elements related to LIN Biao and the Gang of Four. In September 1983, the *Criminal Law* and other relevant regulations were revised to facilitate the deployment of the campaigns. In 1990 and 1996, similar *yanda* campaigns were carried out nationwide. Murray Scot TANNER remarks that on a local administrative level, such campaigns have become an even more regular element of police activity.[30] The *yanda* campaigns can be seen as located at the turning point of campaign development, still being campaigns mainly initiated by a person-centred leadership but also already being law-enforcement campaigns that rely on the institutionalisation of the political-legal system. Further research on *yanda* campaigns was undertaken by Susan TREVASKES who tries to understand the contradiction between professionalism promoted since the start of the open-door reforms and strategies like the reintroduction

22 Chinese: 从重从快，一网打尽.
23 *Strike Hard Decision* (1983), p. 692.
24 Harold M. TANNER (1999).
25 Chinese sources use the term *zhihuibu* (Chinese: 指挥部); LU Hongsheng (2013), p. 92.
26 Harold M. TANNER (1999), p. 87.
27 Harold M. TANNER (1999), p. 87 f.
28 *Strike Hard Decision* (1983).
29 Chinese: 流氓团伙分子.
30 Murray S. TANNER (2005), p. 171.

of the notion of the "enemies of the masses", excessive punishment and mobilisation of the masses, as well as flexible adjudication and multi-agency cooperation.[31] She could not, however, come up with a satisfactory explanation for this obvious conflict but merely questions the long-term effect of such campaigns.

Melanie MANION analysed the use of campaigns in the field of intra-party discipline by focussing on anti-corruption campaigns in the 1980s and 1990s, which she also identifies as enforcement campaigns.[32] According to her, campaigns in the post-MAO era are primarily defined by constituting the exact opposite of routinised bureaucracy[33] which renders it difficult, however, to identify the repeating deployment of campaigns as routine.[34] MANION concludes that the anti-corruption campaigns she analysed, without actually having a deterrent effect but rather giving room for leniency, distorted the development of rule of law and are "antithetical to the order and stability that Chinese leaders see as requisite to economic growth."[35] She also gives reference to the populist element of campaigning by citing LI Lianjing who sees the origin of the campaigns in the "profound frustration with widespread corruption."[36]

The *yanda* campaigns served as the basis for future law-enforcement campaigns like the *sanfei* campaigns or campaigns in the area of environmental protection law. Obviously law-enforcement campaigns in other areas than criminal law exhibit a smaller degree of violence. Reliance on the cooperation of individuals who report deviant behaviour and thus help to maintain social order seems to be a central strategy applied in post-opening campaigns. The integration of the public in government work, however, is not new, as a high level of social control like in China was often only achieved with the active support of groups of Chinese nationals. In her article *From Mass Campaigns to Managed Campaigns: "Constructing a New Socialist Countryside"*, Elizabeth J. PERRY questions the assumption common in contemporary literature that holds that campaigns would disappear as a political means in the course of successive replacement of revolutionary mentors by

31 TREVASKES (2002); TREVASKES (2003).
32 MANION (2004), p. 155 ff.
33 MANION (2004), p. 161.
34 MANION (2004), p. 163. BENNETT however notes that due to the regular occurrence of campaigns, the actors involved indeed developed some kind of routine to cope with campaigns; BENNETT (1977), p. 122.
35 MANION (2004), p. 199.
36 Lianjing LI (2001) cited in MANION (2004), p. 199.

junior technocrats within the leadership ranks and the change in governance from a revolutionary to a more rational and bureaucratic style.[37] She rather proposes that "the legacy of mass campaigns has remained an integral—and under-appreciated—instrument of rule in post-MAO China [...] even in the realm of economic development."[38] She thus wraps together assumptions made by VAN ROOIJ, TREVASKES, and even in part by CELL who postulate a continued use of campaigns in the future and who precisely identify recent campaigns as means of enforcement of legal and economic aims. PERRY defines the concept of "managed campaigns" as a development of Maoist campaigns. Managed campaigns feature several basic elements already incorporated in campaigns of the revolutionary era like focused propaganda to provoke consenting emotions and dedication by the public as well as the underlying concept of struggle and aim to conquer "bureaucratic ossification".[39] Still, managed campaigns are less ambitious but rather pragmatic in their objectives to be achieved and borrow from a much broader scope of techniques and concepts stemming from historical, contemporary, national, as well as international experiences, encased by a "scientific concept of development" as HU Jintao has coined it.[40] Similarly, the term 'struggle' is no longer understood in the sense of socialist class struggle but rather as efforts to be grasped to achieve a 'harmonious society'. Thus, the emphasis is put on scientificity, a key-term of the HU era, while the swift achievement of utopian aims is recognised as unrealistic and even destructive.[41]

Elaborating on his book *Regulating Land and Pollution in China: Lawmaking, Compliance, and Enforcement; Theory and Cases*,[42] Benjamin VAN ROOIJ has written several articles on the subject of the implementation and enforcement of law via campaigns especially in the field of environmental protection law.[43] While assuming that post-MAO campaigns are less political, VAN ROOIJ still admits the political nature of enforcement campaigns and identifies "certain *Yundong* elements"[44] even in today's campaigns. He declares the 'strike hard' campaigns of the early 1980s as the prototype for law-enforcement campaigns in post-MAO China, as the latter still include

37 PERRY (2011).
38 PERRY (2011), p. 31 f.
39 PERRY (2011), p. 43.
40 PERRY (2011), p. 43.
41 PERRY (2011), p. 44 f.
42 VAN ROOIJ (2006 a).
43 Among others VAN ROOIJ (2002), VAN ROOIJ (2006 b), VAN ROOIJ (2009), and VAN ROOIJ (2012).
44 VAN ROOIJ (2009), p. 25.

the characteristic element of striking severely and swiftly coined by DENG.[45] Law-enforcement campaigns share fundamental characteristics with MAO-era campaigns like a top–down hierarchy or an experimental character, but also differ in several aspects. Not only are law-enforcement campaigns less violent[46] and less dependent on the mobilised masses, but also the style of government increasingly relies on a professionalised bureaucracy and a stable legal system.[47] One apparent example is the rejection of mass mobilisation and public punishments and, instead, the application of a public report system that invites Chinese nationals to give notice of corruption or other misbehaviour.[48]

Early literature on campaigns aims to categorise different types of campaigns and to analyse their inner structure in order to give a definition of what is to be understood as a campaign. I conclude that the most important elements of campaigns are the activation and participation of the people, a strong focus on top–down hierarchy from the central to the local level, and an experimental approach where campaigns are first deployed in key-point areas before being applied throughout the country. These elements are still valid today, while the aim of campaigns has shifted towards the focus of law enforcement. With this shift, research also concentrated on the use of campaigns for law enforcement, the first analyses being made in the field of criminal law. The most important finding of these analyses is that the political shift in China towards a focus on legality does not mean the complete renunciation of campaigns as political means. Indeed, in comparison to campaigns in the MAO era, law-enforcement campaigns in contemporary China have shed part of their political nature and one could say that Chinese campaigns and campaigns in Western liberal democracies have become ever more similar. This fact, however, does not deny the political nature of campaigns in general. While the 'strike hard' campaigns still made use of the concept of mass participation, newer research in the field of environmental protection and labour law show a much stronger reliance on a stable bureaucracy and legal system and the renunciation of mass mobilisation. Certain political elements specific to Chinese campaigns, however, can still be found in current law-enforcement campaigns and also, as will be shown in this chapter, in campaigns in the area of immigration law.

---

45 VAN ROOIJ (2009), p. 12 f.

46 VAN ROOIJ however admits that the 'strike hard' campaigns come as an exception from this assumption; VAN ROOIJ (2009), p. 24.

47 VAN ROOIJ (2009), p. 24 f.

48 MANION (2004), p. 160.

II. Definition of 'Campaign'

Before collecting information from newspapers and online sources in order to be able to analyse *sanfei* campaigns in more detail, I need to carve out what 'campaign' means in the context of immigration law. In order to perform a textual analysis on the topic of *sanfei* campaigns, I assess how *sanfei* campaigns are referred to in official documents or newspaper articles. I will use the information that refers to *sanfei* campaigns to analyse the geographical and temporal distribution of campaigns as well as the inner organisation structure of the campaigns to make sense of their deployment and eventually find out their aims and drivers, which finally serves to classify *sanfei* campaigns as regulatory failure campaigns or perhaps as another category of campaigns.

Literature on the subject of campaigns ranges from political campaigns dating back from before the foundation of the People's Republic until today and covers different aspects of campaigning. There is no unified definition for a campaign, rather such a definition has to be deduced from the structure of campaigns that has been identified by different researchers. There is consensus in literature that a campaign interrupts routine administrative work,[49] e. g. by allotting resources to campaign tasks or setting up an *ad-hoc* parallel organisation structure. In general, a campaign comprises different organisation steps, to establish key points where information and instructions are studied, to actually enforce the aims of the campaign at the local level, and to finally sum up and review the campaign's results.

Different approaches in literature mirror the differences of campaigns regarding their geographical, temporal as well as political scope. While aims of campaigns have shifted over time in general, the underlying basic structure has remained similar. Campaigns have always shared certain characteristics like the mobilisation of different agencies at several governmental levels, the focused and intensified enforcement or the encouragement of the people to participate.[50] Because of these consistent characteristics over time, I can still apply certain findings on campaigns of the pre-opening era today. The terminology of BIDDULPH, COONEY, and ZHU, who use the definition of campaigns as "coordinated operations"[51] where tasks, timing, and per-

49 See e. g. MANION (2004), p. 161; Alan P. L. LIU (1971), p. 87.

50 BIDDULPH / COONEY / Ying ZHU (2012), p. 376.

51 Chinese: 统一行动. BIDDULPH / COONEY / Ying ZHU (2012), p. 376. This term was especially used in relation with the *yanda* campaigns; see e. g. TANG Huangfeng (2007).

formance targets are centrally defined and allotted to local level administrative agencies, best summarises the central characteristics of Chinese campaigns. This term originates from a speech of Li Peng,[52] then Premier of the State Council, who used this term in a speech at a National Political-Legal Work Meeting[53] on 18 December 1996 to describe one of the shapes of the 'strike hard' campaigns.[54] A central leadership group as well as local working groups established especially for the administration of the campaign are assigned to coordinate the course of the campaign as well as to gather reports on performance at regular intervals.[55]

Van Rooij shows that contemporary campaigns in China do not differ much from campaigns in Western liberal democracies.[56] This is especially true, since the political, let alone revolutionary, aspect has taken a backseat in recent campaigns that aim for law enforcement.[57] Campaigns in China as well as their Western counterparts temporarily allocate resources in reaction to a distinct problem and merge law and politics and do this in particular in the area of law enforcement, as either feature the support of high-ranking politicians and make use of public media channels.[58] Campaigns are hence a highly efficient means of communication. However, as will be shown in this chapter in particular, Chinese campaigns make use of a distinct organisational structure that is established in an *ad-hoc* manner specifically in order to implement the campaign at different administrative levels and in parallel to the regular administrative structure. Targets identified centrally are then defined prior to their dissemination to the masses directly via discussion meetings or indirectly via mass media. During the climax of a campaign, the previously defined targets are heavily attacked by the masses driven by campaign activists. If the target of a campaign is a distinct social group, this central stage is most visible in the accompanying punishment of individuals who exhibit unwanted behaviour or thinking. Most explicit examples of this are the campaigns against counter-revolutionaries and anti-rightists which both featured public criticism and punishment of the target group. However, targets of a campaign can also be abstract items like production levels that are to be achieved or the education of specific ideological principles.

52 Chinese: 李鹏.
53 Chinese: 全国政法工作会议.
54 Biddulph (2007), p. 135.
55 Biddulph / Cooney / Ying Zhu (2012), p. 376.
56 Van Rooij (2016), p. 229 f.
57 Biddulph / Cooney / Ying Zhu (2012), p. 383.
58 Van Rooij (2016), p. 230.

After a campaign, a review is conducted which evaluates the positive as well as negative outcomes. The central-to-local progression of campaigns, as well as an overlapping structure where bigger movements may consist of several smaller campaigns, also seems to be a specific feature of Chinese campaigns. Summing up, campaigns in China are different from campaigns in Western democracies, not necessarily because of Party leadership and the pursuit of mainly political aims, but rather because of their parallel organisational structure, which is set up in an *ad-hoc* manner in order to implement the campaign's aims, and which is dissolved again after the campaign finished. Even in more recent campaigns that aim to enhance administrative processes and enforcement of legal norms, a high degree of politicisation and Party involvement and parallel organisation structures can be found.

The collection of pertinent information on this chapter's object of my research requires the identification of the relevant Chinese terminology. Campaigns in the sense of the above definition are typically called *yundong*[59] in Chinese as well as in western academic literature. This term has originally and primarily been used to denote movements in the pre-opening era[60] and in a broader sense describes a 'movement'.[61] In a narrower sense and depending on the context, this term can be understood as sport, exercise, motion, agitation, or campaign. Today, literature on campaign-style governance typically refers to this term when talking about *yundongshi zhili*,[62] *yundongshi zhifa*,[63] or *yundongxing zhili jizhi*.[64]

The term *yundong*, however, describes the concept of campaigns in a very general sense. Certain campaigns may more precisely be denoted by specific terms. Apart from the terms 'coordinated action' or 'coordinated operation', that denote an overall political movement, research has identified 'specialist actions' as a different, local shape of campaigns. Biddulph, for example, analyses the case of 'strike hard' campaigns in the early 1980s where a 'coordinated operation'[65] was launched by central-level state organs under the leadership of the Party, while 'specialist actions' or 'specialist struggles'[66] were geographically more confined and deployed under the leadership of a

59 Chinese: 运动.
60 A prominent example is Bennett (1976).
61 Bennett (1976), p. 17, footnote 3.
62 Chinese: 运动式治理; Ni (2014).
63 Chinese: 运动式执法; Tang Xianxing / Yu Yamei (2009).
64 Chinese: 运动型治理机制; Zhou Xueguang (2012).
65 Chinese: 集中统一行动.
66 Chinese: 专项行动, 专项斗争.

local (party) committee.[67] 'Specialist actions' can hence be seen as the local enforcement of the nation-wide 'coordinated operation'. As a prior analysis of the available sources in the context of *sanfei* campaigns revealed, most information on *sanfei* campaigns, for example newspaper articles, denotes campaigns as 'specialist actions' (*zhuanxiang xingdong*). In several official documents on *sanfei* campaigns as well, the described operations are typically called *zhuanxiang (zhengzhi) xingdong*,[68] 'special (punishment) moves' or 'special actions' that are 'launched' (*kaizhan*[69]).[70] During the collection of information on *sanfei* campaigns, I hence primarily focused on the term *zhuanxiang (zhengzhi) xingdong*, but because this term is not necessarily used in secondary literature or in certain official documents, I also took into account literature that talked of *yundong* or *xingdong*.

Summing up, the following aspects serve as main indicators for campaigns and will be used later in the analysis and categorisation of *sanfei* campaigns: First, tasks, timing, and performance targets are defined centrally, which means that a central-level institution defines the main aims of the movement and coordinates its deployment. This institution may be a governmental but also a party body that serves as a coordinating central leadership group. Second, targets derived from these main aims are allotted to local level administrative agencies, and local working groups or committees are established at local levels of deployment, administered by higher-ranking working groups, to which the local working groups report their performance. Third, in an experimental approach, smaller movements are typically deployed in key-point areas before the movement is rolled out in the whole country. Finally, the public is involved in the movement, for example by implementing a public report system.

III. Statistics on Illegal Immigration

Official statistics on illegal immigration are an important source of information as an analysis of these figures allows us to evaluate the necessity of campaigns against illegal immigration. Political statements and newspaper articles often argued that illegal immigration to China was on the rise and had

67 Biddulph (2007), p. 135–136.
68 Chinese: 专项（整治）行动.
69 Chinese: 开展.
70 See the cited 'Implementation Plans' and 'Actions Plans' below.

become a severe problem that had to be tackled using strict enforcement.[71] By assessing available statistical figures, I examined the actual severity of this problem in more detail.[72] I found that although immigration to China sharply increased after 1978 and in the context of the accession to the World Trade Organisation in 2001, it still remains low when compared to immigration to other countries like the U. S. or Germany. Further, as official figures suggest, only a small percentage of foreign nationals stay in China for employment.[73] Although the percentage of foreign nationals who stay in China for employment in comparison to the total number of stays has increased over time, it still remains relatively low.[74] As for the overall distribution of foreign nationals in China, most foreign nationals live in larger cities like Beijing or Shanghai, as well as in Guangdong province.[75]

This section aims to quantify the problem of illegal immigration to China. When assessing official figures published by Chinese authorities, it is important to note that statistical data may be biased, as numbers on illegal immigration are published by the Ministry of Public Security, which pursues a policy of strict enforcement of illegal immigration.[76] As has been noted in the previous part, pressure exerted by higher-ranking authorities may result in an increased and even excessive implementation of administrative meas-

71 See e g. *China to Enact Law to Solve the Problem of Foreign Nationals Illegally Entering, Residing, and Being Employed in China* (中国将立法解决外国人非法入境非法居留非法就业问题)*, NPC Standing Committee Press Release* (2011); *Guide to Interpretation and Application of the 'Exit–Entry Administration Law of the People's Republic of China'* (《中华人民共和国出境入境管理法》释义及实用指南) (2012), p. 23; see also the explanations to the *Exit–Entry Administration Law (Draft)* (2011); *Mid of May to End of August: Beijing Joins Forces to Clean Up 'Sanfei' Foreigners. Almost 200 000 Foreign Nationals Each Day* (5月中旬至8月底　北京集中清理'三非'外国人　每日实有近20万外国人) (2012); Deng Weijin / Xiang (2004).

72 See the statistics regarding immigration to China in general in figure 1.1 and figure 1.2 in the introduction of this study.

73 Guofu Liu (2011), p. 4; figures referred to in Ding Saier (2014), p. 54 f.

74 According to Ding Saier (2014), 515 000, 732 000, and 807 000 foreign nationals stayed in China for employment in 2007, 2009, and 2010 respectively; Ding Saier (2014), p. 54 f. For 2016, the article *Over 900,000 Foreigners Work in Chinese Mainland in 2016* (2017) refers to over 900 000 foreign nationals employed in mainland China, which would be a ratio .12 percent based on a total of 776 030 000 employees in China; Table 4-1 *China Statistical Yearbook* (中国统计年鉴) (2017).

75 Table Appendix 2-1 *Tabulation on the 2010 Population Census of the People's Republic of China* (中国2010年人口普查资料) (2010).

76 See e. g. Yongshun Cai (2000), p. 785 f.

ures resulting in higher figures on illegal immigration. However, the official statistics published by the authorities and the National Bureau of Statistics of China are still the most reliable figures available.

Table 3.1: Number of reported *sanfei* cases [77]

Year	Total *Sanfei* Cases		Deportations		
1995	≈ 10 000				≈ 63 000
2000		122 690		41 172	
2004	16 282				
2005	31 735		7 163		
2006	≈ 36 000		9 560		
2010	23 110				
2011	≈ 20 000				

Table 3.2: Exits and entries of foreign nationals between 2003 and 2017 [78]

Year	Entries of Foreign Nationals	Exits of Foreign Nationals	Entries and Exits of Foreign Nationals	Percentage of Total Entries and Exits
2003	—	—	22 698 600	10.21 %
2004	16 932 500	—	*33 441 688*	*12.16 %*
2005	—	—	*39 386 190*	*13.04 %*
2006	—	—	44 275 000	13.93 %
2007	26 110 000	25 962 000	52 072 000	15.09 %
2008	24 000 000	24 000 000	48 000 000	13.71 %
2009	21 937 480	21 789 520	43 727 000	12.57 %
2010	26 127 000	25 985 000	52 112 000	13.64 %
2011	27 111 000	27 009 000	54 120 000	13.17 %

77 SONG Quancheng (2015); ZHUANG Huining (2007); WANG Mei (2012); WU Chu (2011). An alternative figure for deported foreign nationals in 2006 is 16 000 according to different sources.

Table 3.2: Exits and entries of foreign nationals between 2003 and 2017 (continued)

Year	**Entries of Foreign Nationals**	**Exits of Foreign Nationals**	**Entries and Exits of Foreign Nationals**	**Percentage of Total Entries and Exits**
2012	27 190 196	27 161 304	54 351 500	12.61 %
2013	26 290 200	26 218 900	52 509 100	11.57 %
2014	26 368 945	26 299 146	52 668 091	10.75 %
2015	25 993 128	25 912 103	51 905 231	9.93 %
2016	38 406 186	37 899 243	76 305 429	13.38 %
2017 (first three quarters)	31 565 097	31 201 204	62 766 301	14.17 %
2017	*42 086 796*	*41 601 605*	*83 688 401*	*14.17 %*

Although official statistics do not refer to *sanfei* campaigns directly, the figures can help us understand the relevance of the issue of illegal immigration to China. As newspaper announcements and official statements often refer to rising figures of foreign nationals as well as to illegal activities of foreign nationals and use these figures to legitimate severe police action against illegal immigration, it is reasonable to evaluate the numbers on illegal immigration as reported in the newspaper articles and compare these numbers to relevant numbers of other countries.

The Ministry of Public Security reported a total of 20 000 *sanfei* cases for 2011, one year after the Ministry of Public Security issued its notice that required the setting up of small working groups at the local level, hence at a time when enforcement should have been comparatively efficient. Considering a total of 27 111 000 entries of foreign nationals to China in 2011, the figure of 20 000 *sanfei* cases nationwide is relatively low, especially com-

78 Figures calculated by the author of this study on the basis of official data published on-line by the Bureau of Exit–Entry Administration of the Ministry of Public Security supported by data taken from Deng Ying / Dong / Miao (2015), p. 53. The figures for the exits have been calculated by subtracting the number of entries from the figures for exit and entry together. The figure for the entries in 2012 has been interpolated assuming that the entries in 2013 decreased by .331 percent compared with 2012. The interpolation of the total figures of 2017 assumes a linear increase. The figures for 2004 and 2005 are estimates based on the total number of entries and exits. The figures for 2017 are interpolated estimates. Figures represent person-times (*renci*).

pared to other jurisdictions.[79] The U. S., e. g., report a total of 1 998 609 immigration enforcement actions and 53 082 286 immigrants (using the I-94 scheme) for 2011,[80] Germany reports 71 551 crimes related to immigration law (ausländerrechtliche Straftaten) and 841 695 foreign nationals who entered the country for non-temporary stay[81] in the same year. The number of cases to the number of entered foreign nationals yields a ratio of .0007 for China, of .0850 for Germany[82] and of .0377 for the U. S.

Even when considering an uneven distribution of *sanfei* cases across the country, i. e. a probably higher rate of *sanfei* cases in cities like Guangzhou, Shanghai or Beijing, the ratio of cases to entries of foreign nationals may not be much higher since these cities very likely also report higher figures on entries of foreign nationals. Indeed, as the *Guangdong Daily* reports for 2007 by referring to official police data, about 9 million foreign nationals entered the country via ports in Guangdong province while approximately 7 000 *sanfei* cases were reported in Guangdong in the whole year. A division of both numbers again yields a relatively low ratio of .0038, which is, however, considerably higher than the ratio for the whole country. Furthermore, the cited figures are difficult to interpret. While 7 000 and 13 000 *sanfei* cases are recorded for 2007 and 2008 for the province of Guangdong[83]—which indeed is a remarkable increase—for the city of Guangzhou 4 524 and 5 773 cases are reported for the same years, with an obviously lower growth rate.[84] As pointed out above, higher numbers may refer to higher police activity and do not necessarily indicate a corresponding increase in crimes or offences. As stated in reports, the police in Guangzhou frequently

---

79 See figures in table 3.2.

80 The number of immigrants to the U. S. is calculated by totalling up the figures for foreign nationals apprehended, foreign nationals found inadmissible, initial admissions to ICE detention facilities, foreign nationals returned, and foreign nationals removed; SIMANSKI / SAPP (2012); *2011 Yearbook of Immigration Statistics* (2012), p. 65.

81 *Polizeiliche Kriminalstatistik Bundesrepublik Deutschland: Berichtsjahr 2011* (2012), p. 127; *Migrationsbericht des Bundesamtes für Migration und Flüchtlinge im Auftrag der Bundesregierung: Migrationsbericht 2015* (2016), p. 30. No figures are available on the total number of entries by foreign (non-E. U.) nationals to Germany.

82 Note that this ratio is based only on those foreign nationals who entered the country for non-temporary stay, while the other two ratios are based on all entries of foreign nationals.

83 PAN Xianglong / QIN (2011), p. 85.

84 *Guangzhou Yearbook* (广州年鉴) (1983–2013) 2008, p. 110. *Guangzhou Yearbook* (广州年鉴) (1983–2013) 2009, p. 145.

did not repatriate foreign nationals detained because of illegal activities, but instead set them free after several days of detention because repatriation was expensive and the individuals concerned were often not able to pay for it themselves.[85] Such practice suggests that the same individual may be detained several times, which would increase the number of cases but not the number of individuals engaging in illegal activities.

These numbers suggest that the problem of foreign nationals conducting illegal activities is far less substantial in China, and even in alleged hotspots like Guangdong province, than it is e. g. in Germany or in the U. S. I assume that the relevant figures on *sanfei* cases and foreign immigrants to China are used in Chinese media and reports rather in a suggestive way in order to legitimise police action against foreign nationals. This assumption is supported by the fact that the numbers are often stated without putting them into any context or relation, for example to comparable figures of other countries or of other periods. However, it should also be noted that against the background of insufficient legal norms, a rise of illegal immigration will intensify the problem of insufficient enforcement measures and will make them ever more visible. Hence, although the concrete numbers regarding illegal immigration seem to be relatively low, in the context of outdated legal norms, rising albeit low numbers can easily be perceived as a threat to social order.

B. Conceptual Framework

In order to apply the concept of regulatory failure campaigns to *sanfei* campaigns, I will first analyse the deployment of *sanfei* campaigns and identify patterns of their geographical and temporal scope and distribution and carve out similarities as well as differences with traditional campaign models. I will then classify *sanfei* campaigns as law-enforcement campaigns according to relevant findings in the literature. To finally answer the question whether *sanfei* campaigns can also be classified as regulatory failure campaigns, I will analyse in more detail the structure of the competent authorities and underlying questions regarding top–down hierarchy, responsibilities, and deviations between central and local interests in the following section. The findings of this and of the following section will help to classify *sanfei* campaigns as regulatory failure campaigns with special characteristics.

---

85 LAN (2017 a), p. 103.

In the following section, I lay out the concept of regulatory failure campaigns as coined by BIDDULPH, COONEY, and ZHU. To do this, I first introduce the theoretical framework of two related findings of VAN ROOIJ and HE that serve to explain the concept of regulatory failure campaigns, and analyse the *sanfei* campaigns within this framework. The findings of VAN ROOIJ serve as a basic framework of the concept of law-enforcement campaigns in the context of administrative law, of which exit–entry administration is one part. The analysis of HE shows that the findings of VAN ROOIJ, which are based on campaigns in the area of environment protection law, are also applicable in the area of internal migration.

I. Regulatory Failure in the Context of Exit–Entry Administration

The term 'regulatory failure', although lacking a precise definition,[86] depicts an intervention in the market or other social structures by state regulation, but not necessarily through laws alone, that leads to unwanted outcomes but does not solve the originally targeted problem.[87] The identification of regulatory failure is difficult, as it raises the question what the outcome would have been without the regulation in question.[88] Still, it can be argued that regulatory failure exists when state regulation does not meet its original goal. In the context of exit–entry administration, regulatory failure can be determined when either illegal entry, stay or employment is not prevented or not adequately persecuted by the responsible authorities due to adverse norms or instructions or the lack of appropriate legal regulations.

Regulatory failure may become manifest in weak or adverse legal enforcement or non-compliance especially with central legislation. As I found in the first chapter, certain legal and organisational aspects in the context of exit–entry administration were likely to result in non-compliance or adverse enforcement. Overlapping or contradictory legal norms, as well as poor information sharing between different responsible authorities, resulted in weak enforcement or non-compliance of local public security organs.[89] Experts state that one of the main reasons for the reluctance of local public

86 BALDWIN / CAVE / LODGE (2012), p. 68.
87 STIGLITZ (2009), p. 17 f.; CURRIE (2006), p. 50.
88 BALDWIN / CAVE / LODGE (2012), p. 69.
89 For example regarding the question whether police authorities below county level were allowed to impose sanctions on foreign nationals; see the discussion in section V. of chapter 2 on page 60.

security officials to enforce legal norms in the context of exit–entry administration was the insufficient cooperation between different responsible authorities.[90] On the other hand, vertical incentive structures resulted in excessive punishment by local public security authorities, and hence to adverse enforcement, in order to prevent interference by higher-level authorities.[91] Non-compliance with central-level norms may also be due to the fact that these norms are not suited to local-level implementation. In the context of exit–entry administration, the police is, for example, reported to be burdened with the problem of illegal migrants, as they are often unable to pay fines due to their precarious financial situation.[92]

Regulatory failure may further become manifest in collusive behaviour of local officials and the local public, which again results in non-adherence to regulatory requirements. In the example of Guangzhou, interdependencies between the public and illegal migrants are found, but also between the police and the migrants. Not only do foreign nationals serve the local economy with their trade,[93] but they also provide attractive services at low cost, as in the example of foreign English teachers.[94] The fact that such activities of foreign nationals are possibly illegal is obviously often regarded as a minor issue compared to the benefits of their presence in Guangzhou. But the precarious state of illegal migrants also renders them prone to exploitation by local officials.[95] Literature on international migrants in Guangzhou

90 *China Promotes Opening Up and Foreign Relations by Enacting Norms on Exit–Entry Administration* (中国立法规范出入境管理促进对外开放和交往), *NPC Press Release* (2012).

91 Huang (2018), p. 15.

92 Haugen (2012). In 2009, the Guangzhou police introduced a voluntary repatriation scheme with reduced fines to solve this problem; Haugen (2012), p. 76. See as well Lan (2017 b), p. 55.

93 See Zhigang Li / Lyons / Brown (2012), especially p. 62 ff.; Lan (2017 b), p. 55; Min Zhou / Shenasi / Tao Xu (2016), p. 157.

94 Bredeloup (2012). Haugen refers to foreign students working part-time as English teachers, however often illegally; Haugen (2013 a), p. 15 f.

95 E. g. Haugen reports of officials requiring to pay the repatriation expenses of others (deportation expenses are to be born by the deportee) and of hotels charging bribes to illegally issue a registration proof which was necessary to get an exit visa that would allow to take part in a voluntary repatriation scheme; Haugen (2012), p. 74 f. and 76. Lan reports of agents who help the police to charge illegal fines; Lan (2017 b), p. 57; Lan (2017 a), p. 105. Lan further reports of the police waiting a few minutes inside the police car with blue lights flashing before they actually start their controls, which suggests that they intend to warn those who are informed about the raid; Lan (2017 a), p. 94 f.

further reports of underground banks operating in areas with extensive informal trade activities conducted by foreign nationals, which are controlled by powerful Chinese who bribe the local police in order to get prior warning to raids against illegal immigration.[96]

II. Van Rooij: Campaigns as a Means of Law Enforcement

Van Rooij focuses on campaigns as a means of enforcement of legal norms in the area of administrative law.[97] Law enforcement campaigns are often initiated by political agenda setting that focusses on one specific issue over a certain time span.[98] Van Rooij postulates that in the course of the policy of reform and opening up introduced by Deng Xiaoping in the late 1970s, institutionalisation took place that led to a decrease of the use of political campaigns but also resulted in new problems such as weak legal enforcement and non-compliance, especially with central legislation. While older laws provided wide scope for interpretation that also served local particularities well, newer laws became ever more strict and concrete. This concreteness often resulted in the inapplicability of national norms to local circumstances, which in turn led to non-compliance and weak enforcement.[99] According to van Rooij, these new problems again have made necessary the use of political campaigns, however, now serving as a means of law enforcement rather than a means of introducing or enforcing political guidelines. The increase of autonomy of authorities at the local level often leads to conflicts between central and local administration agencies and the occurrence of local protectionism.[100] Campaigns are used to overcome this unbalanced situation and to re-establish central control over local administration.[101] However, Van Rooij claims that campaigns as a means of law enforcement often achieve only a short-term benefit since they are not able to solve the underlying problems. Still, they are more effective than legal norms due to their ex-

96 Lan (2017 b), p. 55.
97 Among others van Rooij (2002), van Rooij (2006 a), van Rooij (2006 b), van Rooij (2009), and van Rooij (2012).
98 Van Rooij (2016), p. 230.
99 Van Rooij (2006 b), p. 59, 61.
100 Van Rooij (2009), p. 35–37.
101 Van Rooij (2009), p. 38.

perimental and flexible characteristics that are able to address problems in a swifter and more targeted manner.[102]

The main obstacle for legal enforcement and compliance at the local level are highly complex local interdependencies, especially financial ones. At the local level, financial dependencies between governmental agencies, enterprises, and the local population are very strong, resulting in the protection of local enterprises by local government agencies and the local population.[103] Local authorities may be interested in continuing to act against the interest of the central government since fees make up an essential part of their resources.[104] Also, understaffed authorities depend heavily on public participation which creates a strong interdependency between local governments and the public. Therefore, and due to financial dependencies, public complaints against offences committed by local authorities are understandably scarce.[105] Since the economic reforms, administrative responsibilities have been delegated to local authorities, which stripped central organs of local control. Thus, enforcement campaigns may be a reaction to local noncompliance with central norms and an attempt to rebuild central administrative control.[106] Another reason for the execution of enforcement campaigns van Rooij suggests is the reluctance of the central organs to take initiative to improve law enforcement outside of campaigns, which is due to the fact that often central authorities are resistant to public criticism while local authorities are assigned the role of the "scapegoat".[107]

Van Rooij analyses enforcement campaigns in the area of environmental protection law which predominantly took place between 2001 and 2004.[108] These campaigns were only originally designed in a top–down structure and only initially of the same style throughout the whole country. Later in time, the campaigns became increasingly locally diversified in order to target specific local problems.[109] Van Rooij finds that the campaigns did not necessarily lead to an increase of penalties but rather to an increase of inspections which he explains by the interdependencies described above.[110]

---

102 Van Rooij (2006 b), p. 59.
103 Van Rooij (2006 b), p. 62.
104 Van Rooij (2006 b), p. 64.
105 Van Rooij (2006 b), p. 64.
106 Van Rooij (2009), p. 39 f.
107 Van Rooij (2009), p. 40.
108 Van Rooij (2006 b), p. 64 ff.
109 Van Rooij (2006 b), p. 66 f.
110 Van Rooij (2006 b), p. 67.

Obviously, enforcement campaigns do not in every case serve the purpose of enforcing the law. Not only does local protectionism hinder the thorough enforcement of legal norms but also the results of enforcement campaigns are often edited and sugar-coated to convey the impression of being more effective than they actually were.[111] Due to this reason, aside from the use of enforcement campaigns, parallel central administrative structures are built up at local levels, which are meant to re-centralise administrative authorities,[112] serving a similar goal to enforcement campaigns and thus contesting their legitimacy.[113] Against this background, VAN ROOIJ answers the question why campaigns are still used as a means of enforcement with the maintenance of leadership legitimacy being the main driver for the use of campaigns.[114] Other drivers VAN ROOIJ identifies are the ability of campaigns to create "short-term pressure for change"[115] which is helpful in re-establishing central control as well as a particular adverse perception of the effectiveness and applicability of campaigns which is most apparent in the field of criminal justice but less in other realms.[116]

III. HE: Law-Enforcement Campaigns in the Area of Migration

When analysing the Beijing campaigns of 1995 which targeted illegal rural migrants[117] and were carried out in the context of 'strike hard' campaigns, Xin Frank HE observed that lower and upper level governments had different aims and interests, which in the end shaped the campaigns. Due to their economic success, migrants became a source of income to local residents and government and also had a stimulatory impact on general development of the whole region. Also, migrants often had to pay bribes to local officials due to their illegal or at least precarious status as a result of their foreignness, which in turn made the local authorities beneficiaries of the mi-

111 VAN ROOIJ (2009), p. 30 f.
112 This parallel structure is often called "vertical management"; Chinese: 垂直管理; VAN ROOIJ (2009), p. 42 ff.; Alex L. WANG (2018), p. 742.
113 VAN ROOIJ (2009), p. 41.
114 VAN ROOIJ (2009), p. 35.
115 VAN ROOIJ (2009), p. 45.
116 VAN ROOIJ (2009), p. 46 f.
117 Here, intra-national migrants who came to Beijing from rural areas were the target of the campaigns. However, the responsible authorities for intra-national migration are the same as for international migration, namely local public security offices.

grants.[118] These positive effects which migrants had for local residents and the local government led to a resistance at the local level to enforcing central norms and to "legal collusion"[119] as HE calls it: strategies employed by migrants and local officials to circumvent legal provisions, which often involved the demand for unjustified fees by officials in exchange for licenses or protection.[120] On the whole, economic reasons were considered by locals to be more important than or even argued to be the solution for social stability and issues like crime and unrest. Local authorities even would help migrants with issuing official documents or resident permit applications and tried to attract migrants to invest in local marketplaces.[121]

The main concerns of the central government in contrast were social order and stability.[122] Migrant areas are not part of the controlled sphere and were perceived by the central government as a potential threat to their power and thus politically sensitive. This fear was fuelled by comparatively high crime rates within the migrant areas and an overall worse social order situation representing a "major destabilizing factor".[123] Another concern of the central government was the positive economic impact the migrants had with their trade and their comparatively low-priced manufactured products. Restrictive policies against migrants could easily annoy locals as they benefit from cheap products, which in turn would question the legitimacy of central government norms.[124]

Against this background, HE argues that "sporadic campaigns" contribute to both interests making up a compromise. By the means of campaigns, legal enforcement or at least legal awareness takes place, which is of interest to the central government. Also, despite the fact that legal collusion is affected by such campaigns, sporadic campaigns do not completely eliminate it. Moreover, campaigns remind migrants of the illegality of their actions and even might serve the locals in their collusive activities.[125]

The existence of legal collusion in the area of exit–entry administration was already shown in the previous section. Interestingly, campaigns are not necessarily used to combat this phenomenon, but rather may induce certain

118 Xin Frank HE (2003), p. 137 f.
119 Xin Frank HE (2003), p. 129 f.
120 Xin Frank HE (2003), p. 129 f.
121 Xin Frank HE (2003), p. 140 f.
122 Xin Frank HE (2003), p. 139.
123 Xin Frank HE (2003), p. 139 f.
124 Xin Frank HE (2003), p. 140.
125 Xin Frank HE (2003), p. 141.

forms of legal collusion. As for the area of exit–entry administration, HAUGEN reports that the Guangzhou police approached underground African Pentecostal churches and requested them to act as informants on immigration issues.[126] At least for some time, agreements between these churches and the police existed where the police obviously abused their power. The literature often does not explicitly state whether the reported forms of legal collusion happened before, during, or after the deployment of campaigns. At the very least, the cooperation of the police with churches or the exploitation of migrants with illegal status seems to be a side-effect of the campaigns rather than a reason to deploy campaigns. Still, I argue that migrants —regardless of their origin—serve the local economy, which very likely may lead to reluctance to appropriately enforce legal provisions.

One important finding of HE's research is that the campaigns he analysed not only aim at deviant behaviour of migrants but also of local officials and even the public. As legal collusion is a major threat to the central government's striving for control, the use of campaigns is a reasonable method to arouse legal awareness, which is meant to result in legal enforcement. HE shows that many of the patterns of law-enforcement campaigns that VAN ROOIJ has identified in the area of environmental law can also be found in the area of internal migration. Migrant administration—be it of national or international scope—is a task mainly performed by local Public Security offices, which suggests that HE's findings also apply to *sanfei* campaigns. Which of the findings of VAN ROOIJ and HE also apply to *sanfei* campaigns will be discussed at the end of this chapter, after having analysed *sanfei* campaigns in detail.

IV. BIDDULPH, COONEY, and ZHU: Regulatory Failure Campaigns

In their paper *Rule of Law with Chinese Characteristics*, Sarah BIDDULPH, Sean COONEY, and Ying ZHU analyse the role of campaigns as a means of law enforcement in the reform era.[127] They take as an example a campaign which unfolded between 2004 and 2007 to target shortcomings in the wage payment system and conclude that campaigns not only aim to enforce legal provisions but rather are an integral part of law making and law reform. They note that campaigns in the reform era have mainly been analysed for

126 HAUGEN (2013 b), p. 89.
127 BIDDULPH / COONEY / Ying ZHU (2012).

the effects on enforcement practice but less on their impact on law making.[128] The authors criticise the notion that campaigns are understood as "anomaly or as a marker of the incomplete transformation of China's legal system to a more formal or bureaucratically rational system."[129] They question the assumption that because campaigns are rooted in a revolutionary and extralegal past, they are still seen as indications for the immaturity of the Chinese legal system where gaps are filled with campaign-style policing.[130] Instead, campaigns should be regarded as an important element in legislation processes whose impact should be analysed more deeply.

With their understanding of campaigns as an integral part of Chinese governance, Biddulph, Cooney, and Zhu build upon the notion coined by Perry, Heilmann as well as Liebman who state that the contemporary policy style in China embraces the apparent contradictions of populism versus professionalism. Liebman identifies "populist legality" as a means to promote authority and legitimacy of legal institutions by exploiting popular opinions.[131] In this sense, populism, together with political flexibility, is rather used as a tool, which does not necessarily conflict with the path to stronger professionalism. Perry and Heilmann coin the idea of "adaptive governance" which features flexibility and a "guerilla policy style"[132] that has its roots in the revolutionary and Mao eras.[133] While ideological control and mass mobilisation as core components of "guerilla policy style" have decreased with the reform era, inherited techniques like "managed campaigns" (political as well as economical),[134] experimental regulation and policy gen-

128 Biddulph / Cooney / Ying Zhu (2012), p. 374.
129 Biddulph / Cooney / Ying Zhu (2012), p. 374.
130 Biddulph / Cooney / Ying Zhu (2012), p. 374. Dimitrov (2009) for example states that campaign-style enforcement is a sign for the government's inability to solve problems in an efficient way since it is not feasible nor desirable for government agencies to expend so much energy on crisis management. During campaigns, he argues, the involvement of typically multiple agencies with overlapping enforcement portfolios leads to duplicative, uncoordinated, and inconsistent enforcement; Dimitrov (2009), p. 14 f.
131 Liebman (2011).
132 "A low-cost way of local problem-solving and policy generation," as Heilmann states; Heilmann (2011), p. 86 f. This term was originally used by Roderick McFarquhar in a 2008 conference at Harvard.
133 Heilmann / Perry (2011).
134 On "managed campaigns" see the discussion on campaigns above and Perry (2011).

eration, use of model experiences, as well as extensive propaganda work and populism are still applied today.[135]

As for their analysis, BIDDULPH, COONEY, and ZHU define three categories of campaigns in the reform era that all have the aim of law enforcement. They identify campaigns that target crimes, with reference to the *yanda* campaigns, and campaigns directed against problems within the party and the state apparatus, of which the anti-corruption campaigns analysed by MANION are a prominent example. Apart from campaigns targeted against criminal behaviour and campaigns targeted against intra-party deviance and governance shortcomings, they introduce a new category of campaigns that target regulatory failure. Regulatory failure in this context means that local-level officials do not adhere to central-level norms. This non-adherence may be due to limited incentives, vague or non-existent legal norms or inability in general. Regulatory failure campaigns aim to enhance administrative processes in order to suspend regulatory failure. This new category of campaigns has been only little studied before and serves as the focus of their analysis.[136] This third category of campaigns in fact mirrors the authors' new conceptualisation of the role of campaigns in Chinese governance. They state that literature so far has only focused on post-opening campaigns targeted against crime or internal party affairs, and regard post-opening law-enforcement campaigns as political campaigns that have just been transported to a more pragmatic and technocratic framework.[137]

BIDDULPH, COONEY, and ZHU emphasise the influence of this third category of campaigns on the law-making process by highlighting three ways of possible interaction. First, laws may be modified to facilitate the use of campaigns and later remain in force after the campaign has finished. An example of this would be the amendment to the *Criminal Litigation Law* in 1983 in order to allow for swift prosecution. Secondly, laws may be interpreted in a different way during the campaign than they would be otherwise. Especially legal norms which feature somewhat unspecific terminology may be explained in such a way that the campaign's target fits into its definition. Third, additional normative rules may be issued by governmental entities, which are meant to amend or to complete existing laws and regulations.[138]

---

135 HEILMANN / PERRY (2011).

136 BIDDULPH / COONEY / Ying ZHU (2012), p. 376 f.

137 BIDDULPH / COONEY / Ying ZHU (2012), p. 377; the authors cite e. g. BIDDULPH (2007), p. 149, and DUTTON (1995).

138 BIDDULPH / COONEY / Ying ZHU (2012), p. 378 f.

The fact that *sanfei* campaigns target issues related to poor enforcement of exit–entry administration at the local level suggests that they are best classified as regulatory failure campaigns, rather than as campaigns that primarily target criminal behaviour or problems within the party and the state apparatus. However, *sanfei* campaigns target illegal behaviour, too. As BIDDULPH, COONEY, and ZHU state, also "lesser antisocial forms of conduct"[139] may be the target of campaigns that the authors classify as targeting criminal behaviour. Further, regulatory failure campaigns as defined by BIDDULPH, COONEY, and ZHU also serve as a means for the production or alteration of laws and other legal norms or their application and interpretation. In order to prove the hypothesis that *sanfei* campaigns can be classified as regulatory failure campaigns, *sanfei* campaigns first have to meet the characteristic criteria of law-enforcement campaigns and of Chinese campaigns in general. Additionally, they should pursue the major aim of enhancing administrative processes at the local level in order to reduce non-adherence of local officials to central-level norms. After having analysed the deployment of *sanfei* campaigns, I will analyse whether they meet the characteristic criteria of Chinese campaigns and law-enforcement campaigns and finally apply the concept of regulatory failure campaigns to *sanfei* campaigns.

V. Summary

In the following, I will explain the phenomenon of *sanfei* campaigns with the concept of regulatory failure campaigns as coined by BIDDULPH, COONEY, and ZHU. This concept can be regarded as a further development of older concepts on campaigns, especially regarding campaigns as a means of law-enforcement in the context of administrative law, which has been analysed for example by VAN ROOIJ. The main finding of VAN ROOIJ is that campaigns have always been an important part of Chinese governance. Although rooted in their revolutionary past, campaigns have shed most of their ideological nature and have become instruments to enforce political and legal aims. However, specific structures and procedures of current campaigns still testify to their political nature. Above all, the division into several implementation stages, the use of political slogans and a specific vocabulary, as well as the *ad-hoc* establishment of a parallel administrative structure can be regarded as characteristics that identify a movement as campaign. While

139 BIDDULPH / COONEY / Ying ZHU (2012), p. 377.

van Rooij analyses the field of environmental protection within the field of administrative law, He shows that these findings equally apply to the field of internal migration.

The concept of regulatory failure campaigns builds upon the notion of law-enforcement campaigns. It further assumes that, because campaigns are an integral part of Chinese governance, they also stand in close relation not only to law enforcement but also to law making. Regulatory failure is identified as the failure of administrative organs to effectively implement legal norms, which can often be traced back to collusion of local officials and the local public or local enterprises, but which may also be due to a poor legal framework or insufficient communication between relevant authorities. Biddulph, Cooney, and Zhu differentiate their concept of regulatory failure campaigns from campaigns that target criminal behaviour (or illegal behaviour in general) or intra-party deviance. In the context of labour law, the authors show that campaigns have been applied simultaneously to law making and also interacted with law-making processes in order to achieve certain political aims. *Sanfei* campaigns were deployed at the same time as a revision process of exit–entry administration legislation took place and official interpretations on certain legal provisions explicitly refer to campaign work, which suggests a strong connection between *sanfei* campaigns and the revision process of exit–entry administration law. In sum, *sanfei* campaigns share a lot of characteristics with law-enforcement campaigns as analysed by van Rooij or He and also with regulatory failure campaigns as coined by Biddulph, Cooney, and Zhu, although *sanfei* campaigns also target illegal behaviour. I conclude that the concepts discussed in this section, especially the concept of regulatory failure campaigns, are best suited to explain the underlying aims and drivers of *sanfei* campaigns.

C. *Information on* Sanfei *Campaigns*

The classification of *sanfei* campaigns as regulatory failure campaigns requires an analysis of the aims and drivers of *sanfei* campaigns. But in order to assess these aims and drivers, I need to describe the phenomenon of *sanfei* campaigns first. I especially assess where and when and how often these campaigns were deployed. I further assess how *sanfei* campaigns are structured internally, i. e. on which administrative level they are typically organised and which administrative authorities are in charge of the deployment of campaigns. To be able to answer these questions, I examine newspaper articles and available official documents of *sanfei* campaigns.

With a content analysis of newspaper reports and policy documents addressed to administrative officials, I aim to reconstruct the deployment of *sanfei* campaigns throughout China as well as the inner structure of these campaigns.[140] I aim to carve out patterns regarding the local and temporal distribution of *sanfei* campaigns on the basis of the collected information. One main obstacle in this regard is the scarcity of resources and irregular distribution of information. While some campaigns are reported on in detail and in many different newspapers, other campaigns are only mentioned in few sources, which, however, does not necessarily indicate the size of the campaign. Some campaigns may have been conducted without any media report and there is hence no access to relevant information. While for some campaigns I was able to find documents that provide deeper insights into the organisation of the campaign on different administrative levels, other campaigns are only generally covered with announcements on where and when the campaign took place or reports on the amount of *sanfei* foreigners the police detained in the context of a campaign.

A second major drawback of analyses of Chinese media in general is the lack of independent reports. The largest news agencies in the People's Republic of China, Xinhua News Agency and China News Service, are state-owned and newspapers may be urged only to use contents from Xinhua for reports on certain sensitive topics.[141] Due to the lack of independence regarding information sources, information on campaigns may be filtered, altered or biased, which renders a thorough and neutral analysis impossible. One aim of the *sanfei* campaigns, however, was obviously to address the Chinese people via newspapers and other media and encourage them to participate by reporting suspicious foreign nationals. The media also used statistics on rising numbers of foreign nationals who are illegally in China to legitimise the use of campaigns to combat illegal migration, as will be shown below in more detail. The media was used extensively to introduce the deployment of *sanfei* campaigns to the Chinese public, which suggests that it was the aim of the government to address and inform the public and call for action. There-

140 I used WiseSearch (慧科資訊) being the largest Chinese News Database and searched it for keywords like 'sanfei' (三非) or '(zhuanxiang) xingdong' (专项行动). Additionally, I browsed main Chinese news websites for the same keywords using search engines like Google and Baidu where I found several relevant administrative documents.

141 Liebman (2005), p. 45.

fore, I regard the information regarding time and place of *sanfei* campaigns as reliable. Hence, even if the collected data cannot serve as a conclusive overview of the deployment of *sanfei* campaigns, since certain campaigns may not be covered by media reports, the data should provide sound insights regarding the local and temporal distribution of *sanfei* campaigns. Before examining in detail the information collected so far, the sources of information will be analysed.

In general, apart from secondary sources such as articles from academic journals or books, sources of information about *sanfei* campaigns can be classified into four different types. These are local-level campaign action plans, local-level campaign implementation plans, newspaper announcements of future or current campaigns, and newspaper articles and reports on past campaigns. In the following paragraphs, I use examples of newspaper announcements and reports as well as of action and implementation plans to illustrate these different kinds of information and explain the information drawn from these different sources.

Action plans (*gongzuo fang'an*[142]), typically issued by single authorities on a sub-provincial level, contain information on the concrete implementation of the *sanfei* campaign by the relevant local authority. These action plans define the different organisational stages of the campaign, identify the members of the local working group, and assign tasks to these group members. Action plans can be issued by different authorities, not necessarily only by public security authorities. Apart from local public security bureaus, action plans issued by a local tourism bureau or a local education bureau also exist. Such action plans can be found online on websites of local authorities. However, presumably being internal matter, they are not published regularly or openly in any case, which is detrimental to a thorough analysis.

Campaign implementation plans (*shishi fang'an*[143]), which are also issued on a sub-provincial level but by the local government, contain more general information on the implementation of the campaign. These implementation plans assign the responsibility for implementation to the leaders of different local administrative authorities and define different organisational stages for the campaign. Similar to action plans, implementation plans presumably belong to internal matter and are thus only rarely found publicly, e. g. on the internet or in public media.

---

142 Chinese: 工作方案.
143 Chinese: 实施方案.

Newspaper announcements of campaigns that are to be deployed in the near future or that already started in the recent past often start making a case for the deployment of the *sanfei* campaign by stating that illegal immigration has increased severely in recent times. Newspaper announcements typically state the time span for the campaign and give an overview on the targeted types of '*sanfei* foreigners' by describing what exactly is to be understood as 'illegal entry', 'illegal stay', and 'illegal employment'. In some announcements, the Chinese public is requested to report suspicious behaviour of foreign nationals to the local authorities. In certain cases, a phone number is given to report cases to the local public security bureau. However, not every campaign is accompanied by such announcements, while announcements for other campaigns are published broadly in several newspapers at the same time.

Finally, in contrast to announcements, newspaper articles (reports) on campaign work in general report on past campaigns. These reports often refer to achievements of the local public security bureaus that were able to detain or deport a certain number of '*sanfei* foreigners' during a campaign or in a single raid. Although not every newspaper is accessible online and not every campaign is reported on, newspaper articles are a relatively freely accessible source of information. To be sure, the sheer number of articles and newspapers requires a prior limitation to a certain number of important newspapers.

I. Newspaper Announcements and Reports

A typical newspaper announcement starts with a statement that, in order to maintain order in exit–entry administration and in the labour market, the local municipality has just recently launched a campaign to clear out *sanfei* foreigners and that whoever reports such *sanfei* foreigners to the police would be able to receive a reward. Then, the announcement typically explains the concept of *sanfei* foreigners to the public stating that it is an umbrella term for foreign nationals who have entered China, who stay in the country or who are employed without having undergone the relevant administrative procedures. The announcement may also refer to legal norms such as the *Exit–Entry Administration Law* or the *Foreign Nationals Employment Regulations* that require foreign nationals to obtain certain permits in order to enter, stay or work. Such newspaper announcements make clear that illegal activities are to be punished and may lead to deportation. Finally, in order to allow Chinese nationals to report suspicious foreign nationals, a telephone number of the local police department is given. This telephone number is typically the number of the municipal police department and not of an individual local police station. If a reward is to be offered for public assistance, further information on the amount and procedure of application is given.[144]

The newspaper announcement of the 2012 Beijing campaign published in the People's Daily on 15 February 2012 may serve as example to illustrate the structure and contents of such newspaper announcements. While the headline—*"Mid of May to End of August: Beijing Joins Forces to Clean Up 'Sanfei' Foreigners. Almost 200 000 Foreign Nationals Each Day"*—suggests that the daily amount of *sanfei* foreigners in Beijing is as high as 200 000, the text makes clear that this figure includes all foreign nationals in the city.

> We got the information from the municipal police department of Beijing today, that in order to effectively protect the capital's public security and social order concerning foreign nationals, the police forces of Beijing will concentrate on launching a 100-day operation to clean up 'sanfei' foreigners starting from today until end of August. During this time, the municipal police department of Beijing will join forces to strengthen their control of foreign nationals who illegally enter, illegally stay or illegally work (in short 'sanfei') in Beijing.
>
> Currently, along with the economic and social development, Beijing, being the capital of China, has attracted more and more foreign nationals who come to Beijing for work and to live. According to statistics, Beijing hosts nearly 200 000 foreign nationals each day, whose places of residence already cover all administrative districts of the whole city. The police say that with more and more foreign nationals integrating into the Chinese society, some unlawful foreign individuals also seize the opportunity to mingle and wait for their chance to engage in illegal and criminal behaviour. Statistics show that among illegal and criminal foreign nationals, the 'sanfei' problem sticks out prominently, as these kinds of foreign nationals often lack resources for their livelihood, have no fixed residence and no proper occupation,[145] and some even come all the way to China only to engage in illegal or criminal activities.
>
> To target the situation described above, the municipal police department of Beijing will take actions, like investigations in focus communities, controls at important places at regular intervals, or strict examination of visa applications, in order to increase the strength of control of 'sanfei' and other illegal and criminal foreign nationals. The municipal police department of Beijing has decided to collect notices

144 Example based on Xu Tian (2012).
145 Note the reference to 'sanwu'.

on 'sanfei' foreigners from the public during the period of this special operation (telephone number for reports: 010 64 038 685).[146]

Reports on campaigns often refer to official police statements. With reference to these reports they state that in order to target the problem of *sanfei* foreigners, the police launched a campaign starting a few months ago and already investigated a number of cases regarding exit–entry administration with so and so many individuals involved of which some were detained or even deported. The reports may also include achievements of previous campaigns.[147] Other reports, like some newspaper announcements of forthcoming campaigns, analyse the rising number of foreign nationals who come to China for work which, where it happens undocumented, is portrayed as disrupting the public order and leading to loss of fiscal revenue.[148] The problem of rising numbers of foreign nationals and equally rising numbers of illegal entry, stay or employment, however, is rarely underpinned with comparable numbers and data. Rather, relevant figures seem to be used deliberately in order to produce a distorted picture of the threat of *sanfei* foreigners.

II. Implementation Plans

Local-level campaign implementation plans[149] are typically addressed to a wide range of responsible authorities. One example of this kind of internal document is the *Implementation Plan of the City of Fangchenggang for the Launch of the Campaign to Strike on 'Sanfei Individuals'*.[150] Implementation plans are typically issued by the local government at prefecture level and address all relevant institutions that are involved in the topic. A "headquarter" or "commando post"[151] is installed by assigning the positions of a "commander"[152] and his deputies and establishing a headquarter

146 *Mid of May to End of August: Beijing Joins Forces to Clean Up 'Sanfei' Foreigners. Almost 200 000 Foreign Nationals Each Day* (5月中旬至8月底　北京集中清理'三非'外国人　每日实有近20万外国人) (2012).

147 Ke Xiaojun / Ou (2004).

148 Deng Weijin / Xiang (2004).

149 Chinese: 专项行动实施方案.

150 *Implementation Plan of the City of Fangchenggang for the Launch of the Campaign to Strike on 'Sanfei Individuals'* (2011). Fangchenggang is a prefecture-level city in Guangxi province.

151 Chinese: 指挥部.

152 Chinese: 指挥长.

bureau.[153] Prior to the actual campaign, a launching period of one or two weeks is defined in which the main focus lies on the communication of the campaign's aims to the public. Similarly, a conclusion period is defined of about the same duration, when, in most cases, achievements, shortcomings and overall results should be reported to the relevant coordination group at the next higher level.

Implementation and action plans, which will be discussed in the next section in more detail, state that their aim is to safeguard national security and border stability. They argue that with the economic development of China, the number of *sanfei* foreigners has constantly increased. The *Implementation Plan of the City of Fangchenggang for the Launch of the Campaign to Strike on 'Sanfei Individuals'* states that between February 2011 and the promulgation of this plan one month later only, 56 cases involving 519 individuals have been investigated of which 11 constituted criminal cases. This allegedly high number of *sanfei* foreigners is said to be harmful to the national security and border stability and thus needs to be addressed using campaigns.[154] To this end, the *Implementation Plan of the City of Fangchenggang for the Launch of the Campaign to Strike on 'Sanfei Individuals'* sets up a 'headquarter' consisting of the heads or vice heads of almost 20 different governmental authorities at the relevant administrative level like the Municipal Public Security Bureau, the Military Sub-District, the Bureau of Border and Coastal Defence, the Bureau of Transportation or the Bureau of Commerce. In the first stage of the campaign that shall take place from 1 to 10 March 2011, propaganda banners and solid signs shall be installed at streets and ports at the border. Information material shall be disseminated via leaflets and the media in order to raise the public consciousness. In order to increase their ability to chase and arrest *sanfei* foreigners, the border guards shall increase their patrols, and checks of individuals and transportation means shall be intensified at the ports and border check points. Every local police station shall conduct monthly investigations for *sanfei* foreigners at rented houses, places of entertainment, border shops, construction sites or individual enterprises. Until the end of June, campaigns shall be conducted against unregistered marriages between Chinese and Vietnamese nationals led by the Public Security Bureau with support of the Civil Affairs Bureau.

153 See e. g. *Implementation Plan of the City of Fangchenggang for the Launch of the Campaign to Strike on 'Sanfei Individuals'* (2011).

154 *Implementation Plan of the City of Fangchenggang for the Launch of the Campaign to Strike on 'Sanfei Individuals'* (2011).

Until the end of March, the Bureau of Tourism shall conduct campaigns against tour guides without licence (so-called 'wild-horse guides'[155]). Until the end of August, unregistered boats shall be targeted. Finally, increasing attention shall be paid to terrorists and traffickers. In order to prevent future problems, meetings with the Vietnamese authorities shall be conducted. The police shall "handle the cases severely and swiftly",[156] and "resolutely crack down"[157] on trafficking gangs.[158] In order to prevent diplomatic hassle, deportations shall be conducted in an orderly way. Lastly, the Bureau of Transportation and the Border Authorities shall issue regulations concerning illegal passengers of vehicles and ships in order to better combat trafficking.[159] Obviously, while describing a campaign targeting *sanfei* foreigners, this implementation plan also focuses on trafficking, which is due to the fact that the City of Fangchenggang is situated at the Vietnamese–Chinese border.

Both implementation plans and action plans use a distinct, very political vocabulary. The *Implementation Plan of the City of Fangchenggang for the Launch of the Campaign to Strike on 'Sanfei Individuals'* defines six "concrete requirements", which are "strengthening leadership and specifying responsibilities,"[160] "coordinating closely and building up cooperation,"[161] "expanding information and increasing quality,"[162] "asking for instructions and reporting actively,"[163] "participating in funding and increasing the financial coverage,"[164] and "striving for experience and achieving a good conclusion."[165] Similarly, the *Action Plan of the Education Bureau of the City of Changsha on the Launch of the Campaign to Clear Up and Correctively Punish 'Sanfei' Foreigners* defines "increasing awareness and strength-

---

155 Chinese: '野马' 导游.

156 Chinese: 从重从快予以审理. The term 'severely and swiftly' was also used in the context of the 'strike hard' campaigns.

157 Chinese: 坚决打击.

158 *Implementation Plan of the City of Fangchenggang for the Launch of the Campaign to Strike on 'Sanfei Individuals'* (2011).

159 Example taken from *Implementation Plan of the City of Fangchenggang for the Launch of the Campaign to Strike on 'Sanfei Individuals'* (2011).

160 Chinese: 加强领导，明确责任.

161 Chinese: 密切配合，形成合力.

162 Chinese: 拓展信息，增强效果.

163 Chinese: 加强请示，主动汇报.

164 Chinese: 投入经费，加强保障'.

165 Chinese: 摸索经验, 搞好总结. *Implementation Plan of the City of Fangchenggang for the Launch of the Campaign to Strike on 'Sanfei Individuals'* (2011).

ening leadership,"[166] "coordinating closely and strengthening research,"[167] and "summing up experience and expanding quality"[168] as "work requirements".[169] Furthermore, the Changsha action plan defines distinct "implementation stages" with specific dates. These are a "stage of mobilisation and deployment,"[170] of "investigation and fact-finding,"[171] of "comprehensive regulation,"[172] and of "concluding reporting."[173] This political vocabulary as well as the typical segmentation of the movement into distinct stages are indicators for the political nature of these implementation and action plans.

III. Action Plans

Local-level campaign action plans[174] are internal documents geared more narrowly and often focus on a distinct sector that is related to illegal immigration, e. g. tourism or education. Action plans also often combine the target of *sanfei* with other issues like trafficking or religious activities, which shows that these plans are confined to match the local needs—even more than the implementation plans. Examples for this type of documents are the *Action Plan of the Education Bureau of the City of Changsha on the Launch of the Campaign to Clear Up and Correctively Punish 'Sanfei' Foreigners*[175] and the *Action Plan of the Tourism Bureau of the City of Xingtai on the Launch of the Campaign to Clear Up and Correctively Punish 'Sanfei' Foreigners in the Tourism Branch.*[176] Typically, these action plans are issued by local

166 Chinese: 提高认识，加强领导.
167 Chinese: 密切配合，加强研究.
168 Chinese: 总结经验，扩大效果.
169 *Action Plan of the Education Bureau of the City of Changsha on the Launch of the Campaign to Clear Up and Correctively Punish 'Sanfei' Foreigners* (2013).
170 Chinese: 动员部署阶段.
171 Chinese: 调查摸底阶段.
172 Chinese: 全面整治阶段.
173 Chinese: 总结报告阶段. *Action Plan of the Education Bureau of the City of Changsha on the Launch of the Campaign to Clear Up and Correctively Punish 'Sanfei' Foreigners* (2013).
174 Chinese: 专项行动工作方案.
175 *Action Plan of the Education Bureau of the City of Changsha on the Launch of the Campaign to Clear Up and Correctively Punish 'Sanfei' Foreigners* (2013). Changsha is a prefecture-level city in Hunan province.
176 *Action Plan of the Tourism Bureau of the City of Xingtai on the Launch of the Campaign to Clear Up and Correctively Punish 'Sanfei' Foreigners in the Tourism Sector* (2012). Xingtai is a prefecture-level city in Hebei province. As another example

government bureaus of cities at prefecture[177] or county level[178] and address institutions assigned to this bureau. An action plan, e. g., issued by the local educational bureau would address local universities, schools, and other educational institutions. Action plans may explicitly define the targeted persons (e. g. foreign teaching personnel without a proper licence) and set a time limit for the execution of the campaign, which would typically last for fifty or one hundred days.[179] Finally, action plans establish a small leading group by defining the names and positions of its members and different stages for the execution of the campaign. Further, specific tasks during the campaign are assigned. In at least some of the cases found, the head of the small leading group at county or township level was a leading party official while the responsible head of the Public Security bureau held the position of the group's vice chairman.[180]

The analysed action plans explicitly aim at enhancing administrative procedures. The *Action Plan of the Education Bureau of the City of Changsha on the Launch of the Campaign to Clear Up and Correctively Punish 'Sanfei' Foreigners* aims to safeguard and regulate the work processes of the management of foreign teaching personnel by implementing the policies of the higher-ranking administrative level,[181] while the *Action Plan of the Town of Qingxi on the Launch of the Campaign to Clear Up and Correctively Punish 'Sanfei' Foreigners* puts emphasis on setting up a system of cooperation of different authorities in order to "advance the healthy development of the

---

see as well *Action Plan of the Forestry Police Bureau of the City of Jinghong on the Campaign to Clear Up and Correctively Punish 'Sanfei' Foreigners* (2010). Jinghong is a county-level city in the prefecture of Xishuangbanna in Yunnan province.

177 Chinese: 地级市.

178 Chinese: 县级市.

179 Campaigns would typically last for either one month and twenty days or for three months and fifteen days. E. g. they would start on 1 January and last either until 20 February or until 15 April, regardless of the actual amount of days covered.

180 Examples are from Qinghe county, Hebei, Haojiang district of Shantou, Guangdong, as well as Qingxi and Dalingshan townships of Dongguan, Guangdong. *Action Plan of the Town of Qingxi on the Launch of the Campaign to Clear Up and Correctively Punish 'Sanfei' Foreigners* (2014); *Action Plan of the County of Qinghe on the Launch of the Campaign to Clear Up and Correctively Punish 'Sanfei' Foreigners* (2012); Yong/Zhi (2016); Haojiang Office of Shantou Municipal Bureau of Public Security (汕头市公安局濠江分局) (2017).

181 *Action Plan of the Education Bureau of the City of Changsha on the Launch of the Campaign to Clear Up and Correctively Punish 'Sanfei' Foreigners* (2013).

local economy".[182] Although action plans typically focus on a distinct aspect of the aims of *sanfei* campaigns, e. g. by targeting mainly illegal employment or by focusing on a specific sector like education, tourism or even forestry, different authorities are always instructed to work together and establish a parallel organisation structure led by a local leading working group.

IV. Summary

The main sources of information on *sanfei* campaigns on which the following analysis relies are action and implementation plans issued by official bodies as well as newspaper articles and reports. While local-level campaign action and implementation plans are merely for internal use and directed at officials at lower administrative levels, newspaper articles provide the public with information about *sanfei* campaigns. Thus, newspaper articles often feature an educational character when they explain what is to be understood by *sanfei* foreigners or when they state the reasons for the application of campaigns in this politico-legal field. Being internal documents, action and implementation plans focus not so much on explanations but try to legitimise the application of the campaign with legal or political documents of a higher rank or by stating general political aims that make the use of campaign necessary like the safeguarding of national or public security.

D. Drivers and Triggers for the Deployment of Sanfei *Campaigns*

The aim of this section is to identify in more detail the drivers that led to the deployment of *sanfei* campaigns. Based on the information collected from newspaper articles and reports, official documents as well as secondary literature of anthropological studies, this section focuses on triggering events as well as on the addressees of the campaigns. In this section, I first analyse the temporal and geographical distribution of *sanfei* campaigns in order to find out whether or not certain events have triggered the employment of campaigns. While major events certainly may be a reason or justification for the deployment of *sanfei* campaigns, I assume that other aspects, especially

182 Chinese: 促进我镇经济健康良好发展. *Action Plan of the Town of Qingxi on the Launch of the Campaign to Clear Up and Correctively Punish 'Sanfei' Foreigners* (2014).

the making of immigration legislation, also served as underlying drivers for campaigning. I argue that the triggering effect of certain events cannot be understood without acknowledging these underlying drivers. In order to be able to identify in more detail the main objectives of *sanfei* campaigns, I also analyse the main addressees of *sanfei* campaigns and the internal structure between central and local actors within the campaign organisation. The findings collected this way contribute to the understanding of the drivers for *sanfei* campaigns.

I. Temporal and Geographical Patterns

In order to analyse the impact of certain events on the deployment of *sanfei* campaigns, a temporal and geographical analysis of these events and *sanfei* campaigns is useful. With the material collected from newspaper articles and reports, and with official documents as well as secondary literature of anthropological studies evaluated, it is possible to create a time line of campaigns that have been reported on in the media. Admittedly, such a list is not comprehensive, as an analysis of newspaper and on-line reports necessarily incorporates a reporting bias. Thus, smaller campaigns or campaigns deemed not important may not be reported on at all and campaigns with a very local scope are only reported in local newspapers that are not accessible without disproportionate effort. Similarly, because of the lack of accessible data, it is more difficult to gather information on campaigns that were conducted before 2000 as well as on campaigns that only happened very recently. Although not every single campaign can be included in this list, a time line generated this way still can serve as an outline on the chronological development of the campaigns as well as of big or otherwise important events. As the pool of sources that has been searched for informations on *sanfei* campaigns covers the most important national and regional newspapers and on-line news services, the most important campaigns will be represented in this list.[183]

Table 3.3: *Sanfei* campaigns reported in newspapers and online

Place	Date	Source
	1995 (first raids)	speech of vice-minister LIU, 25 April 2014

183 For the sources and methodology of data collection see above footnote 140.

Table 3.3: *Sanfei* campaigns reported in newspapers and online (continued)

Place	**Date**	**Source**
Wuhan	since 2001	*Changjiang Daily* (长江日报), 13 November 2003
Shenzhen	23 December 2001	*Xinxi Daily* (信息日报), 12 January 2002
Shanghai	1 April – 1 July 2002	*Macao Daily News* (澳門日報), 17 July 2002
Shandong province	1 April 2002 –	*Taichung Daily* (大众日报), 14 August 2002
Changsha	2003–2004	*China News Service* (中国新闻社), 12 February 2004
Chongzuo (Ningming)	18 / 19 July 2003	*Nanguo Morning News* (南国早报), 22 July 2003
Dongguan	October 2003	*Taichung Daily* (大众日报), 11 February 2004
Whole country (border region)	10 October 2003 – 10 March 2004	*Southern Daily National Edition* (南方日报全国版), 25 March 2004
Shanghai	November 2003 – April 2004	*Mingpao* (明报), 27 February 2004
Guangdong province	November 2003 – February 2004	*Taichung Daily* (大众报), 27 February 2004
	12–13 November 2003	*2nd ASEM Conference of the Directors-General of Immigration and Management of Migratory Flows in Beijing*
Guangzhou	9 December 2003	*Yangcheng Evening News National Edition* (羊城晚报全国版), 26 February 2004
	1 January 2004	*Guangzhou Regulations (2004) enter into force*
Jilin	February 2006 –	*CCTV News* (CCTV 新闻) 23 September 2006
Xi'an	March 2006 –	*Sanqin Dushibao* (三秦都市报), 25 July 2006
Whole country (60 important cities)	20 April – 20 September 2006	*Global Times* (环球时报), 31 July 2006
Shenzhen (Futian)	3 / 4 July 2006	*Jingbao* (晶报) 7 July 2006
Kunming	6 July 2006	*Chuncheng Wanbao* (春城晚报) 7 July 2006
Henan province	15 May – 20 September 2006	*Dahe Daily* (大河报), 15 May 2006

Table 3.3: *Sanfei* campaigns reported in newspapers and online (continued)

Place	**Date**	**Source**
Foshan	June 2006 –	*Nanfang Daily* (南方日报), 22 June 2006
Zhumadian (Xincai)	12 July 2006	*Sanqin Dushibao* (三秦都市报), 18 July 2006
Shenzhen (Futian)	2 / 3 February 2007 (single raid)	*Oriental Daily News* (東方日報), 8 February 2007
Shenzhen (Futian)	1 October 2007	*Nanfang Daily* (南方日报), 6 February 2007
Wuhan	15 November 2007 (single raid)	*Changjiang Daily* (长江日报), 16 November 2007
Guangzhou	28 July 2008 (1st 'hurricane' campaign)	*New Express Daily* (新快报), 29 July 2008
	8–24 August 2008	*2008 Summer Olympics*
Guangzhou	13 / 14 August 2008 (3rd 'hurricane' campaign)	*Macao Daily News* (澳門日報), 17 August 2008
Guangzhou	28 August 2008 (5th 'hurricane' campaign)	*Guangzhou Daily* (广州日报), 3 September 2008
Guangdong province	End of 2008 –	*Guangxi Daily* (广西日报), 20 July 2010
Shenzhen (Futian)	March 2009 – (fourteen campaigns)	*Shenzhen Special Zone Daily* (深圳特区报), 23 March 2009
	1 October 2009	*60th anniversary of the People's Republic of China*
Guangxi province (border region)	25 March – 31 October 2010	*Guangxi Daily* (广西日报), 3 November 2010
Dongguan	5 April 2010	*Guangzhou Daily* (广州日报), 12 August 2010
	1 May – 31 October 2010	*Expo 2010*
Heshan	"recently"	*Ping'an Nan'ao online* (平安南粤网), 19 May 2010
Chongzuo (Tiandeng)	"recently"	*China News Service* (中国新闻社), 24 June 2010
Guigang (Pingnan)	"recently"	*Guangxi Daily* (广西日报), 23 July 2010
Xishuangbanna (Jinghong)	15 August – 15 October 2010	*Action Plan of the Forestry Police Bureau on the Campaign to Clean Up and Correctively Punish 'Sanfei' Foreigners*, 19 September 2010
Shenzhen	9 September 2010	*Shenzhen Economic Daily* (深圳商报), 10 September 2010

Table 3.3: *Sanfei* campaigns reported in newspapers and online (continued)

Place	Date	Source
Foshan	28 / 29 September 2010	*Southern Metropolis Daily* (南方都市报), 1 October 2010
	12–27 November 2010	*Asian Games 2010*
Shenzhen (Lo Wu)	22 February 2011	*Guangzhou Daily* (广州日报), 24 February 2011
Fangchenggang	1 March – 15 September 2011	*Implementation Plan of the City of Fangchenggang for the Launch of the Campaign to Strike on 'Sanfei Individuals'*, 9 March 2011
	1 May 2011	*Guangdong Interim Provisions (2011) enter into force*
Fuzhou (Dongxiang)	11 August 2011 – (100-day campaign)	*Jiangxi Daily* (江西日报), 23 August 2011
Beijing	15 May – 31 August 2012 (100-day campaign)	*People's Daily* (人民日报), 15 May 2012
Yanbian	15 May – 15 October 2012 (100-day campaign)	*Oriental Morning Post* (东方早报), 25 May 2012
Shenzhen	"recently"	*Shenzhen Econimic Daily* (深圳商报), 29 May 2012
	30 June 2012	*Exit–Entry Administration Law (2012) adopted*
Xingtai	1 August – 15 November 2012 (tourism branch)	*Action Plan of the Tourism Bureau of the City of Xingtai on the Launch of the Campaign to Clear Up and Correctively Punish 'Sanfei' Foreigners in the Tourism Branch*, 2 August 2012
Qinghe	10 September – 15 November 2012	*Action Plan of the County of Qinghe on the Launch of the Campaign to Clear Up and Correctively Punish 'Sanfei' Foreigners*, 10 September 2012
	8 – 14 November 2012	*18th National Congress of the Communist Party of China*
Dehong (Ruili Wanding)	15 January 2013	*Dehong Chang'an Online* (德宏长安网), 22 November 2015
Zhanjiang	28 April 2013	*Nanguo Morning News* (南国早报), 28 June 2013
Zhuhai	9 May 2013	*Ming Pao Daily News (Vancouver)* (明報(溫哥華）), 11 May 2013
	1 July 2013	*Exit–Entry Administration Law (2012) enters into force*

Table 3.3: *Sanfei* campaigns reported in newspapers and online (continued)

Place	**Date**	**Source**
Changsha	19 November 2013 – (50-day campaign)	*China News Service* (中国新闻社), 20 November 2013
Changsha	1 December 2013 – 20 January 2014 (education sector)	*Action Plan of the Education Bureau of the City of Changsha on the Launch of the Campaign to Clear Up and Correctively Punish 'Sanfei' Foreigners*, 12 December 2013
Zhangzhou (Nanjing)	17 April 2014	*Southeast Online* (东南网), 17 October 2014
Guiyang	15 July – 15 October 2014	*Guiyang Evening News* (贵阳晚报), 15 May 2014
	4 September 2014	*Yanbian Regulations (2014) enter into force*
Quanzhou (Shishi Yongning)	29 October 2014	*Haixia Fazhi Online* (海峡法治在线), 13 October 2014
Guangzhou	19 November 2014	*Yangcheng Evening News* (羊城晚报), 24 November 2014
Dehong (Longchuan)	9 December 2014	*Dehong Chang'an Online* (德宏长安网), 15 December 2014
Yulin (Xingye)	"recently"	*China News Service (Guangxi)* (中国新闻网（广西）), 1 June 2015
Fuzhou (Nanfeng)	3 June 2015	*East Day Online* (东方网), 15 June 2015
Shenzhen (Guangming)	17 July 2015	*Administrative Committee of Guangming New District* (光明新区管委会), 20 July 2015
Shantou	20 August 2015	*Nanguo Morning News* (南国早报), 29 October 2015
Chongzuo (Pingxiang)	"first third of September"	*Xinhua Online* (新华网), 16 October 2015
Anhui	July 2015 –	*Phoenix Anhui* (凤凰安徽), 4 January 2016
Guangdong, Guangxi, Yunnan, Xinjiang, Hong Kong (and others)	20 February 2016 – 20 September 2017	*China Youth Daily* (中国青年报), 31 March 2016
Sichuan	20 May – 20 September 2016	*CPD.com.cn* (中国警察网), 14 June 2016

Table 3.3: *Sanfei* campaigns reported in newspapers and online (continued)

Place	**Date**	**Source**
Jiangxi	1 June – 31 August 2016	*Jiangxi Daily* (江西日报), 3 June 2016

According to an official report by YANG Huanning, Vice Minister of the Ministry of Public Security from 2008 to 2015, strikes against *sanfei* foreigners were carried out as early as 1995.[184] As no media coverage on this early crackdown could be found, I assume that it was not a campaign organised on a bigger scale but rather a row of independently organised raids. I analysed newspaper articles as from 2000, since the used keywords did not generate any results for earlier years.

In the years from 2000 to 2002, only a few campaigns can be found in newspaper reports, e. g. in Wuhan, Shenzhen, Shanghai and Shandong province. The campaign in Shanghai is reported to have lasted from April to July, the Shandong campaign also started in April. While these campaigns were only deployed on a relatively narrow geographical scale, the first large-scale campaigns were apparently carried out between October 2003 and March 2004 as well as between April and September 2006. From October 2003 to March 2004 a nationwide campaign in border regions, but also in major cities, was conducted, of which one major target was also *sanfei* foreigners. Some campaigns, e. g. 2003 in Dongguan or a large-scale campaign in 2016 and 2017 in different Chinese provinces as well as in Hong Kong, were also meant to 'catch the snakes',[185] meaning that their target was human trafficking alongside *sanfei* foreigners, especially in the border regions.[186] Other cities where campaigns took place during this time span are Shanghai, Changsha and Guangzhou. A large-scale campaign was launched between 20 April and 20 September 2006 throughout the whole country in "over 60 important cities".[187] More detailed reports on this campaign are available from the cities of Shenzhen, Wuhan, Xi'an, Yiwu, Zhengzhou, and Zhumadian. Smaller, more focused campaigns were carried out in the

184 *Foreign Nationals Report* (2012), p. 515.

185 Chinese: 捕蛇 or 打蛇头.

186 Although the city of Dongguan is not situated at the South-East Chinese border, the action plan targets illegal Vietnamese individuals explicitly.

187 Chinese: 60多个重要城市. *Korean Media Points to High Numbers of Illegally Entering, Illegal Staying and Illegally Employed Foreign Nationals in China: 'Sanfei' Foreigners Weigh on China Mind* (韩媒体指出非法入境、非法滞留、非法就业在中国的外国人很多：'三非'外国人让中国伤脑筋) (2006).

same year in Xi'an in March, in Foshan in June, and in Henan province between mid-May and mid-September. However, there are no reports on strikes against *sanfei* for 2005.

From 2007 and especially starting from the end of 2008, *sanfei* campaigns were increasingly carried out in Guangdong with Shenzhen, Guangzhou, and Foshan as focal cities. In 2008 starting in July, Guangzhou rolled out campaigns in a regular manner. These so-called 'hurricane'[188] campaigns were apparently deployed once a week as their consecutively numbered names suggest. In the following years, comparably many campaigns were deployed in Guangdong province making it a focus area for *sanfei* campaigns. Around March 2009, Shenzhen (Futian) reportedly deployed a series of fourteen campaigns. *Sanfei* campaigns seem to have been carried out in Foshan in a regular manner starting in 2006 at least until 2010.

As from 2010, campaigns lasting for 50 or 100 days in different regions can be found. For example, between March and October 2010, a series of *sanfei* campaigns was deployed in the border regions of Guangxi. These campaigns cover a longer time span, which suggests that they had been planned beforehand and were not just a series of locally confined raids. Indeed, the Ministry of Human Resources and Social Security, the Ministry of Foreign Affairs and the Ministry of Public Security in 2010 jointly issued a *Notice Regarding Questions Concerning the Improvement of Administrative Work Regarding the Employment of Foreign Nationals*[189] in which local-level administrations were required to set up small working groups for the administration of employment of foreign nationals as well as to strike hard on illegal employment of foreign nationals.[190] The first action and implementation plans I could find are also dated 2010.

Starting from 15 May 2012, on the verge of the promulgation of the revised *Exit–Entry Administration Law*, the Beijing Public Security Bureau launched a 100-day campaign[191] to "clean out" foreign nationals having entered China illegally, or living or working in Beijing illegally, thus targeting the above mentioned 'sanfei' population in Beijing. As this was the first major crackdown in Beijing after the Olympic Games in 2008, the campaign gained a lot of media coverage. In the announcement of the campaign,

188 Chinese: 飓风.

189 Chinese: 关于加强外国人就业管理工作有关问题的通知. This notice (Ren She Bu Fa (2010) 33 Hao, Chinese: 人社部发〔2010〕33号) is only for internal use and was not available to the author of this study.

190 Ding Saier (2014), p. 65.

191 Chinese: 百日专项行动.

the authorities asked the public to provide any indications and to report suspicious foreign nationals.[192] According to media reports, the police focused their extensive controls on areas with a high percentage of foreign nationals. The officials examined the documents carried by foreign nationals and also inspected foreign owned businesses as well as businesses that employed foreign nationals.

The People's Daily Overseas Edition reports on 19 May 2012:

> The Beijing police authorities state that during this special operation [i. e. the 100-day campaign starting from 15 May 2012], measures such as thorough investigations in focus districts, periodic controls at important places and strict examinations of visa applications will be taken, in order to strengthen control of offences and crimes committed by 'sanfei' and other foreign nationals. In addition, the public can report via telephone and other means.
> The author points out that in these two days several hundred postings concerning the clearing up of 'sanfei' foreigners on the Weibo platform 'Ping'an Beijing' were forwarded or commented upon, and suggestions and reports of netizens were quickly passed on to the relevant sub-bureaus. If investigation [reveals that the suspicion] is true, the 'sanfei' foreigner will face a fine or detention; depending on the situation it will be decided whether [he or she] will be ordered to leave the country or even deported; if the offence constitutes a crime, [he or she] will be prosecuted according to criminal law.[193]

However, police officers also explained that targeting foreign nationals is not always as simple as the media may make believe:

> An officer of the exit-entry administration division of the Beijing Public Security Bureau, who wishes to remain anonymous, states that they will regularly clean up several entertainment locations, since 'sanfei' foreigners are relatively more concentrated at such places. He says that if there is a report, they have to investigate, but if 'sanfei' foreigners obey the rules and abide by the law in the country, the probability of being checked and repatriated is actually not too high, "because you cannot inspect the visas' expiration dates of a foreign national's family members [each time] you see a foreign national on the streets."[194]

The campaigns in Beijing are said to be a result of an increasing number of reports, mainly published in online media and spread and discussed in weblogs and online communities, about mainly Western foreign nationals being involved in offences or even crimes that finally forced the authorities to intervene.[195] In any case, the implementation of the campaign drew heavily

192 Pan Xiaotian (2012), p. 4.
193 Pan Xiaotian (2012).
194 Zhang Rui (2012), p. 39.
195 On 8 May 2012, a British who held a valid tourist visa was accused for sexually assaulting a young Chinese woman; on 14 May, a Russian cellist rose huge furore

on public reports from Chinese nationals. Considering the huge media coverage, Beijing can be seen as the climax in the development of *sanfei* campaigns. From 2006 until 2013, *sanfei* campaigns received relatively strong media coverage in newspapers, the 2012 Beijing campaign constituting a peak. After the promulgation of the revised *Exit–Entry Administration Law* on 20 June 2012, the media coverage of *sanfei* campaigns decreased somewhat but did not fully stop.

In summary, three waves of increased campaign activity can be identified. The first wave was around the years 2003 and 2004 when the revision process of the *Exit–Entry Administration Law* was initiated, a situation that probably urged the Ministry of Public Security to focus on foreign nationals management work. The second wave was around 2006 and 2007 when a conference on foreign nationals management work initiated by the Ministry of Public Security took place in connection with the Summer Olympics in Beijing.[196] In Guangdong province, however this wave only started in 2008 with the deployment of the 'hurricane' campaigns. The third wave, finally, can be identified around 2012 with a major campaign happening in Beijing, obviously in the context of the promulgation of the revised *Exit–Entry Administration Law*.

II. Triggering Events of *Sanfei* Campaigns

Having structured the geographical and chronological pattern of *sanfei* campaigns, I now use these findings to identify triggering events of the campaigns. Law-enforcement campaigns in the past have often been deployed after incidents that made it indispensable for the political leaders to take action.[197] VAN ROOIJ cites as examples the alleged increase of crimes, especially against women and children, that led to the 'strike hard' campaign in 1983.[198] Other examples are pollution incidents prior to campaigns in

---

mainly on the internet due to his bad behaviour when riding a train. See ZHUANG Qinghong / XU Wenmiao / XU Xiaotong (2012) referred to in LAN (2017 b), p. 52.

196 *The National Public Security Organ's Conference on Foreign Nationals Management Work Was Held in Beijing on the 15th* (全国公安机关外国人管理工作会议15日在北京举行), *Central People's Government Press Release* (2007); see section II. below.

197 VAN ROOIJ (2009), p. 13 f.

198 Murray S. TANNER (2000), p. 102–105

the area of environmental protection,[199] as well as student protests against corruption among officials that were followed by the 1989 anti-corruption campaigns.[200]

In the context of *sanfei* campaigns as well, some researchers point to important events prior to which campaigns have been rolled out.[201] Especially events like the 2008 Summer Olympics in Beijing, the celebration of the 60th anniversary of the People's Republic of China, the 2010 Asian Games in Guangzhou, or the Expo 2010 in Shanghai are mentioned. It may be true that prior to such major events, exit–entry administration becomes more restrictive, which is also reflected in the chronological patterns of *sanfei* campaigns. However, it is problematic to generally relate major events to *sanfei* campaigns, as a lot of campaigns did not happen before such major events. Therefore, I argue that while major events may well trigger *sanfei* campaigns, they are not the most important driver for their deployment in general. Moreover, while campaigns targeting illegal migration indeed have been deployed shortly before such major events as reports from newspapers show, campaigns rolled out before major events did not only target *sanfei* foreigners. As Brady shows, the aims of campaigns on the eve of the Summer Olympics were also "hygiene" and healthcare[202] as well as "spiritual civilization".[203] In fact, Brady even identifies the 2008 Summer Olympics in itself as a huge campaign. All this rather suggests merely that important events are a trigger for campaigns in general, but it should not be conversely assumed that *sanfei* campaigns are only triggered by such big events.

Although literature and sources frequently state that "major events" are often the reason for the deployment of raids and campaigns in the context of exit–entry administration,[204] such a direct causal connection of an event and a specific *sanfei* campaign cannot be identified in every single case. For example, Lan states that *sanfei* campaigns were deployed in 2007 in the preparation for the 2008 Summer Olympics in areas where Africans concentrated.[205] She mentions campaigns happening every two months, obviously referring to the so called 'hurricane' campaigns in Guangzhou described

---

199 Van Rooij (2006 a), p. 101–103
200 Manion (2004), p. 179–181; van Rooij (2009), p. 13 f.
201 Zhigang Li / Lyons / Brown (2012), p. 66; Haugen (2012), p. 75; Lan (2015), p. 294; Lan (2017 b), p. 54.
202 Brady (2009), p. 12 f.
203 Brady (2009), p. 17 f.
204 Lan (2017 a), p. 103.
205 Lan (2015), p. 294.

in the preceding paragraph. Indeed, in January 2007, officially in anticipation of the 2008 Summer Olympics in Beijing, the Ministry of Public Security organised a conference on foreign nationals management work at the national level.[206] Probably as a result, on 31 October 2007, the Ministry of Public Security issued tentative measures on foreign nationals registration.[207] 'Hurricane' campaigns were deployed in Guangzhou during the following months in a regular manner, but also after the end of the Summer Olympics. Between 2007 and 2008, reports on campaigns in Guangdong province by far outnumber reports from other places including Beijing, the host city of the Olympics. If the Summer Olympics really were the main driver for *sanfei* campaigns, *sanfei* campaigns should have been deployed on a large scale in Beijing as well, and they should have stopped after the event. In fact, raids in Beijing conducted prior to the Olympics were obviously mainly targeted against offences like drugs or illegal religious activities and not explicitly against *sanfei* foreigners.[208] While the 'hurricane' campaigns in Guangzhou may well be a response to the conference of foreign nationals management work and related measures, Guangzhou was not a main venue for events in the context of the Summer Olympics, although Hong Kong, which is close to Guangzhou, hosted the equestrian contests. Especially considering the fact that illegal immigration has been identified a problem in Guangdong province at least since 2004, I regard the Summer Olympics as a mere pretext to roll out campaigns in Guangzhou in such a large scale, rather than being the main reason for their deployment. This is supported by the fact that around the same time, the Guangzhou city government had been criticised for not properly administrating foreign population, which arguably pressured them to take action against illegal immigration.[209] In sum, while the 2008 Summer Olympics were officially used as justification for strengthening foreign nationals management work at a national level,[210] which may well have been the reason for an increase of campaigns around

206 *The National Public Security Organ's Conference on Foreign Nationals Management Work Was Held in Beijing on the 15th* (全国公安机关外国人管理工作会议15日在北京举行), *Central People's Government Press Release* (2007); Zhang Huide / Liu Hongbin / Zeng Fanjing (2014), p. 106.

207 *Provisional Measures on the Management of Foreign Nationals Registration by Local Public Security Bureaus* (2007). See Zhang Rui (2013), p. 195.

208 Brea (2007); Weaver (2008).

209 Zhigang Li / Lyons / Brown (2012), p. 66; Huang (2018), p. 15.

210 See the reference to the conference on foreign management work initiated by the Ministry of Public Security, above footnote 206.

2006 in general, the direct connection between the Summer Olympics and the 'hurricane' campaigns in Guangzhou is not fully convincing.

As the example of the Summer Olympics suggests, other drivers may be at least as important as major events in explaining the deployment of *sanfei* campaigns. I argue that, when analysing triggering events for *sanfei* campaigns, the making and promulgation of important legislation or political meetings related to exit–entry administration should also be taken into account. Obviously, campaigning in the context of exit–entry administration started in 2003 and 2004 on a larger scale, or at least newspaper reports on campaigns increased, at a time when the National People's Congress had just instructed the Ministry of Public Security to come up with a first draft law. As a reaction, the Ministry of Public Security issued an order in 2003 to local police stations to improve foreign nationals management work and further dispatched working groups to different places throughout the country to analyse the local implementation of the current legislation.[211] The launch of the *Measures on Rewarding Reports on 'Sanfei' Foreigners* (2004), which featured a system to reward helpful reports of *sanfei* foreigners, can be understood in this context as a reaction of the local government of Guangzhou to these orders and visits by working groups. It is thus reasonable to interpret the campaigns deployed in Guangdong province between November 2003 and February 2004 as a reaction to pressure from the central level to further strengthen control over exit–entry administration.

The fact that campaigns against illegal immigration were initiated in late 2003 can additionally be explained by the fact that the 2nd Asia-Europe Meeting (ASEM) Conference of the Directors-General of Immigration and Management of Migratory Flows was held in Beijing on 11 to 13 November 2003.[212] Vice Minister of Public Security Yang Huanning is reported to have explained on this event that campaigns against *sanfei* foreigners were currently in the focus of police work.[213] Still, as the revision process of the *Exit–Entry Administration Law* was initiated already earlier in 2003, it is reasonable to regard this revision process as an underlying reason for the

211 See section I. of chapter 2 on page 67.
212 Note that the ASEM website dates this event wrongly to the year 2004.
213 *Ministry of Public Security: Chinese Police Currently Launches a New Round of Special Actions Against Illegal Immigration* (公安部：中国警方正开展新一轮的反偷渡专项行动) (2003); Qiu Hongjie (2003).

implementation of local regulations and the deployment of campaigns at the local level.[214]

As a second example of a connection between campaigns and legal norms, the 2012 campaign in Beijing was carried out from 15 May to 31 August 2012, starting only about one month before the revised *Exit–Entry Administration Law* was promulgated on 30 June 2012. Official interpretations of the law refer to these campaigns, which also suggests a strong connection between the campaigns and the new legal provisions.[215] The fact that the legal provision in question was already codified in the 2011 draft law cannot deny the existence of an interrelation, be it that the Beijing campaign was used to legitimise this provision or to test it before taking it into the final law.

Some action plans issued around the time of the promulgation of the revised *Exit–Entry Administration Law* explain that one major aim of the campaign concerned was to create a favourable environment for public security regarding foreign nationals in the relevant city in view of the upcoming 18th National Congress of the Communist Party of China that started on 8 November 2012.[216] Campaigns in Shenzhen were reportedly launched in order to safeguard public security prior to the 'two sessions' and the spring festival.[217] Although the 18th National Congress of the Communist Party of China served as a major event to trigger the deployment of *sanfei* campaigns in this case, it is reasonable to identify the promulgation of the revised *Exit–Entry Administration Law* as the underlying driver here as well.

While it has been shown that major events cannot in every case be identified as the main drivers for *sanfei* campaigns, the promulgation of legislation

---

214 One example are the *Guangdong Measures on Rewarding Reports of 'Sanfei' Foreigners* (2004) introducing a whistle-blower provision that was very likely used in the context of campaigns.

215 An interpretation on Art. 45 of the *Exit–Entry Administration Law* (2012) that defines the duty to report foreign nationals suspected of illegal activities states that it is to be understood as a result from positive experiences of campaigns such as in Beijing; *Guide to Interpretation and Application of the 'Exit–Entry Administration Law of the People's Republic of China'* (《中华人民共和国出境入境管理法》释义及实用指南) (2012), p. 123.

216 *Action Plan of the Tourism Bureau of the City of Xingtai on the Launch of the Campaign to Clear Up and Correctively Punish 'Sanfei' Foreigners in the Tourism Sector* (2012); *Action Plan of the County of Qinghe on the Launch of the Campaign to Clear Up and Correctively Punish 'Sanfei' Foreigners* (2012).

217 *As 'Two Sessions' Come Closer: 'Sanfei' Foreigners Extensively Searched* (兩會期近 深搜「三非」外國人) (2007).

in the context of exit–entry administration does not always trigger the deployment of *sanfei* campaigns either. In Guangdong province, for instance, *Interim Provisions on Administration of and Services to Foreign Nationals* were promulgated in 2011 which can be seen as experimental provisions to the revised law to come and which adopted the report–reward system from the *Guangzhou Regulations*. However, newspaper reports do not suggest a rise in campaign activities between 2011 and 2013, but rather between 2007 and 2009. Similarly, Yanbian introduced local regulations on exit–entry administration only in 2014, which featured a report–reward system similar to that in Guangdong. Again, no reports on campaigns can be found in the major newspapers around this date. Instead, a campaign similar to the one in Beijing of the same year was deployed in Yanbian in 2012.

Summing up these results, I argue that although the deployment of *sanfei* campaigns is triggered by major events to a certain degree, such events cannot be identified as being the sole or most important driver for the deployment of *sanfei* campaigns. The fact that a series of *sanfei* campaigns were introduced without any major event being reported as the reason for their deployment, as well as the fact that the 'hurricane' campaigns in Guangzhou are geographically unrelated to the Summer Olympics that are used to justify their deployment, suggest that other underlying drivers for *sanfei* campaigns exist. The most important underlying driver is the making or promulgation of important legislation in the context of exit–entry administration as in the example of the 2012 campaign in Beijing or the initiation of the revision process of the *Exit–Entry Administration Law* in 2003 and 2004. Still, not every piece of new legislation necessarily leads to the deployment of *sanfei* campaigns or at least to a high degree of media coverage on *sanfei* campaigns. These findings strongly suggest that certain events, like the 2008 Summer Olympics or even very political ones such as the 18th National Congress of the Communist Party of China, only acted as a trigger for the deployment of *sanfei* campaigns because these major events fell at a time when important legislation in the area of exit–entry administration was being revised or promulgated. In any case, a strong connection exists between *sanfei* campaigns and the law-making process in exit–entry administration, which is a characteristic feature of regulatory failure campaigns.

III. Addressees of *Sanfei* Campaigns

If the main aim of *sanfei* campaigns is the abolishment of regulatory failure and the implementation of proper enforcement of legal norms, I assume that *sanfei* campaigns not only address foreign nationals engaging in illegal activities, but also local police officials exhibiting reluctant enforcement behaviour and the public that is requested to support enforcement by reporting. As the analysis of information about *sanfei* campaigns suggests, both the Chinese public and local police officials are addressed in the context of campaigns via newspaper announcements and action or implementation plans respectively. Considering the amount of Chinese information regarding *sanfei* campaigns in comparison to information that is directed to foreign nationals directly in Western languages, one could even argue that the Chinese public and local police officials are the main addressees of the campaigns, while *sanfei* foreigners are merely the 'object' of enforcement.

A major aim of law-enforcement campaigns in the past often has been the re-establishment of central control over reluctant local officials who hinder proper enforcement of central norms at the local level.[218] But the above analysis of action and implementation plans suggests that *sanfei* campaigns primarily aim to establish means to efficiently enforce legal norms, for example co-operation structures that enhance communication and co-operation at all relevant administrative levels. In order to answer the question who *sanfei* campaigns address and which information is communicated to whom, I analyse in the following how *sanfei* campaigns address the foreign population in China and the Chinese public as well as local police officials in charge of exit–entry administration.

1. Communication to Foreign Nationals and the Chinese Public

To illegal immigrants, but also to foreign nationals in general, *sanfei* campaigns are considered to have a deterrent or educative effect.[219] The police aim to communicate that the lenient policy that might have allowed for a certain dimension of illegality in the past is over and tighter control measures as well as harsher punishment are to be expected. The aims of *sanfei* campaigns and often also excerpts of the relevant laws and regulations

218 See e. g. the findings of van Rooij or He discussed above.
219 Cao (2012).

or statements of police officials are communicated to foreign nationals in China via local, mainly English newspapers.[220] Foreign media also report on certain campaigns which may further increase the deterrent and educative effect.[221] However, announcements of campaigns that require the public to report suspects to the police are not found in other languages than Chinese. Information concerning campaigns is also directly introduced to the foreign public by the local police.[222] The fact that illegal immigration is the focus of campaigns already has a deterrent effect, due to the *ad-hoc* character of campaigns which are mostly announced very shortly before or even after the initiation of deployment. However, the *ad-hoc* character of the campaigns also implies that after a short time of 'striking hard', the previous lenient policy may recur. In contrast, frequent campaigns, such as the 'hurricane' campaigns in Guangzhou, communicate that a strict policy will be implemented in the long run.

To the Chinese public, the objectives of *sanfei* campaigns are communicated via newspapers and the internet, most of the contents being in Chinese language. Statistics on rising numbers of immigration and deported *sanfei* foreigners aim to justify the use of campaigns against *sanfei* foreigners, who are outlined as a social group explained by its legal definition in the media. The Chinese public is further requested via newspaper announcements and the media in general to support the local police by reporting suspects. For Guangdong, a legal basis for rewarding reports of illegal activities of foreign nationals has been in force as from 2004,[223] about nine years prior to the establishment of a nationwide legal regulation. But the implementation of reporting systems before 2013 was not limited to Guangdong. The establishment of a system for reporting suspicious foreign nationals to the police can be seen in Foshan and Dongguan, both in Guangdong province,[224] but also in Wuhan and Xi'an.[225] Via the means of campaigns that target illegal behaviour of foreign nationals, the police communicate to the Chinese public that it is taking care of public security and thus helping Chinese na-

220 Quanlin Qiu (2009); Cao (2012).

221 Brea (2007); Weaver (2008); Branigan (2009); Branigan (2012).

222 One example is the amusingly misspelled notice of the Shekou police station in Shenzhen; *Police Station in Shenzhen Posts English Notice: Very Effective, Staff Members Say* (深圳一派出所发全英文公告 工作人员：效果很好 (2013).

223 A report system was codified first in the *Guangdong Measures on Rewarding Reports of 'Sanfei' Foreigners* (2004).

224 Tan / Wen (2006); Xie / Guan (2010).

225 Luo Bin / Xu Rui / Wu Hao (2007); Lu Hua / Li Conghua / Zhao Han (2006).

tionals. The most important notion put across is that the state, in particular the public security organs, is capable of controlling illegal immigration and exit–entry administration in general. To increase the perception that police work is sensible and the established control mechanisms work efficiently, e. g., statistical data is used to suggest that the numbers of crimes and offences committed by illegal migrants are considerable and on the rise but also that the number of foreign nationals prosecuted by the police is increasing. The notion is put across that the police effectively protects social stability by combating unregulated influx of foreign nationals as well as illegal activities among them. By protecting the public order and the security of its nationals the public security apparatus and, eventually, also the political regime is hence able to legitimise itself.[226]

It is tempting to draw a connection between campaigns against illegal immigration and xenophobia. However, the central state media tries not to spur racial or xenophobic notions in order not to harm diplomatic relations.[227] In official statements and documents, *sanfei* campaigns do not specifically target certain groups of foreign nationals. Although government representatives consider China not to be an immigration country,[228] even local media, albeit highlighting local problems with *sanfei* foreigners, do not typically resort to openly xenophobic or racist statements, as the analysis of newspaper articles on *sanfei* campaigns reveals. Furthermore, xenophobic and racist notions are relatively weak among the local residents in hot spots like Guangzhou.[229] LAN even highlights that due to the fact that locals came to terms with African immigrants in Guangzhou and viewed them as potential trading partners, the reward and report system introduced locally did not work as expected.[230] Further, the concrete targets of *sanfei* campaigns differ depending on the place of deployment. While in Beijing mainly Western foreign nationals were targeted and discredited by the media, the target in Guangzhou were primarily African immigrants.[231] However, as other newspaper reports suggest, Africans were also targeted in the Beijing campaigns.[232] In summary, although xenophobic notions may have a certain relevance in the context of the enforcement practice of local police officials,

226 VAN ROOIJ (2009).
227 LAN (2017 a), p. 50.
228 MA Yina (2015).
229 Min ZHOU / SHENASI / Tao XU (2016); LAN (2017 a), p. 107 f.
230 LAN (2017 a), p. 103 f.
231 LAN (2017 a), p. 111.
232 BREA (2007).

xenophobia cannot be identified as being part of any official justification for the deployment of *sanfei* campaigns.

Communication of *sanfei* campaigns to the foreign and to the Chinese public is characterised by statements to justify state action against illegal immigration. Because the police were said to have been struggling with efficient enforcement of legal norms, the notion that the issue was now being tackled using campaigns and that social order and control of exit–entry administration would be reinstated was necessary to be communicated to the public. While foreign nationals were required to abide by the Chinese laws and regulations and to adhere to the relevant registration procedures, the Chinese public was requested to support the police by reporting suspicious foreign nationals to the police and to refrain from collusion with foreign nationals who illegally stay or are illegally employed in China.

2. Communication to Police Officials

In their analysis of law-enforcement campaigns, VAN ROOIJ and HE conclude that apart from actually enforcing legal provisions, campaigns aim to re-establish central control over local-level officials.[233] In the area of environmental protection law as well as registration administration of internal migration, they point to the problem of local officials being reluctant to enforce rules issued by the central government because of the inapplicability of these rules to the local settings. Instead, local officials often benefit from collusive behaviour.[234] Due to local structures in which most participants benefit from illegal behaviour, enforcement of legal norms is severely hindered. Examples of this are enterprises that produce undue emissions but employ large numbers of locals, or foreign nationals illegally staying in China who pay for renting flats and contribute to the local economy, or who can easily be pressed to pay irregular fees for residence and work permits. As a response to such behaviour at the local level, the central government aims to regain control over local structures which is typically achieved through means like propaganda or campaigns.[235]

233 VAN ROOIJ (2009); Xin Frank HE (2003).

234 Xin Frank HE (2003), p. 129 f.

235 See HUANG (2018) who reports that districts under the administration of local police offices with poor performance in foreign nationals management were most likely to be chosen for increased deployment of clean-ups by higher-ranking authorities; HUANG (2018), p. 15 f.

The fact that campaigns against illegal immigration borrow from exit–entry administration legislation by defining their target in legal terms (i. e. *sanfei*) suggests that they primarily aim at law enforcement and hence one of their targets may also be collusion among local officials. Indeed, several aspects of the campaign context serve to increase control of higher-level over lower-level authorities. By the means of the report-reward scheme, e. g., where individuals are asked to report illegal suspects to a higher-level police authority (mostly at the city level), pressure may be imposed on officials of the local police stations[236] to actively reduce illegal activities. The number of arrests and penalties is reportedly used by higher-level authorities in order to calculate a point score, which encourages excessive punishments and raids.[237] On the other hand, districts of local police stations with poor performance ratings are reported to be more likely chosen for clean-ups implemented by higher-ranking public authority organs.[238]

With the assignment of responsibilities in the context of parallel organisation structure during campaigns, the proper implementation of *sanfei* campaign is ensured, which arouses awareness of the relevant legal norms and their importance ascribed by the central government. However, rather than mentioning the problem of collusion, most official documents state that outdated, insufficient or contradicting legal norms were the main reason for local-level authorities to be unable to properly enforce legal provisions. To be sure, collusion on the local level in the context of exit–entry administration does exist to a certain degree. Local officials are reported to exert pressure on *sanfei* foreigners, e. g. by letting them pay the deportation fee for their fellow countrymen, by not issuing necessary documents or by imposing undue fees.[239] Furthermore, local officials are reported to collude with local agents, e. g. by enforcing illegal fees or by getting bribes for warnings before raids.[240] These reported forms of collusion, however, can be identified as a result of the pressure originating in campaign-style enforcement or, in the case of bribes for warnings, as directly related to campaigns and raids. If collusion during a campaign is the result of pressure by higher-level authorities and hence merely a result of campaign-style policing, it is unlikely that collusion had been chosen as a major target of the campaign in the first place.

236 Chinese: 派出所.
237 Huang (2018), p. 15.
238 Huang (2018), p. 15 f.
239 Haugen (2012), p. 74 f.
240 Lan (2017 b), p. 55.

Hence I argue that, rather than collusion, the lack of co-operation of the various responsible authorities on the local administrative levels is the target of *sanfei* campaigns. As the campaigns involve different authorities and set up co-operation structures between them, they communicate the need for a better co-operation between responsible authorities. This co-operation is evaluated as having been insufficient in the past by experts involved in the law-making process of the revised *Exit–Entry Administration Law*.[241] At least since 2010, a parallel administrative structure has been established in the context of exit–entry administration by setting up small working groups that are in charge of administrating the employment of foreign nationals as well as combating illegal employment of foreign nationals.[242] This parallel organisation structure can be interpreted as a local implementation of a *da waiguan* system that serves as a co-ordination platform between the different authorities in charge of exit–entry administration on the relevant local level led by public security organs.[243] Apart from working groups in charge of foreign nationals management, small leading groups for specific *sanfei* campaigns were established according to the implementation and action plans cited above. These leading groups for specific *sanfei* campaigns are not necessarily under the direction of public security organs, but public security organs are always part of the teams. In the example of the *Implementation Plan of the City of Fangchenggang for the Launch of the Campaign to Strike on 'Sanfei Individuals'* (2011), the leading group is chaired by the vice mayor of Fangchenggang,[244] in the example of the *Action Plan of the Tourism Bureau of the City of Xingtai on the Launch of the Campaign to Clear Up*

241 *China Promotes Opening Up and Foreign Relations by Enacting Norms on Exit–Entry Administration* (中国立法规范出入境管理促进对外开放和交往), *NPC Press Release* (2012). This was especially true for the city of Guangzhou; Guobin Zhu / Price (2013), p. 14 f.

242 See the *Notice Regarding Questions Concerning the Improvement of Administrative Work Regarding the Employment of Foreign Nationals* cited above. As the publication of a *Three-Year Action Plan of the City of Guangzhou to Establish Actions to Decidedly Regulate Leasing and Tidy Up Safe and Orderly Leasing (2015–2017)* (Chinese: 广州市出租屋专项整治暨干净整洁平安有序出租屋创建活动3年行动计划（2015～2017）) issued by the Leading Small Group on Non-Locals Service Management Work of Guangzhou City (Chinese: 广州市来穗人员服务管理工作领导小组) suggests, campaigns targeting *sanfei* foreigners are part of foreign nationals management work; Luo Shi (2015).

243 Wei / Zhu Xudong (2009), p. 32.

244 *Implementation Plan of the City of Fangchenggang for the Launch of the Campaign to Strike on 'Sanfei Individuals'* (2011).

and Correctively Punish 'Sanfei' Foreigners in the Tourism Branch (2012), the director of the municipal tourism bureau is assigned head of the leading group.[245] Although these groups are not headed by the relevant public security organs, they still constitute an organisation structure that aims for co-ordination of the different related administrative branches.

IV. Summary

This section demonstrated that *sanfei* campaigns address foreign nationals directly but also the Chinese public and even public security officials. This suggests that *sanfei* campaigns are not only targeted at illegal behaviour of foreign nationals but also address the behaviour of public security officials. A major aim of *sanfei* campaigns is to target regulatory failure in exit–entry administration. Already the temporal and geographical deployment of *sanfei* campaigns suggests that one important driver for the deployment of *sanfei* campaigns was the revision and promulgation of relevant laws and regulations in the field of exit–entry administration, while major events served merely as triggers or justificatory grounds. *Sanfei* campaigns tackle the problem of insufficient enforcement of the relevant legal norms by establishing local-scale *da waiguan* structures or similar parallel organisation structures that aim for the enhancement of communication and co-operation between the local authorities in charge, which in turn aims to improve work flows and, finally, efficient enforcement of legal norms and regulations.

On the other hand, *sanfei* campaigns are used as communication means to convey to the public the notion that the state, more precisely its public security organs, is capable of dealing with the problems of illegal immigration. Not only do the campaigns themselves serve as unmistakeable sign of the increased control of the police over exit–entry administration, but also statistical data is used in the announcements of and reports on *sanfei* campaigns, suggesting that the police has recognised the issue of illegal immigration and already implemented effective measures to cope with it. The reporting systems implement a certain degree of democratic accountability,[246] as citizens can indirectly exert pressure upon local police officials by reporting

245 *Action Plan of the Tourism Bureau of the City of Xingtai on the Launch of the Campaign to Clear Up and Correctively Punish 'Sanfei' Foreigners in the Tourism Sector* (2012).

246 See Alex L. Wang (2018), p. 720, and the conclusion of this study.

suspicious foreign nationals to public security authorities at the municipal or county level. Eventually, the notion that the state is able to deal with illegal immigration serves to strengthen the legitimation of the current leadership of the state.

E. Application of Campaign Models on Sanfei *Campaigns*

A classification of state activity against illegal immigration as campaigns requires an analysis of whether this activity fulfils the preconditions to be a 'campaign' as defined above. In the years after the foundation of the People's Republic of China, political campaigns constituted an important means of communication and implementation of norms. But, as I analysed in the section regarding the conceptual framework of this chapter, campaigns pursue more goals than just propaganda or mere law enforcement. The previous chapter presented systemic problems within the Chinese political system, such as incentive systems that focus on items like numbers of arrests rather than qualitatively evaluating administrative work of local officials, poor intra-administrative communication and restrained sharing of information or overlapping responsibilities. These problems frequently lead to poor enforcement of legal norms or of political aims. While campaigns may intensify the implementation of incentive systems, which can contribute to quick results but are also prone to errors, they frequently also implement *ad-hoc* organisation structures that aim to enhance intra-administrative communication and to coordinate the work of different responsible authorities. Hence, campaigns also serve an important role in enforcing legal provisions and political aims through temporarily reorganising relevant parts of the administrative apparatus. As they are able to resolve certain systemic problems that hamper efficient enforcement of national law at the local level, I argue that campaigns are a crucial means for the enforcement of law within the political system of China.

While campaigns to enforce law are not alien to any legal system, be they liberal constitutional or rather authoritarian systems,[247] campaigns as employed in China differ from law-enforcement campaigns in Western liberal democracies in multiple ways. Apart from the leadership role the Communist Party typically takes in the campaign context, a major characteristic of campaigns in China is the *ad-hoc* establishment of a parallel organisation

247 Van Rooij (2009), p. 49 f.

structure with the aim of implementing the objectives of the campaign. By utilising this parallel organisation structure, aims formulated by the central level are being allocated all the way down to the authorities at the local level. This *ad-hoc* establishment of a parallel organisation structure renders campaigns in China in general much more political in nature than their Western counterparts, which further manifests in the programmatic denomination of the campaigns, of their aims or of their different deployment stages. Finally, as van Rooij argues, law-enforcement campaigns always serve political aims, as the central leadership utilises campaigns as a means to act in accordance with the public will and thus maintain its own legitimacy.[248]

This section aims to clarify whether *sanfei* campaigns can be regarded as law-enforcement campaigns and even as regulatory failure campaigns. To this end, I will compare the characteristics of *sanfei* campaigns against typical characteristics of law-enforcement and regulatory failure campaigns that have been carved out by different scholars of these topics and that were discussed in the introductory part of this chapter.

I. *Sanfei* Campaigns as Law-Enforcement Campaigns

Bennett proposes a typology of campaigns that differs from a mere categorisation by suggesting a non-exclusive scheme of different objectives campaigns may pursue, such as the introduction and popularisation of new policies and the implementation of existing policies, the correction of deviations from public norms or the rectification of malpractices among leading cadres.[249] Bennett argues that most campaigns feature several of his proposed objectives.[250] Of the classification schemes that have been developed in the pre-opening era, Bennett's typology best fits contemporary campaigns such as law-enforcement campaigns. From the set of objectives identified by Bennett, two can be applied to *sanfei* campaigns. The first objective is the introduction and popularisation of new policies and the implementation of existing policies, as the aims of *sanfei* campaigns are first the introduction and popularisation of the concept of *sanfei*—although this concept cannot be said to be new, but at least its strict implementation is novel—and secondly the introduction of new legal norms that are to be es-

248 Van Rooij (2009).
249 Bennett (1976), p. 46.
250 Bennett (1976), p. 46 f.

tablished in the context of the revised *Exit–Entry Administration Law*. The second objective of *sanfei* campaigns is—as Bennett calls it—"correcting deviations" from public norms and "rectifying malpractices" among leading cadres. Not only do the campaigns target deviant, i. e. illegal, behaviour of foreign nationals, but they also target reluctance among local officials who are hesitant to strictly enforce political and legal norms set up by central-level authorities concerning foreign immigrants. Considering certain frictions between central and local authorities I further assume that fostering national integration, an important effect of campaigns identified by Liu,[251] is also an underlying aim of *sanfei* campaigns when they aim to overcome the deviation of local implementation from central directives.

With these findings so far, I argue that *sanfei* campaigns exhibit typical elements of campaign-style policing. Government action targeting *sanfei* foreigners is defined regarding the scope of time and geographical distribution, which is an important indicator for campaigns. As the implementation and action plans suggest, campaigns are typically coordinated by small working groups specifically established in order to implement the campaigns' objectives and define tasks, timing, and targets of the campaigns. This organisation structure as well as the definition of different stages of preparation, implementation and revision is characteristic of campaigns. Although relevant implementation and action plans do not allocate concrete quotas on foreign nationals engaging in illegal activities to be identified by local public security offices, higher-level authorities are reportedly evaluating statistics on foreign nationals management work of local police stations involving scores based on arrests or penalties. In the following, I will apply to *sanfei* campaigns several characteristics of law-enforcement campaigns identified by van Rooij in order to answer the question whether *sanfei* campaigns should be regarded as law-enforcement campaigns as well.

In the introductory part, I set out four main indicators that serve to identify a movement as campaign. These are the centrally led coordination and definition of main aims of the movement, the top-down hierarchy with the establishment of working groups at every administrative level, an experimental approach where campaigns are first deployed in key-point areas, and the involvement of the public in campaign work. In the following, I will apply these indicators on *sanfei* campaigns in order to identify them as law-enforcement campaigns.

---

251 Alan P. L. Liu (1971), p. 111 ff.

1. Central Coordination of *Sanfei* Campaigns

One major characteristic of law-enforcement campaigns, especially in the case of *yanda* campaigns, and of campaigns in China in general is the leading role of the Communist Party. However, BIDDULPH, COONEY and ZHU point out that in the context of regulatory failure campaigns, the organisation of campaigns is conducted by state authorities rather than by Party organs.[252] In VAN ROOIJ's research of law-enforcement campaigns, he also found that the initiators of the campaigns were the State Council or government agencies like the State Environmental Protection Agency and provincial environmental protection bureaus rather than Party committees.[253]

Although the Communist Party does not come to the fore when analysing *sanfei* campaigns, which is in line with the findings of BIDDULPH, COONEY and ZHU, I find references that indicate a centrally led political agenda in the context of *sanfei* campaigns. Party influence at the central level can be traced back to the *Decision by the CPC Central Committee to Further Strengthen and Improve Public Security Work* issued on 18 November 2003, which targeted police work broadly, without explicit reference to campaigns as a means to implement legal norms, and which also addressed the improvement of exit–entry administration and border control, albeit only in one short sentence.[254] The wider *sanfei* movement deployed from October 2003 to March 2004 in different regions was very likely initiated on the basis of internal regulations issued by the Ministry of Public Security in December 2003[255] that aimed to extend the Public Security organs' task of population management to foreign nationals.[256] These internal regulations were probably a response to the *Decision by the CPC Central Committee to Further Strengthen and Improve Public Security Work*.[257]

Although party influence is not very prominent, in several action plans the party secretary of the local Party committee is also designated as leader of

252 BIDDULPH / COONEY / Ying ZHU (2012), p. 383.

253 VAN ROOIJ (2006 b), p. 65 f.

254 *Decision by the CPC Central Committee to Further Strengthen and Improve Public Security Work* (2003).

255 *Regulations on the Coordination Mechanism of Work Division of Foreign Nationals Management Work* (公安机关外国人管理工作分工配合机制规定). These regulations have never been openly published and were not available to the author of this study.

256 ZENG Wei / LIU Jianchang (2005), p. 7; ZHANG Rui (2013), p. 195.

257 *Decision by the CPC Central Committee to Further Strengthen and Improve Public Security Work* (2003).

the relevant working group, which shows that the Communist Party assumes an important role in *sanfei* campaigns. The parallel organisation structure set up in order to implement the campaign's aims and the influence of the Party on several lower administrative levels suggests that *sanfei* campaigns do not rely on existing administrative structures and hence, at least in part, are political in nature.

Summing up, I identify several documents issued by the Central Committee of the Communist Party as well as by the Ministry of Public Security that suggest that a central objective to target illegal activities of foreign nationals existed around 2003. However, these documents seem not to explicitly call for the implementation of campaigns to achieve the political aim of enhancing foreign nationals management work. This suggests that the deployment of campaigns was primarily conducted by lower-level authorities in order to implement central-level instructions by the Party or governmental bodies that were rather general in nature.

2. Top–Down Hierarchy in Organisation Structure

Another central feature of campaigns is a top–down hierarchy where objectives and targets are communicated from the central to local levels. To be sure, it is unlikely that concrete tasks, timing, and performance targets of locally deployed *sanfei* campaigns are defined centrally. The cited implementation and action plans rather suggest that the organisation of most *sanfei* campaigns was arranged at prefecture or county level where relevant authorities defined time and leadership of the campaign. This is consistent with the findings of HUANG who refers to clean-ups initiated by municipal public security authorities on prefecture or county level.[258] As lower-level implementation and action plans typically refer to higher-level plans, I assume a top–down structure within the organisation of *sanfei* campaigns. Some *sanfei* campaigns are reported to have spread across provincial borders or are said to be directly related to central-level documents,[259] which suggests that these campaigns were planned at a level above provincial level. The supra-

258 Guangzhou, being the research focus of the author, is a prefectural-level municipality. HUANG (2018), p. 15.

259 E. g. the bigger movement deployed at supra-provincial level initiated from October 2003 to March 2004 at the border regions of China as well as in other regions like Shanghai, Jilin or Guangdong. ZENG Wei / LIU Jianchang (2005), p. 7; ZHANG Rui (2013), p. 195.

provincial *sanfei* movements in 2003 and 2004 may additionally have been a response to a the different small working groups which had been dispatched on behalf of the Foreign Affairs Committee of the National People's Congress to Jilin, Guangxi, Guangdong, Shanghai and other regions to investigate the local implementation of the old *Exit–Entry Administration Laws*.[260]

Not every single raid against illegal activities of foreign nationals can be attributed to a certain campaign, as raids may also just be a result of pressure exerted by higher-level authorities.[261] But within the organisation of *sanfei* campaigns, I identify a clear top–down hierarchy. As certain bigger movements were deployed at supra-provincial level, this hierarchy probably even may reach up to the national level. Most campaigns are organised at least at prefecture or county level as implementation plans regarding *sanfei* campaigns refer to prefecture-level implementation plans. The action and implementation plans further suggest that reporting to the next-higher coordination entity of the campaign is a typical element of *sanfei* campaigns which is in line with findings of campaigns in general and confirm the existence of a strong top–down hierarchy within the structure of *sanfei* campaigns.

3. Experimental Character of *Sanfei* Campaigns

Campaigns typically exhibit an experimental character when they are first deployed in key-point areas before being applied throughout the country. However, van Rooij found that a characteristic feature of law-enforcement campaigns is rather to start centrally and become more and more diversified as the campaign reaches local administrative levels. While I identify key-point areas for the deployment of *sanfei* campaigns like border areas, "important cities", or Guangdong province, it is not appropriate to say that campaigns were first deployed only in these key-point areas and only later rolled out in other areas of the country. Rather, the collected information suggests that *sanfei* campaigns started with a wide movement in 2003 and 2004 and later spread geographically and became increasingly local and di-

260 *Report of the Foreign Affairs Committee of the National People's Congress on the Results of the Consideration of the Proposal Handed over at the 1st Session of the 10th National People's Congress* (全国人大外事委员会关于第十届全国人民代表大会第一次会议主席团交付审议的代表提出的议案审议结果的报告), *NPC Foreign Affairs Committee Press Release* (2003).

261 Huang (2018), p. 15.

versified in scope and size. Later, major campaigns and single raids always alternated and key-point areas were targeted over a certain time span rather than only in the beginning of the overall movement. One example of such an alternating deployment in a key-point area are campaigns in Guangdong province that were reported to have started in 2003, intensified from 2008 to 2010 as 'hurricane' campaigns, and then continued to persist probably in a less intensive manner afterwards. It is likely that key-point areas in the context of *sanfei* campaigns are for the most part not selected centrally, but that a perceived local need to deploy campaigns led to their local deployment. Furthermore, *sanfei* campaigns allow for local variations when they target illegal employment in the context of education[262] or when they are combined with campaigns targeting human trafficking in border regions.[263]

As the collected data on *sanfei* campaigns is only fragmentary, the resulting picture of the development of *sanfei* campaigns concerning size and geographic distribution may be distorted. From the available data, however, I conclude that *sanfei* campaigns were deployed at supra-provincial level first and later focused at key-point areas. As campaigns were deployed mainly in key-point areas, especially in Guangdong province that also served as experimental region in the context of the revision process of exit–entry administration law, *sanfei* campaigns are an important part of the experimental character of governance. Further, in the context of the revision process of the *Exit–Entry Administration Law*, *sanfei* campaigns served as an experimental framework for legal norms to be codified later, like the 'whistle-blower' provision.

4. Involvement of the Public

As could be illustrated in the previous sections, *sanfei* campaigns integrate the public in different ways. The most prominent example of integrating the public is the establishment of a public report system in several local campaigns where the public is urged to report suspected illegal activities of foreign nationals. Furthermore, the public is introduced to the phenomenon

262 *Action Plan of the Education Bureau of the City of Changsha on the Launch of the Campaign to Clear Up and Correctively Punish 'Sanfei' Foreigners* (2013).

263 *Implementation Plan of the City of Fangchenggang for the Launch of the Campaign to Strike on 'Sanfei Individuals'* (2011).

of 'sanfei' foreigners via the media where the relevant legal provisions are explained briefly to the Chinese public.

As central documents refer to poor law enforcement in the context of exit–entry administration and of insufficient communication between authorities in charge of foreign nationals management work and as implementation and action plans call for enhanced cooperation between the responsible authorities in order to implement the campaign's aim to curb illegal activities of foreign nationals, *sanfei* campaigns not only target illegal behaviour of foreign nationals directly, but also aim at enhancing law enforcement of local public security bureaus. In this regard, they resemble law-enforcement campaigns as analysed by van Rooij. While, as in *yanda* campaigns, the protection of national security and especially social stability is officially stated to be the main driver for the campaigns,[264] *sanfei* campaigns are law-enforcement campaigns targeted at illegal activities of foreign nationals, or, more concretely, illegally entry, illegal stay and illegal employment of foreign nationals. Although it is difficult to identify an official statement on the central level that calls for campaigns as a means to target illegal activities of foreign nationals, central documents point to the problem of poor law enforcement in the context of exit–entry administration and of insufficient communication between authorities in charge of foreign nationals management work.[265] I conclude that these documents exerted pressure on lower-level authorities which then relied on the means of campaigns to tackle the issues raised by the central level authorities.

Within *sanfei* campaigns, a top–down structure parallel to the regular administrative structure is installed in an *ad-hoc* manner and local coordination groups are specifically established in order to implement the campaign's aims and assigned to perform tasks according to a defined time frame. This parallel organisation structure can be regarded as a typical structure of law-enforcement campaigns in China. Furthermore, *sanfei* campaigns also exhibit an experimental character, as they are especially deployed in areas that have been assigned experimental areas of immigration policy and allow for variation when targeting specifically illegal employment in the context of education or also target human trafficking. Finally, with the report system, the public is called on to participate in *sanfei* campaigns.

---

264 See Liu Xiaosen (2003) and e. g. *Implementation Plan of the City of Fangchenggang for the Launch of the Campaign to Strike on 'Sanfei Individuals'* (2011).

265 Zeng Wei / Liu Jianchang (2005), p. 7.

II. *Sanfei* Campaigns as Regulatory Failure Campaigns

As already pointed out above, *sanfei* campaigns fit into two different groups of campaigns as outlined by BIDDULPH, COONEY and ZHU, namely into the group of campaigns targeted against criminal or at least illegal behaviour —although most illegal actions in the area of immigration law do not constitute a crime—and into the group of regulatory failure campaigns. As *sanfei* campaigns single out a certain group of individuals that act in an 'antisocial' way, namely foreign nationals who illegally enter China, who illegally stay in the country or who are employed illegally, hence committing administrative offences according to the legal provisions, I further classify them as campaigns against general criminal behaviour. After all, BIDDULPH, COONEY and ZHU point out that offences not constituting a crime may also fit into this category.[266]

The categorisation of *sanfei* campaigns as regulatory failure campaigns requires that their aim is to target regulatory failure. As shown above, regulatory failure in the context of exit–entry administration can be determined when either illegal entry, stay or employment is not prevented or not adequately persecuted by the responsible authorities due to adverse norms or instructions or the lack of appropriate legal regulations. The analysis in the previous chapter showed that overlapping and contradictory legal norms led to difficulties in law enforcement and vertical incentive structures led to excessive detention of foreign nationals. Also, poor law enforcement was caused by the lack of information sharing, which horizontal communication structures, set up in the context of the deployment of *sanfei* campaigns in an *ad-hoc* manner, aimed to enhance. The analysis above, however, also showed that collusion in the context of exit–entry administration emerged as a by-product of the campaigns rather than being the reason for their deployment. One feature of regulatory failure campaigns as carved out in the definition above is their connection to law-making processes. As could be shown in the previous and the current chapter, law-making processes accompanied the deployment of *sanfei* campaigns. In the following, I elaborate on these findings on *sanfei* campaigns with regard to their connection to law-making processes as well as with regard to their aim to encourage production of local norms that enhance enforcement of legal provisions against illegal immigration, and to combat structures that prevent appropriate enforcement such as collusion or poor information sharing.

266 BIDDULPH / COONEY / Ying ZHU (2012), p. 377.

1. Utilisation of Horizontal and Vertical Organisation Structures

The concept of regulatory failure campaigns defines campaigns as 'coordinated actions'[267] which means that they are led by a superior coordination structure that may consist of different organs jointly acting together or the Communist Party which e. g. temporally sets up a supervisory structure in parallel to administrative authorities. While, e. g., in the context of attracting foreign experts, a series of policy papers and provisions jointly issued by party and government organs exists, this is not the case in the context of combating illegal migration. For 2003, only one party document on the enhancement of police work is available that proves party influence on the central level on police work in general but falls short in proving the leading influence of the party on *sanfei* campaigns or the related revision process of the *Exit–Entry Administration Law*. However, party cadres were installed as heads of the small working groups to implement campaigns work at the local level in some cases, which is characteristic of 'specialist actions' as illustrated by BIDDULPH.[268] While single provisions exist that were jointly issued by the Ministry of Public Security and the Ministry of Foreign Affairs, there seems to be no cooperative action of different ministerial-level organs around 2003 when the campaigns intensified and the law-revision process started. Rather, only the Ministry of Public Security was assigned the task of developing a draft law on exit–entry administration, which led the Ministry of Public Security to exert pressure on its subordinated organs that finally turned to the means of campaigns to enforce the aims set by the Ministry of Public Security. However, I find a strong cooperation between different administrative bodies on the local level where a parallel organisation structure is set up. In short, while I can only assert party involvement at the local level, central-level coordination is virtually limited to instructions of the Ministry of Public Security to its subordinated organs.

A comparison with the findings regarding the vertical and horizontal communication structures from the previous chapter suggests that *sanfei* campaigns utilise a horizontal structure that integrates different administrative branches of a certain administrative level, similar to a local-level *da waiguan* system. Action and implementation plans as the normative basis for the establishment of this structure illustrate that this horizontal structure serves as communication platform to convey the aims and targets of the campaigns.

267 See section II. on page 124.
268 BIDDULPH (2007), p. 135–136.

The articulated aim of the campaigns as laid out in these plans is to reduce the number of foreign nationals who illegally entered or stay in China. To this end, investigations and check-ups are to be deployed in an intensified manner. Vertical incentive structures, however, rather result in the implementation of campaigns or raids, as could be shown in the previous chapter. Extensive imposition of sanctions and deployment of raids may be the result of pressure exerted by higher-ranking authorities, which, on the other hand, would deploy clean-up campaigns in districts of local public security offices that were not able to provide satisfactory statistics on their foreign nationals management work.

In sum, *sanfei* campaigns are deployed in order to target regulatory failure at the local level. Although tackling collusion of local officials with the local public or foreign nationals may be a by-product of *sanfei* campaigns, the major objective of *sanfei* campaigns is the reduction of non-adherence to central-level requirements. *Sanfei* campaigns aim to achieve this objective via the set-up of a horizontal communication structure that forces different responsible administrative branches to temporarily work together. As communication between the different branches as well as information sharing has been identified as having room for improvement in the context of exit–entry administration, the establishment of a horizontal communication structure in the context of *sanfei* campaigns may lead to enhanced cooperation, improved enforcement of legal norms and reduction of regulatory failure. On the other hand, campaigns are reportedly deployed as a reaction to unsatisfactory reports provided by local public security offices to higher-ranking authorities. This suggests that *sanfei* campaigns are regarded by these higher-ranking authorities as a suitable means of reducing regulatory failure in the context of exit–entry administration at the local level.

2. Entanglement of Campaigns with Law-Making Processes

Chapter 2 describes the revision process of the *Exit–Entry Administration Law* that started in 2003 and ended with the promulgation of the revised law in 2012. When the revision process started in 2003, working groups that analysed the implementation of the law already provided the Foreign Affairs Committee of the National People's Congress with information about the problems of legal enforcement. In the same year, the Ministry of Public Security, assigned with the task of working out a draft for a revised law, issued the above mentioned internal regulations which required the local police offices to intensify the administration of foreign nationals. The first nation-wide campaign targeting *sanfei* foreigners that is mentioned in newspaper reports also dates to 2003. Therefore, it is reasonable to identify the initiation of the revision process of the *Exit–Entry Administration Law* as the starting point of a wider movement aimed at the enhancement of the administration of foreign nationals, with a focus on illegal exit and entry, illegal stay, and illegal employment. The end of this bigger movement that incorporated law making as well as campaigns and optimisation of administrative structures can be set to the day of the promulgation of the revised *Exit–Entry Administration Law* in 2012. Official interpretations of the 2012 law refer to *sanfei* campaigns in several cities like Beijing where the implementation of a whistle-blower rule has achieved positive outcomes.[269] Indeed, the fact that the Beijing campaign in 2012 was deployed shortly before the *Exit–Entry Administration Law* was promulgated already suggests a connection between the law and the deployment of *sanfei* campaigns. The final law further codified the whistle-blower provision that had been applied in local regulations and campaigns before. These local provisions providing for the report and reward system can be regarded as experimental provisions that considerably influenced the legislation process. It has to be noted, however, that campaigns targeting *sanfei* foreigners did not cease with the promulgation of the revised *Exit–Entry Administration Law*.

The concept of regulatory failure campaigns focuses on the "impact of these campaigns on law reform"[270]. In the example of the wages campaigns that are illustrated by Biddulph, Cooney and Zhu, apart from a notice that addressed the issue of insufficient enforcement of delayed payments in the construction sector, and a work plan that set out a detailed time schedule and responsibility set-up in order to implement the needed measures,[271] provisional measures were issued that aimed to fix gaps in the current legislation to enhance the enforcement of wage payments.[272] While a comparable notice or work plan issued by a central-level organ is missing in the context of *sanfei* campaigns, the regional provisions in Guangdong province promulgated in 2004 and 2011 served as experimental legal framework in the context of enforcement of legal norms regarding illegal immigration. While the 2004

269 *Guide to Interpretation and Application of the 'Exit–Entry Administration Law of the People's Republic of China'* (《中华人民共和国出境入境管理法》释义及实用指南) (2012), p. 123.
270 Biddulph / Cooney / Ying Zhu (2012), p. 378.
271 Biddulph / Cooney / Ying Zhu (2012), p. 383 f.
272 Biddulph / Cooney / Ying Zhu (2012), p. 385 f.

measures called for the public to support police work by reporting *sanfei* foreigners, the 2011 interim regulations adopted this report-reward system and expanded the authority of the police by assigning the task of conducting investigations on foreign nationals to all police officials and not only to the foreign affairs police branch. The fact that these two provisions were partly included in the revised *Exit–Entry Administration Law* underlines the connection of the *sanfei* campaigns with law reform and the law-making process. Furthermore, the experimental character of the interim provisions in the province of Guangdong in itself can be seen as part of the campaign-style governance in the context of immigration law.[273]

The *Notice on Approval Authority for Orders to Leave* (2008) is another example that shows how the legal framework of exit–entry administration was amended during the period where *sanfei* campaigns were deployed. The *Notice on Approval Authority for Orders to Leave* (2008) allocates the authority to approve an order to leave imposed on a foreign national, which lay solely with the Ministry of Public Security until then, to the public security authorities of the provincial level. Furthermore, it states that its aim is to increase the efficiency of administrative enforcement and explicitly outlines cases of illegal entry, illegal stay and illegal employment where it shall be applied.[274] The revised *Exit–Entry Administration Law* expands the authority of the police regarding an order to leave even further, as any public security organ at or above county level may impose an order to leave according to the new provisions. Finally, the implementation plans on *sanfei* campaigns also called for the establishment of local regulations, e. g. in the context of targeting human trafficking.[275]

Summing up, although the deployment of *sanfei* campaigns did not cease with the promulgation of the 2012 *Exit–Entry Administration Law*, the campaigns are interlinked with law-making processes in several respects. Not only does the revised law codify the whistle-blower rule that was applied during campaign work, but official interpretations even locate the origin of this provision with the deployment of *sanfei* campaigns. Aside from the codification of experimental local provision such as the *Guangdong Interim Provisions on Foreign Nationals Administration* (2011) and the revision of the *Exit–Entry Administration Law*, regulations were amended in the context

273 Compare the findings of van Rooij who identifies campaigns as representing an experimental approach of enforcement. Van Rooij (2016), p. 228.

274 Art. 1 *Notice on Approval Authority for Orders to Leave* (2008).

275 *Implementation Plan of the City of Fangchenggang for the Launch of the Campaign to Strike on 'Sanfei Individuals'* (2011).

of the campaigns and calls to codify regulations can be found in documents that set out the deployment of campaigns. Thus, the characteristic of regulatory failure campaigns to influence, alter and even establish legal rules can also be found in the context of *sanfei* campaigns.

III. Summary

Considering their inner organisation structure as well as their deployment, *sanfei* campaigns can indeed be identified as campaigns in the sense of the term that is typically used in the relevant literature. Moreover, *sanfei* campaigns share a lot of characteristics with law-enforcement campaigns analysed by VAN ROOIJ. Indeed, their use of legal terms like 'sanfei', an abbreviation for 'illegal entry, illegal stay, and illegal employment', implies that *sanfei* campaigns aim to implement legal norms in the context of exit–entry administration. Hence, they should be regarded as law-enforcement campaigns as well. A leadership role of the Communist Party is rather hidden in the context of *sanfei* campaigns. But as other studies have shown that organisation and deployment in the context of regular failure campaigns is typically conducted by government agencies and seldom led by Party committees, the fact that Party influence in the context of *sanfei* campaigns is less prominent does not conflict with the classification of *sanfei* campaigns as regulatory failure campaigns. Moreover, the implementation of *sanfei* campaigns is characterised by a top–down structure in combination with the *ad-hoc* establishment of a parallel organisation structure that is typical of Chinese campaigns in general.

Sanfei campaigns can further be classified as regulatory failure campaigns as they target not only illegal immigration but also inefficient administration of exit and entry of foreign nationals by local public security authorities. Poor enforcement of legal norms against illegal immigration is said to be partly rooted in insufficient information sharing, which *sanfei* campaigns obviously aim to improve by utilising horizontal communication structures. In addition, a distinct relationship between *sanfei* campaigns and the law-making process of the revised *Exit–Entry Administration Law* can be identified. The authority of the police to impose certain administrative penalties, for example, was extended. Local regulations established a whistle-blower rule that required the public to report suspicious foreign nationals to the police. The extended authority to decide on administrative punishment in combination with the whistle-blower provision increased the capacity of the police to target the issue of illegal immigration and also contributed to the implementation of *sanfei* campaigns that aimed to efficiently enforce legal provisions against illegal immigration. Finally, implementation plans on *sanfei* campaigns called for the establishment of local regulations regarding immigration law.

F. Conclusion

Regulatory failure in the context of exit–entry administration may become manifest in non-compliance of local public security offices with legal norms or in weak or adverse enforcement. Reasons for non-compliance or weak or adverse enforcement may be the inapplicability of legal norms in the local context, either due to contradictory legal frameworks or due to regulations that cannot be implemented in certain situations. One example of the latter case is the impossibility of imposing a fee on foreign nationals who are not able to pay, without an option to commute the punishments into detention for example. Other reasons for regulatory failure in the context of exit–entry administration are poor communication between responsible authorities that hampers prosecution and vertical incentive systems that lead to adverse enforcement. Finally, collusion between local public security officials, the local public and foreign nationals may lead to non-compliance with relevant regulations. While contradictions between different legal norms cannot be solved only by using campaigns and campaigns may even increase collusive behaviour resulting in weak enforcement, campaigns are suited for temporarily increasing communication between relevant authorities and exerting pressure upon local-level administration in order to reduce non-compliance or weak enforcement.

Official documents state that the main aim of *sanfei* campaigns is to enforce the law in order to tackle 'illegal migration' and also to enhance foreign nationals management work. This formal reasoning is characteristic of regulatory failure campaigns that aim to enhance administrative processes and are based primarily on legal norms, and suggests that the aim of *sanfei* campaigns is not only to target illegal migration as such, but also to reduce regulatory failure in the context of exit–entry administration. *Sanfei* campaigns establish communication to the public via a report system and utilise a parallel communication and organisation structure that is set up in an *ad-hoc* manner. Both aspects are not only characteristic of campaigns as a means of Chinese governance, but also suggest that *sanfei* campaigns indeed aim to tackle regulatory failure. The report system is used to exert pressure on local public security offices while the horizontal organisation structure enhances communication between the different relevant authorities.

As regulatory failure campaigns, *sanfei* campaigns also stand in close relation to law-making processes in the area of immigration law; more concretely, with the revision process of exit–entry administration law. Although *sanfei* campaigns are said to be triggered by events like the 2008 Summer Olympics or the celebrations of the 60th anniversary of the People's Republic of China, and these events are often used as additional legitimation to deploy campaigns, the chronological distribution of campaigns suggests that legislation work also influenced the deployment of campaigns. Not only did the initiation of the revision process of exit–entry administration law and the start of the deployment of *sanfei* campaigns to a larger extent fall in the same year, but also certain points in time can be identified where political or legal developments happened in the context of foreign national management work at the same time as campaigning intensified, or at least as media coverage about campaign work increased. Finally, the *Exit–Entry Administration Law* (2012) incorporates a whistle-blower rule that is officially said to have its roots in campaigns work.

The analysis of the legislation process suggests that the deployment of *sanfei* campaigns was primarily initiated by public security authorities at prefecture level while the Ministry of Public Security issued notices demanding a stricter management work of foreign nationals. Despite there being no central-level document that explicitly calls for the deployment of campaigns, I argue that *sanfei* campaigns are campaigns that primarily tackle regulatory failure. Campaigns as a means to combat regulatory failure can be regarded as an important element of governance in China as certain structural problems within the Chinese political system exist, such as vertical incentive structures or central-level legal norms that are inapplicable at the local level, both of which lead to poor enforcement of legal norms. As a means to establish parallel organisation structures in an *ad-hoc* manner that serves to enhance communication between relevant administrative organs, regulatory failure campaigns may be an indispensable means to ensure the enforcement of central-level norms within the political system of China. Moreover, campaigns that aim to ensure the enforcement of law also serve a political aim, as the central leadership may utilise such campaigns as a means to act in accordance with the public will and thus maintain and foster its own legitimacy.

Chapter 4: Current Legal Framework of Exit–Entry Administration

A. *Introduction*

This part analyses how the revised *Exit–Entry Administration Law* (2012) contributes to the overall political aim to increase control in the area of immigration administration. Different official statements issued by the government in the context of the revision process of the law pointed out that the revision of the law mainly aimed at targeting illegal immigration framed in the context of 'sanfei', that is illegal entry, illegal stay and illegal employment.[1] The existing legal framework was said to be inadequate to efficiently target illegal immigration to China, as its definitions were not clear enough and its legal provisions were not in line with the newer framework of administrative law. While cooperation and communication between different administrative authorities were tackled using the establishment of horizontal administrative coordination schemes like the *da waiguan* or the *xiao waiguan* system[2] as well as campaigns as a means to enhance coordination between different administration branches,[3] enhanced enforcement of legal norms could only be achieved by revising the legal framework on exit–entry administration, clarifying definitions and bringing it into accord with higher-ranking legislation.

The aim of this chapter is to answer the question whether the revised law supports the political aim of targeting illegal immigration, more concretely illegal entry, illegal stay and illegal employment, or whether it rather protects the foreign national by extending access to legal remedies in comparison with previous legislation. To clarify how the provisions of the law achieve a balance between the aim of bringing legal provisions in line with international standards and the aim of curbing illegal immigration, I analyse

1 See the explanatory part of *Clauses of the Exit–Entry Administration Law (Draft) and Explanations* (出境入境管理法（草案）条文及草案说明), *NPC Press Release* (2011); *Guide to Interpretation and Application of the 'Exit–Entry Administration Law of the People's Republic of China'* (《中华人民共和国出境入境管理法》释义及实用指南) (2012), p. 23 f.

2 See chapter 2.

3 See chapter 3.

the rights foreign nationals may use to challenge police power. This chapter investigates the norms of the *Exit–Entry Administration Law* (2012) in the context of the current framework of administrative law, because only then can questions concerning implementation, enforcement and remedies be understood. The focus of analysis lies on the revised *Exit–Entry Administration Law* (2012), but other legal provisions of administrative and criminal law are taken into account as well in order to clarify the scope of certain provisions of the *Exit–Entry Administration Law*.

The protection of rights often stands in conflict with the aim of tough prosecution by the police. In the context of campaigns, legal norms in the past were amended, interpreted differently or even ignored in order to achieve swift enforcement.[4] Concerning the extension of police power in the context of examination of passports or the imposition of orders to leave, amendments to the legal framework of exit–entry administration have already been determined in the last chapters. As has been shown, the revised *Exit–Entry Administration Law* (2012) indeed contains certain provisions that allow for a swifter enforcement when compared to its predecessor, as certain decisions can now be made by lower-ranking authorities. On the other hand, the legislators of the revised *Exit–Entry Administration Law* obviously tried not to violate international standards in exit–entry administration, as official interpretations argue that certain restrictions regarding the access to legal remedies are in line with international treaties and international practice.[5] Further, courts play an increasingly important role especially in the context of employment of foreign nationals when it comes to the protection of their legal rights. This chapter aims to shed light on how the amended law reconciles these contradicting objectives, i. e. the call for swift and severe enforcement on the one hand and the demand to stay in line with international human rights standards on the other. Furthermore, the role of the courts is analysed where possible.

This chapter is divided into three sections that analyse the aspects of exit and entry, stay, and employment of foreign nationals. While all three sections focus on the scope of legal remedies that foreign nationals may apply against measures imposed on them in the context of exit–entry administration, each section also contributes to the question whether certain aims of the

---

4 BIDDULPH / COONEY / Ying ZHU (2012), p. 378 f.

5 *Guide to Interpretation and Application of the 'Exit–Entry Administration Law of the People's Republic of China'* (《中华人民共和国出境入境管理法》释义及实用指南) (2012), p. 159.

revision of the *Exit–Entry Administration Law* have been fulfilled. The first section analyses the topic of illegal border crossing as well as issuance of exit–entry documents and thereby forms an introduction to the framework of administrative law. It investigates the restriction of legal remedies using the example of visa non-issuance or denial of entry at the border. The first section further discusses the different legal provisions codified in administrative and criminal law that target illegal border crossing. The second section describes repatriation and removal as an example of extended police power. It aims to highlight problems that derive from the conflict between the aim to increase the discretionary power of the police in order to enhance law enforcement and the aim to safeguard the legal rights of foreign nationals. In order to analyse the legal concept of repatriation, the second section first delineates the concept of 'stay rendered improper', which is a prerequisite for repatriation and removal, from illegal stay or registration issues and combines all three aspects under the heading of residence in China. The third section analyses the role of courts in the context of exit–entry administration and does this by looking at the topic of employment of foreign nationals. Apart from severe offences concerning border crossing or human trafficking that are handled by the court, cases where individuals try to challenge decisions regarding exit–entry administration are comparatively rare. In the context of employment, disputes between foreign employees and Chinese employers are much more prevalent. Against this background, this section questions to what degree courts acknowledge the rights of foreign nationals in decisions concerning employment and labour law.

B. Crossing the Border: Restriction of Entry and Exit

One of the motivations to revise exit–entry administration legislation was its outdatedness. Newer, but more general legal provisions conflicted with older, but more specific norms. No normative framework existed to solve such legal conflicts that hence led to ambiguity and finally to hurdles in enforcing the law. The aim of the revision of the law was hence to harmonise the legal revisions of the *Exit–Entry Administration Law* with other relevant laws and to enhance the enforceability of legal provisions in the field of immigration law.

This section aims to answer the question whether the new legal framework of exit–entry administration is able to make use of its enhanced definitions and procedures that are harmonised with the overall framework of administrative law. To answer this question, different aspects of administrative law, such as administrative licences, administrative compulsion as well as administrative punishment, are analysed regarding the conformity of norms of the *Exit–Entry Administration Law* with the relevant higher-ranking legislation. The harmonisation of the revised *Exit–Entry Administration Law* with more general laws like the *Administrative Licence Law*, the *Administrative Compulsion Law*, the *Administrative Punishments Law*, as well as with other laws concerning administrative litigation and reconsideration, suggests that due to fewer conflicting legal norms in comparison with the old legal framework, enforcement of legal provisions in exit–entry administration has been greatly improved. I will examine this assumption in the context of the issuance of exit–entry documents, the restriction of exit and entry at the border, as well as in the context of prosecution of offences regarding illegal border crossing, thereby focusing on the restriction of legal remedies and the clarification of definitions.

One of the most immediate experience of a foreign national with exit–entry administration may be at the border where his or her travel documents are examined. If the border inspection authorities decide positively and let the foreign national cross the border, he or she probably will not think of challenging this decision. However, crossing the border in both directions may be prevented by the authorities and the individual concerned may want to complain against this restriction of his or her movement.

In general, a foreign national may be prevented from entering the country by not being issued a visa, he or she may also be rejected at the border and, finally, an illegal entry may be prosecuted after he or she has managed to cross the border. In the first part of this section, I look into the limitations of legal remedies against the non-issuance of a visa, after having clarified whether a visa can be regarded as administrative licence. I then analyse compulsory measures and compulsory enforcement that may be implemented by border officials in order to restrict exit or entry as well as legal remedies that may be applied against such administrative compulsion. Finally, I examine the legal definition of 'illegal exit or entry' as defined in the *Exit–Entry Administration Law* (2012). As offences in the context of border crossing are not only defined in this law, I analyse in the following the different legal provisions in administrative and criminal law and which legal remedies may be applied against such punishment. By identifying the different offences regarding illegal exit or entry and illegal border crossing, I also carve out the differences between administrative penalties and criminal punishment as well as the resulting legal remedies that may be applied.

I. Non-Issuance or Revocation of Exit–Entry Documents

If a foreign national is not issued a visa or residence permit or his or her exit–entry document has been revoked, he or she may want to apply legal remedies against this decision. A clarification of the legal basis for the decision of the authorities not to issue a visa as well as for the possibilities for the foreign national to file a complaint requires an answer to the question whether a visa is an administrative licence or not. Having answered this question, I look into the legal framework that codifies the different ways to file complaints against decisions of administrative organs and in particular against decisions regarding the non-issuance or revocation of exit–entry documents. After having analysed restrictions of exit and entry in the following section, a conclusion is drawn concerning the compatibility of the practice of Chinese authorities regarding the limitation of legal remedies in cases of non-issuance of visa or exit or entry restrictions with international standards.

1. Exit–Entry Documents as Administrative Licences

One major aim of the revision process of the *Exit–Entry Administration Law* was to better embed its provisions into the framework of administrative law. After the promulgation of the 1985 laws on exit–entry administration, several laws in the area of administrative law have been promulgated, e. g. the *Administrative Licence Law* (2003). As will be analysed in the next section in more detail, the revised *Exit–Entry Administration Law* (2012) serves as *lex specialis* in the area of exit–entry administration that primarily belongs to the realm of administrative law. Other, more basic laws provide the framework for administrative law in general. The *Administrative Licence Law* (2003) codifies the basic legal framework on administrative licences by defining the preconditions for the establishment of administrative licences, as well as relevant punishments and legal remedies in the context of issuance, modification or extension and revocation of administrative licences.

Article 2 *Administrative Licence Law* (2003) defines as administrative license an "act where an administrative organ permits, upon examination according to legal provisions, citizens, legal persons or other organisations to engage in specific activities according to their applications."[6] The licence

6 Art. 2 *Administrative Licence Law* (2003).

issued is hence to be regarded as document to certify this permission. Issuing residence or exit–entry documents is an administrative act assigned to the exit–entry administration authorities or to consulates and embassies. Resident permits are issued by public security organs while visas may be issued by public security organs as well as by consulates or embassies, and these documents may be subject to revocation by the issuing authority.[7] A visa is a certificate to permit an individual to engage in special activities (i. e. entering the country for a special purpose for a defined time span) that is issued by an administrative organ upon examination of an application according to the law (thus apparently constituting an administrative act). This satisfies the requirements laid down in the definition of an administrative licence as stated in Article 2 *Administrative Licence Law* (2003). The same article, however, limits the application of the law to Chinese nationals, legal persons, and other organisations. There is no provision in the *Administrative Licence Law* (2003) stating that foreign nationals should be treated the same as Chinese nationals regarding the application of the law. However, there is no explicit exclusion of non-nationals to apply for an administrative licence either.

Hence in strict accordance with the text,[8] the *Administrative Licence Law* (2003) does not regulate administrative licences issued to foreign nationals and thus documents issued to foreign nationals by an administrative organ should not be handled as an administrative licence according to the *Administrative Licence Law* (2003). However, the *Exit–Entry Administration Law* (2012) mentions several documents that obviously have the quality of an administrative licence, e. g. a work permit (*gongzuo xuke*[9]) that may be issued to foreign as well as to Chinese nationals. It does not state explicitly, however, that visa or other licences issued to foreign nationals should be handled according to the *Administrative Licence Law* (2003). From practice it can be concluded, however, that administrative licences may well be issued to foreign nationals, and foreign nationals may apply for administrative licences, which then—irrespective of certain exceptions discussed below—are handled according to the provisions of the *Administrative Li-*

7 Art. 49, 67 *Exit–Entry Administration Law* (2012).

8 Art. 2 *Administrative Licence Law* (2003) states that "administrative licences according to this law refer to actions of administrative organs to permit specific activities of Chinese nationals, legal entities or other organisations according to their applications" (Chinese: 本法所称行政许可，是指行政机关根据公民、法人或者其他组织的申请，经依法审查，准予其从事特定活动的行为).

9 Chinese: 工作许可.

cence Law (2003).[10] This suggests that the provisions of the *Administrative Licence Law* (2003) also apply to foreign nationals although no legal provision states so.

Neither the *Administrative Licence Law* (2003) nor the *Exit–Entry Administration Law* (2012) or relating regulations or interpretations by the Supreme People's Court or other competent organs explicitly classify visas as administrative licences or as another specific administrative act. Although Article 3 *Administrative Licence Law* (2003) excludes matters such as human resources, financial and foreign affairs from the application of this law, Article 12(1)i explicitly defines activities involving state security and public security as matters where administrative licences may be established. As Chinese literature on the subject suggests, although the exit and entry of foreign nationals may be classified as matter of foreign affairs, the issuance of visas having the aim of controlling exit and entry is rather a matter of public security (*gonggong anquan*[11]), and hence the issuance of visas to foreign nationals should be a matter governed by the *Administrative Licence Law* (2003).[12]

Indeed, the wording in Article 24 *Exit–Entry Administration Law* (2012) stating that during border inspection, foreign nationals shall hand over their "visa or other entry permission certificate" (*qianzheng huozhe qita rujing xuke zhengming*[13]) implies that a visa is also considered an entry permission certificate and thus to be considered an administrative licence. In Chinese literature, it is argued that the missing statement regarding the possible application of the *Administrative Licence Law* (2003) to foreign nationals is beneficial to the discretion of the public security authorities, which may handle licences issued to foreign nationals according to the *Administrative Licence*

---

10 See Luo Haocai / Zhan (1999), p. 175, who—before the *Administrative Licence Law* (2003) entered into force—defined as possible applicants for administrative licences individuals (*geren,* 个人) instead of Chinese nationals (*gongmin,* 公民). Zhang Xingxiang (2003), p. 179 f., stated that also natural persons (*ziranren,* 自然人) should be allowed to apply for an administrative licence, possibly referring to the draft law that still contained this term; an explanation to the draft by the Legislative Affairs Office of the State Council can be found at Zhang Xingxiang (2003), p. 318.

11 Chinese: 公共安全.

12 See Luo Haocai / Zhan (1999), p. 178, who also classify exit–entry permits as licences with the aim to safeguard public security. Zhang Xingxiang (2003), p. 70, classifies foreign national exit–entry permits as 'public security licences' (*gong'an xuke,* 公安许可) having the quality of administrative licences according to the *Administrative Licence Law* (2003).

13 Chinese: 签证或者其他入境许可证明.

Law (2003) but do not have to.[14] However, if the provisions of this law indeed apply to both Chinese nationals and foreign nationals, the provision of Article 21(2) *Exit–Entry Administration Law* (2012) stating that the reasons for prohibiting a foreign national from entering China need not be explained to the foreign national would stand in conflict with the principle of equality and transparency stated in Articles 5, 30, and 38 *Administrative Licence Law* (2003).[15]

The question regarding applicable legal remedies emerges in cases where the issuance of a residence or exit–entry document has been denied or such a permit is to be revoked. Whether or not visas and other licences issued to foreign nationals are to be classified as administrative licences has consequences for the scope of legal remedies. The issuance and revocation of licences is generally governed by the *Administrative Licence Law* (2003) that allows for administrative reconsideration and litigation and even for compensation. But only if a visa is considered an administrative licence can the provisions of the *Administrative Licence Law* (2003) concerning legal remedies be applied, although the right of foreign nationals to contest administrative acts in general should remain unaffected. As a visa obviously grants a permission to an individual to pursue a specific activity, namely to enter the country, it should be assumed that visas are administrative licences and practice shows, e. g. in the case of residence permits or work permits, that foreign nationals are in general entitled to apply for administrative licences. Administrative licences may be applied for via third party if the law doesn't state otherwise.[16] As the *Exit–Entry Administration Law* (2012) remains silent regarding restrictions in this regard, applications for residence and exit–entry documents may thus also be handed in by a representative of the applicant. The *Exit–Entry Administration Law* (2012), however, excludes the non-issuance or extension of residence permits, the non-issuance of stay permits, and the replacement or re-issuance of visas or residence permits from administrative litigation, as will be discussed in the following.

---

14 Lin (2007), p. 135.
15 Lin (2007), p. 135 f.
16 Art. 29 *Administrative Licence Law* (2003).

2. Limitations to Legal Remedies in the Context of Exit–Entry Documents

The fact that the reason for the denial of entry as well as the reason for not issuing a visa need not be explained to the applicant by the authorities[17] already implies that an appeal against such a decision is difficult. There is a "broad wording of exclusion grounds" in Chinese law that leaves a great deal of discretion concerning the approval with the responsible immigration authorities even if the legal documents are valid.[18] For example, the *Exit–Entry Administration Law* (2012) states that a foreign national may be denied entry to the country if he or she is suspected of committing administrative or criminal offences[19] or if the issuing organ "deems it improper to issue a visa".[20] Filing a lawsuit or administrative reconsideration against such discretionary decisions may only result in the examination of the legality of this decision regarding the violation of procedures prescribed by law, the transgression or abuse of power, or the inappropriateness of the decision.[21] As will be shown, however, already the access to legal remedies is limited in certain circumstances, which renders the question concerning the possibility to complain against discretionary decisions subordinate in this context.

Against certain administrative acts, the individual concerned may apply for administrative litigation or administrative reconsideration if he or she disagrees with the decision of an administrative organ. In comparison with administrative litigation, administrative reconsideration is a quicker way to challenge an administrative act. However, the period for bringing an action is in general limited to 60 days for administrative reconsideration,[22] while it amounts to six months for administrative litigation.[23] After 60 days, only administrative litigation is possible and after six months, the concerning administrative act becomes incontestable. Administrative reconsideration stays within the administrative branch where the superior organ of the authority that implemented the administrative act in question reviews the legality and appropriateness of this administrative act. In contrast, filing an

17 Art. 25(2) *Exit–Entry Administration Law* (2012).
18 Opeskin / Perruchoud / Redpath-Cross (2012), p. 141.
19 Art. 21(1)iii *Exit–Entry Administration Law* (2012).
20 Art. 21(1)vi *Exit–Entry Administration Law* (2012).
21 Art. 70 *Administrative Litigation Law* (2014).
22 Art. 9 *Administrative Reconsideration Law* (2009).
23 Art. 46 *Administrative Reconsideration Law* (2009). When filing a complaint against a decision of administrative reconsideration, the period for bringing an action is only 15 days; Art. 45 *Administrative Reconsideration Law* (2009).

administrative case requires the judicial branch to review the lawfulness of the administrative act in question and to finally issue a relevant court decision. As with administrative or criminal litigation, two instances are available in an administrative reconsideration procedure. If the person concerned suspects that the decision made by administrative reconsideration is unjustified, he or she may file an administrative lawsuit to a people's court at the local level. As administrative reconsideration and administrative litigation are considered independent systems, he or she may also directly apply for administrative litigation without having initiated an administrative reconsideration procedure first. However, if a court already decided upon a case, it cannot be challenged again via administrative reconsideration.[24] Although the wording of Article 44 *Administrative Litigation Law* (2014) implies that a law or regulation may require administrative reconsideration before administrative litigation, no such restrictions are mentioned in the *Administrative Licence Law* (2003). If the administrative act has already been through the procedure of administrative reconsideration and a decision has been made that modifies the original administrative act, the defendant in the administrative case shall be the authority that has decided upon the modification. In any other case, the defendant shall be the authority that took the administrative act.[25]

The application of legal remedies in the context of the issuance, extension, or replacement of exit–entry documents is restricted in certain circumstances. The *Exit–Entry Administration Law* (2012) states in Article 36 that the decision of a public security organ not to issue or extend a residence permit, not to issue a stay permit, or not to replace or re-issue a visa or residence permit shall be final and thus may not be subject to administrative litigation or administrative reconsideration. This provision is in line with Article 13(1)iv *Administrative Litigation Law* (2014) that states that suits against "specific administrative acts that shall, as provided for by law, be finally decided by an administrative organ" shall not be accepted for administrative litigation. It is further in line with a similar provision in Article 5 of the *Administrative Reconsideration Law* (2009). Such a restriction does not apply to other licences that the *Exit–Entry Administration Law* (2012) refers to, such as refugee identifications (*nanmin shenfen zhengjian*[26]), permanent residence permits (*yongjiu juliu zhengjian*[27]), or embarkation permits

24 Art. 16(2) *Administrative Reconsideration Law* (2009).
25 Art. 26 *Administrative Litigation Law* (2014).
26 Chinese: 难民身份证件.
27 Chinese: 永久拘留证件.

(*denglun zhengjian*[28]). On first sight, no explicit restrictions concerning administrative reconsideration or administrative litigation exist regarding the non-issuance of a visa or the revocation of a visa or of a residence of stay permit either.

According to Article 13 *Administrative Litigation Law* (2014), generally binding administrative regulations, rules, decisions or orders shall not be accepted for administrative litigation by courts. Only concrete administrative acts directed towards or against a person can be subject to administrative litigation. As it is directed towards a specific person, the issuance or the revocation of a visa or residence or stay permit is such a concrete administrative act. Although neither the *Administrative Reconsideration Law* (2009) nor the *Administrative Litigation Law* (2014) explicitly define the unlawful revocation of a licence as being covered by the scope of application of these two laws, it is possible to argue that a general "infringement upon personal rights, property rights, or other lawful rights and interests"[29] of the foreign national has been established by the revocation of the relevant document. According to Article 6(1)xi *Administrative Reconsideration Law* (2009) or 12(1)xii *Administrative Litigation Law* (2014), administrative reconsideration or litigation may be applied against such a general infringement upon rights. As the revocation of a visa or residence or stay permit is not explicitly excluded from administrative reconsideration or litigation, both ways to take legal action are permissible in principle.

Article 2 *Administrative Reconsideration Law* (2009) as well as Article 2 *Administrative Litigation Law* (2014) restrict the scope of possible plaintiffs to Chinese nationals, legal persons, and other organisations. However, Article 41 *Administrative Reconsideration Law* (2009) as well as Articles 98 and 99 *Administrative Litigation Law* (2014) state that "foreign nationals, stateless persons, and foreign organisations" who apply for administrative reconsideration or apply an administrative lawsuit in the People's Republic of China are also deemed possible plaintiffs.[30] The *Administrative Litigation Law* (2014) further states that "a person subjected to an administrative action"[31] may file a complaint,[32] which should include foreign nationals even outside the territory of the People's Republic of China who are subject to

28 Chinese: 登轮证件.
29 Art. 12(1)xii *Administrative Litigation Law* (2014).
30 Art. 41 *Administrative Reconsideration Law* (2009); Art. 98, 99 *Administrative Litigation Law* (2014).
31 Chinese: 行政行为的相对人.
32 Art. 25 *Administrative Litigation Law* (2014).

decisions of Chinese administrative organs. Although filing administrative litigation or reconsideration needs to be done from within China,[33] persons that are eligible to file a complaint may also, in certain circumstances, file a complaint via an agent.[34] The *Administrative Reconsideration Law* (2009) uses the term "citizen with the right to file administrative reconsideration"[35] to denote individuals who may file a complaint via an agent. However, interpretations of Article 98 *Administrative Litigation Law* (2014) point to the principle of the 'place of occurrence' (*fasheng didian*),[36] which requires that the foreign party files an administrative lawsuit to a Chinese court or attends an administrative lawsuit at a Chinese court and, more importantly, that the administrative action in question was implemented by a Chinese administrative body and occurred within the territory of the People's Republic of China.[37]

According to an official interpretation of the relevant articles of the *Exit–Entry Administration Law* (2012), the provision of the *Exit–Entry Administration Law* (2012) stating that the legal rights of foreign nationals in China shall be protected can only be applied after the foreign national effectively has entered the country, that is, after he or she has successfully passed border control.[38] Hence, a foreign national denied entry to China has no possibility of appeal against this administrative decision as he or she has no right to access legal remedies.[39] The same holds true for the non-issuance of visas as long as the foreign national has not yet entered the territory of the People's Republic of China and successfully passed border control. However, according to this principle, filing a complaint should still be possible

33 Art. 98 *Administrative Litigation Law* (2014); Art. 41 *Administrative Reconsideration Law* (2009).

34 Art. 25 *Administrative Litigation Law* (2014); Art. 10 *Administrative Reconsideration Law* (2009).

35 Chinese: 有权申请行政复议的公民.

36 Chinese: 发生地点.

37 Xin (2014), p. 258; Jiang Bixin (2015), p. 443. This principle results from the provisions of Art. 18, 19 and 20 *Administrative Litigation Law* (2014) that state that an administrative case shall be accepted by the court at the place of the administrative organ concerned, at the place of the reconsideration organ concerned, at the place of the real property involved, or at the place of the plaintiff's location if his or her personal freedom was restricted by a compulsory measure.

38 *Interpretation of the 'Exit–Entry Administration Law of the People's Republic of China'* (《中华人民共和国出境入境管理法》释义) (2012), p. 93 f.

39 *Interpretation of the 'Exit–Entry Administration Law of the People's Republic of China'* (《中华人民共和国出境入境管理法》释义) (2012), p. 93 f.

via an agent. This reading further implies that as soon as the individual has legally entered the territory of the People's Republic of China, he or she is able to file a complaint using both administrative reconsideration and administrative litigation, against the non-issuance or revocation of a visa or a residence or stay permit, notwithstanding the right of the relevant issuing authority not to state the reasons for the non-issuance of the visa. Finally, this notion would be in line with the above mentioned principle of the 'place of occurrence'. In any case, as long as the administrative act has not occurred within the territory of the People's Republic of China, which is the case when a consulate or embassy abroad issues a visa or if a border police officer denies entry of a foreign national, administrative litigation is not admissible according to this logic.

Official interpretations and academic literature explain the fact that foreign nationals have no access to legal remedies against certain decisions with their nature as 'acts of state' or 'sovereign acts' *(guojia xingwei)*.[40] According to explanations of the Supreme People's Court, 'acts of state' as defined in the *Administrative Litigation Law* are acts related to national defence or to foreign affairs, implemented by state organs such as the State Council, the National People's Congress, the Ministry of National Defence or the Ministry of Foreign Affairs in the name of the state.[41] A concise definition of the concrete scope of 'acts of state', however, is missing. The general reading of this explanation is that 'acts of state' are typically directed against other states or governments and include acts such as a declaration of war against another state or the signing of a treaty with another state or international organisation.[42] The *Administrative Litigation Law* (2014) explicitly excludes 'acts of state' from the scope of application of administrative litigation.[43] Although the *Administrative Reconsideration Law* (2009) does not contain a similarly explicit provision, 'acts of state' are also not included

40 Chinese: 国家行为. *Guide to Interpretation and Application of the 'Exit–Entry Administration Law of the People's Republic of China'* (《中华人民共和国出境入境管理法》释义及实用指南) (2012), p. 74, 160; *Interpretation of the 'Exit–Entry Administration Law of the People's Republic of China'* (《中华人民共和国出境入境管理法》释义) (2012), p. 93; Li Jianguo (2013).

41 Art. 2 *Administrative Litigation Law Interpretations* (2000).

42 Jiang Bixin (2015), p. 78; *Interpretation and Application of the 'Administrative Litigation Law of the People's Republic of China'* (《中华人民共和国行政诉讼法》解读与实用) (2015), p. 35; Xin (2014), p. 46.

43 Art. 13 *Administrative Litigation Law* (2014).

in the scope of application of administrative reconsideration.[44] In contrast to 'acts of state', administrative acts may be directed towards specific individuals and, if they are, legal remedies are applicable in general.[45] In the context of exit–entry administration, however, although specific individuals are typically not addressees of 'acts of state',[46] court rulings exist stating that the decision not to issue a travel document to Chinese citizens is an 'act of state' and hence does not fall within the scope of application of administrative litigation.[47]

The underpinning logic is that sovereign states must implement measures to deny certain foreign nationals entry in order to safeguard national security and public order. The right to implement such measures is directly derived from the state's sovereignty.[48] International practice regarding the access to legal remedies in the context of entry into the country differs significantly. Although no duty of a state can be derived from international law,[49] some states allow the foreign national to appeal a decision of the authorities to deny his or her entry, while others deny any access to legal remedies. The member states of the European Union, for example, allow for judicial review of decisions to reject visa applications, although not all of these countries necessarily require the authorities to state the reasons for the rejection.[50] In contrast, U. S. courts regularly apply the 'doctrine of consular non-reviewabilty' (or 'plenary power doctrine') that denies the possibility of

44 Xing et al. (2016), p. 311 f.; Wang Chunye (2017), p. 58; Zhang Chunsheng (1999), p. 163.

45 Art. 2 *Administrative Litigation Law* (2014); Art. 6 *Administrative Reconsideration Law* (2009).

46 Xing et al. (2016), p. 357.

47 See the ruling of a district court in 2017 that states that the decision of a public security authority not to issue a travel permit to Taiwan to a Chinese national should be considered an 'act of state' against which administrative litigation is not applicable; *Decision on Restricting Exit* (2017). In this decision, one can obviously not argue with above mentioned principle of the 'place of occurrence' to deny the applicability of administrative litigation. In another case cited in Li Jianguo (2013) and discussed below, the court—applying the old framework on exit–entry administration law—did not support the view held by the police that the denial of entry due to an entry ban was an 'act of state'.

48 Li Jianguo (2013), p. 41; *Interpretation of the 'Exit–Entry Administration Law of the People's Republic of China'* (《中华人民共和国出境入境管理法》释义) (2012), p. 93; Perruchoud (2012), p. 125.

49 Perruchoud (2012), p. 129, 131 f.

50 *Laws for Legal Immigration in the 27 EU Member States* (2009), p. 37; Art. 13(3) *Schengen Borders Code* (2006); Art. 14(3) *Schengen Borders Code* (2016).

judicial review of decisions to reject visa applications.[51] U. S. immigration authorities are nevertheless required to handle requests by the applicant for reconsideration.[52] Hence, although the view of Chinese academics and official interpretations that the relevant provisions in the Chinese legal framework do not contradict international standards or international practice has to be recognised as valid, the framework of Chinese immigration law in the context of visa applications is still relatively strict when it even denies access to administrative reconsideration. I will discuss the compatibility of the practice of Chinese authorities regarding the denial entry with international standards in the next section in more detail.

II. Restriction of Exit and Entry at the Border

The *Exit–Entry Administration Law* (2012) provides for the prohibition to cross the border which may be decided upon by the border inspection authorities. It may be imposed on foreign as well as on Chinese nationals if they do not hold valid exit–entry documents. Chinese literature classifies such exit restrictions (*buzhun chujing*[53]) and entry restrictions (*buzhun rujing*[54]) differently as administrative licence, administrative penalty, or compulsory measure.[55] But it is crucial to know the kind of administrative act of the concrete exit or entry restriction in order to be able to successfully make use of the appropriate legal remedies.

The old legal framework, based on the 1985 laws, did not clarify whether certain administrative acts should be classified as administrative compulsion, administrative punishment or as another administrative measure. This often resulted in uncertainty among those affected but also among the police and even sometimes among the courts how to identify the applicable legal remedies. One example of such an unclear situation caused by the old legal framework is the case of a Tanzanian national who filed a lawsuit against the Ministry of Public Security. During his stay in China he was punished by a prefecture-level Public Security Bureau for illegal residence as he overstayed his visa and residence permit. He was further ordered to leave before

51 Rosenfield (1955); Saito (2003) p. 18, 20; Chang (2018), p. 1202.
52 *Rivas v. Napolitano* (2013).
53 Chinese: 不准出境.
54 Chinese: 不准入境.
55 Chen Libo (2010); Li Youbiao (2012); Liu Hongxing / Teng (2013); Zhu Jingao (2015).

9 February 2000 and the Ministry of Public Security imposed a five-year re-entry ban. After having returned home, the Tanzanian national acquired a new visa at the Chinese Embassy in Tanzania and re-entered China in March of the same year. The Beijing Municipal Public Security Bureau detained him and deported him in May. The Tanzanian national then filed an administrative lawsuit with the Beijing Second Intermediate People's Court in September 2001 claiming that the denial of entry was an administrative punishment and as such punishing him again for the same action he already had received a punishment for. The Ministry of Public Security argued that the denial of entry ban was an 'act of state' against which no legal remedies were applicable. The court held that the re-entry ban was established legally and should be upheld. However, the court rejected the claim that the denial of entry was an act of state, but denied also that it was an administrative punishment.[56]

The revised legal framework originally aimed to resolve such uncertainties. However, the nature of certain administrative acts, especially regarding the restriction of exit and entry, is still subject to discussion in the Chinese literature. Because individuals who want to cross the border hand their exit–entry credentials over to the border inspection officers who then decide upon the lawfulness of the intended border crossing, some Chinese academics identify this inspection as an administrative licence (*xingzheng xuke*[57]).[58] The concrete decision about the issuance of the permit to cross the border, however, has already been made by another authority to which the individuals applied in advance and which upon their application has issued exit–entry documents, e. g. in the form of a visa or—for Chinese nationals—a passport. Thus, as other academics state, the border inspection itself does not constitute an administrative licence but rather an administrative verification (*xingzheng queren*[59])[60] or a mere administrative decision[61] both of which are neither regulated by the *Administrative Licence Law* nor by the *Administrative Penalty Law*. Furthermore, the mere decision to prohibit from crossing the border does not constitute an administrative compulsory

56 Li Jianguo (2013), p. 40. As the court case is not available in public databases, I need to refer to secondary sources.
57 Chinese: 行政许可.
58 E. g. Liu Hongxing / Teng (2013), p. 50.
59 Chinese: 行政确认.
60 Chen Changfu (2010), p. 89.
61 On the character of an administrative decision see e. g. Hu Jianmiao (2003), p. 157 ff.

measure (*xingzheng qiangzhi*[62]) as held by other scholars who argue that this decision restricts the personal freedom of the individual.[63] This understanding is reflected by the *Exit–Entry Administration Law* (2012) that states that the border inspection officials shall order the relevant individual to return,[64] which rather constitutes an administrative order (*xingzheng mingling*[65]).[66] However, if the individual refuses to follow this order, he or she may be returned or repatriated forcefully which then obviously constitutes a compulsory measure. This section aims to answer the question whether exit or entry restrictions should be regarded as administrative licences or rather as a compulsory measure and which administrative or judicial decisions may underlie this compulsory measure. A considerable amount of the Chinese literature seems to ignore the fact that the compulsory measure of restricting the exit may in some cases be a compulsory enforcement measure. However, as the applicable legal remedies and their effects differ for enforcement measures, I analyse the different circumstances in which exit restrictions may be applied.

1. Legal Framework on Compulsory Measures and Compulsory Enforcement

Before analysing exit and entry restrictions in more detail, this sections investigates the relevant legal framework that outlines compulsory measures. Administrative compulsion is codified in the *Administrative Compulsion Law* (2011). Apart from exit and entry restrictions, the *Exit–Entry Administration Law* (2012) makes use of compulsory measures as defined in the *Administrative Compulsion Law* (2011) in the context of deportation and repatriation, but also when it comes to detention for investigation or the enforcement of administrative acts in general. Compulsory measures defined in the *Exit–Entry Administration Law* (2012) should adhere to the *Administrative Compulsion Law* (2011) that serves as *lex generalis*.

The *Administrative Compulsion Law* (2011) distinguishes between administrative compulsory measures (*xingzheng qiangzhi cuoshi*[67]) and ad-

62 Chinese: 行证强制.
63 Li Youbiao (2012), p. 37.
64 Art. 26 *Exit–Entry Administration Law* (2012).
65 Chinese: 行政命令.
66 On the character of an administrative order see e. g. Hu Jianmiao (2003), p. 146 ff.
67 Chinese: 行政强制措施.

ministrative compulsory enforcement (*xingzheng qiangzhi zhixing*[68]). The former depicts a temporary restriction of the personal freedom or property in order to stop an illegal act, to prevent destruction of evidence, or to avoid damage or the expansion of danger.[69] The latter refers to administrative acts enforced in order to forcefully fulfil legal obligations imposed by administrative organs or courts.[70] Administrative compulsion generally should only be carried out as a last resort, i. e. non-compulsory means should be given preference in order to achieve the desired objective,[71] and administrative compulsion, i. e. both administrative compulsory measures as well as administrative enforcement, may be subject to administrative reconsideration and administrative litigation in general.[72]

In contrast to administrative penalties, which are discussed in the next section in more detail, administrative compulsory measures are not based on the condition that the action against which they are directed is an illegal action. Compulsory measures are of temporary nature and they may occur prior to the action that they aim to prevent. Administrative compulsory actions are directly implemented by an administrative organ.[73] Administrative enforcement measures on the other hand aim to enforce the fulfilment of obligations that result from an administrative or judicial decision. Administrative enforcement measures are based on the precondition that a person did not fulfil his or her obligations as defined in the administrative of judicial decision. In contrast to administrative penalties, administrative enforcement measures do not possess a punitive nature. They further do not establish a new relationship of rights and duties.[74]

a) Administrative Compulsory Measures

Article 9 *Administrative Compulsion Law* (2011) defines as administrative compulsory measures[75] restriction of personal freedom, seizing of premises, facilities or properties, impoundments of properties, as well as freezing of

68 Chinese: 行政强制执行.
69 Art. 2(2) *Administrative Compulsion Law* (2011).
70 Art. 2(3) *Administrative Compulsion Law* (2011).
71 Art. 5 *Administrative Compulsion Law* (2011).
72 Art. 8(1) *Administrative Compulsion Law* (2011); Art. 20(1)ii *Administrative Litigation Law* (2014); Wu Gaosheng (2015), p. 73.
73 Fang / Shi (2011), p. 226 f.
74 Fang / Shi (2011), p. 230 f.
75 Chinese: 行政强制措施.

deposits or remittances. According to Article 10 *Administrative Compulsion Law* (2011), other administrative compulsory measures have to be defined by law in principle, i. e. legal documents adopted by the National People's Congress or its Standing Committee.[76] For matters not already defined by law, compulsory measures may be defined by administrative regulations, except for restricting personal freedom[77] or seizing properties; local matters not already defined by law or by administrative regulations concerning impounding properties or freezing deposits may further be defined by local regulations.[78] Administrative compulsory measures may only be implemented by the administrative organ defined by a law or a regulation and may not be delegated.[79] Before the actual implementation takes place, the party concerned is to be informed of the reasons and grounds as well as of his or her legal rights and remedies, an on-site transcript should be made and signed or sealed by the party concerned.[80] At least two officials should conduct the administrative compulsory measure and identify themselves to the party con-

---

76 According to Art. 7(1) *Legislation Law* (2015).

77 This notion is derived from the provision of Art. 8(1)v *Legislation Law* (2015) that requires compulsory measures or administrative punishment restricting the personal freedom to be codified by law. Although Chinese laws typically talk of "personal freedom of citizens" (Chinese: 公民人身自由), provisions concerning 'personal freedom' should also apply to foreign nationals. See e. g. *Interpretation of the 'Exit–Entry Administration Law of the People's Republic of China'* (《中华人民共和国出境入境管理法》释义) (2012), p. 202, stating that the section of the *Exit–Entry Administration Law* (2012) is codified according to the basic principles of the *Administrative Penalty Law* (2009), which implies that the latter is applicable also in cases where foreign nationals are involved, or the explanations on Art. 3 *Exit–Entry Administration Law* (2012) stating that legal provisions concerning the legal rights regarding civil law, as well as concerning legal remedies in the context public security administration law or criminal law also apply to foreign nationals; *Guide to Interpretation and Application of the 'Exit–Entry Administration Law of the People's Republic of China'* (《中华人民共和国出境入境管理法》释义及实用指南) (2012), p. 32. Official interpretations also state that rights of foreign nationals such as 'personal freedom', 'religious freedom' or 'dignity of human personality' are rights that may not be infringed upon; *Interpretation of the 'Exit–Entry Administration Law of the People's Republic of China'* (《中华人民共和国出境入境管理法》释义) (2012), p. 31. Furthermore, the protection of personal freedom is enshrined in several international conventions.

78 Chinese: 地方性法规. Art. 10(2, 3) *Administrative Compulsion Law* (2011).

79 Art. 17(1) *Administrative Compulsion Law* (2011).

80 Art. 18(1)v, vii, viii *Administrative Compulsion Law* (2011).

cerned.[81] In urgent cases, the notification of the party concerned has to take place within 24 hours after the compulsory measure.[82] If the compulsory measure involves the restriction of the personal freedom of the individual concerned, the relatives have to be informed immediately about the responsible administrative organ that imposes the compulsory measure as well as the reason, the place and the period of implementation.[83] If the compulsory measure involves seizure, the individual involved is to be issued a receipt about the seizure indicating name and address of the individual concerned, the reason, legal basis and period of seizure, a detailed list of the seized items as well as information regarding the applicable legal remedies.[84]

b) Administrative Compulsory Enforcement

The *Administrative Compulsion Law* (2011) defines as different kinds of administrative compulsory enforcement[85] *inter alia* fines and late payment fines, transfer of bank deposits or remittances, auction or deposition of seized or confiscated premises, facilities or properties, removal of obstructions or restoration and substitute execution.[86] While administrative compulsory measures may be defined by laws as well as by administrative and local regulations, administrative enforcement measures may only be set by law.[87] Administrative enforcement measures require that the concerning administrative decision is in force, that the individual in question did not fulfil his or her duties according to this decision within the set period of time and he or she still did not fulfil the relevant duties after having been reminded in

81 Art. 18(1)ii, iii *Administrative Compulsion Law* (2011); ZENG Bin / CHENG Hua (2011), p. 22.

82 ZENG Bin / CHENG Hua (2011), p. 23.

83 Art. 20(1)i *Administrative Compulsion Law* (2011); ZENG Bin / CHENG Hua (2011), p. 23. Art. 43(1)v *Provisions on Handling Administrative Cases* (2012) states that if the relatives cannot be informed on the spot, they shall be notified by phone, text message, fax or other methods immediately after the compulsory measure has been implemented. It is not required to notify the relatives if it is impossible to notify them due to unclear identity or refusal to provide contact information, or due to natural disasters or *force majeure*. The fact that the relatives have been informed as well as the reasons for the failure to do so have to be recorded.

84 Art. 24, 25 *Administrative Compulsion Law* (2011); ZENG Bin / CHENG Hua (2011), p. 23.

85 Chinese: 行政强制执行方式.

86 Art. 12 *Administrative Compulsion Law* (2011).

87 Art. 13 *Administrative Compulsion Law* (2011).

written form to do so and without a valid excuse.[88] More concretely, before carrying out administrative enforcement, the party concerned is to be notified in writing about the time limit and the manner of fulfilment of the legal obligations as well as of the amount of potential fines and the legal rights.[89] The party concerned is entitled to express their arguments regarding this notification.[90]

The administrative organ may only conduct the administrative enforcement measure if it has the right of enforcement.[91] If the right of enforcement of the administrative organ is not defined by law, a court has to decide on the enforcement on behalf of the relevant administrative organ.[92] In contrast to other administrative organs, the public security organs have comprehensive rights concerning the application of administrative compulsion. Hence, only where a law prescribes that a court has to decide on the enforcement measure do the public security organs have to apply to a court for enforcement, while otherwise they may implement the enforcement measure directly.[93] Only in particular cases do the police depend on a decision of a court for enforcement. For example, if the individual did not pay a fine, the police may apply to a court for collection enforcement. If the individual concerned did not discontinue the production or business as demanded, the police has to apply to a court for discontinuation enforcement, but they may actively stop the business in case of imminent danger.[94]

Certain compulsory measures in the area of exit–entry administration include the restriction of personal freedom. This is especially true for the restriction of exit or entry, but also for other measures like detention for investigation, restriction of activities,[95] and repatriation, which will be discussed later in this part. Additionally, border immigration inspection[96] as well as on-site and continued questioning should be classified as compulsory measures.

---

88 Art. 37, 38 *Administrative Compulsion Law* (2011).
89 Art. 35(1) *Administrative Compulsion Law* (2011).
90 Art. 36 *Administrative Compulsion Law* (2011).
91 Zeng Bin / Cheng Hua (2011), p. 28.
92 Art. 13, 53 *Administrative Compulsion Law* (2011).
93 Zeng Bin / Cheng Hua (2011), p. 35.
94 Zeng Bin / Cheng Hua (2011), p. 35.
95 The *Foreign Nationals Exit–Entry Administration Law* (1985) provided for residential surveillance (*jianshi juzhu,* Chinese: 监视居住) instead, which also is classified as compulsory measure.
96 Yu Qun / Ma Shuncheng (2012), p. 119.

2. Legal Remedies Against Restrictions of Exit and Entry

Having analysed the differences between administrative compulsory measures and administrative compulsory enforcement, I will now apply these findings to exit and entry restrictions and analyse whether the fact that an exit or entry restriction is a compulsory measure or compulsory enforcement influences the scope of legal remedies the individual concerned may use. As the revised legal framework omits certain differentiations existing in the old legal framework which are, however, still implicitly applicable, I first examine the relevant provisions of old legal framework that will help understand these differentiations.

As Article 23 *Foreign Nationals Exit–Entry Administration Law* (1985) and Article 8 *Citizen Exit–Entry Administration Law* (1985) defined, exit–entry administration authorities should, e. g. if the individual is currently a party to an unresolved lawsuit, hinder this individual from exiting the country (*buzhun chujing*[97]). This administrative act should be considered an administrative enforcement measure as the authorities would enforce an order of another authority like a court or ministry. In contrast, Article 24 *Foreign Nationals Exit–Entry Administration Law* (1985) and Article 9 *Citizen Exit–Entry Administration Law* (1985) stated that if the individual tried to exit the country illegally, the border authorities should take initiative to prevent him or her from exiting the country (*fangzhi chujing*[98]). Chen Libo classifies decisions on exit restrictions as administrative punishment, while regarding the mere enforcement at the border as administrative enforcement measure.[99] Indeed, although the *Administrative Penalty Law* (2009) does not explicitly account for exit restrictions as a punishment, its Article 8 allows for other administrative penalties defined by law in a non-exhaustive enumeration of administrative penalties. However, Article 12 *Administrative Compulsion Law* (2011) similarly provides a non-exhaustive enumeration of administrative enforcement measures. In any case, the wording of the above cited provision of the *Foreign Nationals Exit–Entry Administration Law* (1985) suggests that a compulsory measure was meant, but not necessarily compulsory enforcement.

According to the *Foreign Nationals Exit–Entry Administration Law* (1985) and the *Citizen Exit–Entry Administration Law* (1985), individu-

97 Chinese: 不准出境.
98 Chinese: 防止出境.
99 Chen Libo (2010), p. 92 f.

als could be prevented from exiting the country if they did not hold valid exit–entry documents (which included holding forged documents or those of others), if they refused to undergo border inspection, if they tried to cross the border elsewhere than at exit–entry ports, if the Ministry of Public Security or the Ministry of National Security had issued a notice of exit restriction, or if laws or administrative regulations required exit restrictions.[100] The old legal framework only explicitly provided for the restriction of entry[101] of foreign nationals who could pose a threat to state security or public order.[102] From the above cited provisions of the 1985 laws I infer, however, that the prevention of individuals from entering or exiting China in itself should not be considered an administrative punishment but merely an administrative compulsory measure, as restrictions of entry and exit were codified in the relevant chapters of the laws concerning exit or entry but not in the chapters on penalties. Furthermore, as discussed above, the physical restriction to exit or enter, i. e. the compulsory measure, should be differentiated from an administrative punishment that may be the basis for the restriction of entry or exit. E. g. in the case where a foreign national does not hold a visa at all, the restriction to exit or enter may not be based on any administrative punishment. Summing up, exit and entry restrictions according to the old legal framework were codified as administrative compulsory measures or as administrative compulsory enforcement, whereas the restriction may or may not be based on an administrative punishment.

The revised *Exit–Entry Administration Law* (2012) does not adopt this clear differentiation of exit and entry restrictions as administrative acts between compulsory enforcement and compulsory measures. In its Articles 12 and 28, the *Exit–Entry Administration Law* (2012) regulates exit restrictions for Chinese and foreign nationals respectively. Instead of distinguishing between exit restrictions as compulsory measure and as compulsory enforcement, the law now uniformly talks of "hindering from exiting" (*buzhun chujing*[103]). However, the differentiation of exit restrictions being applied as compulsory measure and as compulsory enforcement still exists.[104] The regulations of the revised *Exit–Entry Administration Law*

---

100 Art. 23 *Foreign Nationals Exit–Entry Administration Law* (1985); Art. 8 *Citizens Exit–Entry Administration Law* (1985).

101 Chinese: 不准入境.

102 Art. 12 *Foreign Nationals Exit–Entry Administration Law* (1985).

103 Chinese: 不准出境.

104 See Zhu Jingao (2015), p. 145 ff., who finds a continuity from the old to the new legal framework concerning the codification of compulsory enforcement measures,

clarify how to understand the concrete exit or entry restriction of an individual, as the law explicitly defines fine and detention as administrative punishment for illegal exit or entry. Furthermore, as was the case in the old legal framework, the restriction of exit is not codified in the section of legal liabilities but in the sections on exit and entry. Hence, the prevention of individuals from entering or exiting China illegally in itself should not be considered an administrative punishment but an administrative compulsory measure that serves to (re-)constitute a certain legal order. Exit restrictions as measures taken in the context of a lawsuit as well as restrictions that are based on a decision of a public security authority, on the other hand, are compulsory enforcement measures, as they are enforced by the border inspection authorities according to a court notice or decision or on the basis of an administrative decision.

As mentioned, the differentiation between administrative compulsory measures and compulsory enforcement measures has implications for the legal remedies that may be used to challenge the restriction. While administrative litigation or reconsideration against an exit restriction applied as administrative compulsory measure will lead to an examination of the legality of the restriction, challenging the administrative enforcement would only lead to the examination of the legality of the actual enforcement but not to the examination of the legality of the restriction itself. More concretely, exit restrictions imposed on foreign or Chinese nationals should in any case be classified as administrative compulsion when implemented by the border inspection agencies. The decision, however, on which the restriction at the border is possibly based may be an administrative punishment imposed by the police or a court ruling with the aim of enforcing a court decision or to prevent an individual from escaping the country during a pending lawsuit. Entry restrictions are handled similarly, the actual denial of entry to China being administrative compulsion while the possible underlying decision may be an administrative (or even criminal) punishment. However, regarding the legal remedies concerning the refusal of the entry of a foreign national at the border, compare the findings discussed above concerning the refusal to be issued a visa. As long as the foreign national has not legally entered the territory of the People's Republic of China, the application of legal remedies is very limited. Hence, against the prohibition to enter China,

---

although his partial identification of exit restrictions as administrative punishment is problematic.

no legal remedies can be applied.[105] This view is supported by official interpretations that regard decisions to deny entry as 'acts of state' and explain that most countries in the world do not allow for legal remedies against the prohibition to enter the country as a country has no general duty to allow foreign nationals to enter.[106]

3. Restrictions of Entry and Exit in the Context of International Standards

Having analysed the legal framework covering the (non-)issuance and revocation of exit–entry documents as well as the restriction of exit or entry, I will now evaluate this framework in the context of international standards. As the access to legal remedies is limited in the context of visa (non-)issuance or denial of entry and since restrictions of exit may be applied not only on grounds of pending criminal cases but also on grounds of pending civil lawsuits, the question arises whether such practice is in line with international law.[107] As a fundamental principle, a state is responsible for the protection of its nationals and their basic rights.[108] The right to leave a country, the right to enjoy asylum as well as the right of freedom from torture are important mechanisms to preserve basic rights in the context of migration. Although no right exists to enter a country, a state may be obliged to accept the entry of foreign nationals or stateless people in certain circumstances due to the right to enjoy asylum. Furthermore, a state may only expel or return a foreign national to another state if certain preconditions are met.

While the right to leave is explicitly protected by international law as will be discussed below, there is no general right to enter a country laid down in international law, except for the case where this country is the country of origin or in the case of application for asylum. While states shall abide by the principle of non-discrimination when defining who may or may not

105 *Interpretation of the 'Exit–Entry Administration Law of the People's Republic of China'* (《中华人民共和国出境入境管理法》释义) (2012), p. 94. The author of this study was not able to find court decisions regarding a prohibition to enter the Chinese territory based on the current legal framework, which supports the notion that legal remedies are not available or at least not feasible in practice.

106 *Guide to Interpretation and Application of the 'Exit–Entry Administration Law of the People's Republic of China'* (《中华人民共和国出境入境管理法》释义及实用指南) (2012), p. 83.

107 Limitations on access to legal remedies in the context of deportation in an international comparison will be discussed in section 2. on page 267.

108 Shearer / Opeskin (2012), p. 94 f.

enter, there is wide discretionary authority on the classification of different types of migrants, on the relevant conditions for being granted admission, or on the range of exclusionary grounds.[109] Typically, the duration of stay is limited and restrictions are imposed on employment, residence etc. Despite the provisions of the *International Covenant on Civil and Political Rights (ICCPR)* stating that the right to liberty of the person may only be restricted on the basis of a law and when necessary to protect national security, public order, public health or morals or the rights and freedoms of others,[110] most countries interpret the constraint of public security quite widely, especially against the background of the fight against terrorism.[111] States frequently refer to the legitimacy of keeping a distinction between nationals and non-nationals in terms of their legal treatment because this distinction serves a legitimate state objective.[112] This is indeed a basic premise of international human rights law[113] used by some states as excuse for discrimination.

As foreign nationals in general do not possess the right to enter a country, there is also no right of foreign nationals to be granted a visa or a residence permit or to full access to the labour market.[114] Even the *International Convention on the Protection of the Rights of All Migrant Workers and Members of Their Families (ICRMW)*, which is relatively generous in granting rights to migrant workers when compared with other international treaties, allows the state to restrict the access of migrant workers to "limited categories of employment", while this provision only applies to documented migrant workers.[115] Thus, international law cannot easily be said to be viol-

---

109 Perruchoud (2012), p. 131 f.

110 Art. 12(3) *ICCPR* (1966) states that "[t]he above-mentioned rights [i. e. the right to life, the right to liberty and security of person etc.] shall not be subject to any restrictions except those provided by law, that are necessary to protect national security, public order (*ordre public*), public health or morals or the rights and freedoms of others, and that are consistent with the other rights recognized in the present Covenant."

111 Perruchoud (2012), p. 134.

112 E. g. when courts in the U. S. quote the 'doctrine of consular non-reviewabilty' that denies foreign nationals access to legal remedies against decisions of consular officers; Saito (2003).

113 Weissbrodt (2008), p. 45.

114 The ILO *Discrimination (Employment and Occupation) Convention* (1958) being the most relevant treaty in this regard and which China ratified in 2006, only covers the protection of rights of documented migrant workers, which implies that another authority may decide upon the legal status of migrant workers.

115 Art. 52(2)a, b *ICRMW* (1990). China is not signatory to the *ICRMW*, but being a multilateral convention adopted by the United Nations General Assembly, the

ated when Chinese authorities deny a relevant application by not issuing a permit or licence concerning residence or employment, and not even when the reason for decisions not to issue, replace, or extend legal documents such as visa or residence permits as well as the reason for the denial of entry are not explained to the applicant and legal remedies are not applicable. However, without access to legal remedies the foreign national is prevented from contesting infringements of the non-discrimination rule as provided for in Article 2 *ICCPR* and in the *International Convention on the Elimination of All Forms of Racial Discrimination*.[116]

On the other hand, a state may be obliged to allow an individual to enter the country in certain circumstances or at least not to expel or return this person to a specific country due to the right to enjoy asylum and the right of freedom from torture. Article 14 of the *Universal Declaration of Human Rights (UDHR)* defines the "right to seek and to enjoy in other countries asylum from persecution"[117] but limits this right to cases of prosecution that are of political nature and in line with the "purposes and principles of the United Nations"[118]. While the provisions laid down in the *UDHR* have no binding force, China is party to the 1951 *Convention Relating to the Status of Refugees* and the relevant 1967 *Protocol* that lay down more concrete provisions regarding the right to enjoy asylum.[119]

In this context, a certain protection from being expelled or returned is derived from the right of freedom from torture.[120] The so-called *non-refoulement* rule, first laid down in the *Convention Relating to the Status of Refugees*, prohibits states from repatriating foreign nationals if this would result in a threat to his or her life by stating that

> [n]o Contracting State shall expel or return ('refouler') a refugee in any manner whatsoever to the frontiers of territories where his [or her] life or freedom would be

---

ICRMW can be regarded as having exemplary character. States in general reserve the 'sovereign prerogative' to decide upon the access to employment of foreign nationals; Cholewinski (2012), p. 283.

116 Saito (2003), p. 34 f. Saito (2003) illustrates this problem with the 'doctrine of consular non-reviewability' applied by U. S. courts.

117 Art. 14(1) *UDHR* (1948).

118 Art. 14(2) *UDHR* (1948).

119 While the prohibition of torture has been acknowledged as *ius cogens*, i. e. a peremptory norm of international law, it is disputed whether the *non-refoulement* rule that derives from this prohibition also can be regarded as *ius cogens*; Opeskin / Perruchoud / Redpath-Cross (2012), p. 80 f.

120 Perruchoud (2012), p. 134.

> threatened on account of his race, religion, nationality, membership of a particular social group or political opinion.[121]

This rule, however, may be suspended if the refugee in question poses a "danger to the security of the country" or "to the community", the latter presupposing that he or she has been sentenced in a particularly serious criminal case.[122] The principle of *non-refoulement* is also codified in other treaties such as the *Convention against Torture and Other Cruel, Inhuman or Degrading Treatment or Punishment* or the *ICCPR*.[123]

The Chinese *Constitution* (1982) as well as the *Exit–Entry Administration Law* (2012) provide the legal framework for asylum.[124] However, a comprehensive law on asylum has not yet been promulgated and there is no other legal regulation that assigns the task of handling of refugees to a competent authority nor is there any other provision regarding concrete procedures of handling applications for asylum. The UNHCR Beijing Office is mainly responsible for handling refugee claims and determines the refugee status, which is then recognised by the Chinese state.[125] Of major concern in the context of refugee issues is the fact that the Chinese government rejects the recognition of certain refugees, especially nationals of the Democratic People's Republic of Korea (North Korea).[126] As China is bound to the *non-refoulement* rule as laid out above, it must not return individuals to a country where these individuals are likely to be subjected to torture or other inhuman treatment. North Korea is reported to treat individuals who illegally exit the country as defectors subject to criminal law[127] and to inhumane treatment in prison camps,[128] which asks for the application of the *non-refoulement* rule. Even if a North Korean national indeed fled their country of origin in search of a food supply, which would classify them as an economic migrant, they should be regarded as a refugee *sur place*, because their illegal exit will

---

121 Art. 33(1) *Convention Relating to the Status of Refugees* (1951).

122 Art. 33(2) *Convention Relating to the Status of Refugees* (1951).

123 Art. 3 *Convention against Torture and Other Cruel, Inhuman or Degrading Treatment or Punishment* (1984); Art. 7 *ICCPR* (1966).

124 Art. 32 *Constitution* (1982); Art. 46 *Exit–Entry Administration Law* (2012).

125 Lili Song (2018), p. 149.

126 Lili Song (2018), p. 143; Chan / Schloenhardt (2007), p. 227 f. In the *Yanbian Theft and Robbery Case* (2017), a national of the Democratic People's Republic of Korea was repatriated by the provincial public security bureau due to illegal entry and illegal stay.

127 Art. 62 *Criminal Code of the Democratic People's Republic of Korea* (2009).

128 Economic and Social Council (2004), p. 48; Human Rights Committee (2001), p. 4.

be persecuted in their home country.[129] In this context, it is very problematic that North Korean nationals who illegally entered China are reportedly denied access to the UNHCR Office.[130]

In the context of international law, the right to leave and return is codified in the *International Covenant on Civil and Political Rights (ICCPR)* in Article 12,[131] and in Article 8 of the *International Convention on the Protection of the Rights of All Migrant Workers and Members of Their Families (ICRMW)*. The codification of this right is based on relevant provisions laid down in the *Universal Declaration of Human Rights (UDHR)*, which has no binding force by itself, but still serves as the basis for provisions in several international treaties. Article 13 *UDHR* defines the "right to freedom of movement and residence within the borders of each State"[132] and the "right to leave any country […] and to return to his country"[133]. The expression 'his country' obviously refers to the country of nationality of the concerned person.

Although enshrined in different international treaties, the right to leave may be subject to certain restrictions, while the state shall not impose such restrictions arbitrarily.[134] The right to leave a country may only be restricted on the basis of a law and when necessary to protect national security or public order, public health or morals or the rights and freedoms of others.[135] The interpretation of national and public security by states is as loose as it is in the context of entry administration, and it may even result in the prohibition of a national to leave the country.[136] Apart from possible terrorist attacks, reasons for restricting exit may also embrace the evasion of justice or tax paying.[137] To be in line with the provisions of the *ICCPR*, restrictions have to be based on precise and narrow legal grounds, be necessary, and appropriate. They further should impair other rights as little as possible and only be used as last resort.[138]

---

129 Chan / Schloenhardt (2007), p. 225, 226.
130 Chan / Schloenhardt (2007), p. 222; Committee on Economic, Social and Cultural Rights (2005), p. 2 f.
131 Liu Guofu (2006), p. 12.
132 Art. 13(1) *UDHR* (1948).
133 Art. 13(2) *UDHR* (1948).
134 Perruchoud (2012), p. 137.
135 Art. 12(3) *ICCPR* (1966).
136 Perruchoud (2012), p. 137.
137 Perruchoud (2012), p. 138.
138 Perruchoud (2012), p. 138.

The practice described above to prevent foreign nationals from exiting the country on grounds of a pending civil case or on the basis of a court decision in the context of a civil case may contradict international standards if it is not based on this principle of minimum impairment of rights. According to the *Exit–Entry Administration Law* (2012), foreign nationals may not exit the country if a court has decided upon an exit restriction due to a pending civil case.[139] Furthermore, even after the court has made its final decision, exit may be restricted in order to enforce the court decision. Decisions upon exit restrictions will be handled by the court upon application by the plaintiff which should be examined by the courts before approval. Hence, the courts should apply exit restrictions on foreign nationals only as last resort to impair the personal freedom of foreign nationals as little as possible. Literature even argues that exit restrictions do not safeguard the asset in dispute directly, but instead infringe on the right of the individual to free movement and it is hence debatable whether the use of such a means in civil cases in general is in line with international standards.[140] However, an unsecured liability towards a private creditor may well constitute a legitimate reason to implement an exit restriction as a decision of the European Court of Human Rights has shown.[141]

Exit restrictions on foreign nationals who are involved in a civil case in China are imposed on the basis of a legal provision, namely Article 12 *Exit–Entry Administration Law* (2012). The question arises whether they are necessary in a specific case to protect the rights of others which could be argued to be an adequate reason to apply exit restrictions. In this context, the imposition of exit restrictions on grounds of a pending civil case or on the basis of a court decision in the context of a civil case may be in line with international standards only as long as they are applied as last resort and if no other compulsory measure like freezing of bank accounts or compulsory collection can be applied. According to the *SPC Minutes of the Second Meeting on National Foreign Related Commercial and Maritime Adjudication Work (Second Meeting Minutes)* (2005) and the *SPC Guiding Opinions on Foreign-Related Civil and Commercial Cases* (2010), exit restrictions

---

139 Art. 46 *Exit–Entry Administration Law* (2012).

140 Du Wanbian (2013).

141 In the relevant case, the court viewed that an exit restriction in order to "guarantee the interests of [private] creditors" is a "legitimate aim" to protect the rights of others; *Gochev v. Bulgaria* (2009), p. 8. This case was based on Article 2 of *Protocol No. 4 to the European Convention on Human Rights* (1963), of which the contents of are almost identical to those of Article 12 *ICCPR* (1966).

should only be applied with utmost caution, which implies an application only as last resort.[142] However, in a series of court cases, exit restrictions were issued already when the plaintiff was able to prove the existence of an unsettled civil case and applied for an exit restriction "according to the legal provisions".[143] This suggests that courts rather examine formal requirements of the applications. Other academic analyses found that exit restrictions were partly applied together with other preventative measures, which runs counter the premise of applying exit restrictions only as a last resort.[144]

I conclude that the imposition of exit restrictions does not necessarily contradict international standards, not even in the context of civil litigation. However, especially in the context of civil litigation, restrictions should be used as last resort and in a manner that balances the rights of the foreign national with those of the state or the other party. Although the legal framework at least urges Chinese courts to apply exit restrictions in such a cautious way, court practice suggests that a necessary substantive examination of the circumstances is not always conducted, which can eventually lead to restrictions that are not in line with international standards.

III. Prosecution of Administrative and Criminal Offences Concerning Illegal Border Crossing

A clarification of the scope of legal remedies a foreign national may use against the restriction of his or her entry or exit as well as related punishments requires an analysis of the cases in which illegal entry (or exit) is considered an administrative offence and when it is considered a crime. To this end, I investigate the legal framework regarding administrative and criminal punishment and analyse the definition of illegal entry and exit according to the old legal framework as well as to the revised legal provisions of the *Exit–Entry Administration Law* (2012). Finally, these analyses allow a delineation between criminal and administrative offences. Furthermore, this

---

142 Art. 93(2) *SPC Second Meeting Minutes* (2005); Art. 7 *Foreign-Related Civil Cases Guiding Opinions* (2010). See as well the speech of Liu Guixiang, then President of the Fourth Division of the Supreme People's Court Civil Adjudication Court; Liu Guixiang (2011).

143 *Decision on Restricting Exit* (2009); *Decision on Restricting Exit* (2014 a); *Decision on Restricting Exit* (2014 b); *Decision on Restricting Exit* (2015).

144 Du Yixing (2012), p. 82 f.

section aims to evaluate the severity of these sanctions by comparing them with sanctions in other jurisdictions.

While other provisions regarding exit–entry administration are mainly covered by the framework of administrative law, illegal border crossing may also be subject to criminal punishment. Apart from the relevant articles of the *Exit–Entry Administration Law* (2012) discussed above, provisions concerning illegal exit or entry can be found in the *Criminal Law* (2015),[145] but also in the *Regulations on Exit and Entry Border Inspection* (1995), and the *Public Security Administration Punishments Law* (2012). The latter defines the punishment for secretly crossing the national border and for providing the requirements for secretly crossing the national border,[146] as well as the assistance of others in organising[147] or transporting others[148] secretly across the national border.[149] Assistance in illegal exit or entry committed by individuals or legal entities is equally fined according to the provisions of the *Exit–Entry Administration Law* (2012).[150]

Furthermore, The *Regulations on Exit and Entry Border Inspection* (1995) define special penalties the border inspection officials may impose. According to these regulations, individuals entering or leaving the country without legal documents as well as individuals using invalid, third-party, forged or altered documents shall be punished with a fine of RMB 500 to 2 000 or with detention according to the relevant laws and regulations.[151] The assistance to illegally enter or exit the country shall be punished with a fine of RMB 2 000 to 10 000 if this activity does not constitute a crime, and any illegally earned profits shall be confiscated.[152] Apart from being imposed an administrative punishment, foreign nationals who try to enter China without valid documents will be denied entry to the country.[153]

145 The provisions in the *Criminal Law* have remained unchanged since 1997, except for a punishment of detention for one to three years with additional fine for illegally crossing the border for the purpose of joining a terrorist organisation, receiving training on terrorist activities or conducting terrorist activities that was added to Art. 322 in 2015.
146 Art. 62 *Public Security Administration Punishments Law* (2012).
147 Chinese: 协助组织.
148 Chinese: 运送他人.
149 Art. 61 *Public Security Administration Punishments Law* (2012).
150 Art. 72 *Exit–Entry Administration Law* (2012).
151 Art. 32 *Exit–Entry Border Inspection Regulations* (1995).
152 Art. 33 *Exit–Entry Border Inspection Regulations* (1995).
153 Art. 25 *Exit–Entry Administration Law* (2012).

1. Administrative Punishment and Criminal Punishment in the Context of Offences Regarding Border Crossing

Section 3 of Chapter VI of the *Criminal Law* (2015) partly described above and comprising Articles 318 to 323, is directly associated with exit–entry administration and titled "Crimes Against the Control of the National Border (Frontier)" (*fanghai guo(bian)jing guanli zui*[154]). The relevant penalties range from fines, confiscation of property, and criminal detention, up to fixed-term and even life imprisonment. Apart from the criminal offences described above, no other criminal offences are defined in the context of exit–entry administration. As will be shown below in more detail, criminal penalties apply mostly to relatively serious offences whereas administrative punishment applies to similar, but less serious offences. One example is the crime of illegal border crossing and the administrative offence of illegal exit or entry illustrated below. A central characteristic of Chinese immigration law hence is that only relatively severe illegal actions are deemed crimes, while most illegal actions, such as visa overstay, illegal employment, failure to register etc., are considered administrative offences.

Although administrative penalties and criminal penalties both often punish similar illegal actions, they are systematically different. Administrative penalties can be imposed by administrative organs (including organisations that are granted such privilege by law), while criminal penalties are imposed by courts as a result of a criminal proceeding. Administrative penalties belong to the realm of administrative law and are codified in several different laws, the *Administrative Penalty Law* codifying the most general provisions in this context, while criminal punishments are only codified in the *Criminal Law*. Despite the fact that an illegal action that constitutes a crime may be regarded, at the same time, as an administrative offence,[155] the *Administrative Penalty Law* (2009) states that crimes shall not additionally be prosecuted according to administrative law.[156]

From the provisions of the *Administrative Penalty Law* (2009), the following fundamental rules applicable for administrative penalties can be deduced: Administrative penalties can only be imposed by Chinese administrative organs in compliance with the *Administrative Penalty Law* and they can be imposed on Chinese or foreign nationals, on legal persons or other

154 Chinese: 妨害国（边）境管理罪.
155 Fang / Shi (2011), p. 213.
156 Art. 7 *Administrative Penalty Law* (2009).

organisations. The prerequisite for the imposition of an administrative penalty is that the action of the person in question has violated legal provisions and that this action does not constitute a crime. The aim of administrative penalties is to impel the person in question to understand and correct his or her fault via the means of sanctions.[157] Typically, criminal punishment will be imposed on relatively severe offences and the relevant sanctions are also higher than those of administrative punishment.[158]

a) Punishment Based on Criminal Law

Criminal punishment can only be imposed on the basis of a court decision. If the public security organs or the procuratorate identify a certain action as fulfilling the prerequisites of a crime, they shall file a case for investigation according to the *Criminal Litigation Law* (2012).[159] In fact, according to Article 22 *Administrative Penalty Law* (2009), any administrative organ should transfer the relevant case to a judicial organ if an illegal act constitutes a crime. The relevant public security organs have some degree of discretion in deciding whether to file a case for investigation, although the procuratorate may order the public security organs to file the case if it deems that the case should be filed for investigation. However, the procuratorate shall request the relevant public security organs to state the reasons for not filing the case.[160] The fact that the decision whether a certain action constitutes a crime or not lies with the court implies that the police should always hand over a case to a court if it is unclear whether it should be handled as administrative or criminal case, and that the court then either handles it according to criminal litigation or rejects it and hands it back to the police.

In the investigation stage of the file, the public security organs—i. e. the criminal investigation branch of the police or, in case of exit–entry administration, the exit–entry administration branch as well—investigate the circumstances of the case by collecting evidence.[161] During this stage of the case, a criminal suspect may be detained if he or she fulfils the relevant conditions.[162] The investigation stage of the case shall not exceed two months,

157 Xing et al. (2016), p. 163.
158 Ying (2012), p. 21.
159 Art. 107 *Criminal Litigation Law* (2012).
160 Art. 111 *Criminal Litigation Law* (2012).
161 Art. 18 *Criminal Litigation Law* (2012).
162 Art. 113 *Criminal Litigation Law* (2012).

but it may be extended with the approval of the procuratorate of the next higher level.[163] The procuratorate will take over the file from the public security organs and decide upon bringing an action in the relevant criminal court after examination of the case. The final decision whether or not an act constitutes a crime according to the *Criminal Law* (2015) lies with the courts. Against the judgement or order of the first instance made by the court, the defendant may appeal orally or in writing at the court at the next higher level.[164] The judgement of the court of the second instance is the final judgement of this case.[165] If no appeal or protest has been filed within the prescribed time limit against the court judgement (ten days) or against the court order (five days), the judgement or order becomes final. Administrative acts conducted by the public security or national security authorities that are explicitly authorised to conduct these administrative acts by provisions of the *Criminal Litigation Law* (2012) or administrative acts that aim to enforce a final court judgement or court order—unless these administrative acts are conducted illegally or in a way that transgresses the limits of enforcement—cannot be challenged using administrative litigation.[166]

If the public security organs decide that the relevant offence does not constitute a crime, they may punish it according to the *Administrative Penalty Law* (2009) and the *Public Security Administration Punishments Law* (2012) as described below. Unless a specific provision states otherwise, against a decision on administrative punishment made by a public security organ, the individual concerned may apply for administrative reconsideration or administrative litigation as described in the previous part concerning legal remedies against the non-issuance of exit–entry documents.

b) Legal Framework on Administrative Penalties

Most offences codified in the *Exit–Entry Administration Law* (2012) are administrative offences that are to be punished according to the regulations of the *Public Security Administration Punishments Law* (2012) that codifies administrative punishment imposed by the public security organs and which again is based on the *Administrative Penalty Law* (2009) that codifies administrative punishment in the most basic manner and serves as *lex generalis* to

163 Art. 154, 156–158 *Criminal Litigation Law* (2012).
164 Art. 216 *Criminal Litigation Law* (2012).
165 Art. 233 *Criminal Litigation Law* (2012).
166 Art. 1(1)i, vii *Administrative Litigation Law Interpretations* (2018).

the *Public Security Administration Punishments Law* (2012).[167] The provisions in the *Exit–Entry Administration Law* (2012) that codify any form of administrative punishment shall be in line with the provisions of these two laws. Where the *Exit–Entry Administration Law* (2012) does not specify a provision, the relevant provisions of the *Public Security Administration Punishments Law* (2012) and the *Administrative Penalty Law* (2009) will apply.

As it lays out the most basic framework for administrative punishment, I will first look into the provisions of the *Administrative Penalty Law* (2009). The *Administrative Penalty Law* (2009) defines as administrative penalties[168] disciplinary warnings, fines, seizure of illegal gains or confiscation of unlawful property or valuables, order to suspend production or business operations, temporary suspension or revocation of a permit or license, as well as administrative detention.[169] According to Article 9, other administrative penalties involving the restriction of personal freedom shall only be created by law.[170] Furthermore, according to Article 16 *Administrative Penalty Law* (2009), only public security organs may impose administrative penalties involving the restriction of personal freedom. According to Article 30 *Administrative Penalty Law* (2009), administrative penalties shall only be imposed if the circumstances are clear. Before deciding on the administrative penalty, the concerned parties shall be informed of the facts and reasons as well as of their rights.[171]

If the administrative penalty consists of a fine of not more than RMB 50 (RMB 1 000 if the concerned party is a legal person or organisation) or of a warning, a simplified on-the-spot procedure may be applied.[172] In any other case, an ordinary procedure has to be carried out.[173] Decisions of either punishment procedure may be subject to administrative reconsideration or administrative litigation.[174] An ordinary procedure starts with an investigation carried out by the relevant administrative organs conducting inspection and collecting evidence.[175] After this investigation, a decision has to be made by the relevant administrative organ whether to impose an administrative

---

167 Art. 3 *Public Security Administration Punishments Law* (2012).
168 Chinese: 行政处罚.
169 Art. 8 *Administrative Penalty Law* (2009).
170 See above footnote 77.
171 Art. 31 *Administrative Penalty Law* (2009).
172 Art. 33 *Administrative Penalty Law* (2009).
173 Art. 36 *Administrative Penalty Law* (2009).
174 Art. 35, 45 *Administrative Penalty Law* (2009).
175 Art. 36, 37 *Administrative Penalty Law* (2009).

penalty or not, and whether the action should be handled as a criminal case by a court.[176] If the administrative penalty to be decided upon involves an order for production or business suspension, the suspension or revocation of a permit or a license, or the imposition of a "comparatively high fine"[177] the party shall be notified that they have a right to request a hearing without having to pay the expenses.[178] After this hearing, the relevant administrative organ shall decide upon imposing an administrative penalty.[179] When the decision to impose an administrative penalty is made, a notification has to be issued to the relevant parties.[180]

After the decision to impose an administrative penalty has been made, the concerned party shall comply with it within the time limit indicated in the decision.[181] If the concerned party does not comply with the administrative penalty, compulsory measures may be imposed, like additional fines, the auction of seized or frozen property, or the transfer of frozen deposits.[182] The administrative authority may apply to a court for compulsory enforcement.[183] In most cases, however, the public security organs possess administrative enforcement power and are hence not dependent on a court decision in this regard. While defining different administrative penalties and codifying the process of punishment and legal remedy, the *Administrative Penalty Law* (2009) does not codify penalties for specific offences. It rather serves as *lex generalis* to other more specific laws in administrative legislation like the *Public Security Administration Punishments Law* (2012), which I will look at in the following.

The *Public Security Administration Punishments Law* (2012) defines as public security administration punishments[184] a warning, a fine, administrative detention, revocation of a license issued by a public security organ, as well as setting a time limit for exiting China (order to leave) or deport-

176 Art. 38 *Administrative Penalty Law* (2009).
177 Chinese: 较大额罚款. The *Public Security Administration Punishments Law* (2012) has a similar provision stating that the offender shall be informed of his or her rights if the fine amounts to RMB 2000 or more; Art. 98 *Public Security Administration Punishments Law* (2012).
178 Art. 42(1) *Administrative Penalty Law* (2009).
179 Art. 43 *Administrative Penalty Law* (2009).
180 Art. 39, 40 *Administrative Penalty Law* (2009).
181 Art. 44 *Administrative Penalty Law* (2009).
182 Art. 51(1)i, ii *Administrative Penalty Law* (2009).
183 Art. 51(1)iii *Administrative Penalty Law* (2009).
184 Chinese: 治安管理处罚.

ation as additional penalty.[185] The public security administration punishments defined in the 2012 law are the same as those in the original version of the law of 2005. As the authorities headed by the Ministry of Public Security are responsible for enforcement in the context of exit–entry administration, the provisions of the *Public Security Administration Punishments Law* (2012) apply to virtually all punishments imposed in this area.

According to Article 79 *Public Security Administration Punishments Law* (2012), public security organs conduct an investigation to gather evidence. The public security organs may summon individuals who have violated public security administration for investigation upon approval of the person in charge of the public security organ.[186] The reasons for summoning shall be explained to the individual being summoned.[187] If an interrogation takes place it shall not exceed eight hours (twenty-four hours if the circumstances are serious).[188] The transcript of the interrogation shall be presented to the respondent for verification.[189] Transcripts subject to corresponding verification shall also be made of searches of places, articles, or persons involved.[190] The public security organs may confiscate goods to be used as evidence. However, no property lawfully obtained shall be subject to confiscation.[191]

Public security punishments shall be decided upon by a public security organ at county level or above. The decision may be made without a statement by the offender if there is sufficient evidence to prove the facts, but not solely on the basis of a statement of the suspect.[192] A warning or fine less than RMB 500 may be decided upon by local police stations.[193] In contrast to the *Administrative Penalty Law* (2009), the *Public Security Administration Punishments Law* (2012) states that decisions on warnings or fines not exceeding RMB 200 may be made on the spot by an official of the people's police.[194] The differing relevant provision of the *Administrative Penalty Law* (2009) stating that on-the-spot decisions may only be made on warnings or fines not higher than RMB 50[195] suggests that decisions on fines

185 Art. 10 *Public Security Administration Punishments Law* (2012).
186 Art. 82(1) *Public Security Administration Punishments Law* (2012).
187 Art. 82(2) *Public Security Administration Punishments Law* (2012).
188 Art. 83 *Public Security Administration Punishments Law* (2012).
189 Art. 84 *Public Security Administration Punishments Law* (2012).
190 Art. 87, 88 *Public Security Administration Punishments Law* (2012).
191 Art. 89 *Public Security Administration Punishments Law* (2012).
192 Art. 93 *Public Security Administration Punishments Law* (2012).
193 Art. 91 *Public Security Administration Punishments Law* (2012).
194 Art. 100, 101 *Public Security Administration Punishments Law* (2012).
195 Art. 33 *Administrative Penalty Law* (2009).

between RMB 50 and 200 may only be made on the spot by the police while warnings and fines below RMB 50 may also be made by other authorities on the spot. The offender shall be informed of the decision on the public security punishment, of the grounds and reasons as well as of his or her right to make statements and defend himself.[196] Before making a decision upon revoking a licence or imposing a fine of RMB 2 000 or more, the offender has to be notified of the right to request a hearing.[197] In this regard, the *Public Security Administration Punishments Law* (2012) elaborates on the provisions of the *Administrative Penalty Law* (2009) that requires such notification when a "comparatively high fine" is imposed. The public security organ shall issue its decision in written form and inform the offender of the fact that this decision may be subject to administrative reconsideration and administrative litigation.[198] If the offender applies for administrative reconsideration or administrative litigation he or she may file an application for the suspension of enforcement of administrative detention. However, administrative detention may only be suspended if the public security organs decide that the suspension will not result in any danger, or that another individual meets the requirements of being a guarantor or that the offender pays a bail of RMB 200 per day.[199]

2. Definition of Illegal Exit or Entry

The obsolete *Foreign Nationals Exit-Entry Administration Law* of 1985 only provided for the terms 'illegal entry' (*feifa rujing*[200]) and 'illegal exit' (*feifa chujing*[201]) in its Article 29(1), which was virtually the only provision to define penalties in the law at all. No detailed definition of the terms 'illegal entry' or 'illegal exit' was given in the law nor in the 2010 *Foreign Nationals Exit-Entry Administration Law Implementation Rules* that, however, established punishments for illegal exit or entry.[202] As a proper definition was

196 Art. 94 *Public Security Administration Punishments Law* (2012).
197 Art. 98 *Public Security Administration Punishments Law* (2012).
198 Art. 96(1) *Public Security Administration Punishments Law* (2012).
199 Art. 107, 108, 109 *Public Security Administration Punishments Law* (2012).
200 Chinese: 非法入境.
201 Chinese: 非法出境.
202 Art. 40 *Foreign Nationals Exit–Entry Administration Law Implementation Rules* (2010).

missing, every action that went counter to the provisions in the law and the relevant regulations could be deemed as illegal and thus punishable.

Assuming that entering or exiting China in contravention of the legal regulations was deemed illegal, illegal entry (or exit) mainly denoted exit or entry without a valid exit–entry document or entry against the decision of a border administration authority to prohibit the entry according to Article 7 *Foreign Nationals Exit-Entry Administration Law Implementation Rules* (1986). The term 'illegal exit or entry' did not appear as such in the *Foreign Nationals Exit-Entry Administration Law Implementation Rules* (1986), but I assume that the formulation "foreign nationals who illegally enter or exit China" as stated in Article 40 *Foreign Nationals Exit-Entry Administration Law Implementation Rules* (1986) meant to comprise the definition of 'illegal entry' of foreign nationals. The definition of the *Foreign Nationals Exit-Entry Administration Law Implementation Rules* (1986) of certain groups of foreign nationals who may be denied entry to the country suggests that the entry of these groups of foreign nationals should also be considered illegal. According to the old legal framework, foreign nationals could be denied entry to the country when a re-entry ban was still in force, if they suffered from mental disorders or infectious diseases, or if they lacked financial means for self-supply.[203] Further, the suspicion that the individual might commit acts of terrorism, subversion, violence, smuggling, gambling, prostitution, or other activities that may endanger the national security could result in the prevention of entry.[204]

According to Article 71 of the revised *Exit-Entry Administration Law* (2012), "illegal exit or entry" (*feifa chujing rujing*[205])—although not explicitly defined as legal term—primarily denotes exit or entry with a forged, falsified or fraudulently obtained (e. g. by providing wrong statements in the visa application) exit–entry document (visa), or exit or entry with an exit–entry document of someone else. The provision further punishes "otherwise illegal" exit or entry, which obviously covers other ways of exiting or entering the country in an irregular way (e. g. without any required documents at all[206] or against the decision of the relevant authorities). 'Entry' is defined

203 Art. 7 *Foreign Nationals Exit–Entry Administration Law Implementation Rules* (2010); see as well Item 410 *Offences Definitions* (2010).

204 Art. 7(1)vi *Foreign Nationals Exit–Entry Administration Law Implementation Rules* (2010).

205 Chinese: 非法出境入境.

206 *Interpretation of the 'Exit–Entry Administration Law of the People's Republic of China'* (《中华人民共和国出境入境管理法》释义) (2012), p. 206.

as travel from any other country or region, including Hong Kong, Macau and Taiwan, to Chinese mainland.[207] 'Exit', hence, depicts leaving Chinese mainland.

According to the *Administrative Licence Law* (2003), administrative organs that issue an administrative licence shall not change this administrative licence once it has come into effect.[208] This implies that a foreign national may rely on the validity of exit–entry documents properly issued by the competent authorities. Thus, once the foreign national has entered the country holding a valid visa that he or she has not obtained fraudulently, the entry should not be considered illegal in the future. This does not mean, however, that invalid visas lose their invalidity only because the foreign national has successfully passed border inspection. In case the application and examination procedure of a visa retrospectively emerges as incorrect, the police may cancel the visa and order the foreign national to leave the country. Court cases illustrate that a fine or detention due to 'illegal entry' can also be imposed after the entry has taken place. One example case reports that a Vietnamese national was fined due to 'illegal entry' after he had managed to enter the country and only later was found to have entered illegally, i. e. without a valid visa, during a routine check.[209] A foreign national who has entered in a regular way with a valid visa and who later conducts activities for which he or she does not hold valid (entry) documents, should not be punished on grounds of his or her 'illegal entry' as the entry itself was not illegal. Rather, the authorities should argue that the activities of the foreign national are "inconsistent with his or her cause of stay" as stated on the visa as provided for in Article 81 *Exit-Entry Administration Law* (2012). The provisions of Article 81 will be described below in more detail.

Apart from cases where foreign nationals do not possess and produce valid exit–entry documents upon entering China, individuals shall be prevented from entering the country if they are subject to an entry ban, if they have serious diseases, or if they are suspected of harm to national or public security.[210] Foreign nationals shall also be prevented from entering the country if they cannot prove sufficient funds for their stay, or if they are suspected of engaging in activities inconsistent with their visa.[211] Such circumstances may lead to a decision of the authorities to prohibit the foreign

---

207 Art. 89 *Exit–Entry Administration Law* (2012).
208 Art. 8(1) *Administrative Licence Law* (2003).
209 *Yinhai Border Crossing Case* (2014).
210 Art. 25 *Exit–Entry Administration Law* (2012).
211 Art. 25 *Exit–Entry Administration Law* (2012).

national from entering China. The examination of these preconditions shall be conducted either by the consulates or embassies before issuing the visa or by the border security authorities upon entry.[212]

3. Delineation of Criminal Offences Concerning Border Crossing

As some offences covered by the *Exit–Entry Administration Law* (2012) may also constitute a crime, the following part provides an analysis of the concerning acts by delimiting administrative offences from criminal actions. By doing this, it takes into account the findings of the previous parts. According to Article 2 *Public Security Administration Punishments Law* (2012), if an "act of disrupting the public order"[213] is "of social harmfulness"[214] and constitutes a crime as provided for in the *Criminal Law* (2015), it shall be prosecuted criminally. Likewise, Article 7 *Administrative Penalty Law* (2009) states that if an illegal act constitutes a crime, it shall be investigated and prosecuted according to criminal law and no administrative penalty shall be imposed. Thus, only if an act does not constitute a crime may an administrative penalty be imposed.

While, strictly speaking, the crime of illegally crossing the border e. g. should not be prosecuted as illegal entry according to the *Exit–Entry Administration Law* (2012), such criminal action will very likely be targeted in the context of the *sanfei* campaigns as well. As will be shown below in more detail, most offences are only to be punished criminally if they are relatively serious. Illegally crossing the border should, for example, only be punished as a crime if committed three or more times in a row. As the police may in a specific situation not immediately know whether the offence they currently persecute constitutes a crime or just an administrative offence—because they first have to verify the identity of the suspect and examine whether he or she crossed the border illegally in the past already—it is technically not feasible to exclude the persecution of crimes when targeting illegal entry as administrative offence in the context of a campaign.

212 However, practice reveals problems concerning the communication between the public security authorities and the consulates and embassies, which especially relates to entry bans imposed as a result of a repatriation by the police; see section 2. of chapter 2 on page 102.

213 Chinese: 扰乱公共秩序.

214 Chinese: 具有社会危害性.

a) Illegal Border Crossing

Offences regarding illegally crossing the border[215] may be punished according to very different legal provisions as relevant punishments are codified in the *Criminal Law* (2015), in the *Public Security Administration Punishments Law* (2012) as well as in the *Exit–Entry Administration Law* (2012). If the offence of illegally crossing the border (*touyue guo(bian)jing*[216]) constitutes a crime according to Article 322 *Criminal Law* (2015) it shall be punished accordingly. Illegally crossing the border in the sense of the *Criminal Law* (2015) is defined by Article 6 *Interpretations on Handling Criminal Cases Related to Border Obstruction* (2012) more concretely as crossing the border without or with forged, altered, or invalid exit–entry documents, as well as escaping border inspection, crossing the border using exit–entry documents of others, crossing the border under false pretences or under false identity, or crossing the border by other illegal means. While this definition is very similar to the definition in the *Exit–Entry Administration Law* (2012), only "serious circumstances"[217] are to be punished with fixed-term imprisonment, criminal detention, or public surveillance (*guanzhi*[218]) of not less than one year and additional fine according to the provision of Article 322 *Criminal Law* (2015). Apart from that, illegally crossing the border in order to take part in an terrorist organisation, undergo terrorist training, or carry out terrorist activities shall be punished with fixed-term imprisonment of one to three years and additional fine.[219] In general, an offence is typically only punishable as crime if the action is committed intentionally[220] and the

215 Chinese: 违反国（边）境管理法规，偷越国（边）境. The term *'guo(bian)jing'* is meant to consist of the two terms *'guojing'* and *'bianjing'*. While the term *'guojing'* depicts the national border to other states, the term *'bianjing'* depicts the border between mainland China and Hong Kong, Macau, Taiwan and disputed areas; Sun Jianbao (2011). Relevant criminal offences are hence applicable to any border crossing from mainland China to another administrative entity.

216 Chinese: 偷越国（边）境.

217 Chinese: 情节严重.

218 Chinese: 管制.

219 Art. 322 *Criminal Law* (2015).

220 This results from the provisions codified in Art. 14(2) and 15(2) *Criminal Law* (2015) that state that "[c]riminal responsibility shall be borne for intentional crimes" and that "[c]riminal responsibility is to be borne for negligent crimes only when the law so stipulates". Hence, negligence shall not be punished criminally unless explicitly stated in the relevant provision.

person is criminally liable. The attempt to commit a crime is punishable, although with lighter sanctions.[221]

In the academic debate whether or not intention is also a presupposition for an administrative offence to be punishable, there is consensus in the literature that 'three requirements'[222] have to be met—i. e. the existence of facts constituting the offence, the illegality of the offence, and the legal culpability—while intention as well as carelessness of the action already meet the condition of illegality of the offence.[223] This interpretation is supported by the fact that the *Public Security Administration Punishments Law* (2012) defines several offences where intention is explicitly required,[224] which suggests that in general intention is not a prerequisite for an offence to be punishable. The interpretation of the administrative offence of illegally crossing the border as defined in Article 62(2) of the *Public Security Administration Punishments Law* (2012) states that the action should always be considered intended.[225] Similarly, an official interpretation regarding the punishment of illegal stay considers the action always to be intended[226] and hence an administrative offence that shall be punished.[227] As for illegal exit or entry according to Article 71 *Exit–Entry Administration Law* (2012), the action is not generally considered to be intended, but negligence[228] suffices as prerequisite and the committed administrative offence shall be punished more lightly.[229]

The *Border Administration Crimes Note* (2000) defines which circumstances are to be considered as serious or very serious and hence criminally punishable in the sense of the provisions of the *Criminal Law* (2015).[230]

221 See e. g. *Pingxiang Border Crossing Case* (2017).
222 Chinese: 三要件.
223 E. g. Liu Xiaoyuan / Li Liangwan (2017), p. 54 f.; Ying (2012), p. 18.
224 Examples are Art. 25(1)i, 28, 29(1)iv, 35(1)ii, 43(1), 44, 49, 65(1)i, 116(1)iv *Public Security Administration Punishments Law* (2012).
225 Ke Liangdong (2014), p. 528.
226 I. e. the foreign nationals has to be "at fault" (Chinese: 过错).
227 *Guide to Interpretation and Application of the 'Exit–Entry Administration Law of the People's Republic of China'* (《中华人民共和国出境入境管理法》释义及实用指南) (2012), p. 186.
228 Chinese: 过失.
229 *Interpretation of the 'Exit–Entry Administration Law of the People's Republic of China'* (《中华人民共和国出境入境管理法》释义) (2012), p. 204 f. Note the contradiction to practical guidelines for the old law that state that intention is a prerequisite for the offence of illegally entering; Liu Jianchang / Li Xinglin (2012), p. 169.
230 Guofu Liu (2011), p. 120.

According to this circular, illegally crossing the border shall be considered serious if it has happened more than three times in a row despite repeated admonition, if it happens after the suspect committed illegal activities, if the suspect threatens or resorts to violence against officials when crossing the frontier, or if the action seriously affects foreign affairs and has a negative impact. Cases shall be considered very serious if the offence has the aim of escaping criminal persecution or of committing a crime like smuggling or trading drugs.[231] Because the *Border Administration Crimes Note* (2000) was issued by the Ministry of Public Security, however, the interpretations laid down in this document are not undisputed. Academics argue that the Ministry of Public Security transgresses its competence in interpreting legal documents, a task actually assigned to courts, while it is, at the same time, in charge of investigating criminal cases.[232] However, similar standards to denote serious circumstances in the sense of Article 322 *Criminal Law* (2015) have been issued also by the Supreme People's Court in the *Interpretations on Handling Criminal Cases Related to Border Obstruction* (2012).

The *Interpretations on Handling Criminal Cases Related to Border Obstruction* (2012) state that "serious circumstances" in the sense of Article 322 *Criminal Law* (2015) are established if activities damaging national interests have been conducted abroad, if the border has been crossed illegally three times or more or by three people or more who "form a gang",[233] if others are enticed or coerced to illegally cross the border, if the illegal border crossing is organised in collaboration with people or entities abroad, if the illegal border crossing happens within one year after an administrative penalty for illegally crossing the border was imposed, or in other serious circumstances.[234] While this interpretation defines some concrete circumstances where Article 322 *Criminal Law* (2015) shall be applied, the last item still leaves room for further interpretation by the courts. The *Provisions on the Trial of Cases Occuring in Maritime Areas* (2016) issued by the Supreme People's Court add that serious circumstances are also established *inter alia* when entering the territorial waters illegally and not leaving after being banished, or re-entering the territorial waters illegally after having been expelled, or entering the territorial waters within one year after having

231 Art. 1(6) *Border Administration Crimes Note* (2000).

232 Jiang Jianyun (2013), p. 72 f.

233 The expression 'forming a gang' (Chinese: 结伙) suggests that the individuals acted on a common plan of action.

234 Art. 5 *Interpretations on Handling Criminal Cases Related to Border Obstruction* (2012).

been (administratively or criminally) sentenced for having entered the territorial waters illegally, or when illegally entering the territorial waters to engage in fishing activities and these activities do not constitute a crime in itself.[235]

In any case, only offences not covered by the *Criminal Law* (2015) shall be punished as administrative offence. According to Article 62(2) *Public Security Administration Punishments Law* (2012), illegally crossing the border[236] shall be punished with detention of not more than five days or a fine of not more than RMB 500. However, due to the principle of *lex specialis derogat legi generali*, the provisions of the *Exit–Entry Administration Law* (2012) shall take precedence. Article 71 *Exit–Entry Administration Law* (2012) defines the administrative offence of illegal exit or entry as well as evasion of the exit–entry inspection with a punishment of a fine between RMB 1 000 and 5 000 and again refers to "serious circumstances" not further defined where the offence shall be punished with detention of five to ten days and optional fine between RMB 2 000 and 10 000. The provisions regarding the administrative punishments of illegal entry can be applied already during border control, as illegal entry comprises deceiving border inspection officials in order to illegally enter.[237] Offences covered neither by the *Criminal Law* (2015) nor by the *Exit–Entry Administration Law* (2012) may still be punished according to the *Public Security Administration Punishments Law* (2012). However, as Article 71 *Exit–Entry Administration Law* (2012) also includes "crossing the border in other illegal manners", the delineation between the application of this provision and Article 62(2) *Public Security Administration Punishments Law* (2012) should be subject to more detailed interpretations e. g. by the courts.

b) Assistance in and Organisation of Illegal Border Crossing

The assistance in or organisation of illegal border crossing may be punished according to different legal provisions as well. The illegal issuance of application material (e. g. a letter of invitation), the assistance in evading inspection, and the illegal provision of exit or entry documents to foreign nationals illegally residing in China constitute separate administrative offences pun-

235 Art. 3 *Provisions on the Trial of Cases Occuring in Maritime Areas* (2016).

236 Chinese: 偷越国（边）境.

237 *Interpretation of the 'Exit–Entry Administration Law of the People's Republic of China'* (《中华人民共和国出境入境管理法》释义) (2012), p. 204.

ishable according to the *Exit–Entry Administration Law* (2012).[238] Apart from these specific forms of assistance in illegal border crossing, Article 72 *Exit–Entry Administration Law* (2012) more broadly covers the offence of "assisting others"[239] to illegally enter or exit the country, which is to be punished with a fine of RMB 2 000 to 10 000, or with detention of ten to fifteen days and a fine of RMB 5 000 to 20 000 in serious cases with the illegal income confiscated.[240] If the offence is committed by an entity, the persons directly in charge shall be prosecuted accordingly. The entity shall additionally be fined RMB 10 000 to 50 000, any illegal income confiscated.[241]

According to Article 79 *Exit–Entry Administration Law* (2012) the accommodation of illegally entered or residing foreign nationals, the assistance to evade inspection, or the illegal issuance of exit–entry documents shall be punished by a fine of RMB 2 000 to 10 000 or, if the circumstances are serious, RMB 5 000 to 20 000 or detention of five to fifteen days and confiscation of illegal income. An entity committing the above offence shall be punished by a fine of RMB 10 000 to 50 000, the directly responsible individuals shall be persecuted individually.[242]

Further, the illegal issuance of a letter of invitation or other application material shall be punished with a fine of RMB 5 000 to 10 000 or RMB 10 000 to 50 000 if the subject is an entity. The illegal income shall be confiscated and the subject shall assume the expenses for the repatriation of the illegally invited individual. If the subject is an entity, the directly responsible individuals shall be persecuted individually.[243] Additionally, the transport of individuals prohibited from entering or exiting China is punishable with a fine.[244]

While Article 79 *Exit–Entry Administration Law* (2012) covers the illegal provision of exit–entry documents to foreign nationals illegally residing in China, the offence of "assisting others to illegally enter or exit the country" as provided for in Article 72 covers the provision of falsified or modified exit–entry documents or other assistance in order to facilitate the illegal exit or entry.[245] The main focus of Article 79 *Exit–Entry Adminis-*

---

238 Art. 74, 79 *Exit–Entry Administration Law* (2012).
239 Chinese: 协助他人.
240 Art. 72(1) *Exit–Entry Administration Law* (2012).
241 Art. 72(2) *Exit–Entry Administration Law* (2012).
242 Art. 79 *Exit–Entry Administration Law* (2012).
243 Art. 74 *Exit–Entry Administration Law* (2012).
244 Art. 83(2) *Exit–Entry Administration Law* (2012).
245 *Interpretation of the 'Exit–Entry Administration Law of the People's Republic of China'* (《中华人民共和国出境入境管理法》释义) (2012), p. 206; *Guide to In-*

tration Law (2012) lies obviously on the assistance in evading inspection within the country[246] while Article 72 focuses on border crossing.[247] The *Public Security Administration Punishments Law* (2012) further states that "offering others prerequisites to illegally cross the border"[248] shall be punished with detention of five to ten days and an additional fine of RMB 500 to 2 000.[249] Assisting others in organising[250] or transporting others[251] illegally across the border shall be punished with detention of ten to fifteen days and additional fine of RMB 1 000 to 5 000.[252] In cases where the provisions of the *Exit–Entry Administration Law* (2012) do not apply and the activity does not constitute a crime, the provision of the *Public Security Administration Punishments Law* (2012) shall be applied.

According to Article 318 *Criminal Law* (2015), organising illegal border crossing[253] shall be punished with fixed-term imprisonment between two and seven years and additional fine. The fixed-term imprisonment may exceed seven years up to lifelong imprisonment in serious circumstances, i. e. if the offender is the leader of a group organising illegal border crossing, if the offence has happened repeatedly or a large number of individuals is involved in illegal border crossing, if the offence has caused serious injury or death or involves deprivation of personal freedom, if the offender resists inspection, if the sum of illegal earnings is considerably high, or if other particularly serious circumstances are involved.[254]

---

terpretation and Application of the 'Exit–Entry Administration Law of the People's Republic of China' (《中华人民共和国出境入境管理法》释义及实用指南) (2012), p. 173.

246 *Interpretation of the 'Exit–Entry Administration Law of the People's Republic of China'* (《中华人民共和国出境入境管理法》释义) (2012), p. 222 f.; *Guide to Interpretation and Application of the 'Exit–Entry Administration Law of the People's Republic of China'* (《中华人民共和国出境入境管理法》释义及实用指南) (2012), p. 187.

247 However, see *Interpretation of the 'Exit–Entry Administration Law of the People's Republic of China'* (《中华人民共和国出境入境管理法》释义) (2012), p. 208, stating that the provisions of the *Exit–Entry Administration Law* (2012) should in general only be applied when the offence takes place at exit–entry ports.

248 Chinese: 为偷越国（边）境人员提供条件.

249 Art. 62(1) *Public Security Administration Punishments Law* (2012).

250 Chinese: 协助组织.

251 Chinese: 运送他人.

252 Art. 61 *Public Security Administration Punishments Law* (2012).

253 Chinese: 组织他人偷越国（边）境.

254 Art. 318 *Criminal Law* (2015).

Article 1 *Interpretations on Handling Criminal Cases Related to Border Obstruction* (2012) defines what is meant by "organising illegal border crossing" according to the provisions of the *Criminal Law* (2015). According to this interpretation, the leading, planning, or commanding of individuals to illegally cross the border as well as enticing, forcing, or introducing individuals to illegally cross the border under the command of a leading person is to be considered organising illegal border crossing in the sense of Article 318 *Criminal Law* (2015). A "large amount of individuals involved" is given if the amount exceeds ten people; the sum of illegal earnings is to be considered "considerably high" if it exceeds RMB 200 000.[255] The *Interpretations on Handling Criminal Cases Related to Border Obstruction* (2012) further define what is considered a criminal attempt that shall be punished according to Article 23 *Criminal Law* (2015) on the basis of the punishment provided for in Article 318 *Criminal Law* (2015). The offence may or may not have an economic aim and it does not matter whether the head of the organisation personally crosses the border illegally or not.[256]

According to Article 319 *Criminal Law* (2015), fraudulently appropriating passports, visas or other exit–entry certificates[257] in order to help others to cross the border illegally shall be punished with fixed-term imprisonment of not more than three years and additional fine. If the circumstances are serious, the fixed-term imprisonment may range from three to ten years.[258] The illegal provision of forged or modified exit–entry documents like passports or visa, however, is handled separately as will be covered in the next section. According to Article 321 *Criminal Law* (2015), transporting others illegally across the border shall be punished with fixed-term imprisonment, criminal detention, or public surveillance of not more than five years and additional fine. The offence shall be punished with fixed-term imprisonment between five and ten years and additional fine if the circumstances are serious or with fixed-term imprisonment of not less than seven years and additional fine if the transportation has caused serious injury or death or the responsible person resists inspection.[259]

In this regard, the *Interpretations on Handling Criminal Cases Related to Border Obstruction* (2012) again state that a "large amount of individu-

---

255 Art. 1(2) *Interpretations on Handling Criminal Cases Related to Border Obstruction* (2012).

256 Zhang Xuejun (2011), p. 977.

257 Chinese: 弄虚作假，骗取［……］证件.

258 Art. 319 *Criminal Law* (2015).

259 Art. 321 *Criminal Law* (2015).

als having been transported" is given if the amount exceeds ten people; the sum of illegal earnings is to be considered "considerably high" if it exceeds RMB 200 000.[260] If the offences are committed by an entity, the persons directly in charge shall be prosecuted according to the relevant articles of the *Criminal Law* (2015).[261] Serious circumstances according to Article 319 *Criminal Law* (2015) shall be assumed if the amount of relevant exit documents exceeds five, if the sum of illegal gains exceeds RMB 300 000, or if it is "known"[262] to the offender that the individual for whom he or she fraudulently appropriated the exit document is not permitted to exit the country according the national regulations.[263]

Article 2 *Interpretations on Handling Criminal Cases Related to Border Obstruction* (2012) further clarifies that the term 'fraudulent'[264] as used in Articles 319 *Criminal Law* (2015) means the making up of causes for exit, personal data or other proofs relating to exiting the country in order to organise other persons to illegally cross the border. The mentioned exit documents shall comprise passports or international travel documents as passport substitutes, seafarer's certificates, exit and entry permits[265] and travel documents[266] of the People's Republic of China, exit–entry permits for travelling to and from Hong Kong, Macau, and Taiwan, boundary resident's exit–entry certificates, visa and visa endorsements, exit certificates and name lists, and other documents to be examined when exiting the country.[267]

Articles 318 and 319 *Criminal Law* (2015) clash insofar as fraudulently appropriating residence or exit–entry documents in order to organise other persons to illegally cross the border may per definition at the same time constitute the criminal offence of organising illegal border crossing. The relevant interpretations of the Supreme People's Court state that in cases where the offence of organising illegal border crossing also constitutes an offence according to Articles 319 (fraudulent appropriation of exit–entry

260 Art. 4 *Interpretations on Handling Criminal Cases Related to Border Obstruction* (2012).
261 Art. 7 *Interpretations on Handling Criminal Cases Related to Border Obstruction* (2012).
262 Chinese: 明知.
263 Art. 2(3) *Interpretations on Handling Criminal Cases Related to Border Obstruction* (2012).
264 Chinese: 弄虚作假.
265 Chinese: 中华人民共和国出入境通行证.
266 Chinese: 中华人民共和国旅行证.
267 Art. 2(2) *Interpretations on Handling Criminal Cases Related to Border Obstruction* (2012).

documents), 320 (provision of forged exit–entry documents), or 321 (transportation of others illegally across the border), it shall be punished according to the offence with the most severe punishment.[268] Thus, only in situations where the offence of fraudulently appropriating residence or exit–entry documents only constitutes an attempt to organise other persons to illegally crossing the border or in situations where an individual who is not part of the relevant organisation group him- or herself has fraudulently appropriated residence or exit–entry documents, a punishment according to Article 319 *Criminal Law* (2015) is applicable.[269] Furthermore, as an exit–entry document obtained via fraudulent means is not necessarily invalid, its use to cross the border does not in itself constitute an offence in all cases.[270]

Moreover, the criminal offence of organising illegal border crossing[271] is similar to the administrative offence of assistance of illegal exit or entry according to Article 72 *Exit-Entry Administration Law* (2012). If a certain offence does not constitute a crime, it may hence still be punishable according to the relevant provisions in the *Exit–Entry Administration Law* (2012).[272] Literature points to the problem that the term 'assistance'[273] is not clearly defined, especially considering passive assistance or acting as agent.[274] Passive assistance includes e. g. the mere provision of information about illegal border crossing upon request. Agents do not provide active assistance in illegal border crossing, but merely establish the contact to the person who provides assistance. Hence, the definition of "assisting others to illegally exit or enter the country" as provided for in Article 72 *Exit-Entry Administration Law* (2012) is not clear. Official interpretations of this article define it as possibly unremunerated assistance such as forging exit–entry documents, guidance and carriage, "showing pathways to commit crimes"[275] and "educating experiences to commit crimes"[276] as well as facilitating transportation

268 Art. 8 *Interpretations on Handling Criminal Cases Related to Border Obstruction* (2012). If the offence constitutes the organisation of illegal border crossing it will be punished according to Art. 318 *Criminal Law* (2015); Zhang Xuejun (2011), p. 980.
269 Zhang Xuejun (2011), p. 978.
270 Zhang Xuejun (2011), p. 979.
271 Chinese: 组织他人偷越国（边）境.
272 Art. 7 *Administrative Penalty Law* (2009).
273 Chinese: 协助.
274 Tian (2003).
275 Chinese: 指点作案路线.
276 Chinese: 传教作案经验.

or support or entering and exiting transit zones.[277] This interpretation implies that assistance is meant to be more active than passive and that the administrative offence of assistance in illegal exit or entry should be limited to activities at exit–entry ports while the criminal offence may be applied also in other cases.[278] The reading of a more active connotation of 'assistance' is also supported by the fact that the *Public Security Administration Punishments Law* (2012) differentiates between 'assisting to organise' and 'offering prerequisites', of which the letter may comprise passive assistance that is punished less severely. Regardless of the place where the offence is committed, it should be handled as criminal offence as long as the preconditions for a crime are fulfilled. It can be further argued that the scope of the criminal offence should not be interpreted such that it also includes passive assistance, because such a wide interpretation would blur the delineation between criminal and administrative offence.

c) Illegal Provision, Falsification or Fraudulent Appropriation of Residence or Exit–Entry Documents

Article 73 *Exit–Entry Administration Law* (2012) imposes a fine of RMB 2 000 to 5 000 onto individuals fraudulently appropriating residence or exit–entry documents and, in serious circumstances, a fine of RMB 5 000 to 20 000 or detention of ten to fifteen days. If the subject is an entity, the punishment shall be a fine of RMB 10 000 to 50 000 and the directly responsible individuals shall be persecuted individually.[279] Similarly, according to Article 79 *Exit–Entry Administration Law* (2012), individuals illegally offering exit–entry documents to a foreign national illegally residing in China shall also be fined or, in serious circumstances, additionally detained with the illegally appropriated gains confiscated. If the offence is committed by an entity, the persons directly in charge shall be prosecuted accordingly.

---

277 *Interpretation of the 'Exit–Entry Administration Law of the People's Republic of China'* (《中华人民共和国出境入境管理法》释义) (2012), p. 206.

278 *Interpretation of the 'Exit–Entry Administration Law of the People's Republic of China'* (《中华人民共和国出境入境管理法》释义) (2012), p. 208.

279 Art. 73 *Exit–Entry Administration Law* (2012).

The administrative offence of "fraudulent appropriation"[280] applies in cases where a foreign national provides falsified or modified documents, makes up wrong facts, or otherwise provides wrong information to the exit–entry administration authorities in charge of issuing the relevant certificates in order to obtain residence or exit–entry documents.[281] However, the offence does not cover the provision of falsified or modified residence or exit–entry documents which is covered in different provisions already discussed above.

Apart from Article 319 *Criminal Law* (2015) that sanctions fraudulently appropriating passports, visas or other exit documents in order to organise other persons to illegally cross the border as already discussed above, Article 320 more generally states that fixed-term imprisonment of not more than five years and additional fine shall be imposed on individuals offering forged or modified exit–entry documents such as passports or visa or selling such documents. If the circumstances are serious, the fixed-term imprisonment may exceed five years. Additionally to the documents listed in the definition of 'exit documents' in Article 319 *Criminal Law* (2015) cited above, the *Interpretations on Handling Criminal Cases Related to Border Obstruction* (2012) state that the term 'exit–entry documents' as mentioned in Article 320 *Criminal Law* (2015) also shall include any other documents to be examined when entering or exiting the country.[282]

Similarly to the definition of serious circumstances for Article 319 *Criminal Law* (2015) cited above, the *Interpretations on Handling Criminal*

---

280 Chinese: 弄虚作假骗取〔……〕证件. The official English translation of the *Exit–Entry Administration Law* (2012) describes this offence as "obtaining [...] exit–entry credentials by falsification or other fraudulent means." However, according to several interpretations this primarily means the falsification of information in obtaining residence or exit–entry documents rather than directly falsifying such documents; *Interpretation of the 'Exit–Entry Administration Law of the People's Republic of China'* (《中华人民共和国出境入境管理法》释义) (2012), p. 209; *Guide to Interpretation and Application of the 'Exit–Entry Administration Law of the People's Republic of China'* (《中华人民共和国出境入境管理法》释义及实用指南) (2012), p. 175.

281 *Interpretation of the 'Exit–Entry Administration Law of the People's Republic of China'* (《中华人民共和国出境入境管理法》释义) (2012), p. 209; *Guide to Interpretation and Application of the 'Exit–Entry Administration Law of the People's Republic of China'* (《中华人民共和国出境入境管理法》释义及实用指南) (2012), p. 175.

282 Art. 3(1) *Interpretations on Handling Criminal Cases Related to Border Obstruction* (2012).

Cases Related to Border Obstruction (2012) state that if five or more forged or modified exit–entry documents in the sense of Article 320 *Criminal Law* (2015) are offered to others, if the sum of illegal gains exceeds RMB 300 000, or if it is "known"[283] to the offender that the individual to whom he or she offered the exit–entry documents is not permitted to enter or exit the country according the national regulations, or in other serious circumstances, the circumstances shall be considered to be serious.[284]

If the above mentioned criminal offences are committed by an entity, the persons directly in charge shall be prosecuted according to the relevant articles of the *Criminal Law* (2015).[285]

Both the *Criminal Law* (2015) and the *Exit–Entry Administration Law* (2012) use the same terminology for the offence of fraudulently appropriating residence or exit–entry documents, which implies that the definitions are equivalently applicable. Due to the principle that administrative punishment shall not be applied where the offence constitutes a crime,[286] only where the offence does not constitute a crime shall it be handled according to the provisions of the *Exit–Entry Administration Law* (2012). The offence of fraudulently appropriating residence or exit–entry documents only constitutes a crime if it has been conducted in order to organise other persons to illegally cross the border. However, the *Criminal Law* (2015) also provides for the punishment of offering or selling forged or modified exit–entry document. Here as well, the delineation between the application of the relevant provisions of the *Criminal Law* (2015) and Article 79 of the *Exit-Entry Administration Law* (2012) should be subject to interpretations by courts.

4. Penalties Against Illegal Entry and Visa Overstay in International Comparison

The current Chinese legal framework on exit–entry administration provides sanctions for illegal entry and stay that are considerably more severe than those codified in the previous law. Chapter 2 already compares the sanctions of the old and the new law. Only in certain circumstances is illegal

283 Chinese: 明知.

284 Art. 3(2) *Interpretations on Handling Criminal Cases Related to Border Obstruction* (2012).

285 Art. 7 *Interpretations on Handling Criminal Cases Related to Border Obstruction* (2012).

286 Art. 7 *Administrative Penalty Law* (2009).

entry defined as criminal offence that is sanctioned with fixed-term imprisonment of not more than one year, criminal detention or public surveillance and additional fine.[287] In all other cases, the illegal action is considered an administrative offence and sanctioned with RMB 1 000 to 5 000, in severe cases with detention between five and ten days and possibly an additional fine of RMB 2 000 to 10 000.[288] Visa overstay is considered an administrative offence and in severe cases sanctioned with a fine of RMB 500 per day with a maximum fine of RMB 10 000 or with detention of five to 15 days.[289]

In order to evaluate the severity of these sanctions, I compare the handling of illegal entry and visa overstay in China with other jurisdictions. It can be assumed that the legal framework in China provides for relatively severe punishments in order to deter illegal immigration which is a declared target of the revised law. Because it is not possible to assess the sanctions of every country of the world, I primarily concentrate on countries that are cited for comparison in official statements regarding the legal provisions or the revision process of the current Chinese *Exit–Entry Administration Law* but also in academic literature.[290] In this part, I look into relevant sanctions imposed on illegal entry and visa overstay as codified in the current legal frameworks of the Commonwealth of Australia, Canada, the French Republic, the Federal Republic of Germany, the Italian Republic, the State of Japan, the Russian Federation, the Kingdom of Spain, the United Kingdom of Great Britain and Northern Ireland, as well as the United States of America.

I chose France, Germany, Italy, Spain and the United Kingdom as examples in this context, since Chinese officials attended E. U. funded seminars where immigration legislation of European countries was assessed.[291] Apart from E. U. countries, Japan and the U. S., but also Russia, are often referenced in official interpretations, especially in the context of the collection of biometric data.[292] As this suggests that the legal frameworks of these countries were taken into consideration by the legislators of the new *Exit–*

287 Art. 322 *Criminal Law* (2015).

288 Art. 71 *Exit–Entry Administration Law* (2012).

289 Art. 78(1) *Exit–Entry Administration Law* (2012).

290 E. g. Liu Guofu (2008).

291 *Capacity Building For Migration Management in China* (2008); *Capacity Building For Migration Management in China Project Phase II* (2012).

292 E. g. *Interpretation of the 'Exit–Entry Administration Law of the People's Republic of China'* (《中华人民共和国出境入境管理法》释义) (2012), p. 41; *Answers by Officials of the Ministry of Public Security to Journalists on the Implementation of the 'Exit–Entry Administration Law of the People's Republic of China'* (公安部负

Entry Administration Law (2012), it is reasonable to compare the legal provisions concerning sanctions for illegal entry and illegal stay of the Chinese law against the relevant legal provisions of these countries. I further chose the U. S., Canada and Australia as representatives of typical countries of immigration.

In several of the analysed jurisdictions, the same sanction applies for illegal entry and illegal stay. Also, in several jurisdictions illegal entry is handled as a crime. The legal framework of Germany defines illegal entry and illegal stay as a crime that is sanctioned with imprisonment of not more than one year or pecuniary penalty.[293] Similarly, the legal provisions in the United Kingdom sanction illegal entry and illegal stay with imprisonment of not more than six months or a fine of GBP 5 000 (approx. USD 6 500) or both.[294] Japanese law imposes imprisonment with or without work of not more that three years or a fine of not more than JPY 3 000 000 (approx. USD 27 000) on illegal entry and visa overstay.[295] Canadian law imposes a fine up to CAD 50 000 (approx. 38 500 USD) and imprisonment for up to two years on infringements of any provision of the *Immigration and Refugee Protection Act*, which also includes illegal entry and illegal stay.[296]

Not all jurisdictions, however, provide the same sanctions for illegal entry and illegal stay. The French law only defines a sanction for illegal entry, but not for illegal stay, with imprisonment of one year and a fine of EUR 3 750 (amounting to approximately USD 4 250).[297] The Russian legal framework differentiates between illegal entry that is defined as a crime and illegal stay being defined as administrative offence. Accordingly, illegal entry is sanctioned harder with up to two years of imprisonment or a fine of up to RUB 200 000 (approx. USD 2 850),[298] while illegal stay is fined with RUB 2 000 to 5 000 (approx. USD 30 to 70) and optional expulsion.[299] In the U. S., illegal entry is considered a misdemeanour that can be fined and additionally sanctioned with imprisonment up to six months.[300] Additionally

责人就贯彻执行《中华人民共和国出境入境管理法》答记者问), *NPC Standing Committee Press Release* (2012).

293 Art. 95(1) *Residence Act of Germany* (2008).

294 Art. 24(1) *U. K. Immigration Act* (1971, 2016).

295 Art. 70(1) *Japanese Immigration Control and Refugee Recognition Act* (2016).

296 Art. 124(1)(a), 125 *Canadian Immigration and Refugee Protection Act* (2018).

297 Art. L621-2 *French Code on the Entry and Residence of Foreign Nationals* (2019).

298 Art. 322 *Criminal Code of the Russian Federation* (2018).

299 Art. 18.8 *Code of Administrative Offences of the Russian Federation* (2018).

300 Title 8 Sec. 1325 a *United States Code of Laws* (2017).

a civil penalty consisting of a fine of USD 50 to 250 can be imposed.[301] Illegal re-entry is defined as a felony sanctioned with imprisonment up to two years—in certain cases even up to ten or 20 years—and a re-entry ban.[302] Visa overstay, on the other hand, is considered a civil violation that entails a re-entry ban of one or several years.

In some jurisdictions, illegal entry or illegal stay are not considered a crime. According to Italian law, illegal entry and illegal stay is fined EUR 5 000 to 10 000 (approx. USD 5 850 to 11 650).[303] In Spain, illegal stay, but not illegal entry, is considered an administrative offence fined with EUR 501 to 10 000 (approx. USD 600 to 11 650).[304] In Australia, illegal entry and illegal stay is neither considered a crime nor an administrative offence. However, illegal stay entails an re-entry ban and the removal of the individual who has to pay the the cost of the removal. Furthermore, the detention of foreign nationals who illegally stay in Australia is mandatory.[305]

Having compared these legal provisions on illegal entry and illegal stay of different jurisdictions, I conclude that the administration of illegal entry and illegal stay of foreign nationals is handled very differently across different countries and that the Chinese sanctionative system is relatively lenient when it punishes illegal entry and stay with administrative punishments in most cases. Several states define illegal entry as a criminal offence that entails imprisonment between half a year and up to two years and fines mostly amounting between USD 3 000 and 6 500. Japanese law provides even more severe sanctions. Visa overstay is similarly defined as a crime in several countries, although some states that define illegal entry as a crime do not define illegal stay as a crime as well. In comparison to this, the Chinese legal framework defines both, illegal entry and illegal stay, as administrative offences and the related sanctions amount to approximately USD 150 to 1 500 and detention for one to two weeks only. Only in severe cases like repeated illegal entry, a higher fine or imprisonment of up to one year may be imposed, or the offences should be handled as crimes. Of course, the Chinese penalty system is still more severe than the Australian system without any fines. But even in comparison with states where an administrative fine or detention as compulsory measure is imposed on illegal entry or stay, the sanctions and compulsory measures codified in the Chinese framework of

301 Title 8 Sec. 1325 b *United States Code of Laws* (2017).
302 Title 8 Sec. 1326 *United States Code of Laws* (2017).
303 Art. 10 bis(1) *Italian Immigration Provisions* (2009).
304 Art. 53(1), 55(1)b *Spanish Foreign Nationals Law* (2018).
305 *Australian Migration Amendment Act* (1992).

immigration law appear relatively humane. The administrative fine imposed in Spain, for example, is still considerably higher than the equivalent fine in China. Finally, the Chinese framework does not provide for compulsory detention of illegal residents as implemented in the Australian legal framework.[306]

IV. Summary

Exit and entry to China are subject to a detailed legal framework that covers the issuance of visa, restrictions of exit or entry at the border, the prosecution of illegal exit or entry or illegal border crossing, as well as—only outlined briefly here—procedures concerning asylum. Illegal border crossing also comprises trafficking offences, and different provisions exist, both in administrative law as well as in criminal law, that punish the illegal transportation of individuals across the border, illegally crossing the border on one's own, providing forged exit–entry documents or fraudulently obtaining such documents. Hence, a definition of 'illegal entry' cannot simply be made on the basis of administrative law. In fact, criminal activities often depict more severe variations of the administrative offence laid down in the *Exit–Entry Administration Law* (2012). For example, the crime of transporting others illegally across the border obviously also may comprise the illegal exit or entry of these individuals. Illegally entering the country for the third time in a row is considered a criminal activity, while illegally entering only one or two times will be punished as administrative offence. In this regard, campaigns that arguably target 'illegal entry' will necessarily also include the persecution of illegal border crossings, and indeed such campaigns are often linked with campaigns that target trafficking issues.

As for the legal remedies against the prohibition to enter China, a foreign national is left with very little enforceable rights. As it is argued that the decision of a Chinese consulate or embassy abroad not to issue a visa is regarded an 'act of state', the application of administrative reconsideration or administrative litigation is not applicable. The foreign national will also fail to ask for the reasons for the non-issuance, as the authorities are not obligated to tell the applicant the reasons for the denied visa. Similarly, no reasons need to be stated if the foreign national is refused entry to the country

306 It should be noted that New Zealand has a non-punitive approach to illegal immigration similar to Australia's, but never set up a compulsory detention scheme.

at the border. The same logic of limited legal remedies due to the action being an 'act of state' applies here. The limitation of legal remedies of the foreign national against the denial of entry or non-issuance of a visa does not conflict with international standards. Courts in the U. S. for example apply the so-called 'doctrine of consular non-reviewability' that precludes legal remedies against decisions of the authorities not to issue a visa, and such practice is deemed to be in line with international law. Still, in comparison with international practice, the complete denial of access to legal remedies can be regarded as relatively strict, as even in the U. S. the authorities are required to handle reconsideration requests.

In the context of exit restrictions, Chinese courts seem to transgress limitations laid out by international standards that require exit restrictions to be applied only as a last resort. A review of court decisions on the imposition of exit restrictions in the context of civil cases concerning unsettled debts suggests that only a formal examination of the application of the plaintiff is typically conducted. Further, the imposition of other compulsory measures alongside an exit restriction implies that the latter is not applied as last resort. After all, the limitation of legal remedies does not hold in the case of exit restrictions. Finally, China's practice not to grant certain asylum seekers access to the UNHCR Office should be regarded a human rights violation in breach of international law.

I conclude that the revision of the *Exit–Entry Administration Law* was able to resolve most of the previously existing inconsistencies of legal provisions within the framework of administration law. The new law can be regarded as *lex specialis* to more general laws such as the *Administrative Penalty Law* (2009), the *Administrative Compulsion Law* (2011), the *Administrative Licence Law* (2003) or the *Public Security Administration Punishments Law* (2012). While the old law contained detailed provisions regarding time limits of legal remedies that differed from the regulations of the *Administrative Litigation Law*, the new law omits such detailed provisions and the related inconsistencies. The new law further refers to exceptions codified in the *Administrative Litigation Law* regarding the limitation of legal remedies, when it defines decisions on administrative reconsideration as final in certain cases, which illustrates that the current legal framework has indeed been harmonised. However, exit–entry administration law not only relates to administrative acts, such as punishments, compulsion or permissions, but also to so-called 'acts of state', such as the decision not to issue a visa to a foreign national or to deny his or her entry to China, against which no legal remedy is applicable. Hence, while the *Exit–Entry Administration*

Law (2012) for the most part is neatly embedded into the current framework of administrative law, it also contains elements that do not belong to administrative law in the narrow sense. Moreover, the definitions of certain legal terms codified in the *Exit–Entry Administration Law* (2012), such as that of 'illegal entry', still overlap with similar definitions in other provisions of administrative and criminal law, which rather complicates the classification of a specific action as an administrative or a criminal offence.

C. Residence in China: Illegal Stay, Detention and Repatriation

This section investigates the possible legal remedies against administrative punishments or compulsory measures in the context of stay. Sanctions in the context of stay comprise two aspects, the prerequisites that render stay illegal and the consequences that result from illegal stay. The most severe punishment against illegal activities conducted by a foreign national that can be imposed according to administrative law is his or her removal. But this punishment can only be imposed if certain prerequisites are fulfilled, namely: the activities of the foreign national have to have rendered the stay improper. Clarifying what renders stay improper requires a clear definition of illegal stay first. Does illegal stay automatically mean that the continued stay is rendered improper? Does illegal stay also comprise illegal residence? Does illegal stay also include failed registration of a foreign national? In order to assess the consequences that result from illegal stay, these questions need to be answered first. A foreign national may be fined or detained as a punishment, and the police may also issue an order to leave in certain circumstances. The foreign national may further be detained in order to be repatriated. What are the preconditions for such detention? Are legal remedies like administrative reconsideration and administrative litigation always applicable? To answer these questions, administrative punishment needs to be delineated from administrative compulsion.

This section first defines the offence of 'illegal stay' and delineates it from registration issues and stay rendered improper that is a prerequisite for the possibility of the police to impose an order to leave. An order to leave or a deportation, being discussed in the following part, may only be imposed if certain preconditions apply, and it is within the discretion of the police to impose such a punishment. Although detention for investigation, i. e. custody prior to a removal of a foreign national, will typically happen before the execution of the repatriation of the foreign national, this section analyses it after having delineated order to leave, deportation and repatriation, because the difference between administrative punishment and administrative compulsion has to be clarified first, which can be illustrated best with the example of order to leave and repatriation. It will be shown that the police has a certain degree of discretion when it comes to repatriation or deportation. Not only is the imposition of repatriation or deportation non-compulsory, but also legal remedies against such a punishment are restricted. This section will hence also pay attention to the question whether this limitation of legal remedies is in line with international standards. This section eventually aims to answer the question whether the revised legal framework is able to solve the contradiction between the aim to protect the legal rights of foreign nationals as defined in international standards on the one hand and the aim to curb illegal immigration, for example by enhancing the power of the local police, on the other hand.

I. Prosecution of Illegal Stay, Registration Issues, and Inconsistent Behaviour

A definition of 'illegal stay' requires a clarification whether illegal residence also should be regarded as illegal stay. In fact, the Chinese term *feifa juliu* that is translated as 'illegal stay' literally means 'illegal residence', so the question here could be as well whether short-term stay is covered by the offence of 'illegal stay'. I further delineate illegal stay from offences concerning registration of foreign nationals as well as from the concept of 'improper stay'. In order to get a comprehensive idea of the term 'illegal stay', this section first investigates the old legal framework.

1. Illegal Stay and Illegal Residence

In the old *Foreign Nationals Exit-Entry Administration Law* of 1985, 'illegal stay' (*feifa juliu*[307], literally translating to 'illegal residence') was codified in Article 29(1) that generally defined punishments and legal remedies in the context of this law. The old legal framework already included a differ-

307 Chinese: 非法居留.

entiation between short-term stay (*tingliu*[308]) and long-term stay (*juliu*[309]), where the latter was equivalent to a residence status. While a short-term stay was typically already granted with the issuance of a visa and hence no additional document was needed, a residence status required the application of an appropriate permit in addition to the visa. The term 'illegal stay' typically seemed to be covering both, short-term and long-term stay, as virtually all relevant legal provisions covered in the relevant section applied to stay as well as to residence. The *Foreign Nationals Exit–Entry Administration Law* (1985) did not provide for a detailed definition of the term 'illegal stay', neither did the 2010 *Foreign Nationals Exit-Entry Administration Law Implementation Rules* that codified detailed punishments for the offence of illegal stay.[310] According to Article 42 *Foreign Nationals Exit–Entry Administration Law Implementation Rules* (2010), however, 'illegal stay' comprised the failure to register in the context of the application for a residence permit of foreign nationals who needed to apply for a residence permit, e. g. holders of D, Z, X or J-1 visas or individuals who didn't need to apply for a visa to enter China.[311]

The difference between short-term stay and long-term stay (residence) still exists in the revised legal framework,[312] which suggests that the offence of 'illegal stay' (*feifa juliu*[313]) as defined in the revised *Exit–Entry Administration Regulations* (2013) covers both short-term stay and residence as was obviously the case in the old legal framework. Generally speaking, if the foreign national holds a visa that allows him or her to stay, he or she may stay for the stated period that typically does not exceed 180 days. If the foreign national intends to stay longer, he or she has to apply for a residence permit[314] that allows for—probably permanent—residence. According to Article 78 *Exit-Entry Administration Law* (2012), illegal stay in China is punishable. Article 25 *Exit–Entry Administration Regulations* (2013) states that a foreign national shall be deemed to commit the offence of 'illegal stay' if he or she overstays the allowed period of stay as stated on the relevant visa

308 Chinese: 停留.
309 Chinese: 居留.
310 Art. 42 *Foreign Nationals Exit–Entry Administration Law Implementation Rules* (2010).
311 Art. 42 *Foreign Nationals Exit–Entry Administration Law Implementation Rules* (2010).
312 Art. 29 *Exit–Entry Administration Law* (2012).
313 Chinese: 非法居留.
314 Chinese: 外国人居留证件.

or residence permit, if he or she overstays the allowed period of visa-free stay without applying for a stay or residence permit, if he or she moves to a place outside the allowed residence area, or if he or she commits other kinds of illegal stay. As overstaying a visa or residence permit is defined as illegal stay, I conclude that the offence of 'illegal stay' covers both illegal stay and illegal residence. Alike, official interpretations of the cited article state that stay without valid visa or without valid residence permit as well as overstaying the allowed duration of stay should be considered 'illegal stay'.[315]

According to the current provisions, illegal stay or residence shall be punished with a warning or, if the circumstances are serious, with a fine of RMB 500 for each day of illegal residence, or with detention of five to fifteen days. The fine shall not surpass RMB 10 000 in total. A warning or fine of not more than RMB 1 000 shall be imposed on the person assumed to be guardian of a foreign national who is under 16 years old.[316] The accommodation of illegally entered or residing individuals, the assistance to evade inspection, or the illegal issuance of exit–entry documents is also punishable with a fine or with detention of five to fifteen days and confiscation of the illegal income in serious circumstances.[317] The *Exit–Entry Administration Law* (2012) further provides for the confiscation of property illegally appropriated in a restricted area entered by foreign nationals without approval[318] as well as of the income gained from illegally issuing application material to a foreign national or from the illegal accommodation or employment of foreign nationals.[319]

2. Delineation of Illegal Stay from Registration Issues

The process of the registration for temporary stay *(zhusu dengji)*[320] of foreign nationals is described in much more detail in the new law. While the

315 *Guide to Interpretation and Application of the 'Exit–Entry Administration Law of the People's Republic of China'* (《中华人民共和国出境入境管理法》释义及实用指南) (2012), p. 185.

316 Art. 78 *Exit–Entry Administration Law* (2012).

317 Art. 79 *Exit–Entry Administration Law* (2012).

318 Art. 77 *Exit–Entry Administration Law* (2012).

319 Art. 74, 79, 80(2, 3), 74 *Exit–Entry Administration Law* (2012).

320 Chinese: 住宿登记. Note the difference between registration for temporary stay and registration of residence. The former means the registration with a hotel or directly with the local public security office, the latter means the registration in the context of the application for a residence permit.

1985 *Foreign Nationals Exit–Entry Administration Law* and the relevant *Implementation Rules* (2010) only mentioned that foreign nationals had to register for temporary stay,[321] the new law obliges hotels to register their guests according to the 1987 *Measures on Public Security Administration in the Hotel Sector*[322] which state that such a registration has to be carried out within 24 hours.[323] The new law punishes hotels with a warning or, if the circumstances are serious, with a fine of RMB 1 000 to 5 000 if they omit the registration of a foreign national. The hotel shall be punished according to the provisions of the *Public Security Administration Punishments Law* (2012) if it fails to conduct accommodation registration according to the legal provisions.[324] Where foreign nationals reside outside of hotels, they have to register at the local police office within 24 hours after their arrival.[325] Children born to foreign nationals in China have to be registered on the basis of the birth certificates within 60 days after birth at the local police office.[326] The death of a foreign national in China has to be reported to police offices above or at county level according to the relevant regulations which are not referred to in detail in the law. The stay permit will be cancelled upon such a report of death.[327] The refusal of presentation or verification of the relevant legal documents by the foreign national, the legally erroneous procedure of a birth registration or death declaration, the legally erroneous application for modification of registration, the illegal use of legal documents of third persons, as well as the refusal of registration at the local public security authority if staying or living in an accommodation other than a hotel, are punished with a warning or a fine of not more than RMB 2 000.[328] As the new legal framework defines registration issues and the according sanctions separately from the mere offence of illegal stay, I conclude that the offence of illegal stay does not cover the failure of a foreign national to register in China.

According to the old legal framework, 'illegal stay' mainly denoted overstaying the permitted duration of stay or residence as defined by the visa or residence permit, or not to leave the country after being requested by the po-

321 Art. 29, 30 *Foreign Nationals Exit–Entry Administration Law Implementation Rules* (2010).
322 Art. 39(1) *Exit–Entry Administration Law* (2012).
323 Art. 6 *Hotel Public Security Administration Measures* (1987).
324 Art. 76 *Exit–Entry Administration Law* (2012).
325 Art. 39(2) *Exit–Entry Administration Law* (2012).
326 Art. 40(1) *Exit–Entry Administration Law* (2012).
327 Art. 40(2) *Exit–Entry Administration Law* (2012).
328 Art. 76 *Exit–Entry Administration Law* (2012).

lice to do so. Article 42(1) of the *Foreign Nationals Exit-Entry Administration Law Implementation Rules* (2010) defined a punishment against 'illegal stay' in violation of Article 16, 19, or 20 of the *Foreign Nationals Exit-Entry Administration Law Implementation Rules* (2010), which covered the stay without a valid visa or residence permit as well as overstaying the allowed duration of stay as defined on the relevant exit–entry documents. As the term 'illegal stay' was only defined in terms of its legal liability, it could as well be interpreted in a broader sense to also include the failure to register one's stay after having entered the country. However, official opinions and manuals concerning illegal stay only referred to Articles 12, 27 and 29(1) of the *Foreign Nationals Exit-Entry Administration Law* (1985) as well as to Articles 16, 19, 20 and 42(1) of the *Foreign Nationals Exit-Entry Administration Law Implementation Rules* (2010), which implies that registration issues were not covered by the term 'illegal stay' in the old legal framework.[329]

As Article 25 *Exit–Entry Administration Regulations* (2013) also lists "other kinds of illegal stay" in the definition of 'illegal stay', there is no concluding definition of the term in the revised legal framework on exit–entry administration. The *Exit–Entry Administration Law* (2012) provides for penalties if foreign nationals fail to properly register, which may, when interpreting the term in a broader sense, also be considered as 'illegal stay'. However, Article 76 *Exit–Entry Administration Law* (2012) states that it is an offence to fail to register according to Article 39(2) *Exit–Entry Administration Law* (2012) or not to file a modification of a registration item of the permanent residence permit[330] as prescribed by legal provisions. Article 39(2) *Exit–Entry Administration Law* (2012) states that foreign nationals shall register with the local public security authorities within 24 hours after being accommodated, in person or by the provider of the accommodation. Since failure to properly register is defined as a separate offence in the *Exit–Entry Administration Law* (2012) independent from the offence of

329 Item 412 *Offences Definitions* (2010); Liu Jianchang / Li Xinglin (2012), p. 176. Liu Jianchang / Li Xinglin (2012) follow the same structure as laid out in the *Offences Definitions* (2010) which, together with the fact that the book was published by the People's Public Security University of China Press, implies that the information can be seen as equivalent to official.

330 Article 33 *Exit–Entry Administration Law* (2012) non-exhaustively enumerates the following registration items on residence permits: name of the holder, sex, date of birth, cause of residence, period of residence, date and place of issuance, number of passport or international travel document.

illegal stay, the separate handling of registration issues and overstaying a visa or residence permit is reasonable. Moreover, although Article 81 *Exit-Entry Administration Law* (2012) cannot fully clarify in which situations a stay should be understood as being "rendered improper" as will be discussed in the next section, registration issues should also not fall within the scope of this provision, as failing to register does not directly influence the cause of stay. Official definitions and regulations as well as court cases imply that registration issues are not covered by the term 'illegal stay'.[331] In conclusion, failing to register should not be considered as 'illegal stay', although registration issues are closely connected to the offence of 'illegal stay' and could theoretically be subsumed under "other kinds of illegal stay".

3. Activities Inconsistent with the Cause of Stay

The revised legal framework introduces the term 'improper'[332] to describe the stay of a foreign national in Article 81 *Exit–Entry Administration Law* (2012). According to this provision, activities "inconsistent with the cause of stay or residence"[333] rendering the continued stay "improper" may lead to the removal of the foreign national.[334] Moreover, the violation of other laws or regulations, as long as this violation renders the continued stay improper, may also lead to a repatriation according to this provision. If the violations are serious but do not constitute a crime, the suspects may be repatriated on the authority of the Ministry of Public Security whose decision shall be final. Once repatriated, foreign nationals are not allowed to re-enter China within the following ten years.[335] The provision of Article 81 *Exit–Entry Administration Law* (2012) replaces the old Article 16 of the *Exit-Entry Administration Law* (1985) that allowed government authorities to restrict the duration of stay or to revoke the residence status of a foreign national who

331 *Guide to Interpretation and Application of the 'Exit–Entry Administration Law of the People's Republic of China'* (《中华人民共和国出境入境管理法》释义及实用指南) (2012), p. 185; Item 440 *Offences Definitions* (2015), while registration issues are covered by Item 436 *Offences Definitions* (2015); in the *Fuzhou Drug Abuse Case* (2017), the defendant was fined for illegal stay and failing to register by the police separately, which implies that the two offences are handled independently.

332 Chinese: 不适宜.

333 Chinese: 与停留居留事由不相符的.

334 Art. 81 *Exit–Entry Administration Law* (2012).

335 Art. 81 *Exit–Entry Administration Law* (2012).

did not abide by Chinese laws.[336] Official interpretations of this provision state that "cause"[337] of stay in this context is to be understood as the "main aspects"[338] of the stay.[339] The foreign national is regarded as engaging in activities "inconsistent with the cause of stay or residence" if he or she engages in activities that exceed the scope of allowed activities defined on his or her visa or residence permit.[340] Apart from the problem that the law does not define which activities exactly should be regarded "inconsistent with the cause of stay or residence", the term 'improper' is not defined and it seems hence unclear at first whether in this context 'improper stay' can be understood as equivalent to 'illegal stay'.

Although an official interpretation states that the provision regarding 'improper stay' regulates the restriction of the duration of stay and the removal of foreign nationals,[341] from a systematic point of view it cannot be regarded as a general provision to codify the procedures regarding the removal of foreign nationals, as it is found in Chapter VII on "Legal Liability", which implies that an order to leave, if applied in this context, should be understood as administrative punishment. Moreover, Article 62 already sets out the basic framework for the repatriation of a foreign national.[342] The provision of Article 81 *Exit–Entry Administration Law* (2012) hence codifies an administrative punishment by essentially defining the legal consequence of a violation of Article 37 *Exit–Entry Administration Law* (2012) that requires foreign nationals not to engage in activities inconsistent with the cause of their stay and to leave China before the prescribed limit of stay.[343]

The authorities obviously are granted a certain degree of discretion, since the provision defines the removal as optional. In fact, an order to leave shall

336 *Guide to Interpretation and Application of the 'Exit–Entry Administration Law of the People's Republic of China'* (《中华人民共和国出境入境管理法》释义及实用指南) (2012), p. 192.
337 Chinese: 理由.
338 Chinese: 重要方面.
339 *Guide to Interpretation and Application of the 'Exit–Entry Administration Law of the People's Republic of China'* (《中华人民共和国出境入境管理法》释义及实用指南) (2012), p. 190.
340 *Guide to Interpretation and Application of the 'Exit–Entry Administration Law of the People's Republic of China'* (《中华人民共和国出境入境管理法》释义及实用指南) (2012), p. 190.
341 *Guide to Interpretation and Application of the 'Exit–Entry Administration Law of the People's Republic of China'* (《中华人民共和国出境入境管理法》释义及实用指南) (2012), p. 190.
342 See the sections below on the differentiation between the different forms of removal.
343 Art. 37 *Exit–Entry Administration Law* (2012).

only be imposed if the activity of the foreign national fulfils two prerequisites, namely it has to be inconsistent with the cause of stay or residence and it has to render the continued stay improper. Hence, an activity that is inconsistent with the cause of stay or residence without rendering the continued stay improper (probably a rather minor transgression of the legal provisions) shall not be punished with an order to leave. In this context, whether the stay or residence of the foreign national is considered to have been rendered improper due to his or her activities lies within the decision power of the public security organs. In any case, the provisions concerning 'improper stay' should be regarded independently from the offence of 'illegal stay', since an activity that fulfils the prerequisite of 'illegal stay' obviously does not necessarily render the continued stay improper.

As an example, I take that working with a visa other than a Z visa or an R visa—which implies that no work permit can be produced—will be considered illegal employment rather than illegal stay. Such an activity may be additionally considered to be inconsistent with the cause of stay according to Article 81 *Exit–Entry Administration Law* (2012). According to official interpretations, activities inconsistent with the cause of stay not only comprise illegal stay but also entering areas not open to foreign nationals without permission or illegally conducting interviews or religious services in China.[344] Court decisions have shown that Article 81 may be imposed in addition to a punishment imposed for illegal employment.[345] Hence, the provision of Article 81 can be regarded as a general definition of the administrative punishment of an order to leave or deportation respectively rather than defining a distinct administrative offence. This interpretation further supports the reading that this provision should be treated separately from the definition of the offence of 'illegal stay'.

The legal remedies for administrative acts as discussed above may also be applied to challenge a fine or detention imposed as administrative punishment in the context of illegal stay or registration issues. Criminal litigation law is not applicable here, since the offences discussed are codified as administrative offences only. In the context of stay and residence of foreign nationals in China, limitations on the access to administrative litigation or

344 *Interpretation of the 'Exit–Entry Administration Law of the People's Republic of China'* (《中华人民共和国出境入境管理法》释义) (2012), p. 228.

345 See the *Hangzhou Illegal Emplyoment Case* (2014) where working without a work permit was additionally punished with an order to leave according to Art. 81(1) *Exit–Entry Administration Law* (2012).

administrative reconsideration may apply in the context of repatriation and deportation, which I will analyse in detail in the next part.

II. Repatriation and Deportation as Examples of Administrative Compulsion and Administrative Punishment

The removal of an individual from a country for whatever reason may be the result of criminal punishment or administrative punishment. Deportation leading to removal may be imposed as primary punishment or as secondary punishment alongside another (primary) punishment, but removal may also not be the result of a punishment at all. Furthermore, the actual removal of the individual, i. e. when he or she is forcefully put into a plane to leave the country, may be based on a judicial decision or an administrative notice and there may be an order to leave that is finally enforced. Against some of these judicial or administrative decisions or acts, the individual may or may not apply certain legal remedies. In order to identify the possible legal remedies that may be applied, a proper terminology on the different decisions and acts has to be established. A problem especially arises when applying terms stemming from the legal system of one country to that of another. To make clear what exactly I refer to with each term, a definition of these terms is made in the following paragraph.

1. Order to Leave, Deportation and Repatriation

In English legal literature, the terms 'expulsion' and 'deportation' or 'removal' are typically used for administrative acts constituting a decision for a compulsory measure or its enforcement.[346] Removal typically means the administrative act of repatriating individuals who illegally stay in the country or whose entry has been denied. While the term 'deportation' is more often associated with punishment or at least with a forceful removal,[347] the term 'repatriation' also depicts the voluntary return to one's home country. Finally, repatriation may also refer to the restoration of a prior nationality.

346 Perruchoud (2012) p. 143.
347 Title 8 Sec. 1227 *United States Code of Laws* (2017).

In the official English translations of the Chinese laws, however, the terms 'repatriation' and 'repatriation measure' are used for the terms *qianfan*[348] and *qiansong (cuoshi)*[349] in the *Exit–Entry Administration Law* (2012), meaning the act of being removed from the territory of the state, while 'deportation'—apart from other grammatical constructions like "being expelled" (*beichu quzhu*[350]) etc.—is used for *quzhu*[351] denoting a punishment of being removed from the country. A third term, *xianqi chujing*[352], is used to denote an 'order to leave' that may be enforced by the means of repatriation (*qiansong*). Neither the *Administrative Penalty Law* (2009) nor the *Administrative Compulsion Law* (2011) talk of *quzhu* or *qianfan*. The terms are used, however, in the *Exit–Entry Administration Law* (2012) and in the *Public Security Administration Punishments Law* (2012), suggesting that orders to leave, deportations and repatriations at least in the context of administrative law are mainly decided upon or enforced by the public security authorities. The Chinese terms do not clearly differentiate between administrative decisions or compulsory measures in this regard but rather between penalties and compulsion. Article 10(2) *Public Security Administration Punishments Law* (2013) lists *quzhu* as a type of administrative penalty, which implies that the term *quzhu* depicts an administrative penalty. Article 35 of the *Criminal Law* (2015) codifies *quzhu chujing*[353] as an independent or supplemental penalty which can be imposed on foreign nationals. Thus, deportation (*quzhu*) may be imposed as administrative punishment, but also as criminal penalty. In the following, 'deportation' is used to denote the term *quzhu*, 'repatriation' is used for *qiansong*, and *xianqi chujing* is translated as 'order to leave', in accordance with the official translations. Where the concrete removal of a foreign national is meant, this is additionally emphasised by using the term 'removal'.

The use of the term *qianfan* is not clearly defined in Chinese law as administrative act, punishment or compulsory measure but it is rather used to describe the repatriation of Chinese nationals back to China without clarifying whether or not this repatriation constitutes an administrative penalty of the foreign country. Article 75(1) *Exit–Entry Administration Law* (2012) states that a Chinese national may be prohibited from exiting China when he

348 Chinese: 遣返.
349 Chinese: 遣送措施.
350 Chinese: 被处驱逐.
351 Chinese: 驱逐.
352 Chinese: 限期出境.
353 Chinese: 驱逐出境.

or she has been repatriated by another country or region because he or she entered this country or region illegally. Article 12(1)iv states that Chinese nationals also may be prohibited from exiting China (again) when they have been repatriated by another country or region because they were not allowed to exit China due to a criminal or administrative penalty. Furthermore, the term *qianfan*, apart from its use to describe the repatriation of Chinese nationals, seems to be used as an umbrella term for all kinds of deportation, repatriation, or order to leave, which is suggested by the use of this term in the title of Chapter VI of the *Exit–Entry Administration Law* (2012) specifically devoted to deportation and repatriation: *"diaocha he qianfan"*[354].

Article 26 *Exit–Entry Administration Law* (2012) finally introduces the term *fanhui*[355], which should be translated as 'order to return'.[356] This measure is implemented where a foreign national is not allowed to pass border control. It may be enforced as compulsory measure.[357] Neither the 'order to return', however, nor its enforcement should be understood as administrative punishments. If the enforcement of the 'order to return' has no effect, the foreign national may be repatriated as will be discussed in the following.

Article 62 *Exit–Entry Administration Law* (2012) lists circumstances in which a foreign national may be 'repatriated' (*qiansong chujing*[358]). According to this provision, a foreign national may be repatriated if he or she has been ordered to leave the country within a time limit but did not adhere to this order, if he or she is prohibited from entering China, if he or she is illegally residing or employed in China, or if other laws or administrative regulations require repatriation. While all of these circumstances constitute violations of the law and repatriated individuals may be refused entry to China within one to five years from the date of repatriation, this measure seems not to constitute an administrative penalty in itself since it is not classified under Chapter VII of the law that outlines administrative penalties, but under Chapter VI that lists compulsory measures. Also, under Chapter VII in Article 81, the administrative penalty of 'deportation' (*quzhu chujing*[359]) can be found involving a re-entry ban of ten years. This re-entry ban is argued to be a necessary measure to maintain the order of exit–entry admin-

354 Chinese: 调查和遣返.

355 Chinese: 返回.

356 Art. 26 *Exit–Entry Administration Law* (2012).

357 *Interpretation of the 'Exit–Entry Administration Law of the People's Republic of China'* (《中华人民共和国出境入境管理法》释义) (2012), p. 184.

358 Chinese: 遣送出境.

359 Chinese: 驱逐出境.

istration and safeguard national security and should hence not be regarded as punishment in itself.[360] As repatriation and deportation are codified in different chapters of the law, it is reasonable to interpret them as qualitatively different. Official interpretations identify repatriation as codified in Article 62 as measure that targets individuals who do not possess a right of residence.[361] Hence, repatriation should be regarded as an administrative act to enforce the obligation to return of the individual and to restore the public and legal order. The *Exit–Entry Administration Law* (2012) *inter alia* specifies illegal stay and illegal employment as possible reasons for repatriation,[362] which should be interpreted in such a way that after the sentence for illegal stay or illegal employment has been served, the individual may be repatriated if he or she has lost his or her right of residence due to his or her illegal stay or illegal employment.

According to Yu and Ma, repatriation (*qiansong chujing*) is classified as administrative compulsory measure (*qiangzhi cuoshi*).[363] While deportation has to be decided upon by a higher ranking authority[364] and is executed according to the *Regulations on the Enforcement of Compulsory Measures on Foreign Nationals to Exit* (1992),[365] a repatriation measure may be decided upon and enforced by public security organs at or above county level.[366] Until 2012, decisions regarding repatriations had to be approved by the next

360 *Guide to Interpretation and Application of the 'Exit–Entry Administration Law of the People's Republic of China'* (《中华人民共和国出境入境管理法》释义及实用指南) (2012), p. 156.

361 *Guide to Interpretation and Application of the 'Exit–Entry Administration Law of the People's Republic of China'* (《中华人民共和国出境入境管理法》释义及实用指南) (2012), p. 157.

362 Art. 62(1)iii *Exit–Entry Administration Law* (2012). More concretely, repatriation should be understood as the enforcement of Art. 3(2), 37 or 43 *Exit–Entry Administration Law* (2012); *Interpretation of the 'Exit–Entry Administration Law of the People's Republic of China'* (《中华人民共和国出境入境管理法》释义) (2012), p. 185.

363 Yu Qun / Ma Shuncheng (2012), p. 131.

364 I. e. a public security authority at provincial or ministerial level; Art. 2(1)i–iii,v *Regulations on the Enforcement of Compulsory Measures on Foreign Nationals to Exit* (1992).

365 *Regulations on the Enforcement of Compulsory Measures on Foreign Nationals to Exit* (1992), jointly issued by the Supreme People's Court, the Supreme People's Procuratorate, the Ministry of Public Security, the Ministry of Foreign Affairs and the Ministry of Justice.

366 Art. 58 *Exit–Entry Administration Law* (2012); Art. 2(1)iv *Regulations on the Enforcement of Compulsory Measures on Foreign Nationals to Exit* (1992).

higher public security authority.[367] In any case, the provisions of the *Regulations on the Enforcement of Compulsory Measures on Foreign Nationals to Exit* (1992) imply that repatriation should be seen as administrative compulsory measure and, more concretely, as compulsory enforcement (*qianzhi zhixing*).[368]

Article 64(1) *Exit–Entry Administration Law* (2012) allows for administrative reconsideration when "opposing the repatriation measure" (*qiansong chujing cuoshi bufu*[369]). Here, as official interpretations of this provision suggest,[370] *qiansong chujing* or *qiansong chujing cuoshi* is considered a compulsory measure (*qiangzhi cuoshi*) regardless of whether the underlying administrative decision constitutes a penalty or not. The term *qiansong cuoshi* may hence be best translated as 'removal', i. e. the act of physically removing a foreign national from the territory of the state, e. g. to enforce an order to leave that the foreign national did not comply with.

Article 63 *Exit–Entry Administration Law* (2012) as well as Article 29(3) *Foreign Nationals Exit–Entry Administration Regulations* (2013) state that if a "repatriation or deportation cannot be executed immediately" (*wufa liji zhixing qiansong chujing, quzhu chujing de*[371]), the individual shall be detained. This suggests that *quzhu chujing* shoud also be regarded as compulsory measure or at least as the immediate enforcement of the punishment of *quzhu*. Article 35 *Criminal Law* (2015), however, suggests that the term *quzhu chujing* is not meant as compulsory measure but as individual or supplementary punishment. Whether or not a compulsory measure is meant in

367 Art. 183 *Provisions on Handling Administrative Cases* (2003); Art. 192 *Provisions on Handling Administrative Cases* (2006). According to Art. 220 *Provisions on Handling Administrative Cases* (2012), the power of approval lies with the authorities at county level or above.

368 Yu Qun / Ma Shuncheng (2012), p. 133.

369 Chinese: 遣送出境措施不服.

370 *Interpretation to the Exit–Entry Administration Law of the People's Republic of China* (中华人民共和国出境入境管理法释义) (2012), p. 128; *Interpretation of the 'Exit–Entry Administration Law of the People's Republic of China'* (《中华人民共和国出境入境管理法》释义) (2012), p. 169; *Guide to Interpretation and Application of the 'Exit–Entry Administration Law of the People's Republic of China'* (《中华人民共和国出境入境管理法》释义及实用指南) (2012), p. 159: "Second, administrative compulsory measures such as continued interrogation, detention for investigation, restriction of activities, that are carried out in the process of exit–entry administration [...]" (Chinese: 二是继续盘问, 拘留审查、限制活动范围、遣送出境措施等行政强制措施是出境入境管理过程中所采取的［……］).

371 Chinese: 无法立即执行遣送出境、驱逐出境的.

the context of deportation has thus to be inferred from the context. Often additional words like "measure" (*cuoshi*[372]) or "to execute" (*zhixing*[373]) imply that a compulsory measure or the actual enforcement is meant.

Since compulsory measures should only be enforced if the desired result cannot be achieved by other means,[374] in cases of illegal stay or illegal employment, repatriation should only be applied in severe circumstances where the further stay or residence of the foreign national would be rendered "improper"[375] according to an official interpretation.[376] This interpretation, hence, suggests that repatriation should be applied cautiously and always only as last resort. Further, as repatriations interfere considerably with personal rights, Article 62(1)iv *Exit–Entry Administration Law* (2012) restricts the application of repatriation to cases where laws or administrative regulations require a repatriation and implicitly excludes lower-level legal documents like local regulations, meaning that repatriation is not admissible solely on the basis of a local regulation.[377] The fact that Article 62 *Exit–Entry Administration Law* (2012) defines repatriation as optional underlines this reading as well as the official interpretation that repatriation should in general only be applied in concrete situations after having taken into consideration the "spirit of the law."[378]

Except for the case where the Ministry of Public Security decides on the deportation (*quzhu*) of the foreign national, an order to leave the country within a certain time limit (*xianqi chujing*[379]) may be issued by public security authorities, which may finally be enforced by the means of repatriation as a compulsory measure. The specified time limit for such an order to leave shall not exceed fifteen days.[380] Article 81 *Exit–Entry Administration Law*

372 Chinese: 措施.
373 Chinese: 执行.
374 Art. 5 *Administrative Compulsion Law* (2011).
375 Chinese: 不再适宜.
376 *Interpretation of the 'Exit–Entry Administration Law of the People's Republic of China'* (《中华人民共和国出境入境管理法》释义) (2012), p. 185. Regarding the term 'improper', see the discussion on Art. 81 *Exit–Entry Administration Law* (2012) above.
377 *Interpretation of the 'Exit–Entry Administration Law of the People's Republic of China'* (《中华人民共和国出境入境管理法》释义) (2012), p. 185.
378 Chinese: 法律精神. *Interpretation of the 'Exit–Entry Administration Law of the People's Republic of China'* (《中华人民共和国出境入境管理法》释义) (2012), p. 186.
379 Chinese: 限期出境.
380 Art. 33 *Exit–Entry Administration Regulations* (2013).

(2012) states that foreign nationals who carry out activities inconsistent with their cause of stay or residence or who violate legal regulations in a way that it "renders their further stay or residence improper"[381] may be ordered to leave China within a specified time limit (*xianzhi chuqing*). Where foreign nationals infringe upon provisions of the *Exit–Entry Administration Law* (2012) in a serious way but their infringement does not constitute a crime, the Ministry of Public Security may decide upon their deportation. As this kind of deportation is classified in Chapter VII of the *Exit–Entry Administration Law* (2012) that covers legal responsibility, it should be considered an administrative penalty as already discussed above. The decision of the Ministry of Public Security shall be final and is thus not subject to administrative reconsideration or administrative litigation. The restriction on reconsideration and litigation, however, is only part of the second sentence of the relevant provision covering "serious circumstances" that allow the Ministry of Public Security to decide. What exactly is to be considered a case with serious circumstances is neither mentioned in the law nor defined in the relevant *Exit–Entry Administration Regulations* (2013). Being an administrative penalty, an order to leave in general allows for both, administrative reconsideration and administrative litigation. An order to leave can be imposed apparently by any public security organ at county level or above,[382] as the law does not state otherwise.

After being repatriated, individuals are prohibited from re-entering China within one to five years.[383] The concrete period of time during which the repatriated individual is prohibited re-entry to China shall be specified by the authority that decides on the repatriation.[384] After being deported, the re-entry ban shall amount to ten years.[385] If the repatriation cannot be executed immediately, the individual shall be detained.[386] The *Foreign Nationals Exit–Entry Administration Regulations* (2013) define inclement weather or poor health conditions of the individual concerned as possible reasons for the adjournment of repatriation.[387] The expenses for repatriation shall be paid by the individual concerned. If the reason for repatriation is illegal

381 Chinese: 不适宜在中国境内继续停留居留情形的.
382 Art. 70 *Exit–Entry Administration Law* (2012).
383 Art. 62 *Exit–Entry Administration Law* (2012).
384 Art. 31 *Exit–Entry Administration Regulations* (2013).
385 Art. 81(3) *Exit–Entry Administration Law* (2012).
386 Art. 63 *Exit–Entry Administration Law* (2012); Art. 29(3) *Exit–Entry Administration Regulations* (2013).
387 Art. 29 *Exit–Entry Administration Regulations* (2013).

employment, the expenses shall be borne by the employer if the individual concerned is not able to pay for him- or herself. In any other case, if the individual concerned is not able to bear the expenses, the individual or entity guaranteeing for the stay shall pay the expenses.[388]

The *Provisions on the Procedures for Handling Administrative Cases by Public Security Organs* (2012) list possible countries and regions a foreign national may be repatriated to. Apart from the state of his or her nationality, this can be the country of residence, the country of birth, the country of exit before having entered China, or any other country which permits his or her entry.[389] The relevant article does not state which of these countries or regions shall be preferred. It is hence unclear, whether e. g. the country of nationality of the foreign national shall be given preference over the country of his or her last entry to China. In theory, these provisions allow for the removal of an individual whose nationality cannot be clarified or who is stateless to any other country. In practice, however, this is only possible if a repatriation agreement or a similar law enforcement treaty exists between the People's Republic of China and the receiving country.[390]

Article 30 of the *State Security Law* (1993/2009) provided for the 'order to leave' and 'deportation' of foreign nationals[391] who violated this law.[392] This provision, however, was abolished with the 2015 revision of the *State Security Law*. Furthermore, individuals who enjoy consular protection and who are therefore exempt from certain legal sanctions may be declared as *persona non grata* in accordance with international law,[393] which is commonly denoted with the term 'diplomatic punishment' (*waijiao chufa*[394]) in Chinese literature.[395]

Taking together all these findings, I conclude that the provisions in Articles 62 and 64 of the *Exit–Entry Administration Law* (2012) concerning repatriation (*qiansong*) shall be regarded as basic legal framework concerning the procedure of repatriation (removal) of foreign nationals, regardless of whether the underlying administrative decision is an administrative punishment or not and without differentiating between administrative or judicial

388 Art. 32 *Exit–Entry Administration Regulations* (2013).
389 Art. 221 *AdministrativeCasesHandlingP2012*.
390 Other practical problems of removal will be discussed below.
391 Chinese: 境外人员.
392 Art. 30 *State Security Law* (1993); Art. 30 *State Security Law* (2009).
393 Art. 23 *Vienna Convention on Consular Relations* (1963).
394 Chinese: 外交处罚.
395 Research Institute for Prosecution Theory of the Supreme People's Procuratorate (最高人民检察院检察理论研究所) / Cai Yaqi (2013).

decisions that are enforced in the concrete case. In contrast, the provisions in Article 81 of the *Exit–Entry Administration Law* (2012) as well as relevant provisions concerning deportation (*quzhu*) or order to leave (*xianqi chujing*) in the *Criminal Law* (2015) and the *Public Security Administration Punishments Law* (2012) are deemed to only regulate deportation or order to leave as administrative punishment. Furthermore, while deportation has a compulsory character and may be enforced immediately, an order to leave sets a certain period of time during which the foreign national shall leave the country. Only if the foreign national does not comply with the order to leave, his or her repatriation (removal) is enforced. Notwithstanding this, repatriations may also be enforced after the handling of certain punishments, e. g. those regarding illegal entry, illegal stay or illegal employment. Finally, the term *qianfan* does not describe a specific administrative act performed by a Chinese administrative organ, but rather serves as umbrella term for repatriation, deportation and removal enacted by Chinese or foreign authorities.

2. Limitations to Legal Remedies against Deportation or Repatriation

As has been outlined above, order to leave, deportation and repatriation constitute different kinds of administrative actions that imply different legal remedies. While an order to leave constitutes an administrative penalty and repatriation is typically considered to be an administrative enforcement measure, deportation may denote an administrative or a criminal penalty. Finally, the enforcement of a deportation, i. e. the concrete removal of the foreign national from the Chinese territory, is also considered an administrative enforcement measure. Depending on the kind of administrative act or court decision that underlie the order to leave, the deportation or the repatriation, different legal remedies can be applied by the concerned foreign national.

An order to leave, being an administrative punishment imposed by the public security organs at and above county level, is subject to administrative reconsideration and administrative litigation. According to the *Public Security Administration Punishments Law* (2012) an order to leave can also be imposed as supplemental penalty,[396] which also is subject to administrative reconsideration and administrative litigation.

As on-site questioning, continued questioning, detention for investigation, restriction of activities, as well as repatriation are considered admin-

396 Art. 10(1)iv *Public Security Administration Punishments Law* (2012).

istrative compulsory measures, the *Administrative Compulsion Law* (2011) is the basis for the implementation of these measures. Of these measures, continued questioning, detention for investigation, restriction of activities, as well as repatriation are considered compulsory measures restricting personal freedom.[397] A basic principle for the implementation of compulsory measures is the use of such measures as supportive and temporary means without punitive character.[398] Thus, as soon as the facts to verify the illegality of an activity are clear, the compulsory measure has to be terminated. Furthermore, a prerequisite for executing detention for investigation is that the omission of such detention would have a negative impact on the clarification of the facts.[399]

Repatriation (*qiansong chujing*[400]), the actual removal of the foreign national, is a compulsory measure with the aim to enforce an order to leave and hence itself is not deemed an administrative penalty.[401] Against administrative compulsion, regardless of whether it is an administrative compulsory measure or compulsory enforcement, the individual concerned may generally apply for administrative reconsideration or administrative litigation as described in the sections above. However, the *Exit–Entry Administration Law* (2012) limits the access to legal remedies in the case of repatriation to administrative reconsideration. As Article 64 *Exit–Entry Administration Law* (2012) states, for some compulsory measures like continued questioning, detention for investigation, restriction of activities, or repatriation the decision laid down by administrative reconsideration shall be the final decision. However, strictly speaking, this formulation leaves open whether administrative litigation is really impossible here, as administrative litigation is

397 *Guide to Interpretation and Application of the 'Exit–Entry Administration Law of the People's Republic of China'* (《中华人民共和国出境入境管理法》释义及实用指南) (2012), p. 150.

398 *Guide to Interpretation and Application of the 'Exit–Entry Administration Law of the People's Republic of China'* (《中华人民共和国出境入境管理法》释义及实用指南) (2012), p. 148.

399 *Guide to Interpretation and Application of the 'Exit–Entry Administration Law of the People's Republic of China'* (《中华人民共和国出境入境管理法》释义及实用指南) (2012), p. 152.

400 Chinese: 遣送出境.

401 *Interpretation of the 'Exit–Entry Administration Law of the People's Republic of China'* (《中华人民共和国出境入境管理法》释义) (2012), p. 169; *Guide to Interpretation and Application of the 'Exit–Entry Administration Law of the People's Republic of China'* (《中华人民共和国出境入境管理法》释义及实用指南) (2012), p. 148.

always possible without prior administrative reconsideration. Nevertheless, official interpretations of this provision explicitly state that administrative litigation is neither allowed against the decision of administrative reconsideration nor against the original administrative action.[402]

Deportation, of which the enforcement is considered a compulsory measure as well, may be imposed as criminal penalty or as administrative penalty. In certain circumstances, deportation may be imposed as administrative penalty by the Ministry of Public Security according to the *Exit–Entry Administration Law* (2012). The punishment is then enforced immediately and is neither subject to administrative consideration nor to administrative litigation, nor, obviously, is its enforcement. According to the *Public Security Administration Punishments Law* (2012), deportation may further be imposed as supplemental penalty. The provisions of the *Exit–Entry Administration Law* (2012) only state that against a decision concerning deportation made by the Ministry of Public Security administrative litigation or reconsideration cannot be applied, but it remains silent about cases where other administrative organs make such a decision.[403] This implies that if an administrative decision on deportation is made by a public security organ other than the Ministry according to the relevant provisions of the *Public Security Administration Punishments Law* (2012), this restriction of legal remedies does not hold. The *Exit–Entry Administration Law* (2012) in its provisions concerning repatriation, however, *inter alia* refers to repatriation on the basis of other laws or administrative regulations,[404] which suggests that the limitation of the legal remedies to administrative reconsideration also applies to repatriations applied as means of enforcement in the context of a deportation imposed by this public security organ. Taken these findings together, the decision on deportation can be subject to administrative litigation and administrative reconsideration, while the enforcement of the decision on deportation can only be subject to administrative reconsideration, as long as the deportation has not been decided upon by the Ministry of Public Security. When imposed as criminal penalty, criminal litigation is admissible, which allows for appeal once. In any case, legal remedies against

---

402 *Guide to Interpretation and Application of the 'Exit–Entry Administration Law of the People's Republic of China'* (《中华人民共和国出境入境管理法》释义及实用指南) (2012), p. 159; *Interpretation of the 'Exit–Entry Administration Law of the People's Republic of China'* (《中华人民共和国出境入境管理法》释义) (2012), p. 188.

403 Art. 81(2) *Exit–Entry Administration Law* (2012).

404 Art. 62(1)iv *Exit–Entry Administration Law* (2012).

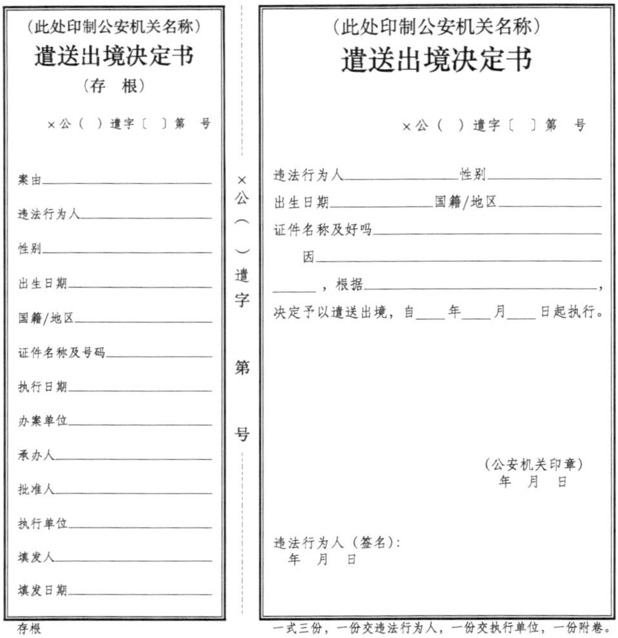

（此处印制公安机关名称）
遣送出境决定书
（存　根）
×公（　）遣字〔　〕第　号
案由＿＿＿＿
违法行为人＿＿＿＿
性别＿＿＿＿
出生日期＿＿＿＿
国籍/地区＿＿＿＿
证件名称及号码＿＿＿＿
执行日期＿＿＿＿
办案单位＿＿＿＿
承办人＿＿＿＿
批准人＿＿＿＿
执行单位＿＿＿＿
填发人＿＿＿＿
填发日期＿＿＿＿
存根

×公（　）遣字　第　号

（此处印制公安机关名称）
遣送出境决定书
×公（　）遣字〔　〕第　号
违法行为人＿＿＿＿性别＿＿＿＿
出生日期＿＿＿＿国籍/地区＿＿＿＿
证件名称及好吗＿＿＿＿
因＿＿＿＿
＿＿＿，根据＿＿＿＿，
决定予以遣送出境，自＿＿年＿＿月＿＿日起执行。
（公安机关印章）
年　月　日
违法行为人（签名）：
年　月　日
一式三份，一份交违法行为人，一份交执行单位，一份附卷。

Figure 4.1: Written decision on repatriation issued by public security authorities[405]

the enforcement of an administrative decision or court judgement can only be used to evaluate the legality of the enforcement itself and cannot be used to evaluate the underlying decision or court ruling.

a) Suspension of Administrative Acts

An important question in the context of repatriation is whether the removal of a foreign national can be stopped or suspended by filing a complaint to the relevant authority or a court. During the procedure of administrative reconsideration, an administrative act shall generally not be suspended.[406] However, the authority receiving the request (which may be the same authority that executes the administrative act or a higher-ranking authority) may

405 Example taken from Yu Qun / Ma Shuncheng (2012), p. 134.
406 Art. 21 *Administrative Reconsideration Law* (2009).

suspend the execution of the administrative action if it deems it necessary or if the person concerned applied for the suspension of the administrative act in question because the execution of the administrative act would lead to irreversible damage and the suspension would not undermine the administrative order or public interest.[407] Alike, the *Public Security Administration Punishments Law* (2012) states that the individual concerned may apply for the suspension of the execution of administrative detention as administrative punishment, and if the public security organs in charge hold that no danger to the public[408] will result from the suspension, the execution of the administrative detention may be suspended upon bail of a guarantor who meets the relevant requirements.[409] The suspension of an administrative act can also be required by other legal provisions.[410] The possibility to apply for suspension of administrative acts during administrative reconsideration is important in the context of an order to leave or repatriation since it opens the possibility to a fair review of the relevant case. As the repatriation of the foreign national would result in a situation where he or she has no more opportunity to exercise his or her rights once he or she has left the territory of the People's Republic of China, one could indeed argue that a successful repatriation indeed could lead to irreversible damage to the rights of the foreign national.

Similar provisions regarding the suspension of an administrative act exist in the context of administrative litigation. According to Article 56 *Administrative Litigation Law* (2014), filing administrative litigation and acceptance by a court will not imply the suspension of the execution of the administrative act in question. However, the defendant, i. e. the state authority against which a lawsuit is filed, may suspend the execution of the administrative action if it deems it necessary.[411] The plaintiff may file a request for suspension of the administrative act.[412] If the court deems the non-suspension to result in "irreparable losses"[413] and the suspension would not infringe national or public interest, it may decide on the suspension of the administrative act and

407 Art. 21(1)i–iii *Administrative Reconsideration Law* (2009); Wu Gaosheng (2015), p. 151.

408 Chinese: 社会危险.

409 Art. 107 *Public Security Administration Punishments Law* (2012); Wu Gaosheng (2015), p. 151–152.

410 Art. 21(1)iv *Administrative Reconsideration Law* (2009).

411 Art. 56(1)i *Administrative Litigation Law* (2014).

412 Art. 56(1)ii *Administrative Litigation Law* (2014).

413 Chinese: 难以弥补的损失.

issue an appropriate ruling.[414] The court can also issue a ruling for suspension if it deems that the execution of the administrative act would infringe the national or public interest.[415] Finally, the suspension of an administrative act may be required by other legal regulations.[416] A ruling to suspend or not to suspend the execution of an administrative act may be subject to administrative reconsideration by one of the parties once.[417] Although administrative litigation can not be applied in the context of repatriation or deportation on the basis of a decision by the Ministry of Public Security, a request for suspension of an administrative act can be filed in the context of administrative litigation against an order to leave or any other administrative act as long as the legal remedies are not limited as stated by a law.

b) Compatibility with International Standards

The authority of a state to allow foreign nationals to enter the territory also implies its authority to order foreign nationals to leave. However, here again, the state is bound by international law.[418] The breach of conditions of the stay is generally considered a reason for expulsion, and the burden of proof is then shifted to the individual.[419] Deportation is the factual execution of an expulsion order. Deportation is also used by states as a supplemental punishment of crimes, sometimes combined with a bar to re-enter the country.[420] Human rights like the right to dignity, to non-discrimination, not to be subject to torture or inhuman treatment,[421] or the right to family life must be considered in the context of expulsion. Especially the obligations of a state to protect children and the unity of family limit the authority to expel

---

414 Art. 56(1)iii *Administrative Litigation Law* (2014).

415 Art. 56(1)iii *Administrative Litigation Law* (2014).

416 Art. 56(1)iv *Administrative Litigation Law* (2014).

417 Art. 56(2) *Administrative Litigation Law* (2014).

418 Perruchoud (2012), p. 143.

419 Perruchoud (2012), p. 143.

420 See Stumpf (2013) on the combination of criminal and immigration law to criminalise illegal immigration as well as to use deportation as a punishment of criminal offences.

421 Possible torture as well as inhuman or degrading treatment or punishment in the state to which the individual is deported to is considered an hindrance to deportation (i. e. prohibition of *refoulement* codified *inter alia* in Art. 33(1) *Convention Relating to the Status of Refugees* (1951), Art. 3 *Convention against Torture and Other Cruel, Inhuman or Degrading Treatment or Punishment* (1984), or Art. 7 *ICCPR* (1966)).

foreign nationals.[422] It has to be noted that states may not expel their own nationals, e. g. by the means of depriving their nationality.[423]

It is considered an international standard that irregular migrants may be subject to expulsion.[424] Basic procedural guarantees including the possibility to review the expulsion decision are enshrined in international law, but only apply to foreign nationals who are "lawfully in the territory of a State".[425] Where "compelling reasons of national security" exist, these basic procedural guarantees do not apply.[426] The burden of proof to provide reasons against the expulsion decision rests with the foreign national, which makes these guarantees only a weak legal protection.[427] Some states apply procedures that do not allow for appeal or review in specific circumstances. For example, in the U. S., a crime can lead to deportation that cannot be contested.[428] Also, if a foreign national arrives at the U. S. border without proper immigration documents, he or she can be removed immediately in an expedited removal procedure and the relevant decision of the official of the Department of Homeland Security is final.[429] In regular removal procedures in the U. S. however, an appeal against a decision of an immigration judge is possible.[430] The European Court of Human Rights highlighted the requirement of an "effective possibility of challenging the deportation or refusal-of-residence order",[431] which implies that in countries that are party to the *European Convention on Human Rights* legal remedy against deportation orders are effective in general. While there is no consensus internationally whether basic procedural rights such as the right to receive a notice of the expulsion decision and the right to challenge this decision should apply to undocumented immigrants as well,[432] the *ICRMW* provides for even more

422 Perruchoud (2012), p. 143.
423 Some states do, however, apply this means when it does not lead to statelessness; Perruchoud (2012), p. 145.
424 Perruchoud (2012), p. 144.
425 Art. 13 *ICCPR* (1966).
426 Art. 13 *ICCPR* (1966).
427 Perruchoud (2012), p. 144.
428 Stumpf (2013), p. 94.
429 Title 8 Sec. 1225 b(1)(A)(i) *United States Code of Laws* (2017). However, as discussed above, a request by the foreign national for reconsideration has to be accepted.
430 Title 8 Sec. 1362 *United States Code of Laws* (2017); Title 8 Sec. 1003.38 *United States Code of Federal Regulations* (2018).
431 See *Al-Nashif v. Bulgaria* (2002), in reference to Art. 13 and 8 of the *European Convention on Human Rights*.
432 Perruchoud (2012), p. 145.

comprehensive guarantees for migrant workers of any legal status, including the right to be informed in a language they understand and the right to have the decision reviewed, again with the exception of "compelling reasons of national security".[433] Currently, the *ICRMW* is signed only by a small number of states and China is not party to this convention. It is hence difficult to state that it is recognised international practice to allow any foreign national, regardless of his or her legal status, access to basic procedural guarantees in the context of expulsion. In any case, expulsion decisions have to be made on an individual basis. Collective expulsions are not permitted under customary international law.[434]

Except for a decision made by the Ministry of Public Security to remove a foreign national, the Chinese legal framework allows for administrative reconsideration against repatriation and the individual concerned is informed in written form beforehand about his or her repatriation and the reasons thereof. The deportation decision of the Ministry of Public Security requires a serious violation of the provisions of the *Exit–Entry Administration Law*,[435] but does not explicitly refer to reasons of national security. Hence, it can be argued that the relevant provision stands in contradiction to the provision of the *ICRMW* and the *ICCPR*, which only allows the expulsion of foreign nationals without access to a review procedure where "compelling reasons of national security" exist. However, as there is no international consensus about the applicability of procedural rights to undocumented migrants and international practice deviates from the general requirement of access to legal remedies in certain situations, it is difficult to regard this provision as in conflict with international standards. Where a deportation is imposed as supplemental or individual punishment according to the *Criminal Law* (2015),[436] an appeal may be filed to the relevant court. If an order to leave is imposed by the public security organs, the foreign national may file an administrative lawsuit. In summary, from an analysis of the relevant legal norms, the Chinese legal framework on deportation and repatriation does not contradict international legal practice. The Chinese practice to impose a re-entry ban on foreign nationals who have been deported can also

433 Art. 22(3), 22(4) *ICRMW* (1990).

434 *Čonka v. Belgium* (2002); Perruchoud (2012), p. 145 f. See as well Art. 22(1) *ICRMW* (1990).

435 Art. 81(2) *Exit–Entry Administration Law* (2012).

436 Art. 35 *Criminal Law* (2015).

not be considered a violation of international standards, as it is generally accepted international practice.[437]

III. Detention for Investigation

Before being repatriated from China, a foreign national may be detained for investigation. Detention for investigation can be regarded as a last resort the police may turn to in cases where the identity of the foreign national to be repatriated remains unclear after continued questioning or other investigations or in cases where it is suspected that the foreign national may escape the execution of repatriation.

The 2012 *Exit–Entry Administration Law* states that measures like on-site questioning, continued questioning, investigative detention, restriction of activities, and repatriation shall be executed by the local public security authorities at county level or above or the exit–entry border inspection authorities.[438] Questioning shall be conducted according to the provisions of the *Police Law* (2012) and the *Public Security Administration Punishments Law* (2012).[439] On-site questioning shall be conducted if a person is suspected of violating exit–entry administration while continued questioning is permitted only if the person is suspected of exiting or entering the country illegally or assisting others in exiting or entering the country illegally, suspected of illegal residence or employment being a foreign national, or if the person is suspected of affecting national security, disrupting the public order, or of any other illegal or criminal action.[440] In contrast to the relevant provisions of the old legal framework of 1985 that only codified detention for investigation for individuals suspected of illegal entry or illegal stay,[441] the revised legal framework extends the scope of application. According to

437 Title 8 Sec. 1182(9)(A) *Code of Laws of the United States of America* (2015); Art. 11 *Gesetz über den Aufenthalt, die Erwerbstätigkeit und die Integration von Ausländern im Bundesgebiet* (2018); Art. 320(7)(B) *[U. K.] Immigration Rules* (2019)

438 Art. 58 *Exit–Entry Administration Law* (2012).

439 Art. 59 *Exit–Entry Administration Law* (2012).

440 Art. 59 *Exit–Entry Administration Law* (2012). Chinese law typically assigns the term *fanzui* (犯罪) to a crime while *weifa* (违法) depicts any illegal action whether criminal or not. The expression *weifa fanzui huodong* (违法犯罪活动) obviously depicts both criminal and other illegal actions even though, logically, the term *fanzui* is already comprised in the broader term of *weifa*.

441 Art. 27 *Foreign Nationals Exit–Entry Administration Law* (1985).

the 2012 *Exit–Entry Administration Law*, the prerequisites to detain a foreign national for investigation are the same as for continued questioning.[442]

According to Article 60 *Exit–Entry Administration Law* (2012), detention for investigation may be applied if on-site and subsequent continued questioning did not clarify a suspected illegal activity of a foreign national. Detention for investigation may also be used where a foreign national is to be repatriated or deported to prevent escape. However, a prerequisite for the facultative compulsory measure of detention for investigation is that the foreign national has been questioned beforehand and the continued questioning did not dispel the suspicion.[443] In any case, a decision on detention for investigation shall be issued to the foreign national. The duration of detention for investigation shall not be longer than 30 days with the option of extension up to 60 days after approval of the public security authorities, the entry-exit border inspection authorities, or the local people's government of the next higher level.[444] According to Article 61 *Exit–Entry Administration Law* (2012), in certain circumstances where detention is not permissible, the individual's activities shall be restricted instead. The restriction of activity shall not exceed 60 days. If it turns out that the measure of detention for investigation is "not applicable",[445] the suspect shall be released immediately. The *Exit–Entry Administration Regulations* (2013) state that the transfer of the suspect to the detention house or repatriation facility shall be executed within 24 hours.[446]

Although the law defines a fixed period of detention for investigation and restriction of activity, these periods shall be counted from the day on which the identity of the foreign national is clarified.[447] Thus, it is basically possible to keep a foreign national under detention for an unlimited period of time by contending that his or her identity has not been clarified yet.[448] This

442 Art. 60 *Exit–Entry Administration Law* (2012).

443 *Interpretation of the 'Exit–Entry Administration Law of the People's Republic of China'* (《中华人民共和国出境入境管理法》释义) (2012), p. 178.

444 Art. 60 *Exit–Entry Administration Law* (2012).

445 Chinese: 不应当拘留审查的.

446 Art. 29 *Exit–Entry Administration Regulations* (2013).

447 Art. 60(3) *Exit–Entry Administration Law* (2012).

448 The *Provisions on Handling Administrative Cases* (2003) explicitly stated that the length of detention for investigation should end with the clarification of identity and subsequent removal of the foreign national (see Art. 184), which basically allowed for indefinite detention. The *Provisions on Handling Administrative Cases* (2006) restricted the maximum period of detention for investigation to two months and the maximum period for restriction of activity to six months (see Art. 193), regardless

provision is justified by the fact that repatriation would not be possible where the nationality and identity of the individual is unclear.[449] However, Article 216 *Provisions on the Procedures for Handling Administrative Cases by Public Security Organs* (2012) states that where the nationality of a foreign national is unclear and where it is impossible to ascertain his or her real nationality, the foreign national shall be treated according to the nationality declared by him or her or as stateless. This implies that the period to clarify the identity of the foreign national is limited to the period of internal investigation by the relevant authorities on the nationality of the foreign national and not his or her identity. However, a similar legal structure exists in criminal litigation where criminal suspects may be detained as long as their legal status is unclear in order to clarify their identity.[450]

During the procedure of administrative reconsideration, no additional evidence shall be collected by the authorities from the applicant or individuals or organisations concerned.[451] This essentially means that, where detention for investigation is subject to administrative reconsideration, the police are not allowed to subsequently look for additional evidence proving that the individual detained is under reasonable suspicion, but the authorities have to argue on the basis of the facts that were collected before the decision for detention for investigation was made. This does not imply, however, that the authorities have to suspend their investigation altogether, since further investigation is done to collect evidence for the offence of the individual, which then may be used to impose administrative or criminal

of whether the identity of the foreign national was clear. A longer period was only possible upon approval of the public security organs at provincial level in case the individual could not be repatriated immediately and his or her release would endanger (public) security and only until his nationality was finally clarified and the foreign national could hence be removed. The wording of the 2006 provisions implies that this provision originally was meant to only govern cases where a foreign national was detained for repatriation but timely repatriation was hindered due to the difficulty to clarify his or her nationality (see Yu Qun / Ma Shuncheng (2012), p. 123). However, the revised *Provisions on Handling Administrative Cases* (2012), which abolish the 2006 provisions, do not contain such a ruling any more and stick to the wording of the *Exit–Entry Administration Law* (2012), implying that this provision is no longer meant to only cover the above mentioned case.

449 *Interpretation of the 'Exit–Entry Administration Law of the People's Republic of China'* (《中华人民共和国出境入境管理法》释义) (2012), p. 180.

450 Art. 158(2) *Criminal Litigation Law* (2012); Dutton (2005), p. 275 f. Detention in these cases has to be approved by a police authority at or above county level; Art. 126 *Provisions on Handling Criminal Cases* (2012).

451 Art. 24 *Administrative Reconsideration Law* (2009).

punishment. The administrative reconsideration organ shall issue a decision on the subject within 60 days, in complex cases this period may be extended by another 30 days.[452] Finally, the *Administrative Reconsideration Law* (2009) provides for legal consequences if administrative authorities do not comply with the legal provisions. Administrative litigation is not admissible against detention for investigation.[453]

Thus, when being questioned or detained, a foreign national is entitled to refuse to accept the compulsory measure and to file an application for reconsideration. However, this does not mean that the compulsory measure will immediately be stopped. As has been discussed in the case of repatriation already, only if the authority that receives the application for reconsideration explicitly requesting the suspension of the execution of the administrative act deems it necessary to suspend the execution of the questioning or detention will the execution of the administrative act be suspended. The provisions of the *Administrative Reconsideration Law*, however, leave it up to the administrative organ in charge to decide upon the suspension of the execution of the administrative act in question.

1. Legal Remedies against Detention for Investigation in Comparison with International Standards

China has ratified several international treaties and is hence bound to the relevant provisions. Examples of treaties ratified by the People's Republic of China are the *International Covenant on Economic, Social and Cultural Rights (ICESCR)*, the *United Nations Convention against Transnational Organized Crime* and the *Convention on the Rights of the Child.* China further has subscribed to the *International Convention on the Elimination of All Forms of Racial Discrimination* and the *Convention Relating to the Status of Refugees* all of which contain provisions concerning (im)migration. However, China has only signed but not ratified the *ICCPR.*

Notwithstanding this, certain provisions of the *ICCPR* concerning arbitrary detention are still applicable to China. The Working Group on Arbitrary Detention of the Office of the United Nations High Commissioner for Human Rights (OHCHR) concluded in its 2004 *Report* that Article 9 *ICCPR*

452 Art. 31 *Administrative Reconsideration Law* (2009).
453 Art. 64(1) *Exit–Entry Administration Law* (2012).

is binding even on states not party to the treaty, since its contents can be regarded as customary international law.[454]

Moreover, as China is party to the *Vienna Convention on the Law of Treaties* (1969), it is "obliged to refrain from acts which would defeat the object and purpose of a treaty" that it has signed with reservation of ratification.[455] Article 9 *ICCPR* requires detention to be non-arbitrary and lawful[456] and states that any detention may be challenged before a court[457] and that unlawful detention is subject to compensation.[458]

Official interpretations of the relevant provisions state that the limitation of legal remedies against compulsory measures in the context of exit–entry administration to administrative reconsideration is in line with international treaties and customs.[459] Further, the establishment of a specific detention scheme for foreign nationals is argued to be in line with international practice.[460] International standards, however, require the possibility of judicial review of the detention of foreign nationals. Therefore, with regard to the measure of detention for investigation, the statement that the limitation to administrative reconsideration is in line with international standards is dubious.

According to Article 9 *ICCPR*, detention has to be lawful and non-arbitrary. Detention is only lawful if it is executed on the basis of legal norms that are codified in a law. Administrative norms cannot serve as primary basis for detention.[461] Furthermore, neither the legal norms nor their application shall be arbitrary, which means that detention has to be applied in a reasonable way and only if necessary.[462] In other words, detention shall be a "proportionate means to achieve a legitimate aim,"[463] i. e. it shall be applied only if no other, less restrictive means can be applied.

---

454 Art. 53 OHCHR Working Group on Arbitrary Detention (2003); Vohra (2007), p. 53.

455 Art. 18 *Vienna Convention on the Law of Treaties* (1969).

456 Art. 9(1) *ICCPR* (1966).

457 Art. 9(4) *ICCPR* (1966).

458 Art. 9(5) *ICCPR* (1966).

459 *Guide to Interpretation and Application of the 'Exit–Entry Administration Law of the People's Republic of China'* (《中华人民共和国出境入境管理法》释义及实用指南) (2012), p. 159.

460 *Interpretation of the 'Exit–Entry Administration Law of the People's Republic of China'* (《中华人民共和国出境入境管理法》释义) (2012), p. 178.

461 See Nowak (1993), p. 171, cited in Vohra (2007), p. 56.

462 UN Human Rights Committee (1990).

463 Humans Rights and Equal Opportunity Commission (1998).

The Working Group on Arbitrary Detention states in its 2002 *Report* that a temporary detention is justified in performing identity checks, but "any deprivation of liberty must be proportionate to the aims pursued".[464] According to the *Convention on the Rights of the Child*, detention of a child shall only be applied as last resort and for as short a time as possible.[465]

A uniform definition of detention is missing, it can, however, be deduced from definitions in various legal documents. The 1990 *UN Rules for the Protection of Juveniles Deprived of their Liberty* state that

> [d]eprivation of liberty means any form of detention or imprisonment or the placement of a person in another public or private custodial setting from which this person is not permitted lo leave at will, by order of any judicial, administrative or other public authority.[466]

According to the 1999 *UNHCR Revised Guidelines on Applicable Criteria and Standards Regarding to the Detention of Asylum Seekers*, detention, more broadly, covers all kinds of "confinement within a narrowly bounded or restricted location."[467] Thus, while detention covers both criminal and administrative detention, it can be distinguished from mere restriction of movement.[468]

In the case of detention for investigation, the decision of the public security authorities on administrative reconsideration are deemed final and no administrative litigation is hence possible, which renders this form of detention unlawful according to Article 9(1) *ICCPR*. The limited access to legal remedies in combination with the fact that detention for investigation, at least theoretically, may be extended indefinitely provided that the identity of the foreign national remains unclear, renders the means of detention for investigation a very dubious instrument.

IV. Summary

The topic of repatriation and removal of foreign nationals cannot be analysed in sufficient depth without carving out the preconditions for the imposition of an order to leave or deportation. As the analysis in the first part of this section showed, the decisive question is whether the activity of the indi-

464 Art. 12 OHCHR Working Group on Arbitrary Detention (2002).
465 Art. 37(b) *Convention on the Rights of the Child* (1989).
466 Cited in Vohra (2007), p. 51.
467 UN High Commissioner for Refugees (1999), p. 3.
468 Vohra (2007), p. 50 f.

vidual is suitable to render his or her ongoing stay improper. The stay of an individual is not automatically deemed to be improper if this individual committed an administrative or criminal offence of whatever severity. Illegal stay comprises illegal residence and illegal short-term stay, but it does not include offences in the context of registration of foreign nationals, and both offences are technically not a necessary precondition for the stay to be rendered improper. This implies that the decision regarding the improperness of stay lies with the public security organs that, moreover, also may not impose an order to leave or deportation. Obviously, hence, the public security organs are granted a large amount of discretion in the context of repatriation and removal of foreign nationals.

The last part of this section analysed the measure of detention for investigation. The revised *Exit–Entry Administration Law* contains several measures that are only applicable to foreign nationals and that are defined as compulsory measures. Of these, continued questioning, detention for investigation, restriction of activities and repatriation cannot be contested using administrative litigation and only administrative reconsideration is applicable. Detention for investigation and restriction of activities, defined as replacement for detention for investigation for certain cases, may only be applied if on-site questioning and continued questioning could not clarify the suspiciousness of the foreign national. Hence, the application of detention for investigation is limited to a certain group of foreign nationals. However, the fact that access to a review by a court is restricted renders this measure incompatible with international law that requires access to judicial review for any form of detention. Hence, regardless of the fact that detention for investigation allows for infinite detention of unidentified foreign nationals as could be shown above, this measure should be regarded as contradictory to international standards.

This section aimed to answer the question whether the new legal framework of exit–entry administration solves the conflict of aims as on the one hand the legal rights of foreign nationals shall be protected in accordance to international standards and on the other hand the enforcement of legal norms shall be increased in part by enhancing the power of discretion of police officials. The extension of police power has already been pointed out in the context of passport inspections. The revised *Exit–Entry Administration Law* removes the requirement for the approval of the Ministry of Public Security for an order to leave. While such an extension of power surely contributes to improved enforcement of legal norms, it needs to be balanced by appropriate access to legal remedies for the individual concerned to take action against misapplication of the law. The second part of this section has shown that the revised legal framework on exit–entry administration codifies access to legal remedies in much more detail in comparison to the old legal framework. While access to legal remedies is possible in most situations, legal remedies in the context of detention for investigation and repatriation are limited to administrative review. If the Ministry of Public Security decides on the deportation of a foreign national, even administrative review cannot be applied. In the context of detention for investigation this limitation to legal remedies stands in conflict with international customary law, according to which any detention without access to a court review shall be regarded as illegal arbitrary detention. I conclude that the fulfilment of the aim of the revision of the *Exit–Entry Administration Law* to increase swift and efficient enforcement has been surpassed in the context of detention for investigation, rendering it a questionable measure.

D. Being Employed as a Foreign National in China

Court cases with regard to illegal entry and stay in China are relatively rare.[469] Although a considerable number of criminal cases concerning border crossing or human trafficking exists, this is not true for cases in the context of administrative law. Admittedly, legal remedies in the context of exit–entry administration are restricted in certain situations like denial of entry, non-issuance of visa abroad, detention of investigation or repatriation and removal. But for circumstances where administrative litigation is generally admissible, I was unable to find a considerable amount of cases where individuals try to challenge decisions of public security authorities in the context of exit–entry administration. However, in the context of employment courts play a much more important role, as disputes between foreign employees and Chinese employers are much more prevalent. This part, hence, takes the context of employment of foreign nationals in China as an example to examine the question to what degree courts acknowledge rights of foreign nationals.

Article 25 of the *International Convention on the Protection of the Rights of All Migrant Workers and Members of Their Families (ICRMW)* requires

469 A search in openly accessible on-line databases revealed only few cases between 2012 and 2018 where foreign nationals filed a lawsuit against a decision of a public security organ in exit–entry administration matters.

at least equal treatment of migrant workers and nationals of the state regarding remuneration for employment. The *ICRMW* further states that the illegality of stay or employment of migrant workers shall not result in the deprivation of this right. This section aims to answer the question whether illegally employed foreign nationals are able to claim monetary compensation for their work. In order to answer this question, this section looks at both the legal provisions regarding illegal employment of foreign nationals as well as at court practice, which allows us to understand the actual options for enforcement of remuneration claims. By examining the question regarding the right to remuneration of illegally employed foreign nationals, this section analyses the role of courts in the context of employment of foreign nationals. The findings further help to assess whether courts are influenced by campaign-style governance or rather act independently from campaign work.

I. Definition of Illegal Employment

Before being able to assess whether the provisions of the new law allow for remuneration claims of illegally employed foreign nationals, the legal definition of illegal employment in the current Chinese legal framework has to be clarified. The concept of illegal employment first of all raises the question of what should be understood as employment, especially in the context of employment of foreign nationals. Does illegal work denote the same as illegal employment? Does employment in comparison to work require monetary remuneration? Is self-employment also considered employment? In order to answer these questions, the following part aims to clarify the legal concept of employment of foreign nationals in China. Furthermore, in order to clarify in what way the new legal framework provides for a more distinct definition of illegal employment, this part first analyses the definition of illegal employment in the context of the legal framework of 1985. As will be shown, defining the term 'illegal employment' is not as straightforward as it may seem, as not only is the concept of 'employment' hard to grasp, but also the underlying legal concept of 'work' is undefined. After having analysed the definition according to the old law, I analyse the definition of 'illegal employment' as outlined in the *Exit-Entry Administration Law* (2012). As the concept of 'illegal work' is used alongside 'illegal employment' in literature and legal provisions, I analyse the differences and relationship between both terms and, more generally, also between 'work' and 'employment'. I also look at the sanctions for illegal employment and answer the question whether these sanctions are in line with international standards.

1. Illegal Employment According to the 1985 Law

The term 'illegal employment' (*feifa jiuye*[470]) did not exist in the legal provisions until 2012. However, Article 44 of the 1986 *Foreign Nationals Exit-Entry Administration Law Implementation Rules* stated that foreign nationals who "privately seek employment without approval of the Ministry of Labour or responsible authorities"[471] should be punished by having their employment terminated and additionally paying a fine.[472] As it was not explicitly stated that an employer had to exist in order to establish employment in the sense of these regulations, it was unclear whether self-employment was also covered by this provision. As from 1994, the *Foreign Nationals Exit-Entry Administration Law Implementation Rules* also provided for punishment of the employing entity, which could be required to bear the cost of removal of the foreign national in severe cases where a deportation was applicable.[473]

While neither the 1985 *Exit-Entry Administration Law* nor the 1986 *Foreign Nationals Exit-Entry Administration Law Implementation Rules* defined 'illegal employment', the *Foreign Nationals Employment Regulations* (1996) define "employment of foreign nationals in China" as a remunerated labour activity of foreign nationals who do not possess the right of permanent residence.[474] While this definition strictly speaking is only valid within the context of the *Foreign Nationals Employment Regulations* (1996), it may also be applicable to superior legal norms, as there are no other definitions regarding the employment of foreign nationals. As will be shown below in more detail, the terms 'illegal employment' and 'illegal

470 Chinese: 非法就业.

471 Chinese: 未经中华人民共和国劳动人事部批准私自谋职.

472 Art. 44 *Foreign Nationals Exit–Entry Administration Law Implementation Rules* (1986).

473 Art. 44 *Foreign Nationals Exit–Entry Administration Law Implementation Rules* (1994). Note that Art. 29 *Foreign Nationals Employment Regulations* (1996) states that if a foreign national is deported due to refusing inspection of his or her employment permits, deportation cost may be borne by the employer or the foreign national.

474 Art. 2(2) *Foreign Nationals Employment Regulations* (1996).

work' (*feifa gongzuo*[475]) are used alongside each other in different legal provisions. It is unclear at first whether both terms depict the same legal concept or illegal employment should be considered a specific form of illegal work. However, the *Offences Definitions* (2010) issued by the Ministry of Public Security define 'illegal work'[476] as an offence that is to be punished according to Article 44(1) *Foreign Nationals Exit–Entry Administration Law Implementation Rules* (2010) and hence comprises employment.[477]

The 1985 *Exit-Entry Administration Law* stated that employment was generally prohibited for individuals without permanent residence and for foreign exchange students, unless permitted by the Chinese government. Article 2 *Foreign Nationals Employment Regulations* (1996) limits the application of this rule, i. e. the need to hold a work permit in order to be allowed to work in China, to "foreign nationals without permanent residence status", which leaves it unclear what kind of permission, if any, would be required for foreign nationals who hold a permanent residence status. Hence, if the foreign national holds a permanent residence status, his employment without a valid work permit cannot be classified as 'illegal employment' by referring to the provisions of the *Foreign Nationals Employment Regulations* (1996) only.

The above definition of "employment of foreign nationals in China" as provided in the *Foreign Nationals Employment Regulations* (1996) is limited to remunerative labour activities. While this does not imply that non-remunerated labour activities are *per se* legal, remuneration is an important characteristic of employment.[478] However, while remunerative activities that have not been approved by a responsible authority would definitely count as 'illegal employment', there was no clear answer regarding non-remunerative labour activities under the old legal framework. The problem that the legal provisions were unclear regarding the question whether only remunerated labour activities would be regarded as employment of foreign nationals is also highlighted in official explanations of the relevant articles of the revised *Exit-Entry Administration Law* (2012) as will be shown below.

475 Chinese: 非法工作.
476 Chinese: 非法工作.
477 See as well Item 410 *Offences Definitions* (2010).
478 Liu Jianchang / Li Xinglin (2012), p. 208.

2. Illegal Employment According to the 2012 Law

'Illegal employment' (*feifa jiuye*[479]) is defined by Article 43 *Exit-Entry Administration Law* (2012) as either working without having obtained a work permit or a residence permit for work as required by legal provisions (i. e., for legal employment both permits are required), or working beyond the scope specified in the work permit, or, as a foreign student, working beyond the defined scope of jobs or period in violation of the provisions regarding the administration of foreign work-study students. Article 80 *Exit-Entry Administration Law* (2012) states that being illegally employed, illegally employing someone else, as well as providing reference for illegal employment constitute a punishable offence. It is not clear, however, which activities count as 'working', as there is no legal definition of 'work' in Chinese legislation. In the following, I aim to clarify whether the term 'work' is limited to employment relations or whether the definition in Article 43 *Exit-Entry Administration Law* (2012) also covers other kinds of work such as self-employment or work that is conducted in China on the basis of an employment relationship with a legal entity in a foreign country.

a) Definition of Illegal Employment and Employment of Foreign Nationals

The terms 'illegal work' (*feifa gongzuo*[480]) and 'illegal employment' are often used interchangeably in both the legal and the political context.[481] The definition of illegal employment referring to work in Article 43 *Exit-Entry Administration Law* (2012) suggests that both terms indeed mean quite similar concepts. While no explanation concerning the differences between the two concepts existed before, official interpretations of the revised *Exit-Entry Administration Law* (2012) cast some first light on this problem. One interpretation states that the law now uses the term 'illegal employment' because this concept is regarded as being more precise than the term 'illegal work', since 'illegal employment' allegedly depicts the participation of the foreign national in the labour market that is regulated by the state.[482] It is argued that

479 Chinese: 非法就业.
480 Chinese: 非法工作.
481 E. g. in the context of campaigns.
482 *Interpretation of the 'Exit–Entry Administration Law of the People's Republic of China'* (《中华人民共和国出境入境管理法》释义) (2012), p. 133.

the state has the responsibility to secure access to the labour market for its nationals, which in turn legitimises the state restricting access to the labour market for foreign nationals. It is, however, still unclear whether 'employment' is only confined to labour relations and whether illegal work constitutes a wider concept of which illegal employment is only a special kind. Further, if the latter is true, it is unclear how illegal work other than illegal employment would be punished, if at all. While the above interpretation can explain why one term was preferred over the other, it fails to define the exact scope of illegal employment. In the following sections, I analyse the question regarding the scope of 'illegal employment' from different points of view.

As the differentiation of the terms 'illegal employment' and 'illegal work' cannot clarify the definition of 'illegal employment' but rather raises new questions, I will in a next step analyse the definition of 'employment of foreign nationals' in order to answer these questions. As already stated above, the *Regulations on the Management of Employment of foreign nationals in China* (1996) define "employment of foreign nationals in China" as a remunerated labour activity without the right of permanent residence.[483] The regulations refer to a "right of residence"[484] which obviously means permanent residence here, as legal employment in China is only possible with a residence permit. The Chinese law does not explain or define the concept of 'labour remuneration'[485]. According to Article 4 of the *Wages Composition Regulations* (1990), total wages[486] include wages based on time or piece-work, bonuses, subsidies, allowances, as well as payments for overtime work and special payments.[487] The same definition is used by the Supreme People's Court to outline the term 'labour remuneration'.[488] The definition of 'total wages' does not include specific forms of payment like pensions or other welfare benefits, food subsidies, lectures, medical payments or share or bond interest.[489] However, while labour remuneration obviously includes total wages, it is unclear whether it only covers monetary

483 Art. 2(2) *Foreign Nationals Employment Regulations* (1996).
484 Chinese: 定居权.
485 Chinese: 劳动报酬.
486 Chinese: 工资.
487 Art. 4 *Wages Composition Regulations* (1990).
488 *SPC Labour Remuneration Interpretation* (2013).
489 Art. 11 *Wages Composition Regulations* (1990).

goods or also includes material remuneration or social security, as such a wide interpretation is applied by courts.[490]

When applying these findings to the term 'illegal employment', another complication arises. While labour remuneration seems to be a requirement for the employment of foreign nationals, it is not a precondition for an activity to be considered as 'illegal employment', as stated by an official interpretation of Article 43 *Exit-Entry Administration Law* (2012).[491] According to an official report of the Law Committee of the National People's Congress, delegates of the committee questioned the ability to check the existence of remuneration in every case and thus the formulation of remuneration as a precondition was omitted.[492] In fact, the *Exit-Entry Administration Law* (2012) does not explicitly refer to remuneration but only to work.[493] This interpretation is supported by the fact that, in the process of investigating a relevant case, the police shall record not only the arranged wages and (already received as well as to be received) remuneration, but also relevant "benefits".[494] This approach again does not lead to a clarification of the scope of illegal employment. Arguably it may be easier for the police to prosecute administrative offences if the existence of remuneration is irrelevant, however this argument cannot fully convince. Where an employment contract has been signed illegally, it is easy to identify illegal employment as both parties obviously pursued the goal to set up an employment relationship. In such a case, omitting the examination regarding remuneration should indeed facilitate prosecution. Where no employment contract exists,

490 *Langfang Labour Remuneration Case* (2016); *Nanyang Labour Remuneration Case* (2015).

491 *Guide to Interpretation and Application of the 'Exit–Entry Administration Law of the People's Republic of China'* (《中华人民共和国出境入境管理法》释义及实用指南) (2012), p. 120.

492 Item 5 *Report by the Law Committee of the National People's Congress on Amendments of the 'Exit–Entry Administration Law of the People's Republic of China (Draft)'* (全国人民代表大会法律委员会关于《中华人民共和国出境入境管理法（草案)》修改情况的汇报), *NPC Press Release* (2012).

493 Art. 43 *Exit–Entry Administration Law* (2012).

494 Chinese: 利益. Liu Jianchang / Li Xinglin (2012). Whether these benefits depict monetary payments not included in wages or (monetary) remuneration or whether this term also covers non-monetary remuneration is unclear. However, see *Shanghai Illegal Employment Case* (2015) where the court found that the fact that the claimant paid accommodation and plane tickets in exchange for the work of three foreign nationals suffices to establish a labour relationship and whether any remuneration was paid or not would not affect the determination of illegal employment.

however, the fact that remuneration is not a precondition for illegal employment only raises the question of how to determine the existence of illegal employment. Obviously, non-monetary remuneration can be used by courts to determine the existence of a labour relationship.[495] This problem can probably be solved by analysing what constitutes 'work', as will be done below. However, I first elaborate on the application of 'illegal employment' on self-employment in the next section.

b) Legal Provisions on Visa Application

In the next step, I look into the legal provisions regarding the application of visas in order to clarify whether 'illegal employment' can be applied to self-employment as well. The *Exit–Entry Administration Regulations* (2013) define the various types of visas foreign nationals may apply for, depending on the intended cause of stay.[496] For 'work', a Z or R visa is needed. As the R visa only applies for foreign experts who are subject to a somewhat different employment scheme, I will focus on the application of the Z visa that is needed for the employment of regular foreign nationals. As for the application of a Z visa an invitation of the future employer is needed, 'work' in this context only depicts an employment relationship and not self-employment. Thus, it is reasonable to interpret the term 'work' in the context of immigration legislation in a narrow sense, only depicting employment by a Chinese (legal) person. If the employer is not situated within the Chinese territory, working for this employer in China is obviously not considered 'work' in the sense of Article 43 *Exit-Entry Administration Law* (2012): no work permit is needed for such kind of business or non-business visits but only an M or F visa, although such activities should actually be considered work. If Article 43 *Exit-Entry Administration Law* (2012) is interpreted strictly, it is relatively easy to circumvent the complicated application procedures for a Z visa by transferring wages to a foreign entity that effectively employs and pays the employee in China. This way, no employment relationship will be set up within China and the employee will only need an M visa to enter the country, which has to be renewed, however, every three months.

495 *Shanghai Illegal Employment Case* (2015).
496 Art. 6) *Exit–Entry Administration Regulations* (2013).

Another way would be to establish a 'representative office'[497] and act simultaneously as chief representative and executive officer of the foreign parent company. Such a representative office has no legal capacity and hence cannot sign contracts on its own; it also may not conduct profit-oriented activities.[498] But of course the foreign parent company can take over this role. While in general Chinese staff of representative offices has to be employed via qualified local human resources service companies (a so-called 'Foreign Enterprise Service Companies') that sign labour contracts with the staff and place them at the disposal of the representative offices,[499] the chief representative of a foreign representative office and up to three other foreign representatives may be employed by the foreign parent company directly.[500] Either way, it is difficult to speak of self-employment in China in this context. The staff employed by the representative office via such a human resources service company are paid by this service company and the total expenses are then invoiced to the representative office. As from 2010, the parent company has to have been in existence for at least two years.[501] At least until 2017, the registration certificate for a representative office had to be renewed annually.[502] In practice, African traders in the Pearl River Delta indeed use their own foreign enterprise to establish a representative office in China of which they also act as chief representative.[503] This way, it is possible for them to become *de facto* self-employed in China and conduct certain profit-oriented activities by means of the parent company without the need for a Z or R visa. As soon as an employment relationship with a human resources service company is set up, however, a Z visa is needed.

Schemes such as using an M visa to enter China and being paid by the foreign enterprise or acting as chief representative and executive officer of the foreign parent company at the same time, however, undermine the argumentation of the official interpretation cited above, which states that the term 'illegal employment' is preferred over 'illegal work' in the law because it better depicts the connection to the labour market that the state wants to

497 Chinese: 外国企业常驻代表机构.

498 Art. 2 *Representative Office Registration Regulations* (2013).

499 Lavener (1996), p. 37; Mahony (2015), p. 159 f.

500 Art. 11 *Representative Office Registration Regulations* (2013).

501 Art. 23(1)ii *Representative Office Registration Regulations* (2013).

502 Art. 2 *Representative Office Registration Notice* (2010). This notice has been repealed according to the *SAIC Regulatory Documents Review Annoucenment* (2017), which does not necessarily imply that the requirement for annual renewal has been repealed as well.

503 Gilles (2015), p. 31 f.

protect. It is hence difficult to imagine that 'work' in the context of immigration law should really be interpreted that strictly. With such a narrow interpretation of 'work', at least, self-employment would not be covered by Article 43 of the *Exit-Entry Administration Law* (2012).

In fact, self-employment is generally bound to a business licence that is a prerequisite to running an enterprise in China. Foreign nationals are only allowed to establish a partnership[504] together with a Chinese partner (as of 2010), a 'wholly-foreign owned enterprise'[505] or a joint venture, or any other form of company according to the *Company Law* (1993). Note that a representative office as described above is not a legal entity and self-employment in a legal sense can hence not be established via this means. It is not possible for a foreign national to set up an 'individual industrial and commercial household'[506] or an 'individual proprietorship enterprise'[507]. A foreign national will only be issued a business licence for the types of enterprise foreign nationals are allowed to establish. Thus, self-employment for foreign nationals is virtually only possible within the context of establishing an own enterprise according to the relevant legal provisions.[508] In this context, however, running an enterprise without a required business licence will be handled according to the provisions concerning operating a business without licence rather than as illegal employment. After all, executive officers of foreign enterprises in China also need to hold a Z (or R) visa,[509] which suggests that not holding such a visa constitutes 'illegal employment'. The fact that executive officers have to hold a Z or R visa as well implies that 'illegal employment' is also applicable to self-employment.

504 Chinese: 合伙企业.

505 Chinese: 外商投资企业.

506 Chinese: 个体工商户. Art. 2 *Individual Household Regulations* (2011) that restricts the application for this kind of enterprise to Chinese nationals.

507 Chinese: 独资企业. See Art. 47 *Individual Proprietorship Enterprises Law* (1999) stating that this law does not apply to foreign investment.

508 Although the *Wholly Foreign-Owned Enterprises Law* (2016) does not codify a minimum amount for the registered capital (the *Company Law* did until 2013; Art. 26, 81 *Company Law* (2005)), a minimum registered capital is still *de facto* required in practice.

509 Item 2 *Foreign Nationals Illegal Employment Notice* (1994); Item 1 *Yunnan Foreign Nationals Employment Regulations* (1995). Note that different versions of the *Foreign Nationals Illegal Employment Notice* (1994) exist, some of which do not explicitly state that executive officers have to hold a Z visa. However, all versions do state that "every foreign national who holds a post or works in China" has to hold a Z visa, which obviously includes executive officers as well.

c) Basic Prerequisites for Work

The most straightforward approach to analysing the definition of 'work' is to find out its most basic prerequisites, be it the minimum income, the minimum return over investment, or the minimum taxes to be paid, that require a business licence, as this would *de facto* demarcate 'work' from 'non-work'. It would then be possible to argue that an activity for which a business licence is needed counts as 'illegal work' if no such licence is at hand. However, a definition of the basic prerequisites in this context is missing. Only as recent as 2017, two legal documents shed light onto this issue: the draft of a new *E-Commerce Law*[510] and the revised *Measures on Investigation of Unpermitted and Unlicenced Businesses* (2017). Both documents introduce a new class of business activities that do not require a business licence without further elaborating upon the subject. The relevant literature assumes that the scope of such activities would include e. g. setting up stands at morning or evening markets or bazaars.[511] The *Measures on Investigation of Unpermitted and Unlicenced Businesses* (2017) as well as the draft of the *E-Commerce Law* both refer to the "sale of agricultural by-products, of articles of daily life, or engaging in informal service activities using one's personal skills for which according to the law no licence is needed".[512] However, this formulation refers to a legal definition laid down in other legal documents that do not yet exist. Hence, a concise delineation of the scope of such business activities that do not require a business licence is still missing.

As there is neither a concise legal definition of 'work' nor of 'labour remuneration' as has been shown above, it is unclear which amount of freelance work for which kind of remuneration should be regarded as illegal work of a foreign national. E. g. offering a small translation service even without any remuneration, material or monetary, could already be covered by the above definitions. But the same activities also could be classified as informal service activities that may be exempt from the requirement to apply for a business licence beforehand. With the current definition of 'illegal employment', hence, a considerable scope of discretion rests with the public security authorities.

510 *E-Commerce Law (Draft)* (2017).
511 WANG Fangyi (2017), p. 14.
512 Chinese: 销售农副产品、日常生活用品，或者个人利用自己的技能从事依法无须取得许可的便民劳务活动. The 2017 draft of the *E-Commerce Law* refines the first two items to "sale of self-produced agricultural by-products and sale of cottage industry products" (Chinese: 销售自产农副产品、销售家庭手工业产品).

d) Sanctions for Illegal Employment

As illegal employment is mainly considered to be an illegal working relationship, sanctions apply to the foreign national illegally employed as well as to the employer, be it an individual or a legal entity, who illegally employs a foreign national. Furthermore, acting as an intermediary in the context of illegal employment is also fined. However, while the provisions for illegal exit or entry and illegal stay are spread over multiple articles in the *Exit–Entry Administration Law* (2012), there is only one article concerning illegal employment. As a foreign national, being illegally employed is punished with a fine of RMB 5 000 to 20 000 or, if the circumstances are serious, additionally by detention of five to fifteen days.[513] As for the employer, the direct illegal employment of foreign nationals shall be punished by a fine of RMB 10 000 for each illegal employee, the total sum shall not exceed RMB 100 000. Furthermore, the provision of references for illegal employment shall be punished by a fine of RMB 5 000, the total sum shall not exceed RMB 50 000. If the provision of references is conducted by an entity, the total sum shall not exceed RMB 100 000.[514] In any case, the illegal income of the employer (but not of the employee) shall be confiscated.[515] Although the fines regarding illegal employment are higher for employers in absolute figures, it can be argued that fines are relatively harder for employees than for employers, who typically have greater financial leeway.[516]

According to the *Foreign Nationals Employment Regulations* (2017), labour administrations shall revoke work permits of foreign nationals who refuse inspections of their work permit by labour administrations, change their employers or jobs without permission, or prolong their terms of employment without authorisation, and the labour administrations shall request the relevant public security authority to withdraw the qualification of these foreign nationals to stay in China.[517] If the foreign nationals are subsequently to be repatriated, the costs of repatriation shall be borne by the employer or by the foreign nationals in question.[518]

While the illegally gained income of the employer may be confiscated, the income of the foreign national is not subject to seizure according to the

513 Art. 80(1) *Exit–Entry Administration Law* (2012).
514 Art. 80(2) *Exit–Entry Administration Law* (2012).
515 Art. 80(3) *Exit–Entry Administration Law* (2012).
516 Zou (2016), p. 8.
517 Art. 28 *Foreign Nationals Employment Regulations* (2017).
518 Art. 28 *Foreign Nationals Employment Regulations* (2017).

current legal framework, notwithstanding a punishment due to illegal employment as well as a possible repatriation because the continued stay has been rendered improper. Whether the foreign national is able to enforce his or her claims regarding income or compensation in case the employment relation was illegal shall be answered in the next section. Article 25 of the *ICRMW* states that migrant workers shall not receive a treatment less favourable than nationals of the state of employment regarding their remuneration, and they shall not be deprived of this right because their stay or employment status is or becomes irregular. Although the provisions of the *ICRMW* do not apply to the stateless, this means that a foreign national shall be compensated for his or her work even if this work was conducted in an illegal employment context. However, as the *ICRMW* remains silent regarding punishments, a punishment for illegal employment may still be admissible. In this regard, although the confiscation of illegally gained income can only be imposed onto the employer, while the employee may be fined, there is no explicit provision in the *Exit–Entry Administration Law* (2012) that assures that the foreign national may retain his or her income in any case. Hence, the question regarding the equal treatment of illegally employed foreign nationals can only be answered by looking at the actual enforcement of the relevant legal provisions. As will be shown below, current court practice often supports the principle of equal compensation when a general service relationship is assumed that allows for compensation claims in cases of illegal employment, but the entitlement of the foreign national to remuneration is not always asserted in court decisions.

e) Subsumption

Summing up the findings, although a concise legal definition of 'work' is missing, there are efforts to exclude certain activities from the scope of activities for which a business licence is needed. Hence, a foreign national should be able to conduct work in this context without the need to establish an enterprise, a representative office or an employment relationship. Probably, the concept of informal service activities already exists in practice and the police would not persecute small-scale freelance work of foreign nationals as described above. However, the fact that no business licence is needed for certain kinds of work can only indicate that such activities are also allowed for foreign nationals without work visa. I further argue that illegal employment primarily depicts an illegal employment relationship either without or on the basis of an invalid employment contract. As executive officers also need to hold a visa that allows for work in China, illegal employment is applicable in the context of self-employment in general as well. Finally, legal pathways exist that allow for working activities in China by establishing an employment relationship with a legal entity in a foreign country. The above findings suggest that 'illegal employment' denotes work of any kind without holding a proper visa, while the scope of activities that count as work is not precisely defined. Hence, 'illegal employment' is indeed more or less congruent with 'illegal work'. As long as an activity neither counts as employment nor as self-employment from the Chinese perspective, as in the example of simultaneously acting as chief representative of a representative office and as executive officer of the foreign parent company, 'illegal employment' cannot be construed.

II. Framework Regarding Employment of Foreign Nationals

Having clarified the scope of 'illegal employment' allows me to analyse the employment relationship. The most important question in this regard is in which situations illegal employment may appear. What will happen, for example, in a situation where an employer, whose duty it is to apply for a work permit for the foreign national, fails to do so? May an employment relationship be based only on a labour contract or only on a work permit? If the legal provisions cannot solve such questions, how would courts decide in these circumstances? As has been already pointed out above, the *ICRMW* demands that foreign nationals shall not receive a treatment less favourable than nationals regarding their remuneration. But would a foreign national in China actually be able to claim compensation if the employment relationship is deemed illegal?

In order to answer these questions, I assess how employment relationships between foreign nationals and Chinese employers are established or terminated. I particularly analyse the procedures a foreign national and his or her employer have to go through in order to establish, change or terminate a legal employment relationship. On that basis I investigate in which situation an employment relationship may be deemed illegal. This way, this part sets out the framework that allows an exploration of the question regarding court decisions on the possibility to claim compensation in illegal employment cases that will be answered in the next section.

1. Establishment of a Legal Employment Relationship

In chapter 2, I looked into the procedures that are necessary in order to establish a labour relationship between a foreign employee and a Chinese employer as laid down in the *Foreign Nationals Employment Regulations* (1996). In this section, I also take into account the 2017 amendment of these regulations. After the employer has successfully applied for a foreign nationals employment licence and a letter of visa notification, the foreign national will be sent the letter of visa notification and the employment licence with which he or she applies for a working visa (Z or, as from 2013, R visa). After the foreign national has entered China and signed the employment contract with the Chinese employer, the latter shall apply for a foreign nationals employment permit, the actual work permit for the foreign national, within 15 days. Within 30 days after entry, the foreign national shall apply for a residence permit on the basis of his or her exit–entry documents and the foreign nationals employment permit. Until 2017, foreign experts would be issued a foreign expert permit that serves as a work permit on the basis of the successful application for an expert visa (R visa). According to the *Foreign Nationals Employment Regulations* (2017), the responsible authorities for the administration of the employment of foreign nationals in China are the human resource and social security authorities at provincial level as well as those at prefecture level.[519]

As from April 2017, employers use an online management system to apply for the foreign nationals employment licence with the State Administration of Foreign Experts Affairs (SAFEA),[520] an authority at the sub-ministerial level that was integrated into the Ministry of Science and Technology[521] in April 2018.[522] The foreign employee also uses the online system to apply for his or her work permit. With the new system, the application for foreign national expert certificates and foreign nationals employment permits is merged and a unified foreign national work permit[523] is issued.[524] The authorities use a points-based system to determine the expert status of

519 Art. 4 *Foreign Nationals Employment Regulations* (2017).
520 Chinese: 国家外国专家局.
521 Chinese: 科学技术部.
522 Paragraph 3(3) *Work Permit System Notice* (2017).
523 Chinese: 外国人工作许可证.
524 Paragraph 4 *Work Permit System Notice* (2017).

the foreign national.[525] The application process concerning working visa and residence permit, however, remains the same as described above. This procedure already implies that employment in China is only possible with a valid labour contract, a valid work permit and, additionally, a valid residence permit allowing for work. If one of these documents becomes invalid or cannot be produced, the employment relationship may be deemed illegal by the public security organs or by courts.

2. Extension of an Employment Relationship

In order to be able to legally stay in China, the foreign national to be employed needs a work permit. The validity of this work permit, however, is bound to a valid labour contract. The *Foreign Nationals Employment Regulations* (2017) hence require that the work permit ceases to be valid with the expiration of the labour contract. With the expiration of the labour contract, the employer shall report the expiration of the contract to the human resources and social security authorities as well as to the public security authorities and return the employment permit as well as the residence permit of the foreign national who shall leave the country.[526] This procedure implies that the foreign national cannot stay longer than the labour contract is valid, as this would result in illegal stay of the foreign national.[527]

According to the *Foreign Nationals Employment Regulations* (2017), labour contracts with foreign nationals may only cover a maximum period of five years, and after this time, the labour contract may be renewed.[528] Hence, a work permit also has a maximum validity of five years.[529] A desired extension of the work permit has to be applied for at the relevant human resource and social security authorities within 30 days before the expiration of the contract.[530] After the extension of the work permit has been approved, the foreign national has to change his residence permit accordingly with the

525 See the *(Tentative) Classification Standards for Foreign Nationals Working in China* (外国人来华工作分类标准（试行）) appended to the *Work Permit System Notice* (2017).

526 Art. 21 *Foreign Nationals Employment Regulations* (2017).

527 This probably contradicts Art. 49(2), 51 *ICRMW* (1990) that states that migrant workers shall not be regarded to be in an illegal situation due to the mere fact that the labour relationship was terminated.

528 Art. 18 *Foreign Nationals Employment Regulations* (2017).

529 Work permits typically have a validity of one year.

530 Art. 19 *Foreign Nationals Employment Regulations* (2017).

local public security authorities.[531] According to the *Labour Contract Law* (2012), the employer has to hand over a document to prove the dissolution or termination of the labour contract to the employee and has to handle the transfer of the employee's social insurance account.[532] The fact that it is the task of the employer to apply for the work permit or for its extension raises the question how the foreign national can protect him- or herself against inaction of the employer. As will be shown below, courts handle cases where the employer failed to apply for a work permit or for its extension very differently. Although newer court decisions more often ruled in favour of the foreign national, the variety of rulings leaves the foreign national in an insecure situation.

3. Change of Employer

Employment can further only be legally established with one specific employer.[533] As the administration of employment of foreign nationals rests with the local authorities, establishing a new employment relationship outside the jurisdiction of the current authority implies that a new work permit has to be issued which also renders dual employment illegal. The legal provisions state that if the foreign national changes his employer and the new employer is located within the jurisdiction of the relevant human resources and social security authority in charge of the administration of his or her current employment, the change of employer shall be approved by this authority. If the new employer is located outside the said jurisdiction, however, or the new position differs from the one with the current employer, the foreign national has to re-apply for a new work permit.[534] The change of the employment location or employer has to be reported to the local public security authorities.[535] For the change of employer, a document proving the termination of the former labour contract issued by the former employer—a so-called release letter—is needed,[536] which implies that it is prohibited to

531 Art. 20 *Foreign Nationals Employment Regulations* (2017).
532 Art. 50 *Labour Contract Law* (2012).
533 This probably contradicts Art. 39(2) *ICRMW* (1990) as it *de facto* denies a right to freely choose the place of residence.
534 Art. 24 *Foreign Nationals Employment Regulations* (2017).
535 Art. 20 *Foreign Nationals Employment Regulations* (2017).
536 See e. g. Beijing Bureau of Human Resources and Social Security (2018); Shanghai Bureau of Human Resources and Social Security (2018).

have more than one employer as a foreign national in China. The limitation to only one employer and only one jurisdiction is implied also by the fact that the employment licence on which the work permit is based defines a specific employer at a specific location. However, as long as the employer remains the employing party of the labour contract and hence bears the legal responsibility, the foreign national may factually work at another affiliated company.

III. Illegal Employment Handled by Courts

In the course of investigating the procedures for establishing, extending, or changing an employment relationship, I concluded that an employment relationship is only legal if a valid labour contract and a valid work permit is at hand. While the work permit is only valid if the underlying labour contract is valid, the labour contract again only becomes valid with the issuance of a work permit. Further, the employer has the duty to apply for this work permit or for its extension. This section eventually aims to answer the initial question of this section by focusing on the possible claims a foreign national can make in case the employment relationship is deemed illegal due to the fact that no work permit was applied for or that the work permit was not extended. The scope of possible claims is mainly bound to the question whether a factual labour relationship or a general service relationship can be established between a foreign national and a Chinese employer.

The *Labour Contract Law* (2007) states that a labour contract is wholly or partly invalid if it violates "mandatory provisions of laws or administrative regulations".[537] This implies that a valid employment contract is a precondition for foreign nationals being able to make use of their rights resulting from an employment relationship.[538] In this regard, the *SPC Work Dispute Cases Interpretation* (2013) states that if foreign nationals sign a labour contract with a Chinese employer without holding a valid work permit, courts shall interpret the labour relationship as non-existent.[539] However, in cases where the foreign national holds an expert certificate[540] and a work permit for

537 Art. 26(1)iii *Labour Contract Law* (2007).
538 Zou (2016), p. 7.
539 Art. 14(1) *SPC Work Dispute Cases Interpretation* (2013).
540 Chinese: 外国专家证.

foreign experts[541] the labour relationship shall still be recognised.[542] Thus, only where both the work permit and the labour contract of the non-expert foreign national are valid can an employment relationship be legally established. The question arises whether the foreign national can still claim compensation for his work that has been conducted under a legally non-existent labour relationship.

The concept of a factual labour relationship, i. e. a labour relationship where no written labour contract exists, seems in practice not to be applicable to non-expert foreign nationals. The concept of a factual relationship means in general that if a Chinese worker is a "member"[543] of an enterprise or another entity and is paid for labour, he or she is considered a *de facto* employee if no written work contract has been signed.[544] In the case of (non-expert) foreign nationals, however, as the work permit will only be issued on the basis of a signed labour contract,[545] working without a labour contract will be rather deemed as having established a general service relation[546] where only the *General Principles of Civil Law* and the *Contract Law*, but not the *Labour Contract Law* can be applied, which, in the case of a proper labour relationship, is in general applicable to foreign-related civil relations as well.[547] In the following section, I analyse court practice in this regard.

1. Claims Resulting from an Illegal Employment Relationship

An analysis of court decisions on labour disputes involving foreign nationals reveals different approaches to the question which claims may result from an illegal employment relationship. Apart from the question how courts decide on the existence of a factual labour relationship or a general service relation, this analysis also reveals the court practice regarding the legal consequences in situations where the employer failed to apply for a work permit

541 Chinese: 外国专家来华工作许可证.

542 Art. 14(2) *SPC Work Dispute Cases Interpretation* (2013). See *Shenzhen Labour Dispute Case* (2016) for a case where the latter provision was applied.

543 Chinese: 成员.

544 Art. 1(2) *Labour Law Opinions* (1995).

545 According to Art. 16 *Foreign Nationals Employment Regulations* (1996).

546 Chinese: 劳务关系 or 雇佣关系.

547 Art. 43 *Foreign-Related Civil Relations Law* (2010). Courts may, however, take a valid work permit as indication for the existence of an employment relation; *Shenzhen Labour Remuneration and Economic Compensation Case* (2014).

or its extension. Courts may reject the accusations of the foreign national and decide that the foreign national was illegally employed because no valid work permit could be produced. In one case, an enterprise that illegally employed a foreign national without applying for a work permit later cancelled the labour contract by drawing upon the excuse of illegal employment to avoid being held responsible for illegal breach of the contract that had never officially entered into force.[548] When the foreign national claimed his rights, the court only found that no employment relation existed and decided to fine the employee for illegal employment while the employer was not fined at all. Most courts, however, construed the relevant regulations in such a way that without a work permit, a general service relation between the employer and the employee is set up, but no employment relationship.[549] Thus, if no work permit has been issued, the employer is not liable to bear any social contributions or other charges that would result from a labour contract. Further, the employer shall bear the responsibility to only employ foreign nationals with valid work permit and is responsible for the application for the work permit on behalf of the foreign national, according to Article 16 *Foreign Nationals Employment Regulations* (2017). Hence, the court may find that the foreign national's claims for compensation are justified due to the employer's duty to apply for a work permit or its extension.[550] In cases where the work permit expired over time and the employer failed to renew it, the courts typically assumed a labour relation only for the time the work permit was valid and handled the remaining as general service relation.[551]

Some courts applied the provisions of the *SPC Work Dispute Cases Interpretation* (2008) stating that where the labour contract is deemed void, the payment shall be calculated according to the salary for the relevant work, period, job and position.[552] This interpretation can be seen to be in line with international standards that require equal treatment of foreign migrant workers, regardless of their legal status, and nationals regarding remunera-

548 *Beijing Labour Dispute Case* (2014).

549 *Guangdong Labour Dispute Case* (2008); *Shenzhen Economic Compensation Dispute Case* (2013); *Jiangsu Labour Dispute Case* (2015); *Guangzhou Labour Dispute Case* (2016).

550 *Shanghai Economic Compensation Case* (2015).

551 *Shenzhen Economic Compensation Dispute Case* (2013); *Guangzhou Labour Dispute Case* (2016 a).

552 *Guangdong Labour Dispute Case* (2008); Art. 14 *SPC Work Dispute Cases Interpretation* (2008).

tion.[553] In one case, the court found that the provisions of the *Labour Contract Law* (2012) concerning the payment of employees with invalid labour contracts[554] and concerning the liability of compensation of the party that caused the invalidity of the labour contract[555] were applicable where the employer had signed a labour contract with a foreign national who did not hold a valid work permit.[556] The assumption of an invalid labour contract implies a better protection of rights of the foreign national compared to the non-recognition of a labour relation, because on the basis of an invalid labour contract, certain rights as provided for in the *Labour Contract Law* can be claimed. The *SPC Work Dispute Cases Interpretation* (2013) does not explicitly state that in cases where the foreign national does not hold a valid work permit the labour contract shall be regarded invalid, but rather the labour relation shall be deemed as non-existing.[557] Still, a number of regional court interpretations, e. g. of Beijing, Zhejiang and Guangdong, state that in such a situation the labour contract shall be regarded as invalid.[558]

While court decisions that completely ignore the rights of the foreign national are rare and courts typically acknowledge a general service relation that would at least entitle the foreign national to receive his or her payment, the broad range of different decisions demonstrates uncertainty regarding the enforceability of labour rights, where it remains possible for foreign nationals to end up in unfavourable situations. In any case, without a work permit that has to be applied for by the employer, there is no possibility for the employee to get a residence permit, which may result in illegal employment or illegal stay. Because the handling of the work permit is the task of the employer, the employee is dependent on him or her, not only where the foreign national needs to get a work permit in the first place, but also in cases where he or she wants to change the employer or has to renew his or her work permit. Hence, the employer can exert high pressure on the foreign national as he or she can threaten the foreign national with cancelling the labour contract or exploit the foreign national by not applying for a work permit.

553 Art. 9(1) *Migrant Workers (Supplementary Provisions) Convention* (1975); Art. 25 *ICRMW* (1990). Note that China did not ratify either of these international treaties.
554 Art. 28 *Labour Contract Law* (2012).
555 Art. 86 *Labour Contract Law* (2012).
556 *Jiangsu Labour Dispute Case* (2015).
557 Art. 14(1) *SPC Work Dispute Cases Interpretation* (2013).
558 Art. 15 *Beijing Labour Dispute Minutes* (2009); Art. 4 *Zhejiang Labour Dispute Opinions* (2009); Art. 18 *Guangdong Labour Dispute Minutes* (2008).

2. Claims Resulting from Work-Study

According to the *Labour Law Opinions* (1995), work-study[559] does not require a labour contract and no formal labour relation will be established,[560] a principle also applied by courts.[561] According to the revised framework of exit–entry administration law, work-study may only be conducted by foreign nationals who hold a residence permit for study and it has to be approved by the university or college where the foreign student is currently enrolled as well as by the local public security office.[562] Work-study can be regarded as a form of internship although its aim is also to support students financially.[563] As from 2012, apart from the work-study scheme that requires holding an X-2 visa and an appropriate residence permit as well as being enrolled at an appropriate university or college,[564] internships of foreign nationals in China are generally handled the same way as a formal employment relationship requiring a Z visa, a work permit and an appropriate residence permit. While work-study does not count as employment legally, an underlying (factual) labour relationship is assumed in certain situations although no labour contract has been formally signed, as court decisions on cases involving Chinese working students show.[565] Based on these court decisions, foreign nationals should be able to assert their compensation claims based on the existence of a factual labour relationship.

IV. Summary

Illegal employment as it is defined in the *Exit–Entry Administration Law* (2012) depicts primarily a relationship between a foreign national and a Chinese employer that lacks proper documentation. Employment of foreign nationals is only possible with one specific employer in China. According to the 2012 legal framework, remuneration is no prerequisite for illegal employment, which allegedly makes it easier for the police to prosecute rel-

559 Chinese: 勤工助学.
560 Art. 2(1)xii *Labour Law Opinions* (1995).
561 *Suqian Personal Damage Compensation Case* (2014).
562 Art. 22 *Exit–Entry Administration Regulations* (2013).
563 Art. 4 *Work Study Measures* (2007).
564 Which universities or colleges are appropriate is regulated in local provisions that differ greatly concerning the scope of work or remuneration.
565 *Shanghai Personal Damage Compensation Case* (2015); *Nanjing Labour Dispute Case* (2010).

evant cases, but also raises the question how illegal employment should be determined and eventually how to delineate work from non-work activities. Employment in China is hence not as clearly defined as it may seem at first glance. Strict regulations regarding the employment of foreign nationals make it easy for them to slip into illegality.

International law, such as the *ICRMW*, requires that foreign nationals may not be subject to discrimination regarding their remuneration, even if their stay or employment is illegal. The *Exit–Entry Administration Law* (2012) punishes the employer of an illegally employed foreign national with confiscation of the illegal gains and a fine, while the punishment for the illegally employed foreign nationals is a fine or, in severe cases, detention. Hence, the foreign national may retain the remuneration he or she received during the illegal employment relationship, but the law remains silent about the right of foreign nationals to claim compensation in cases of illegal employment. Hence, it is not possible to deduce from the legal provisions alone whether the Chinese legal framework protects the foreign national in a way that guarantees the right to receive compensation.

In several cases, courts referred to regulations on the remuneration of Chinese citizens in the context of an illegal work relationship and in this regard equated the legal status of foreign nationals with that of Chinese citizens. The courts found that on the basis of these regulations, foreign nationals are entitled to claim compensation from the Chinese employer. In other cases, however, courts ruled that the employment relationship was nonexistent and the foreign national was employed illegally and hence could not claim remuneration. While no legal provisions exist in the Chinese framework of exit–entry administration law that contradict the *ICRMW*, Chinese court practice is mainly in line with the non-discrimination rule. Chinese courts thus can act as mediators by protecting the rights of foreign nationals. But, as practice shows, courts may also decide to the disadvantage to the foreign national, and even oppose international standards. In any case, the fact that several court decisions which at least implicitly supported the claims of foreign nationals or acknowledged claims resulting from a general service relationship were made by courts at times and places where campaign-style governance was promoted,[566] suggests that courts act independently from campaign-style policies that typically require quick and appropriate results.

E. Conclusion

As pointed out in chapter 2, the aim of the revision of exit–entry administration law was to keep up with social development and to increase control in the area of exit–entry administration, which essentially meant that the legal framework to identify and punish illegal entry, illegal stay and illegal employment had to be amended but also the provisions regarding the introduction of foreign talent had to be improved. Further, the legal norms regarding immigration legislation had to be aligned with newer legislation. As the former legal framework posed enforcement problems, the harmonisation of the different norms was regarded as crucial. As could be shown, the latter aim, i. e. making the legal norms of the *Exit–Entry Administration Law* (2012) fit the framework of administration law, has indeed been largely achieved. This becomes particularly apparent in the context of legal remedies where the old legal framework only provided for a very general norm while the revised law differentiates between different administrative penalties and compulsory measures that allow for different legal remedies.

As for the improved framework to tackle so called ‘sanfei’ foreign nationals, the analysis of the new law reveals a mixed picture. Penalties have been increased and certain definitions have been clarified, which will make a positive contribution to law enforcement. However, although the revised law provides for new or amended definitions of ‘illegal entry’ (or exit), ‘illegal stay’ and ‘illegal employment’, it still offers a certain degree of discretion

566 E. g. *Guangdong Labour Dispute Case* (2008) in 2008, falling within a period of extensive campaign work in Guangdong province; e. g. *Shenzhen Labour Dispute Case* (2016) and *Guangzhou Labour Dispute Case* (2016) falling within the period of a three-year action plan (2015–2017) to strengthen campaign work against illegal immigration in Guangzhou (see *Guangzhou Further Steps Up Crackdown on Illegal Foreigners* (2015)) and also within the period of an anti-smuggling campaign that also targeted illegal immigration (see He Chunzhong (2016)). On the other hand, when the Beijing court decided in 2014 that due to a missing work permit, the foreign national was illegally employed resulting in a fine for the foreign national and the rejection of any claims against the employer, it was already two years ago that larger campaigns against illegal immigration were deployed in Beijing; *Beijing Labour Dispute Case* (2014).

to the police and the courts, e. g. by providing non-comprehensive lists in the definitions. Most offences in the field of exit–entry administration are not considered crimes, which suggests that foreign nationals are treated relatively leniently in comparison to other states, like e. g. Germany, where overstaying a visa is considered a crime. Indeed, in comparison with other countries the Chinese system of sanctions is relatively lenient. However, while crimes are handled by independent courts, administrative offences can be decided by the police and the Ministry of Public Security directly. The fact that most offences are handled within the scope of administrative punishment or administrative enforcement essentially allows the police to act in a relatively flexible and swift way without the influence of courts or the procuratorate, even where the personal freedom of a foreign national is heavily restricted as in the examples of repatriation or deportation. Additionally, legal remedies are limited, *inter alia*, in the context of repatriation, which does not imply a lenient handling of foreign nationals. The codification of a detention scheme that violates international law because no access to effective court review is allowed, underlines this notion.

Chinese authorities can revoke legal documents or remove a foreign national from the Chinese territory. The right to remove a foreign national is argued to be a manifestation of state sovereignty.[567] Consistent with this notion is that the Chinese constitution only recognises certain rights of Chinese nationals. Although it states that "China protects the lawful rights and interests of foreign nationals,"[568] it does not specify these rights and interests and also does not define so-called everyman's rights that would apply to Chinese nationals, foreign nationals and the stateless alike. However, the access of foreign nationals to legal remedies has been largely improved in comparison to the former legal framework that only allowed for legal remedies against administrative punishment in the form of fines or detention. Apart from specific situations where the law explicitly limits access to legal remedies, a foreign national has the same access to legal remedies as a Chinese citizen as long as he or she is situated within the territory of the People's Republic of China. Moreover, most aspects concerning the restriction of legal remedies, for example in the context of the non-issuance of visa and even for the most part in the context of deportation, are in line with international standards or international practice. In sum, although the Chinese legal framework on exit–entry administration is relatively strict regarding

567 Perruchoud (2012), p. 143.
568 Art. 32 *Constitution* (2004).

access to legal remedies, it cannot be said to be overly limiting or not in line with generally accepted international practice.

Access to the Chinese employment market is highly restrictive and both residence and employment are in general limited in time.[569] Foreign employees, especially those without permanent residence, are highly dependent on their Chinese employers. Not only do they have to rely on their future employer applying for a work permit on their behalf on time, but their residence permit is also bound to a valid employment contract. A change of the employer always requires the approval of the local labour administrations. If the new workplace is in a different administrative district or the new position is different from what is indicated on the work permit, the foreign national has to go through the application procedures for a work permit and a residence permit anew. This makes it difficult to change the employer and again increases the dependence of the employee.[570] Furthermore, fines are relatively high for foreign employees, and occasional court practice shows that even when employers are responsible for the employment relationship becoming illegal because they fail to apply for a work permit, they may not be fined accordingly because the court only takes into account the illegal activity of the foreign national who works without a valid permit. In such a case, the foreign national has no practical way to assert his or her claims resulting from the employment relationship. Although such court decisions may be rare, they exemplify the possibility for the foreign national to end up in an adverse legal position within the current legal framework. Quite in contrast to the above findings, however, that identify a rather weak position of the foreign national, Chinese courts regularly decide in favour of the foreign national when it comes to the question whether compensation claims are enforceable against the employer. The *ICRMW* states that migrant workers shall not be treated less favourably regarding remuneration than nationals of the relevant state. Thus, the interpretation of some courts that an illegal employment relationship can be regarded as general service relationship from which certain rights for compensation arise is in line with international standards.

In comparison with the old legal framework as discussed in chapter 2, the revised law has to a large extent achieved its aim to increase government and police control in the area of exit–entry administration. One example for the extension of control is the power to examine passports that the revised

569 Zou (2016).
570 Zou (2016), p. 6.

law grants all public security authorities at county level and above while the former law only assigned this task to the foreign affairs police. Alike, while the old legal framework made it necessary that an order to leave be approved by the Ministry of Public Security or, as from 2008, the public security organs at the provincial level, the decision regarding an order to leave to a foreign national lies with the public security organs at or above county level according to the revised law. Also, the requirement that repatriations need to be approved by the public security organ of the next higher level has been revoked. Other examples for increased control are the provision that the reason for the non-issuance of a visa does not have to be explained to the foreign national, or the fact that the decision by the Ministry of Public Security upon deportation of a foreign national cannot be challenged. The introduction of a visa for foreign experts in combination with the more detailed definitions of illegal activities further implies that the legislators aimed to increase control over immigration issues by classifying foreign nationals and handling certain groups of foreign nationals in a different manner than others. The enhanced provisions regarding legal remedies in the revised legal framework in combination with court practice, however, illustrate that foreign nationals enjoy a much larger scope of enforceable legal remedies in comparison with the former legal framework, although legal remedies are limited in certain areas like visa application or repatriation and deportation. Finally, the fact that Chinese courts rule in favour of foreign nationals even during campaigns against illegal immigration suggests that courts are less affected by campaign-style governance than public security organs in the context of exit–entry administration.

Chapter 5: Reform of Immigration Law: An Example of Symbolic Governance?

This study aims to answer the question how the law-making process of the revised *Exit-Entry Administration Law* and the deployment of campaigns against illegal behaviour in the context of immigration law interact. The main findings showed that the aim of the government to strengthen control in immigration was pursued via different means to tackle regulatory failure in the context of exit–entry administration: experimental legislation, law enforcement campaigns, revision of legal norms, institutional reform and establishment of parallel administrative structures. These different means do not stand alongside each other as self-contained systems, rather they are intertwined in several ways.

First, campaigns make use of a certain organisational structure that has also been applied in institutional reforms, namely the so called *da waiguan* system where new specialised administrative entities are set up for specific purposes, comprising of representatives of different involved ministerial branches. One example of such a structure is the establishment of the Working Group for Cooperation between Ministries in Foreign Nationals Management Work as well as of the several working groups with the task to organise and implement *sanfei* campaigns, which comprise of representatives of the local public authority, the human resources and social security, as well as of education, tourism or other relevant authorities.

Second, the law-revision process makes use of experimentation when it integrates certain norms that have been applied before on a locally confined scope, e. g. the interim provisions in Guangdong province. Moreover, as the whistle-blower provision introduced in 2012 shows, the new law not only draws on experimental norms that have been previously introduced locally, but it also incorporates measures that originate in campaign-style policing. The extension of police authority to impose administrative punishments like orders to leave or the adjustment of the definition of 'illegal employment' not to require monetary remuneration also enable swifter enforcement of legal norms. While campaigns that aim to enforce legal norms themselves already can be regarded as an experimental approach to law enforcement,[1] it

1 See van Rooij (2016), p. 228.

is evident that the use of campaigns, of which the reporting of suspects to the police by the public is a major aspect, has had an impact on the law-making process when the final law codifies a whistle-blower provision.

This suggests that campaigns are not only driven by the law-making process or *vice versa*, but that an overarching political aim to tackle problems in immigration law led to both the deployment of campaigns on the one hand and the revision of the law on the other hand. I conclude that the Chinese government used a combined approach of symbolic and factual governance in the area of immigration law. This combined approach becomes primarily manifest in the deployment of campaign-style enforcement and the parallel revision of legal provisions. The law-making process and the deployment of campaigns are interdependent. The law needed to be revised in order to better fit international standards and the overall legal framework of administrative law, but the revised legal regulations at national level were difficult to implement at the local level. To avoid the law not achieving visible local result, campaigns were deployed to exert pressure on local officials and to communicate that the state is tackling the problem of illegal immigration even at the local level. With reference to legal norms that are to be enforced, in turn, the deployment of campaigns is justified. While the reason to apply this combined approach may primarily be a rather pragmatic one, such an approach can also help to increase the legitimation of the ruling leadership, as will be shown in the following.

A. *Summary of the Findings*

This study examined several drivers to the development of immigration law, one of which are economic reforms. The 1980 *Nationality Law* and the 1985 *Foreign Nationals Exit–Entry Administration Law* were promulgated in the context of the opening of China to the outside world. To strengthen economic relations in the international context, an improved legal framework of exit–entry administration was needed and, as a basis for the legal differentiation of Chinese nationals and foreign nationals, a law to codify nationality was promulgated. In the context of ongoing economic reforms, new aspects of exit–entry administration, such as the attraction of foreign experts or a green-card system, became necessary and were codified in supplemental provisions. While these developments show the direct influence of economic reforms to immigration law, the revision process of the *Exit–Entry Administration Law* was also indirectly driven by the economic reforms. Because market reforms were only deemed to succeed against the background of a comprehensive administrative legal framework that allowed state organs to be held responsible, legislative work in this area of law intensified, resulting in the promulgation of the *Administrative Litigation Law*, the *Administrative Reconsideration Law*, the *Administrative Penalty Law*, and the *Administrative Compulsion Law* to name only a few. As the framework of administrative law developed, the contradictions between the new provisions and the old immigration law became evident. The provision of a series of regulations and local provisions on exit–entry administration over time could not resolve the complexity and contradictions of the legal basis and a revision of the *Exit–Entry Administration Law* to harmoniously integrate it into the framework of administrative law was necessary.

With China's accession to the World Trade Organisation in 2001, immigration to China increased, which is another driver to the revision process of the *Exit–Entry Administration Law*. This driver, however, is probably best understood in the context of symbolic legitimation. Although the numbers of foreign nationals who entered China increased considerably around 2001, in relation to the Chinese population, the ratio of foreign nationals even in China's biggest cities has always been considerably low compared to other countries. Official statements justify the promulgation of the new *Exit–Entry Administration Law* in 2012 with the rising numbers of *sanfei* foreigners that allegedly accompanied the increase of immigration to China in general. However, current statistics reveal that the problem of *sanfei* foreigners even in cities like Guangzhou, which are identified by the media and in academic literature as hot spots of illegal immigration, is minor compared with similar problems of illegal immigration in other countries, especially countries of immigration. While an increase of illegal migration can certainly be determined, the greater driving force to amend the legal framework on exit–entry administration was, hence, the complicated and contradictory legal framework that hampered efficient law enforcement, while the problem of illegal immigration itself can only be regarded as a secondary stimulus. Still, in the context of symbolic legitimation as discussed below, the increase in immigration was taken as a proxy for actual outcomes of governance reform in the context of immigration law.

Insufficient communication and cooperation posed a problem to law enforcement in the context of immigration law. Organisational administrative structures to enhance cooperation between different authorities in the context of exit–entry administration and foreign nationals management exist on local levels as well as on a supra-ministerial level. However, as the establishment of a new working group on foreign nationals management work in 2003 suggests, these structures have not been able to efficiently tackle the problem of insufficient communication between the relevant agencies, at least not without additional political pressure in the form of campaigns. The revised *Exit–Entry Administration Law* encourages the establishment of a platform to share information concerning immigration between different responsible authorities in the context of digitisation of exit–entry administration such as the use of biometric data. The full implementation of this platform, however, has yet to be realised. To tackle the problem of regulatory failure that resulted from insufficient communication and cooperation between the different authorities, so-called *sanfei* campaigns were deployed. The campaigns aimed to enhance the enforcement of legal provisions regarding foreign nationals who illegally entered China, illegally stayed in China or were illegally employed in China. However, *sanfei* campaigns were also used to convey the message to the public that the government and the local public security authorities were tackling the problem of illegal immigration and hence incorporate factual and symbolic aspects of governance.

Rather than identifying campaigns as merely enforcing the law or the law being influenced by campaigns, both depict forms of governance that are deployed in parallel in the context of immigration, guided by an overarching political aim to strengthen control in exit–entry administration. *Sanfei* campaigns explicitly refer to the legal framework using the definitions of illegal entry, stay and employment as codified in the law and can hence be identified as law-enforcement campaigns. Legal norms on the other hand, first at the local level in an experimental way, but later also at the national level, have been amended to facilitate law enforcement, e. g. by extending the decision making power of public security organs concerning administrative punishments and compulsory measures, and also to codify a whistle-blower rule, both of which contribute to the deployment of campaigns. In this regard, an interaction between law enforcement campaigns and law-making processes is evident, in which both governance instruments rely on and refer to each other. Neither the revision process of exit–entry administration law nor the deployment of *sanfei* campaigns can be explained without reference to the other governance instrument, while both instruments as well as said institutional reforms in administrative structures can be regarded as manifestations of the political aim to strengthen control in exit–entry administration.

The findings of this study develop the theoretical framework on the function of campaigns in the context of law and its enforcement as coined primarily by VAN ROOIJ and BIDDULPH, COONEY and ZHU. As VAN ROOIJ states, "[c]ampaigns are organized in reaction to weak law enforcement due to local protectionism. In addition, campaigns serve political goals as they offer a way for China's central leadership to maintain legitimacy by showing a willingness to act against public incidents."[2] He thus views campaigns as a form of law enforcement that depends on a legal framework already promulgated, albeit it may introduce new norms only later to be codified in law.[3] However, he also identifies a legitimating function of campaigns.[4] BIDDULPH, COONEY and ZHU state that regulatory failure campaigns are a new type of campaign to be differentiated from campaigns targeting criminal (or, more general, illegal) behaviour and from campaigns that target intra-party deviation. BIDDULPH, COONEY and ZHU further state that regulatory failure campaigns are often accompanied by law-making processes and in such cases influence the law-making process via different means. Hence, the three authors analyse campaigns that are deployed prior to or during the promulgation of law.

The campaigns analysed by VAN ROOIJ or by BIDDULPH, COONEY and ZHU were deployed either before or after the promulgation of legal provisions that they referred to. Campaigns that aim to be law-enforcement campaigns logically need legal provisions promulgated beforehand. BIDDULPH, COONEY, and ZHU, on the other hand, state that the deployment of regulatory failure campaigns often results in the promulgation of new legal provisions. *Sanfei* campaigns were deployed prior to the promulgation of the revised law and have continued to be deployed after the new law came into force. It is thus difficult to identify *sanfei* campaigns as pure law-enforcement campaigns as described by VAN ROOIJ. But *sanfei* campaigns cannot be identified as pure regulatory failure campaigns either, because they also incorporate elements of campaigns targeted against illegal behaviour. Also, in contrast to the wages campaign analysed by BIDDULPH, COONEY, and ZHU, *sanfei* campaigns lack a unified, centrally initiated national movement and are hence rather a local-level implementation of national legislation (albeit not on the lowest administrative level). This again, more resembles local law-enforcement campaigns as described by VAN ROOIJ. *Sanfei* campaigns hence share characteristics of regulatory failure campaigns, but also of law-

2 VAN ROOIJ (2009), p 2.

3 VAN ROOIJ (2006 b), p. 314.

4 According to VAN ROOIJ, "[campaigns] continue to be organized, mainly for two reasons: targeting scarce enforcement resources and reacting to public outcry and incidents in order to maintain confidence in the state and ultimately legitimacy." VAN ROOIJ (2009), p. 52.

enforcement campaigns and even of campaigns that are targeted against illegal behaviour, similar to 'strike hard' campaigns.

I therefore argue that the interconnection of campaigns with law making procedures cannot serve as a basis for classification as either regulatory failure or law-enforcement campaign. Rather, I identify the interlinkage with law making processes through developing new or altering existing legal provisions as one of several functions a campaign can have. Other functions are, for example, the enforcement of legal norms or the communication of certain political aims. *Sanfei* campaigns conflate the function of being interlinked with law making with a communication function, for example when they promote legal provisions or exert pressure on local officials in order to push local-level enforcement of the law. Moreover, I argue that a campaign does not necessarily have to be deployed as a unified nation-wide movement in order to be interlinked with law-making processes. In the case of *sanfei* campaigns, an interlinkage of campaigns with law-making processes exists where local provisions developed during the deployment of campaigns become implemented into legal provisions at the national level. But *sanfei* campaigns evolved as a multitude of small-scale local campaigns rather than being officially initiated at national level, such as the wages campaign described by Biddulph, Cooney, and Zhu.

The deployment of campaigns in the context of immigration law illustrates that it is no longer feasible to distinguish between a 'routine mode' and a 'crisis mode' as described in literature on campaigns.[5] At first glance, *sanfei* campaigns only seem to solve problems that they create in the first place and their benefit is not evident. But a closer look at the subject reveals that in the context of immigration law, campaigns and the law are mutually dependent and constitute two forms of governance that complement each other. In contrast to older literature that depicts campaigns and the law as modes of crisis and routine where the former and the latter are mutually exclusive, I argue that today, Chinese leadership has managed to incorporate both forms of governance in a holistic way to enforce certain political aims and at the same time to foster its legitimacy.

During the deployment of *sanfei* campaigns, no increase in the severity of punishment can be determined in concurrence with a collaboration of the police, the procuratorate and the courts in order to 'swiftly and severely' prosecute illegal actions, as is reported for 'strike hard' campaigns. Although an increase in police controls and in the number of penalties can be

5 E. g. Heilmann (2016).

assumed during campaigns, the punishments provided in the revised law, albeit harsher in comparison to the ones in the old law, are still relatively mild in international comparison. Legal remedies have been consolidated and extended in the new *Exit-Entry Administration Law*, of which the revision process happened in parallel to the deployment of campaigns. In addition, at least some courts protect the interests of foreign employees, which shows that the codified legal remedies and protections are indeed being enforced. Thus, taken together, the overall situation is very different from that during the 'strike hard' campaigns, although *sanfei* camapaigns also bear a similar notion of combating illegal activities.

Biddulph, Cooney and Zhu state that the coordination of and between different agencies, also including the courts, is a typical feature of Chinese campaigns—not only of 'strike hard' campaigns, but also of the more recent regulatory failure campaigns—which differentiates Chinese campaigns from their Western counterparts.[6] In the context of *sanfei* campaigns, the police are in fact a recipient of campaign communication and pressure is exerted on local officials via campaign-style governance. However, a similarly strong influence by campaigns on the courts cannot be determined, which at least in the context of employment of foreign nationals protect the legal rights of individuals and which are also not directly addressed in action and implementation plans regarding campaign-work. I hence argue that an important objective of *sanfei* campaigns is communication to local police officials and to the Chinese public in order to unveil illegal activities of foreign nationals and promote strict and formal enforcement.

While the courts and the procuratorate are not addressed in the campaign context, this study demonstrates that administrative organs were coordinated during *sanfei* campaigns in order to tackle regulatory failure at the local level. Hence, I conclude that although *sanfei* campaigns lack a typical characteristic of Chinese campaigns when they do not address the courts, they still "involve central coordination between different agencies of state, allocation of tasks, and performance quotas both across different agencies and down the administrative hierarchy to local levels",[7] which can only be implemented in the context of the Chinese authoritarian system.

---

6 Biddulph / Cooney / Ying Zhu (2012), p. 393.
7 Biddulph / Cooney / Ying Zhu (2012), p. 393.

B. Symbolic Legitimation as Explanatory Approach

The concept of symbolic legitimation coined by WANG[8] helps explain the parallel use of campaigns and law making in order to achieve the political aim to increase control in the context of immigration law. Using the description of symbolic and factual governance, campaigns can be classified as a more symbolic form of governance, while law depicts rather a factual form of governance. Undoubtedly, campaigns and the law-making process both contain certain elements of factual and symbolic governance. While law making may be less symbolic than campaign-style policing, it is still used in part in a symbolic manner. In the example of immigration law, the codification of the symbolic whistle-blower rule only restates an already established legal concept, namely the right (and duty) of a citizen to report illegal behaviour to the police. Hence, this provisions communicates to the public that the state is taking care of the problem of illegal activities of foreign nationals, while at the same time establishing a mechanism for public supervision of local officials, who are forced to take action and to be accountable to the public. Campaigns are, similarly, not entirely symbolic, as they are used to establish communication channels and additional administrative structures to enhance regulation in an efficient, albeit temporary, way. During *sanfei* campaigns, parallel administrative structures with the aim to tackle regulatory failure in the context of immigration administration are established. Courts act independently from campaign work showing that the protection of legal rights of foreign nationals is safeguarded and the law is hence applied in a functional way.

In the context of immigration law, the deployment of campaigns and the application of law (as well as the process of law making) take place over the same time span, and both in their symbolic and factual aspects complement each other and are dependent on one another. While campaign-style governance relies on law enforcement as legitimation, law enforcement on the local level can often only be accomplished with the use of campaigns. Hence, it is difficult to distinguish between a mode of crisis and of normalcy when looking at the enforcement of immigration law that is accompanied by *sanfei* campaigns. Rather, at least in the context of immigration law, factual and symbolic aspects of governance are used in combination. It is important to note that in general the intention to use a specific measure in a factual

8 Alex L. WANG (2018).

or in a symbolic way cannot be determined.[9] Measures that may have been intended to be factual in the beginning probably turn out to be rather symbolic and are only later utilised as such. Still, I identify certain aspects of specific governance measures that are most likely intended to be symbolic from the very beginning, like certain communication functions of both the law-making process and campaigns.

I argue that in the context of immigration law, campaigns have a lasting effect on law making not only by impelling the adoption of certain provisions that strengthen police control over immigration issues, but also through the adoption of provisions that incorporate elements of campaign-style governance, such as the whistle-blower rule, into law. As citizens already have the right to report illegal actions to the police according to the *Police Law*, this provision only restates already existing general rules and hence has merely a symbolic function. To be sure, whistle-blower provisions are not alien to Chinese law. They also exist in laws like the *Environmental Protection Law* (2016), the *Circular Economy Promotion Law* (2008), the *Counterterrorism Law* (2015) or the *Counterespionage Law* (2014). However, most of these legal provisions can also be found in areas where campaigns are deployed regularly, and campaigns probably have a similar effect on law making in these areas as well. The official statements that the whistle-blower provision in the *Exit-Entry Administration Law* (2012) is rooted in campaigns against illegal immigration underlines the lasting effect of campaigns on law making in immigration law.

I argue that the lasting effect of campaigns on law making and legal provisions is not related to their being unambiguously classified as regulatory failure campaigns. Rather the effect on law making and legal provisions is a function of contemporary campaigns in general. A certain campaign may possess different functions that are characteristic of regulatory failure campaigns, of campaigns targeted against illegal behaviour or of campaigns targeted against intra-party deviance. However an unambiguous classification does not accurately reflect the actual nature of today's campaigns. The lasting effect on law making and legal provisions may result in elements of campaign-style governance being codified in the law, such as whistle-blower rules. In this event, the so-called 'crisis mode' enters the realm of the 'routine mode'[10] and becomes part of it, making both inseparable. While it may be possible to identify times where campaigns are not deployed, an

9 Alex L. Wang (2018), p. 714, 723 f.
10 As referred to in Heilmann (2016), p. 150.

alternation of a crisis and a routine mode cannot be determined any longer, because the former is explicitly included in the latter. Rather than in alternation, both modes exist in parallel and in reference to each other. I argue that this relationship of law and campaigns represents a style of governance that is characteristic of the Chinese autocratic system and that is applied by the leadership to legitimate itself and the system.

As WANG argues, Chinese governance relies in part on symbolic governance, such as the deployment of campaigns as a means of communication, to legitimise the governing regime.[11] State action is in part used to communicate to the public or to state officials and to convey the notion that the state cares and addresses problems, alongside its factual application which may still be effective.[12] However, the efficiency of state action is irrelevant for symbolic governance to be effective.[13] Communication is probably the most important function of campaigns as a form of symbolic governance. The parallel application of campaigns and law making in the context of immigration law is an example of the application of a combination of factual and symbolic governance. I argue that both elements of governance are needed in the context of the Chinese political system due to its particularities. The interaction of *sanfei* campaigns and the revision of the *Exit–Entry Administration Law* is an example of how the combination of factual and symbolic governance supports the legitimation of the leadership.

The law cannot be efficiently enforced without the use of campaigns, because local-level authorities pursue aims that differ from those of the national level. Hence, legal aims declared in national-level norms may not be applied as intended at the local level, resulting in the loss of authority of central level authorities. The means of institutional reforms and structural reorganisation (in part in the context of campaigns) are applied to enhance communication between the central level and the local level. The means of campaigns is additionally used to foster hierarchical instruction authority and also to convey to the public that the central level is able to reach down to the local level and is able to control political problems.

On the other hand, campaigns cannot be applied without a legal or at least a normative basis either, because this would also undermine the authority of the central level. By referring to legal norms in campaign work, the state conveys the notion that campaigns are not applied arbitrarily but

11 Alex L. WANG (2018), p. 702, 710.
12 Alex L. WANG (2018), p. 718.
13 Alex L. WANG (2018), p 703, 723.

they are based on legitimately constituted norms. This argumentation can be applied both to the outside when persecuting illegal behaviour, but also to the inside when persecuting internal misbehaviour like corruption. On the other hand, law making itself also conveys the notion to the public that the state is addressing a certain problem. When the courts are seemingly not affected by the deployment of campaigns, as in the example of immigration law, the notion of a reliable legal system is underlined which in turn legitimises the use of campaigns as an enforcement instrument.

It remains to be seen whether the courts will be excluded from future campaign-style governance. If the courts remain unaffected by campaign-style governance, this could be regarded as a step towards a 'rule of law' with Chinese characteristics where, although campaigns are used as a temporary means of enforcement, the individual could still rely on a relatively independent judiciary. However, the exclusion of the courts may be a particularity specific to the case of immigration law. From the point of view of central government, the exclusion of courts from law-enforcement campaigns may strongly contribute to legitimation of the regime, because on the one hand campaigns can be used as a form of symbolic governance, but on the other hand this would not undermine the confidence of fundamental principles of a society governed by law.

C. Conclusion

This study showed that the revision of exit–entry administration law and the deployment of campaigns targeting illegal immigration were primarily driven by the perception of regulatory failure in the context of exit–entry administration. This perception resulted in the the aim to increase control by central government and the leadership over immigration issues. To this end, central political aims had to be implemented at the local levels which was achieved through a combined approach of law revision and deployment of campaigns. The harmonisation of legal norms, but also the enhancement of intra-administrative communication was used as a means to achieve the aim of effective and efficient enforcement of laws. Campaigns not only served as important means to exert pressure and implement *ad-hoc* organisational structures that served the aim of enhanced communication and information sharing, but also as a means to communicate to the public that the leadership recognised and addressed the issue of illegal immigration. Together with the framing of illegal immigration as a considerable threat to social and public security, this eventually served the legitimation of the central leadership.

This study showed that campaigns are an integral part of contemporary governance in China, especially in the context of immigration law, together with experimental legislation and ongoing institutional reform. Used as a means for law enforcement, campaigns cannot be regarded as an alien element in governance. Rather, they are connected to law making and law enforcement in several ways. On the one hand, law-enforcement campaigns contribute to law making by utilising an experimental approach of legislation that can be observed in different areas of Chinese law and not only in the context of immigration law. In the context of exit–entry administration, experimental interim provisions on a local level go hand in hand with the deployment of law-enforcement campaigns. While the campaigns offer new approaches to law enforcement like the participation of the public via a whistle-blower rule, the legal norms facilitate the deployment of campaigns by extending the enforcement power of the public security organs. On the other hand, campaigns make use of similar institutional reforms and organisational models established typically in regular administrative structures. In the context of exit–entry administration, the *da waiguan* system is an example of a regular administrative structure where different administrative branches are joined to strengthen administrative cooperation. Campaigns, too, make use of parallel administrative structures to strengthen administrative cooperation between different administrative bodies in order to implement the campaign aims. It is exactly this interrelation between different means of governance that is characteristic of China and campaigns should hence be regarded as inalienable part of Chinese governance. In the example of exit–entry administration, the aim of enhanced control over immigration issues was tackled by combining the revision process of the law with the deployment of campaigns. While the efficient enforcement of national-level laws on the local level relies heavily on campaigns, campaigns, in turn, receive their legitimation from legal norms. In this context, the legitimacy of the central leadership in China could only be maintained with the combination of both means of governance, which explains the use of campaigns in parallel to the law revision process in the area of Chinese immigration law.

List of References

A. *Laws, Regulations, Political Directives, Treaties and Court Cases*

Action Plan of the County of Qinghe on the Launch of the Campaign to Clear Up and Correctively Punish 'Sanfei' Foreigners (2012): *Action Plan of the County of Qinghe on the Launch of the Campaign to Clear Up and Correctively Punish 'Sanfei' Foreigners (Qing Zheng Ban Han [2012] 51 Hao)* (清河县开展清理整治'三非'外国人专项行动工作方案（清政办函〔2012〕51号）). URL: www.qinghexian.gov.cn/index.aspx?lanmuid=46&sublanmuid=277&id=1425 (visited on 8 August 2017).

Action Plan of the Education Bureau of the City of Changsha on the Launch of the Campaign to Clear Up and Correctively Punish 'Sanfei' Foreigners (2013): *Action Plan of the Education Bureau of the City of Changsha on the Launch of the Campaign to Clear Up and Correctively Punish 'Sanfei' Foreigners (Chang Jiao Tong [2013] 273 Hao)* (长沙市教育局关于开展旅游行业开展清理整治'三非'外国人专项行动工作方案（长教通〔2013〕273号）). URL: www.csedu.gov.cn/news/62889.html (visited on 22 November 2015).

Action Plan of the Forestry Police Bureau of the City of Jinghong on the Campaign to Clear Up and Correctively Punish 'Sanfei' Foreigners (2010): *Action Plan of the Forestry Police Bureau of the City of Jinghong on the Campaign to Clear Up and Correctively Punish 'Sanfei' Foreigners (Jing Sen Gong [2010] 56 Hao)* (景洪市森林公安局清理整治'三非'外国人专项行动工作方案（景森公〔2010〕56号）). URL: xxgk.yn.gov.cn/Z_M_012/Info_Detail.aspx%3FDocumentKeyID%3D3CE90768B5464E7CA02251D2097E2F63 (visited on 8 August 2017).

Action Plan of the Tourism Bureau of the City of Xingtai on the Launch of the Campaign to Clear Up and Correctively Punish 'Sanfei' Foreigners in the Tourism Sector (2012): *Action Plan of the Tourism Bureau of the City of Xingtai on the Launch of the Campaign to Clear Up and Correctively Punish 'Sanfei' Foreigners in the Tourism Sector (Xing Lü Zi [2012] 29 Hao)* (邢台市旅游局关于开展旅游行业开展清理整治'三非'外国人专项行动工作方案（邢政字〔2012〕29号）). URL: www.xtlyj.gov.cn/group/newsshow.asp?NewsID=103 (visited on 22 November 2015).

Action Plan of the Town of Qingxi on the Launch of the Campaign to Clear Up and Correctively Punish 'Sanfei' Foreigners (2014): *Action Plan of the Town of Qingxi on the Launch of the Campaign to Clear Up and Correctively Punish 'Sanfei' Foreigners (Qing Zheng Ban [2014] 60 Hao)* (清溪镇开展清理整治'三非'外国人专项行动工作方案（清府办〔2014〕60号）). URL: www.dongguan.gov.cn/007331929/0201/201607/c516a4eb3ce943fea5087eaea4ceec42.shtml (visited on 8 August 2017).

Administrative Compulsion Law (2011): *Administrative Compulsion Law of the People's Republic of China* (中华人民共和国行政强制法), *promulgated on 30 Juni 2011 and entered into force on 1 January 2012*. URL: www.pkulaw.cn/fulltext_form.aspx?Gid=153701 (visited on 27 June 2017).

Administrative Licence Law (2003): *Administrative Licence Law of the People's Republic of China* (中华人民共和国行政许可法)*, promulgated on 27 August 2003 and entered into force on 1 July 2004*. URL: www.pkulaw.cn/fulltext_form.aspx?Gid=49280 (visited on 27 June 2017).

Administrative Litigation Law Interpretations (2000): *Interpretation Regarding Several Questions Concerning the Enforcement of the 'Administrative Litigation Law of the People's Republic of China'* (最高人民法院关于执行《中华人民共和国行政诉讼法》若干问题的解释)*, promulgated on 8 March 2000 and entered into force on 10 March 2000*. URL: www . pkulaw . cn / fulltext _ form . aspx ? Gid = e3fef157898345b5bdfb (visited on 18 March 2018).

Administrative Litigation Law Interpretations (2018): *Interpretation of the Supreme People's Court on the Application of the 'Administrative Litigation Law of the People's Republic of China'* (最高人民法院关于适用《中华人民共和国行政诉讼法》的解释)*, promulgated on 6 February 2018 and entered into force on 8 February 2018*. URL: www.pkulaw.cn/fulltext_form.aspx?Gid=309904 (visited on 18 March 2018).

Administrative Litigation Law (1989): "Administrative Litigation Law of the People's Republic of China (中华人民共和国行政诉讼法), promulgated on 4 April 1989 and entered into force on 1 October 1990". In: *Gazette of the State Council of the People's Republic of China* (中华人民共和国国务院公报) 7, 1989, pp. 296–307.

Administrative Litigation Law (2014): *Administrative Litigation Law of the People's Republic of China* (中华人民共和国行政诉讼法)*, promulgated on 4 April 1989 and entered into force on 1 October 1990, last amended on 1 November 2014*. URL: www.pkulaw.cn/fulltext_form.aspx?Gid=239820 (visited on 27 June 2017).

Administrative Penalty Law (1996): "Administrative Penalty Law of the People's Republic of China (中华人民共和国行政处罚法), promulgated on 17 March 1996 and entered into force on 1 October 1996". In: *Gazette of the Supreme People's Court of the People's Republic of China* (中华人民共和国最高人民法院公报) 3, 1996, pp. 75–80.

Administrative Penalty Law (2009): *Administrative Penalty Law of the People's Republic of China* (中华人民共和国行政处罚法)*, promulgated on 17 March 1996 and entered into force on 1 October 1996, last amended on 27 August 2009*. URL: www.pkulaw.cn/fulltext_form.aspx?Gid=167113 (visited on 27 June 2017).

Administrative Reconsideration Law (2009): *Administrative Reconsideration Law of the People's Republic of China* (中华人民共和国行政复议法)*, promulgated on 29 April 1999 and entered into force on 1 October 1999, last amended on 27 August 2009*. URL: www.pkulaw.cn/fulltext_form.aspx?Gid=167114 (visited on 27 June 2017).

Al-Nashif v. Bulgaria (2002): *Case of Al-Nashif v. Bulgaria, Application No. 50963/99*. URL: hudoc.echr.coe.int/eng?i=001-60522 (visited on 1 February 2019).

Australian Migration Amendment Act (1992): *Migration Amendment Act [of the the Commonwealth of Australia], adopted on 6 May 1992*. URL: www.legislation.gov.au/Details/C2004A04315 (visited on 4 March 2019).

Beijing Labour Dispute Case (2014): *Labour Dispute Case between Liu Jinxiang and Nuance Communications (Beijing), Inc. (2014) Chao Min Chu Zi Di 10102 Hao* (刘锦湘与纽昂司软件技术（北京）有限公司劳动争议一审民事裁定书（2014）朝民初字第 10102 号). URL: wenshu.court.gov.cn/content/content?DocID=7ca8658a-b4f2-48ee-9598-234d23e34de9 (visited on 27 June 2017).

Beijing Labour Dispute Minutes (2009): *Minutes of the Discussion Meeting High Court of Beijing and the Municipal Labour Dispute Arbitration Commision on Questions Concerning the Application of Law in Labour Dispute Cases* (北京市高级人民法院、北京市劳动争议仲裁委员会关于劳动争议案件法律适用问题研讨会会议纪要)*, issued on 7 October 2009*. URL: www.pkulaw.cn/fulltext_form.aspx?Gid=d1e9b73f039976a0547c734300f2a717bdfb (visited on 26 March 2018).

Border Administration Crimes Note (2000): "Notification on the Standards for Filing Directly Received Cases of Crimes of Disrupting the Administration of the Border and Relevant Issues (关于妨害国（边）境管理犯罪案件立案标准及有关问题的通知), promulgated and entered into force on 31 March 2000". In: *Selection of Judicial Documents* (司法业务文选) 18, 2000, pp. 1–7.

Canadian Immigration and Refugee Protection Act (2018): *Immigration and Refugee Protection Act [of Canada], adopted on 1 November 2001, last amended on 31 July 2018*. URL: laws-lois.justice.gc.ca/eng/acts/I-2.5/ (visited on 4 March 2019).

Circular Economy Promotion Law (2008): *Circular Economy Promotion Law of the People's Republic of China* (中华人民共和国循环经济促进法)*, promulgated on 29 August 2008 and entered into force on 1 January 2009*. URL: www.pkulaw.cn/fulltext_form.aspx?Gid=655ad4b68f55f896bdfb (visited on 4 March 2019).

Citizens Exit–Entry Administration Law (1985): "Law of the People's Republic of China on the Administration of the Exit and Entry of Citizens (中华人民共和国公民出境入境管理法), promulgated on 22 November 1985, entered into force on 1 February 1986". In: *Gazette of the State Council of the People's Republic of China* (中华人民共和国国务院公报) 33, 1985, pp. 1112–1115.

Code of Administrative Offences of the Russian Federation (2018): *Code of Administrative Offences of the Russian Federation (Кодекс Российской Федерации об административных правонарушениях), adopted on 20 December 2001, last amended on 27 December 2018*. URL: www.pravo.gov.ru/proxy/ips/?docbody=&nd=102074277 (visited on 4 March 2019).

Common Program (1948): "Common Program of the Chinese People's Political Consultative Conference (中國人民政治協商會議共同綱領), promulgated on 29 September 1949". In: *The New China* (新中華) 12.20, 1948, pp. 40–43.

Company Law (1993): *Company Law of the People's Republic of China* (中华人民共和国公司法)*, promulgated on 29 December 1993 and entered into force on 1 July 1994*. URL: www.pkulaw.cn/fulltext_form.aspx?Gid=96c8140a5ce8d3a8bdfb (visited on 5 January 2018).

Company Law (2005): *Company Law of the People's Republic of China* (中华人民共和国公司法)*, promulgated on 29 December 1993, amended on 27 October 2005 and entered into force on 1 June 2006*. URL: www.pkulaw.cn/fulltext_form.aspx?Gid=e54c465cca59c137bdfb (visited on 4 March 2019).

Čonka v. Belgium (2002): *Case of Čonka v. Belgium, Application No. 51564/99*. URL: hudoc.echr.coe.int/eng?i=001-60026 (visited on 2 February 2019).

Constitution (1982): "Constitution of the People's Republic of China (中华人民共和国宪法), promulgated and entered into force on 4 December 1982". In: *Gazette of the State Council of the People's Republic of China* (中华人民共和国国务院公报) 20, 1982, pp. 851–874.

Constitution (2004): "Constitution of the People's Republic of China (中华人民共和国宪法), promulgated and entered into force on 14 March 2004". In: *New Laws and Regulations Monthly* (新法规月刊) 5, 2004, pp. 4–17.

Contract Dispute Jurisdiction Case (2017): *Appeal Case on the Jurisdiction of Disputes on a Joint Venture Contract on Developing Real Estate between Guangxi Lihui Investment Ltd. and Wang Yuanye* (广西丽汇投资有限公司与王原野（Wang Yuanye）合资合作开发房地产合同纠纷管辖权异议上诉案). URL: www.pkulaw.cn/case/pfnl_a25051f3312b07f32b91c8e7a1f5a8d5639c5274f0e00067bdfb.html (visited on 28 August 2018).

Convention against Torture and Other Cruel, Inhuman or Degrading Treatment or Punishment (1984): *Convention against Torture and Other Cruel, Inhuman or Degrading Treatment or Punishment, adopted and opened for signature, ratification and accession by General Assembly resolution 39/46 of 10 December 1984*. URL: www.ohchr.org/Documents/ProfessionalInterest/cat.pdf (visited on 18 March 2019).

Convention on the Rights of the Child (1989): *Convention on the Rights of the Child, adopted and opened for signature, ratification and accession by General Assembly resolution 44/25 of 20 November 1989*. URL: www.ohchr.org/Documents/ProfessionalInterest/crc.pdf (visited on 3 March 2019).

Convention Relating to the Status of Refugees (1951): *Convention Relating to the Status of Refugees, adopted on 28 July 1951 by the United Nations Conference of Plenipotentiaries on the Status of Refugees and Stateless Persons convened under General Assembly resolution 429 (V) of 14 December 1950*. URL: www.ohchr.org/Documents/ProfessionalInterest/refugees.pdf (visited on 3 March 2019).

Counterespionage Law (2014): *Counterespionage Law of the People's Republic of China* (中华人民共和国反间谍法)*, promulgated and entered into force on 1 November 2014*. URL: www.pkulaw.cn/fulltext_form.aspx?Gid=eff4fdc4b2f3457cbdfb (visited on 4 March 2019).

Counterterrorism Law (2015): *Counterterrorism Law of the People's Republic of China* (中华人民共和国反恐怖主义法)*, promulgated on 27 December 2015 and entered into force on 1 January 2016*. URL: www.pkulaw.cn/fulltext_form.aspx?Gid=f694f0bd49b816eabdfb (visited on 4 March 2019).

Criminal Code of the Democratic People's Republic of Korea (2009): *The Criminal Code of the Democratic People's Republic of Korea* (조선민주주의인민공화국 형법), *adopted on 3 March 1950, last amended in April 2009*. URL: wipolex.wipo.int/en/text/330165 (visited on 4 March 2019).

Criminal Code of the Russian Federation (2018): *Criminal Code of the Russian Federation (Уголовный кодекс Российской Федерации), adopted on 24 May 1996, last amended on 27 December 2018*. URL: www.pravo.gov.ru/proxy/ips/?docbody=&link_id=1&nd=102041891 (visited on 4 March 2019).

Criminal Law (1979): "Criminal Law of the People's Republic of China (中华人民共和国刑法), promulgated on 1 July 1979 and entered into force on 1 January 1980". In: *People's Judicature* (人民司法) 7, 1979, pp. 10–24.

Criminal Law (2015): *Criminal Law of the People's Republic of China* (中华人民共和国刑法)*, promulgated on 1 July 1979, revised on 14 March 1997 and entered into force on 1 October 1997, last amended on 29 August 2015*. URL: www.pkulaw.cn/fulltext_form.aspx?Gid=256346 (visited on 27 June 2017).

Criminal Litigation Law (2012): *Criminal Litigation Law of the People's Republic of China* (中华人民共和国刑事诉讼法)*, promulgated on 7 July 1979, revised on 14 March 2012 and entered into force on 1 January 2013*. URL: www.pkulaw.cn/fulltext_form.aspx?Gid=6d5f42efc8724124bdfb (visited on 4 March 2019).

Current Summary of Work Sharing of Public Security Organs in the Administration of Criminal Cases (n. d.): *Current Summary of Work Sharing of Public Security Organs in the Administration of Criminal Cases* (现行公安机关刑事案件管辖分工汇总)*, issued by the Second Bureau of the Legal Office of the Ministry of Public Security* (公安部法制局二处). URL: pkulaw.cn/fulltext_form.aspx?Db=lawexplanation&Gid=e4b548dc522995d9998fc53b3640ff30bdfb (visited on 6 May 2019).

Decision on Restricting Exit (2009): *Decision on Restricting Exit in the First Instance Credit Dispute Between Shaoxing Haiming Textile Co., Ltd., and Mohammad Nasim Jallat Khan (2009) Shao Shang Wai Chu Zi Di 22 Hao* (绍兴县海明纺织品有限公司与 Mohammad Nasim Jallat Khan 民间借贷纠纷一审限制出境裁定书(2009)绍商外初字第 22 号). URL: wenshu.court.gov.cn/content/content?DocID=da2d20e4-c1be-4884-9ccc-12a73dce1765 (visited on 27 July 2018).

Decision on Restricting Exit (2014 a): *Decision on Pre-Trial Preservation and Non-Litigious Enforcement in the Credit Dispute Between Zhuang Jinping and Wu Ziren and Yu Qinmin (2014) Rong Min Bao Zi Di 188 Hao* (庄金平与吴自仁、俞琴民间借贷纠纷诉前保全与非诉执行审查案件民事裁定书（2014）榕民保字第 188 号). URL: wenshu.court.gov.cn/content/content?DocID=80eb73c1-8fe5-4443-af3b-b363e09288db (visited on 27 July 2018).

Decision on Restricting Exit (2014 b): *Decision on Pre-Trial Preservation and Non-Litigious Enforcement [in the Dispute] Between Zhang Li and Chen Jinlong and Yang Jinxiu (2014) Rong Min Bao Zi Di 718 Hao* (张丽与陈金龙、杨锦秀诉前保全与非诉执行审查案件裁定书（2014）榕民保字第 718 号). URL: wenshu.court.gov.cn/content/content?DocID=e1e14ca4-7c3c-462a-9865-3912f65b8e5c (visited on 27 July 2018).

Decision on Restricting Exit (2015): *Decision in the First Instance Credit Dispute Between Tianjin Bangxin Microfinance Co., Ltd., and Li Jingtai (2015) Yi Zhong Min Wu Chu Zi Di 0120 Hao* (天津邦信小额贷款有限责任公司与李京泰企业借贷纠纷一审民事裁定书（2015）一中民五初字第0120号). URL: wenshu.court.gov.cn/content/content?DocID=4f61de51-20d7-426c-b216-90e791bf4e05 (visited on 27 July 2018).

Decision on Restricting Exit (2017): *First-instance Decision in the Administrative Case between Chen Hai and Hebei Municipal Public Security Office, Administrative Decision of the People's Court of Luyang District of Hefei City, Anhui (2017) Wan 0103 Xing Chu 10 Hao* (程海与合肥市公安局一审行政裁定书，安徽省合肥市庐阳区人民法院行政裁定书（2017）皖0103行初10号). URL: wenshu.court.gov.cn/content/content?DocID=693aa776-0ee6-40d2-9885-a7b601545060 (visited on 16 April 2019).

Discrimination (Employment and Occupation) Convention (1958): *Convention Concerning Discrimination in Respect of Employment and Occupation, adopted at Geneva, 42nd ILC session, 25 June 1958*. URL: www.ilo.org/dyn/normlex/en/f?p=NORMLEXPUB:12100:0::NO::P12100_ILO_CODE:C111 (visited on 4 March 2019).

Environmental Protection Law (2016): *Environmental Protection Law of the People's Republic of China* (中华人民共和国环境保护税法)*, promulgated on 25 December 2016 and entered into force on 1 January 2018*. URL: www.pkulaw.cn/fulltext_form.aspx?Gid=78d5d4163c8fba53bdfb (visited on 4 March 2019).

Exit and Entry Administration Regulations (1964): "Regulations on the Entry, Exit, Transit, Residence and Travel Administration of Foreign Nationals in China (外国人入境出境过境居留旅行管理条例), promulgated and entered into force on 13 April 1964". In: *Gazette of the State Council of the People's Republic of China* (中华人民共和国国务院公报) 6, 1964, pp. 112–114.

Exit Restrictions Relaxing Notification (1984): *Notification of the Ministry of Public Security about the Conscientious Implementation of Document Gongfa (Jing) 59 to Further Relax the Restrictions on Exiting the Country for Private Affairs* (公安部关于认真贯彻执行公发（境）59号文件进一步放宽因私出国的通知)*, promulgated on 22 November 1984*. URL: www.chinalawedu.com/news/1200/22598/22604/22708/2006/3/xu8791345511136002372-0.htm (visited on 6 June 2017).

Exit–Entry Administration Law (2012): "Law of the People's Republic of China on Exit and Entry Administration (中华人民共和国出境入境管理法), promulgated on 30 June 2012, entered into force on 1 July 2013". In: *New Laws and Regulations* (司法业务文选) 26, 2012, pp. 3–21.

Exit–Entry Administration Regulations (2013): "Regulations on the Administration of the Exit and Entry of Foreign Nationals (外国人入境出境管理条例), promulgated on 3 July 2013, entered into force on 1 September 2013". In: *New Laws and Regulations* (司法业务文选) 32, 2013, pp. 11–19.

Exit–Entry Border Inspection Regulations (1995): "Regulations of the People's Republic of China on the Exit–Entry Border Inspection (中华人民共和国出境入境边防检查

条例), promulgated on 6 July 1995 and entered into force on 1 September 1995". In: *Gazette of the State Council of the People's Republic of China* (中华人民共和国国务院公报) 20, pp. 799–806.

Foreign Nationals Employment Regulations (1996): *Regulations on the Management of Employment of Foreign Nationals in China* (外国人在中国就业管理规定), *promulgated on 22 January 1996 and entered into force on 1 May 1996*. URL: www.pkulaw.cn/fulltext_form.aspx?Gid=14378 (visited on 7 June 2017).

Foreign Nationals Employment Regulations (2017): *Regulations on the Management of Employment of Foreign Nationals in China* (外国人在中国就业管理规定), *promulgated on 22 January 1996 and entered into force on 1 May 1996, last amended on 13 March 2017*. URL: www.pkulaw.cn/fulltext_form.aspx?Gid=6c34d660e4fca24fbdfb (visited on 25 July 2018).

Foreign Nationals Employment Regulations (1987): *Several Regulations on the Employment of Foreign Nationals Without Residence Permit and Exchange Students in China* (关于未取得居留证件的外国人和来中国留学的外国人在中国就业的若干规定), *promulgated on 5 October 1987*. URL: www.pkulaw.cn/fulltext_form.aspx?Gid=9310 (visited on 8 January 2018).

Foreign Nationals Exit Provisional Regulations (1954): "Provisional Measures on the Exit of Foreign Nationals (外国侨民出境暂行办法), promulgated and entered into force on 10 August 1954". In: *Compilation of Statutes of the Central People's Government – 1954 (January–September)* (中央人民政府法令汇编——1954 年（1 月至9 月）). Vol. 5, 1982. Beijing: Legal Press (法律出版社), pp. 37–38.

Foreign Nationals Exit–Entry Administration Law (1985): "Law of the People's Republic of China on the Administration of the Exit and Entry of Foreign Nationals (中华人民共和国外国人入境出境管理法), promulgated on 22 November 1985, entered into force on 1 February 1986". In: *Gazette of the State Council of the People's Republic of China* (中华人民共和国国务院公报) 33, 1985, pp. 1107–1111.

Foreign Nationals Exit–Entry Administration Law Implementation Rules (1986): "Implementation Rules on the Law of the People's Republic of China on the Administration of the Exit and Entry of Foreign Nationals (中华人民共和国外国人入境出境管理法实施细则), promulgated and entered into force on 27 December 1986". In: *Gazette of the State Council of the People's Republic of China* (中华人民共和国国务院公报) 34, 1986, pp. 1060–1069.

Foreign Nationals Exit–Entry Administration Law Implementation Rules (1994): "Implementation Rules on the Law of the People's Republic of China on the Administration of the Exit and Entry of Foreign Nationals (中华人民共和国外国人入境出境管理法实施细则), promulgated and entered into force on 27 December 1986, revised on 13 July 1994". In: *Gazette of the State Council of the People's Republic of China* (中华人民共和国国务院公报) 17, 1994, pp. 772–781.

Foreign Nationals Exit–Entry Administration Law Implementation Rules (2010): "Decision of the State Council about the Revision of the 'Implementation Rules on the Law of the People's Republic of China on the Administration of the Exit and Entry of Foreign Nationals' (国务院关于修改《中华人民共和国外国人入境出境管理

法实施细则》的决定), promulgated and entered into force on 24 April 2010". In: *New Laws and Regulations* (司法业务文选) 21, 2010, pp. 25–34.

Foreign Nationals Exit, Entry, and Stay Provisional Regulations (1951): "Provisional Regulations on the Exit, Entry, and Stay of Foreign Nationals (外国侨民出入及居留暂行规则), promulgated and entered into force on 28 November 1951". In: *Compilation of Statutes of the Central People's Government – 1951* (中央人民政府法令汇编——1951年). Vol. 2, 1982. Beijing: Legal Press (法律出版社), pp. 100–101.

Foreign Nationals Illegal Employment Notice (1994): *Notice on Stopping Illegal Employment of Foreign Nationals in China* (关于制止外国人在华非法就业的通知)*, issued on 31 October 1994*. URL: www.hrssgz.gov.cn/zcfg/ldfgzh/201101/t20110113_138000.htm (visited on 15 May 2018).

Foreign Nationals Management Work Coordination Regulations (2003): *Regulations on the Coordination Mechanism of Public Security Organs in Foreign Nationals Management Work* (公安机关外国人管理工作分工配合机制规定)*, published in December 2003*. URL: xxgk.hengshui.gov.cn/eportal/ui?pageId=793322&articleKey=1333587&columnId=792600 (visited on 12 September 2017).

Foreign Nationals Report (2012): "Report on the Administrative Work Concerning Exit-Entry, Residence, and Employment of Foreign Nationals (关于外国人入出境及居留、就业管理工作情况的报告), 25 April 2012". In: *Yearbook of the National People's Congress* (全国人民代表大会年鉴), pp. 514–517.

Foreign Nationals Residence Registration Provisional Regulations (1954): "Provisional Measures on Residence Registration of and Issuance of Residence Certificates for Foreign Nationals (外国侨民居留登记及居留证签发暂行办法), promulgated and entered into force on 10 August 1954". In: *Compilation of Statutes of the Central People's Government – 1954 (January–September)* (中央人民政府法令汇编——1954年（1月至9月）). Vol. 5, 1982. Beijing: Legal Press (法律出版社), pp. 33–34.

Foreign Nationals Travel Administration Regulations (1982): "Regulations of the Ministry of Public Security, the General Staff Headquarters, the Ministry of Foreign Affairs, and the National Bureau of Tourism on the Administration of Foreign Nationals Travelling in China (公安部、总参谋部、外交部、国家旅游局关于外国人在我国旅行管理的规定), promulgated on and entered into force as of 9 October 1982". In: *Comprehensive Volume of Laws and Regulations of the People's Republic of China* (中华人民共和国法律法规全书). Vol. 8, 1994. Beijing: Chinese Democratic Legal System Press (中国民主法制出版社), pp. 513–514.

Foreign Nationals Travel Provisional Regulations (1954): "Provisional Measures on the Travel of Foreign Nationals (外国侨民旅行暂行办法), promulgated and entered into force on 10 August 1954". In: *Compilation of Statutes of the Central People's Government – 1954 (January–September)* (中央人民政府法令汇编——1954年（1月至9月）). Vol. 5, 1982. Beijing: Legal Press (法律出版社), pp. 35–36.

Foreign Nationals Treatment Instructions (1948): "Instructions of the Central Authorities on the Policy Regarding the Treatment of Foreign Nationals in China (中央关于

对待在华外国人的政策的指示), issued on 7 February 1948". In: *Anthology of Documents of the Central Committee of the Communist Party of China* (中共中央文件选集). Vol. 17, 1984. Beijing: Press of the Central Party School of the Communist Party of China (中共中央党校出版社), pp. 35–39.

Foreign-Related Civil Cases Guiding Opinions (2010): *Guiding Opinions of the Supreme People's Court on Further Doing Good Work in the Trial of Foreign-Related Civil and Commercial Cases in Border Areas* (最高人民法院关于进一步做好边境地区涉外民商事案件审判工作的指导意见). URL: www.lawinfochina.com/display.aspx?lib=law&id=8702 (visited on 4 August 2016).

Foreign-Related Civil Relations Law (2010): *Law of the People's Republic of China on the Application of Law in Foreign-Related Civil Relationships* (中华人民共和国涉外民事关系法律适用法)*, published on 28 October 2010, entered into force as of 1 April 2011*. URL: www.pkulaw.com/fulltext_form.aspx?Gid=139684 (visited on 27 June 2017).

Fraudulent Appropriation of Exit Documents Case (1999): *Case on the Fraudulent Appropriation of Exit Documents by Yuan Mingang and Bao Huamin* (袁闵钢、包华敏骗取出境证件案). URL: www . pkulaw . cn / case / pfnl_a25051f3312b07f3d02da32c651c59ab34c658b4c6e07890bdfb.html (visited on 28 August 2018).

French Code on the Entry and Residence of Foreign Nationals (2019): *Code on the Entry and Residence of Foreign Nationals and the Right of Asylum (Code de l'entrée et du séjour des étrangers et du droit d'asile), adopted on 24 November 2004, last amended on 1 March 2019*. URL: www.legifrance.gouv.fr/affichCode.do?cidTexte=LEGITEXT000006070158 (visited on 4 March 2019).

Funds Missappropriation Case (2012): *Case on the Misappropriation of Funds by Zhao Shuwei – State Officials May Not Renounce Chinese Nationality* (赵书伟挪用公款案——国家工作人员不得退出中国国籍). URL: www . pkulaw . cn / case / pfnl_a25051f3312b07f3361772b2fb6988679afea7375953fc98bdfb.html (visited on 28 August 2018).

Fuzhou Drug Abuse Case (2017): *Criminal Case on Sheltering Others for Drug Abuse of Lin Jian* (林某1容留他人吸毒案). URL: www . pkulaw . cn / case _ es / pfnl_a25051f3312b07f308851ae1c7ccee754b4ee9e91be43e2fbdfb.html (visited on 27 March 2018).

Gochev v. Bulgaria (2009): *Case of Gochev v. Bulgaria, Application No. 34383/03*. URL: hudoc.echr.coe.int/eng?i=001-95947 (visited on 1 February 2019).

Guangdong Interim Provisions on Foreign Nationals Administration (2011): *Interim Provisions of Guangdong Province on Administration of and Services to Foreign Nationals* (广东省外国人管理服务暂行规定)*, promulgated on 1 March 2011 and entered into force on 1 May 2011*. URL: www.gdfao.gd.gov.cn/Item/7983.aspx (visited on 5 February 2018).

Guangdong Labour Dispute Case (2008): *Appeal Case on Labour Dispute between Michael Deng and Zymbo Electrical Appliance Manufacturing Co., Ltd.* (邓米高（Michael Deng）与中山深宝电器制造有限公司劳

动争议纠纷再审案). URL: www . pkulaw . cn / case _ es / pfnl _ a25051f3312b07f3b908ec1ea0c14f35e0174e8d03a07481bdfb . html (visited on 26 March 2018).

Guangdong Labour Dispute Minutes (2008): *Guiding Opinions of the High Court of Guangdong and the Provinvial Labour Dispute Arbitration Commision on Several Questions Concerning the Application of the Labor Dispute Mediation and Arbitration Law and the Labour Contract Law* (广东省高级人民法院、广东省劳动争议仲裁委员会关于适用《劳动争议调解仲裁法》、《劳动合同法》若干问题的指导意见), *issued on 23 June 2008*. URL: www.pkulaw.cn/fulltext_form.aspx?Gid=611d79073b349a06760b54fe56f5c477bdfb (visited on 26 March 2018).

Guangdong Measures on Rewarding Reports of 'Sanfei' Foreigners (2004): *Measures on Rewarding of People Contributing to the Reporting of 'Sanfei' Foreigners* (举报'三非'外国人有功人员的奖励办法), *entered into force on 1 January 2004*. URL: www.southcn.com/news/gdnews/gdanounce/200402260589.htm (visited on 5 February 2018).

Guangzhou Labour Dispute Case (2016): *Labour Dispute Case between Ricefield (Guangdong) Nutritional Products Co., Ltd., and Li Zhong (2016) Yue 01 Min Zhong 18242 Hao* (赖斯菲尔得（广东）营养产品有限公司与李忠（Li Zhong）劳动争议二审民事判决书（2016）粤01民终18242号). URL: wenshu.court.gov.cn/content/content?DocID=1c614535-f32f-474e-8212-a72401104af2 (visited on 26 March 2018).

Guangzhou Labour Dispute Case (2016 a): *Labour Dispute Case 2016 Min Zhong 5310 between Yang Huarong and Shenzhen Worldway Expat Consulting Co., Ltd., and Guangzhou Worldway Expat Consulting Co., Ltd.* (杨华蓉与深圳市世贸通出国咨询有限公司、广州市世贸通出国咨询有限公司劳动争议2016民终5310案). URL: www . pkulaw . cn / case _ es / pfnl_a25051f3312b07f316734654fddad161288270fe87b741a3bdfb.html (visited on 27 March 2018).

Hangzhou Illegal Emplyoment Case (2014): *First Instance Decision in the Administrative Case of Benjamin David Salyers against the Yuhang Bureau of the Hangzhou Municipal Public Security Bureau, Administrative Case Decision of the People's Court of Yuhang District of Hangzhou City (2014) Hang Yu Xing Chu Zi Di 30 Hao* (Benjamin David Salyers 与杭州市公安局余杭区分局行政处罚一审行政判决书，杭州市余杭区人民法院行政事判决书（2014）杭余行初字第30号). URL: wenshu.court.gov.cn/content/content?DocID=a1e0fc5e-19c2-49b5-bc55-60662a31d2f2 (visited on 28 May 2018).

Hong Kong Basic Law (1990): "Basic Law of the Hong Kong Special Administrative Region of the People's Republic of China (中华人民共和国香港特别行政区基本法), promulgated on 4 April 1990 and entered into force on 1 July 1997". In: *Gazette of the State Council of the People's Republic of China* (中华人民共和国国务院公报) 7, 1990, pp. 231–257.

Hotel Public Security Administration Measures (1987): *Measures on Public Security Administration in the Hotel Sector* (旅馆业治安管理办法), *promulgated and entered into force on 10 November 1987*. URL: www.pkulaw.cn/fulltext_form.aspx?Gid=3566 (visited on 24 May 2017).

Hukou Regulations (1958): "Regulations on Household Registration (中华人民共和国户口登记条例), promulgated on 9 January 1958". In: *Gazette of the State Council of the People's Republic of China* (中华人民共和国国务院公报) 2, 1958, pp. 44–48.

ICCPR (1966): *International Covenant on Civil and Political Rights, adopted and opened for signature, ratification and accession by General Assembly resolution 2200A (XXI) of 16 December 1966*. URL: www.ohchr.org/Documents/ProfessionalInterest/ccpr.pdf (visited on 3 March 2019).

ICRMW (1990): *International Convention on the Protection of the Rights of All Migrant Workers and Members of Their Families, adopted by General Assembly resolution 45/158 of 18 December 1990*. URL: www . ohchr . org / Documents / ProfessionalInterest/cmw.pdf (visited on 3 March 2019).

Implementation Plan of the City of Fangchenggang for the Launch of the Campaign to Strike on 'Sanfei Individuals' (2011): *Circular of the Government Bureau of the City of Fangchenggang on the Publication of the Implementation Plan of the City of Fangchenggang for the Launch of the Campaign to Strike on 'Sanfei Individuals' (Fang Zhengban Fa [2011] Di 35 Hao)* (防城港市人民政府办公室关于印发防城港市开展打击'三非人员'专项行动实施方案的通知 (防政办发〔2011〕第35号)). URL: www.fcgs.gov.cn/csgk/rwfcg/wmcs/201106/t20110630_9259.html (visited on 31 January 2018).

Individual Household Regulations (2011): *Regulations on Individual Industrial and Commercial Households* (个体工商户条例)*, promulgated on 16 April 2011 and entered into force on 1 November 2011*. URL: www.pkulaw.cn/fulltext_form.aspx?Gid=b4591cbbe748b440bdfb (visited on 5 January 2018).

Individual Proprietorship Enterprises Law (1999): *Individual Proprietorship Enterprises Law of the People's Republic of China* (中华人民共和国个人独资企业法)*, promulgated on 30 August 1999 and entered into force on 1 January 2000*. URL: www.pkulaw.cn/fulltext_form.aspx?Gid=10604c99b1eaee54bdfb (visited on 5 January 2018).

Interpretations on Handling Criminal Cases Related to Border Obstruction (2012): *Interpretations of the Supreme People's Court and the Supreme Procuratorate of the People's Republic of China on Handling of Criminal Cases of Obstructing Border (Frontier) Control* (最高人民法院、最高人民检察院关于办理妨害国（边）境管理刑事案件应用法律若干问题的解释)*, promulgated and entered into force on 20 December 2012*. URL: www.pkulaw.cn/fulltext_form.aspx?Gid=7dc0af8d3ef6b155 (visited on 19 December 2017).

Italian Immigration Provisions (2009): *Consolidated Text of the Provisions Governing Immigration and Rules on the Status of Foreign Nationals (Testo unico delle disposizioni concernenti la disciplina dell'immigrazione e norme sulla condizione dello straniero), adopted on 25 July 1998, last ameded 15 July 2009*. URL: www.cliclavoro.gov.it/normative/decreto_legislativo_25_luglio_1998_n.286.pdf (visited on 4 March 2019).

Japanese Immigration Control and Refugee Recognition Act (2016): *Immigration Control and Refugee Recognition Act [of Japan]* (出入国管理及び難民認定法)*, adopted on 1 November 2009, last amended on 28 November 2016*. URL: elaws.e-gov.go.jp/search/elawsSearch/elaws_search/lsg0500/detail?lawId=326CO0000000319 (visited on 4 March 2019).

Jiangsu Labour Dispute Case (2015): *Labour Dispute Case between Chiang Yu-chen and Jiangsu SFT Photoelectrics Co., Ltd. (2015) Su Shen Er Min Shen Zi Di 02153 Hao* (姜昱丞与江苏史福特光电股份有限公司劳动争议再审复查与审判监督民事裁定书（2015）苏审二民申字第 02153 号). URL: wenshu.court.gov.cn/content/content?DocID=da457885-d407-4aec-886e-73b43e5beb18 (visited on 26 March 2018).

Labour Contract Law (2012): *Labour Contract Law of the People's Republic of China* (中华人民共和国劳动合同法)*, promulgated on 29 June 2007, amended on 28 December 2012 and entered into force on 1 July 2013*. URL: www.pkulaw.cn/fulltext_form.aspx?Gid=7ab5e7d605f859e6bdfb (visited on 4 March 2019).

Labour Law Opinions (1995): *Opinions on Several Question Concerning the Implementation of the 'Labour Law of the People's Republic of China'* (关于贯彻执行《中华人民共和国劳动法》若干问题的意见)*, promulgated by the Ministry of Labour on 4 August 1995*. URL: www.pkulaw.cn/fulltext_form.aspx?Gid=13739 (visited on 27 June 2017).

Langfang Labour Remuneration Case (2016): *Work Dispute Case between Chi Junguo and Asimco Meilian Braking Systems (Langfang) Co. Ltd. (2016) Ji 10 Min Zhong 3167 Hao* (迟俊国与亚新科美联制动（廊坊）系统有限公司劳动争议案（2016）冀 10 民终 3167 号). URL: www.pkulaw.cn/case/pfnl_1970324845592728.html (visited on 7 June 2017).

Legislation Law (2000): "Legislation Law of the People's Republic of China (中华人民共和国立法法法), promulgated on 15 March 2000 and entered into force on 1 July 2000". In: *Gazette of the Standing Committee of the National People's Congress of the People's Republic of China* (中华人民共和国全国人民代表大会常务委员会公报) 2, 2000, pp. 112–127.

Legislation Law (2015): *Legislation Law of the People's Republic of China* (中华人民共和国立法法法)*, promulgated on 15 March 2000 and entered into force on 1 July 2000, last amended on 15 March 2015*. URL: www.pkulaw.cn/fulltext_form.aspx?Gid=9073d435178b9633bdfb (visited on 27 June 2017).

Measures on Investigation of Unpermitted and Unlicenced Businesses (2017): *Measures on the Investigation and Punishment of Unpermitted and Unlicenced Businesses* (无证无照经营查处办法)*, promulgated on 6 August 2017 and entered into force on 1 October 2017*. URL: www.pkulaw.cn/fulltext_form.aspx?Gid=300763 (visited on 5 January 2018).

Migrant Workers (Supplementary Provisions) Convention (1975): *Convention Concerning Migrations in Abusive Conditions and the Promotion of Equality of Opportunity and Treatment of Migrant Workers, adopted at Geneva, 60th ILC session, 24 June

1975. URL: www.ilo.org/dyn/normlex/en/f?p=NORMLEXPUB:12100:0::NO::P12100_ILO_CODE:C143 (visited on 4 March 2019).

Nanjing Labour Dispute Case (2010): *Appeal Case on Labour Dispute between Guo Yi and Jiangsu Yifeng Pharmacy Chain Co., Ltd.* (郭懿诉江苏益丰大药房连锁有限公司劳动争议案). URL: gongbao . court . gov . cn / Details / c66ff5b19208390bcfa3757da764d8.html (visited on 27 June 2017).

Nanyang Labour Remuneration Case (2015): *Appeal Case on Labour Remuneration between Gong Yongqi and Xichuan Powder Metallurgy Co. Ltd. (2015) Nan Min Lao Zhong Zi Di 00017 Hao* (龚永岐与淅川县粉末冶金有限公司追索劳动报酬纠纷上诉案（2015）南民劳终字第00017号). URL: www.pkulaw.cn/case/pfnl_1970324845938306.html (visited on 7 June 2017).

Nationality Law (1980): "Nationality Law of the People's Republic of China (中华人民共和国国籍法), promulgated and entered into force on 10 September 1980". In: *Gazette of the State Council of the People's Republic of China* (中华人民共和国国务院公报) 13, 1980, pp. 383–384.

Nationality Law Implementation Explanations (1996): "Explanations of Some Questions by the Standing Committee of the National People's Congress Concerning the Implementation of the Nationality Law of the People's Republic of China in the Hong Kong Special Administrative Region (全国人民代表大会常务委员会关于《中华人民共和国国籍法》在香港特别行政区实施的几个问题的解释), promulgated on 15 March 1996 and entered into force on 1 July 1997". In: *Gazette of the Standing Committee of the National People's Congress of the People's Republic of China* (中华人民共和国全国人民代表大会常务委员会公报) 4, 1996, pp. 97–98.

Nationality Law Implementation Explanations (1998): "Explanations of Some Questions by the Standing Committee of the National People's Congress Concerning the Implementation of the Nationality Law of the People's Republic of China in the Macao Special Administrative Region (全国人民代表大会常务委员会关于《中华人民共和国国籍法》在澳门特别行政区实施的几个问题的解释), promulgated on 29 December 1998 and entered into force on 20 December 1999". In: *Gazette of the Standing Committee of the National People's Congress of the People's Republic of China* (中华人民共和国全国人民代表大会常务委员会公报) 6, 1998, p. 691.

Nationality Ordinance (1909): "Nationality Ordinance of the Great Qing (大清國籍條例), promulgated and entered into force on 18 March 1909". In: *Bulletin of Commercial Affairs* (商務官報) 7, 1909, pp. 34–38.

Notice on Approval Authority for Orders to Leave (2008): *Notice of the Ministry of Public Securtiy on Adjusting the Approval Authority for Orders to Leave* (公安部关于调整限期出境审批权限的通知), *issued on 3 March 2008*. URL: www.pkulaw.com/fulltext_form.aspx?Db=chl&Gid=28eef133d6b41673bdfb (visited on 23 April 2018).

Notice Regarding Questions of the Proper Participation of Foreign Workers in the Social Insurance System (2011): *Notice Regarding Questions of the Proper Participation of Foreign Workers in the Social Insurance System* (关于做好在我国境内就业的外国人参加社会保险工作有关问题的通知), *promulgated on 5 October 2011 and entered into force on 2 December 2011*. URL: www.pkulaw.cn/fulltext_form.aspx?Gid=ad8f45d7b00cd138bdfb (visited on 4 March 2019).

Notification to Pool Administration of the Exit of Chinese Citizens for Private Purposes at the Ministry Public Security (1956): *Notification of the State Council to Pool Administration of the Exit of Chinese Citizens for Private Purposes at the Ministry Public Security* (国务院关于我国公民因私事出国的管理工作由公安部统一掌握的通知), *promulgated on 14 November 1956*. URL: www.pkulaw.cn/fulltext_form.aspx?Gid=bd7a1f0d594330d5bdfb (visited on 28 August 2018).

Offences Definitions (2010): *Opinions on Definitions and the Application of Public Security Administration Offences* (违反公安行政管理行为的名称及其适用意见), *issued on 17 December 2010*. URL: www.pkulaw.cn/fulltext_form.aspx?Gid=167772 (visited on 15 August 2017).

Offences Definitions (2015): *Opinions on Definitions and the Application of Public Security Administration Offences* (违反公安行政管理行为的名称及其适用意见), *issued on 23 November 2015*. URL: www.pkulaw.cn/fulltext_form.aspx?Gid=286682 (visited on 15 August 2017).

Opinions on Foreign Talent Regarding the Implementation of the Plan of Attracting Foreign Highly Skilled Talent (2008): *Opinions of the Talents Coordination Group of the Central Government on Foreign Talent Regarding the Implementation of the Plan of Attracting Foreign Highly Skilled Talent* (中央人才工作协调小组关于实施海外高层次人才引进计划的意见), *promulgated and entered into force on 23 December 2008*. URL: www.pkulaw.cn/fulltext_form.aspx?Gid=4d06e69942deff05bdfb (visited on 4 March 2019).

Outline to Promote Measures for Administration According to Law (2004): *Outline to Promote Measures for Administration According to Law* (国务院全面推进依法行政实施纲要). URL: www.npc.gov.cn/npc/xinwen/fztd/yfxz/2004-04/20/content_330047.htm (visited on 4 March 2019).

Overseas Chinese Exit and Entry Provisional Regulations (1951): "Provisional Measures on the Exit and Entry of Overseas Chinese (華僑出入國境暫行辦法), promulgated and entered into force on 2 August 1951". In: *Gazette of the People's Government of Jiangxi* (江西政報) 8, 1951, p. 104.

Passport and Visa Regulations (1980): *Regulations of the People's Republic of China on Passports and Visas* (中华人民共和国护照、签证条例), *promulgated on and entered into force as of 13 May 1980*. URL: www.pkulaw.com/fulltext_form.aspx?Db=chl&Gid=162781 (visited on 6 June 2017).

Permanent Residence Measures (2004): *Measures for the Administration of Examination and Approval of Foreign Nationals' Permanent Residence in China* (外国人在中国永久居留审批管理办法), *promulgated and entered into force on 15 August 2004*. URL: www.pkulaw.cn/fulltext_form.aspx?Gid=2ac1e934acd51b51 (visited on 18 December 2017).

Pingxiang Border Crossing Case (2017): *First Instance Decision in the Criminal Case of Li Haiyan and Si Langzhengxia Illegally Crossing the Border, Criminal Case Decision of the People's Court of Pingxiang City in the Guangxi Zhuang Autonomous Region*

(2017) Gui 1481 Xing Chu 37 Hao (李海燕、斯郎正呷偷越国（边）境一审刑事判决书，广西壮族自治区凭祥市人民法院刑事判决书（2017）桂1481刑初37号). URL: wenshu.court.gov.cn/content/content?DocID=2e298b02-3fc5-4736-bf28-a79400991278 (visited on 27 April 2018).

Police Law (1995): *People's Police Law of the People's Republic of China* (中华人民共和国人民警察法), *promulgated and entered into force on 28 Feburary 1995*. URL: www.pkulaw.cn/fulltext_form.aspx?Gid=b0c32881807d97d5bdfb (visited on 20 February 2018).

Police Regulations (1957): *People's Police Regulations of the People's Republic of China* (中华人民共和国人民警察条例), *promulgated and entered into force on 25 June 1957*. URL: www.pkulaw.cn/fulltext_form.aspx?Gid=5d76b30108de1765bdfb (visited on 24 April 2018).

PRD Reform and Development Framework (2008): *Reform and Development Framework for the Pearl River Delta Region (2008–2020)* (珠江三角洲地区改革发展规划纲要（2008–2020年）), *issued in December 2008*. URL: www.economia.gov.mo/public/docs/EETR_PDR_RD/introduction/sc/prd_rd_outline_sc.pdf (visited on 6 February 2018).

Protocol No. 4 to the European Convention on Human Rights (1963): *Protocol No. 4 to the Convention for the Protection of Human Rights and Fundamental Freedoms, Securing Certain Rights and Freedoms Other Than Those Already included in the Convention and in the First Protocol Thereto*. URL: www.echr.coe.int/Documents/Convention_ENG.pdf (visited on 26 July 2018).

Provisional Measures on the Management of Foreign Nationals Registration by Local Public Security Bureaus (2007): *Provisional Measures on the Management of Foreign Nationals Registration by Local Public Security Bureaus* (公安派出所外国人住宿登记管理办法（试行）), *promulgated on 31 October 2007 and entered into force on 1 January 2008*. URL: www.pkulaw.cn/fulltext_form.aspx?Gid=91f92b31d1e70947bdfb (visited on 4 March 2019).

Provisional Rules on Introducing Overseas Talented People (1983): *Provisional Rules on Introducing Overseas Talented People* (关于引进国外人才工作的暂行规定), *promulgated on and entered into force as of 26 September 1983*. URL: www.pkulaw.com/fulltext_form.aspx?Db=chl&Gid=162031 (visited on 9 January 2018).

Provisions on Handling Administrative Cases (2003): *Provisions on the Procedures for Handling Administrative Cases by Public Security Organs* (公安机关办理行政案件程序规定), *promulgated on 26 August 2003 and entered into force on 1 January 2004*. URL: www.pkulaw.cn/fulltext_form.aspx?Gid=49400 (visited on 2 January 2018).

Provisions on Handling Administrative Cases (2006): *Regulations for the Procedure of Administrative Cases by Public Security Organs* (公安机关办理行政案件程序规定), *promulgated and entered into force on 26 August 2003, last amended on 29 March 2006*. URL: www.pkulaw.cn/fulltext_form.aspx?Gid=79188 (visited on 2 January 2018).

Provisions on Handling Administrative Cases (2012): *Regulations for the Procedure of Administrative Cases by Public Security Organs* (公安机关办理行政案件程序规定)*, promulgated and entered into force on 26 August 2003, last amended on 3 December 2012*. URL: www.pkulaw.cn/fulltext_form.aspx?Gid=191634 (visited on 2 January 2018).

Provisions on Handling Administrative Reconsideration Cases (2002): *Provisions on the Procedures for Handling Administrative Reconsideration Cases by Public Security Organs* (公安机关办理政复议案件程序规定)*, promulgated on 2 December 2002 and entered into force on 1 January 2003*. URL: www.pkulaw.cn/fulltext_form.aspx?Gid=49400 (visited on 2 January 2018).

Provisions on Handling Criminal Cases (1998): *Provisions on the Procedures for Handling Criminal Cases by Public Security Organs* (公安机关办理刑事案件程序规定)*, promulgated and entered into force on 18 March 1987, last amended on 14 May 1998*. URL: www.pkulaw.cn/fulltext_form.aspx?Gid=20168 (visited on 2 January 2018).

Provisions on Handling Criminal Cases (2012): *Provisions on the Procedures for Handling Criminal Cases by Public Security Organs* (公安机关办理刑事案件程序规定)*, promulgated and entered into force on 18 March 1987, last amended on 13 December 2012*. URL: www.pkulaw.cn/fulltext_form.aspx?Gid=191739 (visited on 6 December 2017).

Provisions on Providing Entry and Residence Conveniences to Foreign Highly Skilled Persons and Investors (2002): *Provisions on Providing Entry and Residence Conveniences to Foreign Highly Skilled Persons and Investors* (关于为外国籍高层次人才和投资者提供入境及居留便利规定)*, promulgated and entered into force on 24 April 2002*. URL: www.pkulaw.cn/fulltext_form.aspx?Gid=c127d0cf913be760bdfb (visited on 4 March 2019).

Provisions on the Trial of Cases Occuring in Maritime Areas (2016): *Provisions of the Supreme People's Court on Several Issues Concerning the Trial of Cases Occurring in Maritime Areas under the Jurisdiction of China (II)* (最高人民法院关于审理发生在我国管辖海域相关案件若干问题的规定(二）)*, promulgated on 1 August 2016 and entered into force on 2 August 2016*. URL: www.pkulaw.cn/fulltext_form.aspx?Gid=d68551f0253e20e5bdfb (visited on 27 April 2018).

Public Security Administration Punishments Law (2005): "Public Security Administration Punishments Law of the People's Republic of China (中华人民共和国治安管理处罚法), promulgated on 28 August 2005 and entered into force on 1 March 2006". In: *Gazette of the State Council of the People's Republic of China* (中华人民共和国国务院公报) 30, 2005, pp. 5–7.

Public Security Administration Punishments Law (2012): *Public Security Administration Punishments Law of the People's Republic of China* (中华人民共和国治安管理处罚法)*, promulgated on 28 August 2005 and entered into force on 1 March 2006, last amended on 26 October 2012*. URL: www.pkulaw.cn/fulltext_form.aspx?Gid=188539 (visited on 27 June 2017).

Quality Examination and Appraisal Regulations (2016): *Regulations Concerning the Examination and Appraisal of the Quality of Law Enforcement by Public Security Organs* (公安机关执法质量考核评议规定), *promulgated on 14 January 2016 and entered into force on 1 March 2016*. URL: www.pkulaw.cn/fulltext_form.aspx?Gid=ffb8869fe220d6acbdfb (visited on 4 March 2019).

Regulations on the Enforcement of Compulsory Measures on Foreign Nationals to Exit (1992): *Regulations on the Enforcement of Compulsory Measures on Foreign Nationals to Exit* (关于强制外国人出境的执行办法的规定), *promulgated and entered into force on 31 July 1992*. URL: www.pkulaw.cn/fulltext_form.aspx?Gid=9092364a6ff77714bdfb (visited on 27 June 2018).

Representative Office Registration Notice (2010): *Notice on Further Strengthening the Administration of Registration of Permanent Representative Offices of Foreign Enterprises* (关于进一步加强外国企业常驻代表机构登记管理的通知), *issued on 1 April 2010*. URL: www.pkulaw.cn/fulltext_form.aspx?Gid=6f1688f95ce6ce6ebdfb (visited on 14 January 2018).

Representative Office Registration Regulations (2013): *Regulations on the Administration of Registration of Resident Representative Offices of Foreign Enterprises* (关于进一步加强外国企业常驻代表机构登记管理的通知), *promulgated on 19 November 2010 and entered into force on 1 March 2011, last amended on 18 July 2013*. URL: www.pkulaw.cn/fulltext_form.aspx?Gid=bd068023482f0cccbdfb (visited on 14 January 2018).

Residence Act of Germany (2008): "Act on the Residence, Employment and Integration of Foreign Nationals in the Federal Republic of Germany (Gesetz über den Aufenthalt, die Erwerbstätigkeit und die Integration von Ausländern im Bundesgebiet) of 23 May 1949, in the version of 25 February 2008, last amended on 23 December 2014". In: *Bundesgesetzblatt* 1, 2008, pp. 162–214.

Rivas v. Napolitano (2013): *Hilario Rivas v. Janet Napolitano, No. 09-56843 (9th Cir. 2013)*. URL: cases.justia.com/federal/appellate-courts/ca9/09-56843/09-56843-2013-03-28.pdf (visited on 5 August 2018).

SAIC Regulatory Documents Review Annoucenment (2017): *Announcement of the State Administration for Industry and Commerce on Issuing the Results of the Review of Regulatory Documents* (工商总局关于公布规范性文件清理结果的公告), *issued on 8 November 2017*. URL: www.pkulaw.cn/fulltext_form.aspx?Gid=93709874b7bf5f82bdfb (visited on 14 January 2018).

Schengen Borders Code (2006): *Regulation (EC) No 562/2006 of the European Parliament and of the Council of 15 March 2006 Establishing a Community Code on the Rules Governing the Movement of Persons Across Borders (Schengen Borders Code)*. URL: eur-lex.europa.eu/LexUriServ/LexUriServ.do?uri=OJ:L:2006:105:0001:0032:EN:PDF (visited on 5 August 2018).

Schengen Borders Code (2016): *Regulation (EC) No 2016/399 of the European Parliament and of the Council of 9 March 2016 on a Union Code on the Rules Governing the Movement of Persons Across Borders (Schengen Borders Code)*. URL: eur-lex.europa.eu/legal-content/EN/TXT/PDF/?uri=CELEX:32016R0399 (visited on 5 August 2018).

Shanghai Economic Compensation Case (2015): *Appeal Case on Economic Compensation between Leng Hong and China HP Co., Ltd. Shanghai Branch (2015) Hu Er Zhong Min San (Min) Zhong Zi Di 1384 Hao* (冷虹与中国惠普有限公司上海分公司经济补偿金纠纷二审民事判决书（2015）沪二中民三（民）终字第1384号). URL: wenshu.court.gov.cn/content/content?DocID=4c1527e6-5dfd-49ae-af11-d80100fb8c1e (visited on 24 July 2018).

Shanghai Illegal Employment Case (2015): *First Instance Decision in the Administrative Case of New Global Electronics (Shanghai) Co., Ltd. against the Songjian Bureau of the Shanghai Municipal Public Security Bureau, Administrative Case Decision of the People's Court of Songjiang District of Shanghai City (2015) Song Xing Chu Zi Di 44 Hao* (原告纽播电子（上海）有限公司不服被告上海市公安局松江分局治安管理行政处罚决定一审行政判决书，上海市松江区人民法院行政判决书（2015）松行初字第44号). URL: wenshu.court.gov.cn/content/content?DocID=7052bf28-9713-4d1f-8574-634b0b0c0063 (visited on 15 May 2018).

Shanghai Personal Damage Compensation Case (2015): *Appeal Case on Compensation of Personal Damage between Li Shuaishuai and Shanghai General Fushi Refrigeration Equipment Co., Ltd. and Shanghai Business & Information College* (李帅帅诉上海通用富士冷机有限公司、上海工商信息学校人身损害赔偿纠纷案). URL: gongbao.court.gov.cn/Details/0a9888ee5ed65e5766b746b73b8913.html (visited on 27 June 2017).

Shenzhen Economic Compensation Dispute Case (2013): *Economic Compensation Dispute Case between Shenzhen Sharch Design Co., Ltd., and Martin Larronde* (深圳市尚合建筑设计有限公司诉Martin Larronde（马丁·劳伦德）经济补偿金纠纷案). URL: www . pkulaw . cn / case _ es / pfnl _ a25051f3312b07f3f22365687c1708de993db19920897166bdfb . html (visited on 27 March 2018).

Shenzhen Labour Dispute Case (2016): *Labour Dispute Case between James Hodgkiss and Shenzhen Airlines (2016) Yue 03 Min Zhong 16274 Hao* (James Hodgkiss与深圳航空有限责任公司劳动争议二审民事判决书（2016）粤03民终16274号). URL: wenshu.court.gov.cn/content/content?DocID=d9d6843a-5c71-477d-979a-a8510100671c (visited on 26 March 2018).

Shenzhen Labour Remuneration and Economic Compensation Case (2014): *Labour Remuneration and Economic Compensation Dispute Case between UMC Electronics (Shenzhen) Co., Ltd., UMC Electronics (Dongguan) Co., Ltd., and Okuyama Ken* (三和盛科技电子（深圳）有限公司、三和盛电子科技（东莞）有限公司与Okuyama Ken追索劳动报酬及经济补偿纠纷案). URL: www.pkulaw.cn/case_es/pfnl_a25051f3312b07f363ead25c4ae20584ad5b87b0d436511abdfb.html (visited on 27 March 2018).

Social Insurance Law (2010): *Social Insurance Law of the People's Republic of China* (中华人民共和国社会保险法), *promulgated on 28 October 2010 and entered into force on 1 July 2011*. URL: www . pkulaw . cn / fulltext _ form . aspx ? Gid = 83649bdaef86fe17bdfb (visited on 4 March 2019).

Spanish Foreign Nationals Law (2018): *Organic Law on the Rights and Freedoms of Foreign Nationals in Spain and their Social Integration (Ley Orgánica sobre derechos y libertades de los extranjeros en España y su integración social), adopted on 11 January 2000, last amended 4 September 2018*. URL: www.boe.es/eli/es/lo/2000/01/11/4/con (visited on 4 March 2019).

SPC Labour Remuneration Interpretation (2013): *Interpretation of the Supreme People's Court on Several Issues concerning the Application of Law in the Trial of Criminal Cases of Refusal to Pay Labour Remunerations* (最高人民法院关于审理拒不支付劳动报酬刑事案件适用法律若干问题的解释). URL: www.pkulaw.cn/fulltext_form.aspx?Gid=193347 (visited on 7 June 2017).

SPC Second Meeting Minutes (2005): *Minutes [by the Supreme People's Court] of the Second Meeting on National Foreign Related Commercial and Maritime Adjudication Work* (第二次全国涉外商事海事审判工作会议纪要). URL: www.pkulaw.cn/fulltext_form.aspx?Gid=78927 (visited on 26 June 2017).

SPC Work Dispute Cases Interpretation (2008): *Interpretations of the Supreme People's Court on Several Questions on the Application of the Law in the Trial of Work Dispute Cases* (最高人民法院关于审理劳动争议案件适用法律若干问题的解释). URL: www.pkulaw.cn/fulltext_form.aspx?Gid=111865 (visited on 26 March 2018).

SPC Work Dispute Cases Interpretation (2013): *Interpretations of the Supreme People's Court on Several Questions on the Application of the Law in the Trial of Work Dispute Cases (IV)* (最高人民法院关于审理劳动争议案件适用法律若干问题的解释（四））. URL: www.pkulaw.cn/fulltext_form.aspx?Gid=1ff9ffbccbff92b0bdfb (visited on 27 June 2017).

State Council Institutional Reform Decision (2018): *Decision of the First Session of the Thirteenth National People's Congress on the State Council Institutional Reform Proposal* (第十三届全国人民代表大会第一次会议关于国务院机构改革方案的决定), *adopted on 17 March 2018*. URL: www.pkulaw.cn/fulltext_form.aspx?Gid=338647c8fdce77a4bdfb (visited on 7 May 2018).

State Security Law (1993): *State Security Law of the People's Republic of China* (中华人民共和国国家安全法), *promulgated and entered into force on 22 February 1993*. URL: www.pkulaw.cn/fulltext_form.aspx?Gid=a849de1f54e52a13bdfb (visited on 4 March 2019).

State Security Law (2009): *State Security Law of the People's Republic of China* (中华人民共和国国家安全法), *promulgated and entered into force on 22 February 1993, last amended on 27 August 2009*. URL: www.pkulaw.cn/fulltext_form.aspx?Gid=22e0b4a025e2ab17bdfb (visited on 4 March 2019).

Strike Hard Decision (1983): "Decision Regarding Striking Hard Blows Against Criminal Activities (Excerpt) (中共中央关于严厉打击刑事犯罪活动的决定（节录））, promulgated on 25 August 1983". In: *Selected Readings of Important Documents Since the Third Plenary Session of the Eleventh Central Committee* (十一届三中全

会以来重要文献选读). Vol. 2, 1987. Beijing: People's Press (人民出版社), pp. 690–694.

Structural Reforms Explanations (2018): *Explanations on the Structural Reform Plans of the State Council* (关于国务院机构改革方案的说明)*, 13 March 2018*. URL: www.gov.cn/guowuyuan/2018-03/14/content_5273856.htm (visited on 26 March 2018).

Suqian Personal Damage Compensation Case (2014): *Appeal Case on Compensation of Personal Damage between Wang Jun and Jiangsu Qiangwei Rubber & Plastic Science and Technology Co., Ltd and Xuzhou College of Industrial Technology* (王俊诉江苏强维橡塑科技有限公司、徐州工业职业技术学院人身损害赔偿纠纷案). URL: gongbao.court.gov.cn/Details/834faec177fa6c26753185ed911a9f.html (visited on 27 June 2017).

U. K. Immigration Act (1971, 2016): *Immigration Act [of the United Kingdom], adopted on 28 October 1971, last amended on 12 May 2016*. URL: www.legislation.gov.uk/ukpga/1971/77/contents (visited on 4 March 2019).

UDHR (1948): "Universal Declaration of Human Rights, adopted and proclaimed by UN General Assembly Resolution 217 A (III) of 10 December 1948". In: *Refugee Survey Quarterly* 27.3, 2008, pp. 149–182.

United States Code of Federal Regulations (2018): *Code of Federal Regulations [of the United States of America] (2018)*. URL: www.govinfo.gov/app/collection/cfr/2018/ (visited on 4 March 2019).

United States Code of Laws (2017): *Code of Laws of the United States of America (2017)*. URL: www.govinfo.gov/app/collection/uscode/2017/ (visited on 4 March 2019).

Vienna Convention on Consular Relations (1963): *Vienna Convention on Consular Relations, done at Vienna on 24 April 1963*. URL: legal.un.org/ilc/texts/instruments/english/conventions/9_2_1963.pdf (visited on 4 March 2019).

Vienna Convention on the Law of Treaties (1969): *Vienna Convention on the Law of Treaties, done at Vienna on 13 May 1969*. URL: legal.un.org/ilc/texts/instruments/english/conventions/1_1_1969.pdf (visited on 4 March 2019).

Wages Composition Regulations (1990): *Regulations on the Composition of Gross Wages* (国家统计局关于工资总额组成的规定)*, published on and entered into force as of 1 January 1990*. URL: www.pkulaw.com/fulltext_form.aspx?Gid=4555 (visited on 7 June 2017).

Wholly Foreign-Owned Enterprises Law (2016): *Wholly Foreign-Owned Enterprises Law of the People's Republic of China* (中华人民共和国外资企业法)*, promulgated on 12 April 1986, last amended on 3 September 2016*. URL: www.pkulaw.cn/fulltext_form.aspx?Gid=565613090e841b27bdfb (visited on 5 January 2018).

Work Permit System Notice (2017): *Notice of the State Administration of Foreign Experts Affairs, the Ministry of Human Resources and Social Security, the Ministry of Foreign Affairs, and the Ministry of Public Security on Comprehensively Implementing a Work Permit System for Foreign Nationals in China* (国家外国专家局、人力资源社会保障部、外交部、公安部关于全面实施外国人来华工作许可制度的通知),

promulgated on 28 March 2017 and entered into force on 1 April 2017. URL: www.pkulaw.cn/fulltext_form.aspx?Gid=05e9adf3a8f1ddebbdfb (visited on 28 March 2018).

Work Study Measures (2007): *Administration Measures for Work-Study of Students at Universities and Colleges* (高等学校学生勤工助学管理办法)*, promulgated by the Ministry of Education and the Ministry of Civil Affairs on 26 June 2007*. URL: www.pkulaw.cn/fulltext_form.aspx?Gid=2c335ea790ec33a9bdfb (visited on 24 July 2018).

Yanbian Foreign Nationals Administration Regulations (2014): *Regulation on the Administration of Foreign Nationals in Yanbian Korean Autonomous Prefecture* (延边朝鲜族自治州外国人管理条例)*, promulgated and entered into force on 9 April 2014*. URL: www.pkulaw.cn/fulltext_form.aspx?Gid=17614831 (visited on 24 May 2017).

Yanbian Theft and Robbery Case (2017): *Enforcement Case on Theft and Robbery of Cui Qiang* (崔强盗窃罪、抢劫罪一案执行案). URL: www.pkulaw.cn/case_es/pfnl_a25051f3312b07f3f9ed2531ef98495b10f9f5a35a905c1abdfb.html (visited on 27 March 2018).

Yinhai Border Crossing Case (2014): *First Instance Decision in the Criminal Case of Wu Wenping Illegally Crossing the Border, Criminal Case Decision of the People's Court of Yinhai District of Beihai City in the Guangxi Zhuang Autonomous Region (2014) Yin Xing Chu Zi Di 34 Hao* (武文平偷越国境一案一审刑事判决书，广西壮族自治区北海市银海区人民法院刑事判决书（2014）银刑初字第34号). URL: wenshu.court.gov.cn/content/content?DocID=9e9309ac-0461-4724-beea-1e556bd4f6b3 (visited on 15 January 2018).

Yunnan Foreign Nationals Employment Regulations (1995): *Regulations on the Strengthening of the Administration of Employment of Foreign Nationals in Yunnan* (关于加强外国人在我省就业管理的有关规定)*, promulgated and entered into force on 20 March 1995*. URL: www.pkulaw.cn/fulltext_form.aspx?Gid=96a263e032c29f793900e816cd2355edbdfb (visited on 15 May 2018).

Zhejiang Labour Dispute Opinions (2009): *Opinions of the First Civil Division of the High Court of Zhejiang on Several Questions Regarding the Handling of Labour Dispute Cases* (浙江省高级人民法院民一庭关于审理劳动争议案件若干问题的意见)*, issued on 16 April 2009*. URL: www.pkulaw.cn/fulltext_form.aspx?Gid=27c6524202f3e1f5e3598c4d3f283e1ebdfb (visited on 26 March 2018).

B. Monographs, Articles in Periodicals, Edited Volumes and Reports

2011 Yearbook of Immigration Statistics (2012). Washington, D.C.: Department of Homeland Security Office of Immigration Statistics.

Ahl, Björn; Pilar Czoske (2016): "Migration, the Law and 'One Belt, One Road'". In: *Legal Dimensions of China's Belt and Road Initiative*. Ed. by Lutz-Christian Wolff; Chao Xi. Hong Kong: Wolters Kluwer, pp. 393–416.

Answers by Officials of the Ministry of Public Security to Journalists on the Implementation of the 'Exit–Entry Administration Law of the People's Republic of China' (公安部负责人就贯彻执行《中华人民共和国出境入境管理法》答记者问), *NPC Standing Committee Press Release* (1 July 2012). URL: www.npc.gov.cn/huiyi/cwh/1127/2012-07/01/content_1728616.htm (visited on 21 February 2017).

"As 'Two Sessions' Come Closer: 'Sanfei' Foreigners Extensively Searched (兩會期近深搜「三非」外國人)" (2007). In: *Oriental Daily News* (東方日報) 8 February (2007), A35.

Bakken, Børge (1993): "Crime, Juvenile Delinquency and Deterrence Policy in China". In: *The Australian Journal of Chinese Affairs* 30 (1993), pp. 29–58.

Baldwin, Robert; Martin Cave; Martin Lodge (2012): "Regulatory Failure". In: *Understanding Regulation: Theory, Strategy, and Practice*. 2nd ed. Oxford: Oxford University Press, pp. 68–82.

Beijing Bureau of Human Resources and Social Security (2018): *Matters Relating to the Alteration of Position and Employer for Foreigners*. URL: www.ebeijing.gov.cn/feature_2/WorkingInBeijing/ChangeOfEmploymentPermitInformation/t1126513.htm (visited on 28 March 2018).

"Beijing People's Government: Foreigners Free to Choose Hotels" (2003). In: *Beijing Review* 6 February (2003), p. 47.

Beijing Statistical Yearbook (北京统计年鉴) (2017). Beijing: Beijing Municipal Bureau of Statistics (北京市统计局).

Bennett, Gordon A. (1976): *Yundong: Mass Campaigns in Chinese Communist Leadership*. Berkeley: Center for Chinese Studies, University of California.

——— (1977): "China's Mass Campaigns and Social Control". In: *Deviance and Social Control in Chinese Society*. Ed. by Amy Auerbacher Wilson; Sidney L. Greenblatt; Richard W. Wilson. New York: Praeger, pp. 121–139.

Biddulph, Sarah (2007): *Legal Reform and Administrative Detention Powers in China*. Cambridge: Cambridge University Press.

——— (2017): "Justice at the Margins: Notions of Justice in the Punishment of Prostitution". In: *Justice: The China Experience*. Ed. by Flora Sapio et al. Cambridge: Cambridge University Press, pp. 312–355.

Biddulph, Sarah; Sean Cooney; Ying Zhu (2012): "Rule of Law with Chinese Characteristics: The Role of Campaigns in Lawmaking". In: *Law & Policy* 34.4 (2012), pp. 373–401.

Bodomo, Adams (2010): "The African Trading Community in Guangzhou: An Emerging Bridge for Africa–China Relations". In: *The China Quarterly* 203 (2010), pp. 693–707.

Border Control Department of the Ministry of Public Security (公安部边防管理局) (3 July 2008 a): *Exit and Entry Border Inspection General Stations and Subordinate Immigration Control Checkpoints* (出入境边防检查总站及下属出入境边防检查站). URL: www.mps.gov.cn/n2254996/n2254997/c3892969/content.html (visited on 3 January 2018).

——— (29 April 2008 b): *Introduction to Public Security Border Control* (公安边防简介). URL: www.mps.gov.cn/n2256217/n2256222/index.html (visited on 26 March 2018).

——— (2 May 2016 a): *Schematic Diagram of the Chinese Public Security Exit–Entry Administration System* (中国公安出入境管理系统示意图). URL: www.mps.gov.cn/n2254996/n2254997/c3892992/content.html (visited on 3 January 2018).

——— (2 May 2016 b): *Structure and Divison of Functions of the Chinese Public Security Exit–Entry Administration Authorities* (中国公安出入境管理机构设置与职责分工). URL: www.mps.gov.cn/n2254996/n2254997/c3892992/content.html (visited on 3 January 2018).

Bork-Hüffer, Tabea; Yuan Yuan-Ihle (2014): "The Management of Foreigners in China: Changes to the Migration Law and Regulations during the Late Hu–Wen and Early Xi–Li Eras and Their Potential Effects". In: *International Journal of China Studies* 5.3 (2014), pp. 571–597.

Brady, Anne-Marie (2009): "The Beijing Olympics as a Campaign of Mass Distraction". In: *The China Quarterly* 197 (2009), pp. 1–24.

Branigan, Tania (16 July 2009): *Africans Protest in China After Nigerian Dies in Immigration Raid*. URL: www.theguardian.com/world/2009/jul/16/china-african-protesters-immigration-raid (visited on 28 February 2018).

——— (19 June 2012): *Africans in China Protest After Death of Expat*. URL: www.theguardian.com/world/2012/jun/19/foreigners-protest-china-death-expat (visited on 28 February 2018).

Brea, Jennifer (26 September 2007): *Beijing Police Round Up and Beat African Expats*. URL: www.theguardian.com/world/2007/sep/26/china.internationalcrime (visited on 18 January 2018).

Bredeloup, Sylvie (2012): "African Trading Post in Guangzhou: Emergent or Recurrent Commercial Form?" In: *African Diaspora* 5 (2012), pp. 27–50.

Briefing of the 12th Session of the Standing Committee of the 6th National People's Congress (第六届全国人民代表大会常务委员会第十二次会议简况), *NPC Law Committee Press Release* (8 December 2000). URL: www.npc.gov.cn/npc/cwhhy/content_5946.htm (visited on 6 March 2015).

Briefing of the 13th Session of the Standing Committee of the 6th National People's Congress (第六届全国人民代表大会常务委员会第十三次会议简况), *NPC Law Committee Press Release* (8 December 2000). URL: www.npc.gov.cn/npc/cwhhy/content_5947.htm (visited on 6 March 2015).

Cai, Yongshun (2000): "Between State and Peasant: Local Cadres and Statistical Reporting in Rural China". In: *China Quarterly* 163 (2000), pp. 788–805.

Cai, Yongshun (2014): *State and Agents in China: Disciplining Government Officials*. Stanford: Stanford University Press.

Cao, Yin (18 May 2012): *Beijing Gets Stricter with Welcome*. URL: usa.chinadaily.com.cn/weekly/2012-05/18/content_15326765.htm (visited on 18 March 2018).

Capacity Building For Migration Management in China (2008). International Labour Organization. URL: www.ilo.org/beijing/what-we-do/projects/WCMS_141650/lang--en/index.htm (visited on 12 September 2018).

Capacity Building For Migration Management in China Project Phase II (2012). International Labour Organization. URL: www.ilo.org/beijing/what-we-do/projects/WCMS_195963/lang--en/index.htm (visited on 12 September 2018).

Cell, Charles P. (1981): "The Utility of Mass Mobilization Campaigns in China: A Partial Test of the Skinner-Winckler Compliance Model". In: *Organizational Behavior in Chinese Society*. Ed. by Sidney L. Greenblatt; Richard W. Wilson; Amy Auerbacher Wilson. New York: Praeger, pp. 121–139.

"Central Committee Issues 'Plan to Deepen the Reform of the Party and State Institutions' (中共中央印发《深化党和国家机构改革方案》)" (2018). In: *Ideological and Political Work Studies* (思想政治工作研究) 4 (2018), pp. 8–19.

Chan, Elim; Andreas Schloenhardt (2007): "North Korean Refugees and International Refugee Law". In: *International Journal of Refugee Law* 19.2 (2007), pp. 215–245.

Chang, Robert S. (2018): "Whitewashing Precedent: From the Chinese Exclusion Case to Korematsu to the Muslim Travel Ban Cases". In: *Case Western Reserve Law Review* 68.4 (2018), pp. 1183–1222.

Changsha Says No to 'Black Foreign Teachers', Clears Up 'Sanfei' For 50 Days (长沙对'黑外教'说No 为期50天的清理'三非') (20 November 2013). URL: www.chinanews.com/edu/2013/11-20/5524219.shtml (visited on 6 February 2018).

Chen Changfu (陈昌福) (2010): "A Brief Introduction to the 'Nationality Law of the People's Republic of China': Focusing on the Problem of Dual Citizenship of Overseas Chinese (《中华人民共和国国籍法》简介——以华侨'双重国籍'问题为中心)". In: *Journal of Shanghai Institute of Socialism* (上海市社会主义学院学报) 6 (2010), pp. 9–15.

Chen Ji (陈冀); Li Shu (李舒); Ji Ming (季明) (2008): "New Issues in Administrating Foreign Nationals (外国人管理新课题)". In: *Outlook Weekly* (瞭望) 10 (2008), pp. 60–61.

Chen Libo (陈立波) (2010): "Analysis of the Type of Action of Border Inspection (出入境边防检查的行为模式分析)". In: *Tribune of Political Science and Law* (政法论坛) 6 (2010), pp. 85–94.

Chen Xiang (陈翔) (2009): "Guangzhou Strictly Investigates Illegal Entry, Illegal Stay and Illegal Employment (广州严查非法入境非法居留非法就业)". In: *Guangzhou Daily* (广州日报) 21 May (2009), A04.

Cheng Xianshu (程贤淑) (2013): "Suburban Residents Will Be Able to Apply for Exit–Entry Documents Nearby – Awaiting Regulations on Industry Sectors and Time Limits for Employment of International Students (郊区居民将可就近办理出入境证件——留学生就职行业和期限有待规定)". In: *Shanghai Evening Post* (新闻晚报) 9 January (2013), A1–12.

Chetail, Vincent (2013): "International Legal Protection of Migrants and Refugees: Ghetto or Incremental Protection? Some Preliminary Comments". In: *Migration, Human Rights, and Development: A Global Anthology*. Ed. by Anne T. Gallagher. New York: International Debate Education Association, pp. 139–148.

China Promotes Opening Up and Foreign Relations by Enacting Norms on Exit–Entry Administration (中国立法规范出入境管理促进对外开放和交往), *NPC Press Release* (2 July 2012). URL: www.npc.gov.cn/huiyi/cwh/1127/2012-07/02/content_1728589.htm (visited on 21 February 2017).

China Statistical Yearbook (中国统计年鉴) (n. d.). Beijing: National Bureau of Statistics of China (中华人民共和国国家统计局).

China Statistical Yearbook (中国统计年鉴) (2017). Beijing: National Bureau of Statistics of China (中华人民共和国国家统计局).

China to Enact Law to Solve the Problem of Foreign Nationals Illegally Entering, Residing, and Being Employed in China (中国将立法解决外国人非法入境非法居留非法就业问题), *NPC Standing Committee Press Release* (26 December 2011). URL: www.npc.gov.cn/huiyi/cwh/1124/2011-12/26/content_1683101.htm (visited on 6 March 2015).

China's Projected Regulations to Introduce the Collection of Fingerprints in Exit–Entry Administration (我国拟立法规定将指纹采集引入出境入境管理), *NPC Standing Committee Press Release* (26 December 2011). URL: www.npc.gov.cn/huiyi/cwh/1124/2011-12/26/content_1683140.htm (visited on 6 March 2015).

Cholewinski, Ryszard (2012): "International Labour Migration". In: *Foundations of International Migration Law*. Ed. by Brian Opeskin; Richard Perruchoud; Jillyanne Redpath-Cross. Cambridge: Cambridge University Press, pp. 283–311.

Chung, Jae Ho (2001): "Reappraising Central–Local Relations in Deng's China: Decentralization, Dilemmas of Control, and Diluted Effects of Reform". In: *Remaking the Chinese State: Strategies, Society, and Security*. Ed. by Chien-min Chao; Bruce J. Dickson. London: Routledge, pp. 46–75.

Clarke, Donald C. (1985): "Concepts of Law in the Chinese Anti-Crime Campaign". In: *Harvard Law Review* 98 (1985), pp. 1890–1908.

Clauses of the Exit–Entry Administration Law (Draft) and Explanations (出境入境管理法（草案）条文及草案说明), *NPC Press Release* (31 December 2011). URL: www.npc.gov.cn/huiyi/cwh/1124/2011-12/31/content_1685108.htm (visited on 21 February 2017).

Committee on Economic, Social and Cultural Rights, ed. (13 May 2005): *Consideration of Reports Submitted by States Parties under Articles 16 and 17 of the Covenant – Concluding Observations of the Committee on Economic, Social and Cultural Rights: People's Republic of China (including Hong Kong and Macao) (E/C.*

12/1/Add. 107). URL: documents-dds-ny.un.org/doc/UNDOC/GEN/G05/422/45/PDF/G0542245.pdf (visited on 24 July 2018).

Currie, Carolyn (2006): "A New Theory of Financial Regulation: Predicting, Measuring and Preventing Financial Crises". In: *The Journal of Socio-Economics* 35 (2006), pp. 48–71.

Decision by the CPC Central Committee to Further Strengthen and Improve Public Security Work (2003) (18 November 2003): *Decision by the CPC Central Committee to Further Strengthen and Improve Public Security Work* (中共中央关于进一步加强和改进公安工作的决定). URL: cpc.people.com.cn/GB/64184/64186/66691/4494638.html (visited on 15 August 2017).

Delegates of the Standing Committee of the National People's Congress Propose the Elimination of 'Dual Nationality' (全国人大常委会委员建言消除'双重国籍'), *NPC Press Release* (27 April 2012). URL: www.npc.gov.cn/huiyi/cwh/1126/2012-04/27/content_1719882.htm (visited on 12 February 2016).

Deng Weijin (邓伟进); Xiang Bo (向波) (2004): "Bringing the 'Sanfei' Foreigners Under Control (整治老外'三非')". In: *Changsha Evening News* (长沙晚报) 11 February (2004).

Deng Xiaoping (邓小平) (1994 a): *Selected Works of Deng Xiaoping* (邓小平文选). Vol. 2. Beijing: People's Press (人民出版社).

——— (1994 b): *Selected Works of Deng Xiaoping* (邓小平文选). Vol. 3. Beijing: People's Press (人民出版社).

Deng Ying (邓莹); Dong Qingqian (董庆前); Miao Lü (苗绿) (2015): "Spreading the Word About Ten Years of Efficient Visa Measures to Push Forward the Facilitation of China's Visa Policy (将十年有效签证措施推广，推动我国签证政策便利化)". In: *Annual Report on Chinese International Migration (2015)* (中国国际移民报告(2015)). Ed. by Wang Huiyao (王辉耀); Liu Guofu (刘国福); Miao Lü (苗绿). Beijing: Social Sciences Academic Press (社会科学文献出版社), pp. 51–65.

Dimitrov, Martin K. (2009): *Piracy and the State: The Politics of Intellectual Property Rights in China*. New York: Cambridge University Press.

Ding Rui (丁瑞); Jiang Boren (姜博仁) (2013): "On Countermeasures for the Handling of 'Sanfei Cases' (论'三非案件'处置对策)". In: *Legal System and Society* (法制与社会) 1.1 (2013), pp. 76, 113.

Ding Saier (丁赛尔) (2014): *Regulation of Labour Migration: Legal and Institutional Choice* (外国人入境工作管理：法律和制度选择). Beijing: Legal Press (法律出版社).

Du Wanbian (杜万鞭) (2013): "On Countermeasures to Problems Raised by 'Three Illegals' Foreigners (论'三非'问题综合治理的对策)". In: *Journal of Yunnan Police Officer Academy* (云南警官学院学报) 2 (2013), pp. 40–44.

Du Yixing (杜以星) (2012): "Several Practical Issues Concerning Measures on Exit Restrictions in Civil Procedures (民事诉讼中限制出境措施的若干实务问题)". In: *Journal of Law Application* (法律适用) 4 (2012), pp. 81–85.

Dutton, Michael R. (1995): “Dreaming of Better Times: ‘Repetition with a Difference’ and Community Policing in China”. In: *Positions: East Asia Cultures Critique* 3.2 (1995), pp. 418–447.

——— (2005): *Policing Chinese Politics: A History*. Durham: Duke University Press.

E-Commerce Law (Draft) (2017) (7 November 2017): *Request for Comments on the E-Commerce Law (Draft for Second Deliberation)* (电子商务法（草案二次审议稿）征求意见). URL: www.pkulaw.cn/fulltext_form.aspx?Db=protocol&Gid=6cde170abe8178280dfa3146df38f528bdfb (visited on 5 January 2018).

Economic and Social Council, ed. (2004): *Commission on Human Rights: Report on the Sixtieth Session (15 March–23 April 2004) (E/2004/23, E/CN.4/2004/127)*. URL: documents-dds-ny.un.org/doc/UNDOC/GEN/G04/162/00/PDF/G0416200.pdf (visited on 24 July 2018).

Edin, Maria (March 2003): “State Capacity and Local Agent Control in China: CCP Cadre Management from a Township Perspective”. In: *The China Quarterly* 173 March (2003), pp. 35–52.

Exit–Entry Administration Law (Draft) (2011) (31 December 2011): *Exit–Entry Administration Law (Draft) Clauses and Draft Explanation* (出境入境管理法（草案）条文及草案说明)*, NPC Standing Committee Press Release*. URL: www.npc.gov.cn/huiyi/cwh/1124/2011-12/31/content_1685108.htm (visited on 6 March 2015).

Exit–Entry Administration Law Draft: Establishing a Unified Data Administration Platform to Enable Data Sharing (出入境管理法草案: 建立统一管理信息平台实现信息共享)*, NPC Standing Committee Press Release* (24 April 2012). URL: www.npc.gov.cn/huiyi/cwh/1126/2012-04/24/content_1718646.htm (visited on 6 March 2015).

Explanations Regarding the ‘Law of the People’s Republic of China on the Administration of the Exit and Entry of Foreign Nationals (Draft)’ (关于《中华人民共和国外国人入出境管理法（草案）》的说明)*, NPC Press Release* (26 August 1985). URL: www.npc.gov.cn/wxzl/gongbao/2000-12/26/content_5001704.htm (visited on 9 January 2018).

Fang Shirong (方世荣); Shi Youqi (石佑启) (2011): *Administrative Law and Administrative Litigation Law* (行政法与行政诉讼法). 2nd ed. Beijing: Peking University Press (北京大学出版社).

Feng Lei (丰雷) (2006): “Almost Half of Foreign Nationals in Guangdong are Long-Term Residents of Shenzhen: First Round of Foreign Nationals in Shenzhen Were Granted ‘Green Card’ in First Half of the Year, Illegal Entered, Illegal Staying, Illegal Employed Foreign Nationals Will be Focus of Crack Down (全省近半外国人常住深圳：深圳首批外国人‘绿卡’上半年发放，将重点打击非法入境、居住、就业的外国人)”. In: *Southern Metropolis Daily* (南方都市报) 28 March (2006), A08.

Foreign Affairs Committee of the National People’s Congress Launches Investigation in Qingdao on the Amendment of the Exit–Entry Administration Law (外事委在青岛开展出境入境管理法修改立法调研)*, NPC Standing Committee Press Release* (6 May

2011). URL: www.npc.gov.cn/huiyi/cwh/1124/2011-05/06/content_1682737.htm (visited on 6 March 2015).

Gilles, Angelo (2015): "The Social Construction of Guangzhou as a Translocal Trading Place". In: *Journal of Current Chinese Affairs* 44.4 (2015), pp. 17–47.

Greenblatt, Sidney Leonard (1977): "Campaigns and the Manufacture of Deviance in Chinese Society". In: *Deviance and Social Control in Chinese Society*. Ed. by Amy Auerbacher Wilson; Sidney L. Greenblatt; Richard W. Wilson. New York: Praeger, pp. 82–120.

Guangzhou Further Steps Up Crackdown on Illegal Foreigners (22 July 2015). URL: www.globaltimes.cn/content/933245.shtml (visited on 1 March 2019).

Guangzhou Statistical Yearbook (广州统计年鉴) (2017). Beijing: Guangzhou Municipal Bureau of Statistics (广州市统计局).

Guangzhou Yearbook (广州年鉴) (1983–2013). Guangzhou: Chinese Communist Party Guangzhou Committee (中共广州市委员会).

Guide to Interpretation and Application of the 'Exit–Entry Administration Law of the People's Republic of China' (《中华人民共和国出境入境管理法》释义及实用指南) (2012). Beijing: Chinese Democratic Legal System Press (中国民主法制出版社).

Haojiang Office of Shantou Municipal Bureau of Public Security (汕头市公安局濠江分局) (1 July 2017): *Haojiang District Launches Campaign to Clear Up and Correctively Punish 'Sanfei' Foreigners* (濠江区开展清理整治'三非'外国人行动). URL: www.haojiang.gov.cn/%E6%94%BF%E5%8A%A1%E5%85%AC%E5%BC%80/%E5%B7%A5%E4%BD%9C%E5%8A%A8%E6%80%81/%E6%94%BF%E5%8A%A1%E8%A6%81%E9%97%BB/2017-1/%E6%BF%A0%E6%B1%9F%E5%8C%BA%E5%B1%95%E5%BC%80%E6%B8%85%E7%90%86%E6%95%B4%E6%B2%BB%E2%80%9C%E4%B8%89%E9%9D%9E%E2%80%9D%E5%A4%96%E5%9B%BD%E4%BA%BA%E8%A1%8C%E5%8A%A8.aspx (visited on 8 August 2017).

Haugen, Heidi Østbø (2012): "Nigerians in China: A Second State of Immobility". In: *International Migration* 50.2 (2012), pp. 65–80.

——— (2013 a): "China's Recruitment of African University Students: Policy Efficacy and Unintended Outcomes". In: *Globalisation, Societies and Education* 11 (2013), pp. 315–334.

——— (2013 b): "African Pentecostal Migrants in China: Marginalization and the Alternative Geography of a Mission Theology". In: *African Studies Review* 56.1 (2013), pp. 81–102.

He Chunzhong (2016): "Ministry of Public Security: Mainland and Hong Kong Police Joined Forces to Track Down About 3 000 Illegal Foreign Immigrants (公安部：大陆香港警方联手查获非法入境外籍人员近3000人)". In: *China Youth Daily* (中国青年报) 31 March (2016).

HE, Xin Frank (2003): "Sporadic Law Enforcement Campaigns as a Means of Social Control: A Case Study from a Rural-Urban Migrant Enclave in Beijing". In: *Columbia Journal of Asian Law* 17.1 (2003), pp. 121–145.

HEILMANN, Sebastian (2008): "Policy Experimentation in China's Economic Rise". In: *Studies in Comparative International Development* 43 (2008), pp. 1–26.

——— (2011): "Policy-Making through Experimentation: The Formation of a Distinctive Policy Process". In: *Mao's Invisible Hand*. Ed. by Sebastian HEILMANN; Elizabeth J. PERRY. Cambridge (Massachusetts): Harvard University Press, pp. 62–101.

——— (2016): *Das politische System der Volksrepublik China*. 3rd ed. Wiesbaden: Springer VS.

HEILMANN, Sebastian; Elizabeth J. PERRY (2011): "Embracing Uncertainty: Guerrilla Policy Style and Adaptive Governance in China". In: *Mao's Invisible Hand*. Ed. by Sebastian HEILMANN; Elizabeth J. PERRY. Cambridge (Massachusetts): Harvard University Press, pp. 1–29.

HOLLIFIELD, James F.; Philip L. MARTIN; Pia M. ORRENIUS (2014): "The Dilemmas of Immigration Control". In: *Controlling Immigration: A Global Perspective*. Ed. by James F. HOLLIFIELD; Philip L. MARTIN; Pia M. ORRENIUS. 3rd ed. Stanford: Stanford University Press, pp. 3–34.

HU Jianmiao (胡建淼) (2003): *Administrative Law* (行政法学). Beijing: Peking University Press (北京大学出版社).

HU Zhangwei (胡张炜); ZHAO Wei (赵伟); CHEN Wanning (陈婉宁) (2011): "New Exploration on Patterns of Foreign Nationals Management Work of Local Police Stations (派出所外国人管理工作模式新探)". In: *Public Security Science Journal – Journal of Zhejiang Police College* (公安学刊——浙江警察学院学报) 4 (2011), pp. 79–83.

HUANG, Guangzhi (2018): "Policing Blacks in Guangzhou: How Public Security Constructs Africans as Sanfei". In: *Modern China* 48.4 (2018), forthcoming.

HUMAN RIGHTS COMMITTEE, ed. (27 August 2001): *Consideration of Reports Submitted by States Parties under Article 40 of the Covenant – Concluding Observations of the Human Rights Committee: Democratic People's Republic of Korea (CCPR/CO/72/PRK)*. URL: documents-dds-ny.un.org/doc/UNDOC/GEN/G01/443/78/PDF/G0144378.pdf (visited on 24 July 2018).

HUMANS RIGHTS AND EQUAL OPPORTUNITY COMMISSION, ed. (11 May 1998): *Those Who've Come Across the Seas: Detention of Unauthorised Arrivals*. URL: humanrights.gov.au/sites/default/files/document/publication/h5_2_2.pdf (visited on 14 November 2017).

Interpretation and Application of the 'Administrative Litigation Law of the People's Republic of China' (《中华人民共和国行政诉讼法》解读与实用) (2015). Beijing: Legal Press (法律出版社).

Interpretation of the 'Exit–Entry Administration Law of the People's Republic of China' (《中华人民共和国出境入境管理法》释义) (2012). Beijing: People's Public Security University of China Press (中国人民公安大学出版社).

Interpretation to the Exit–Entry Administration Law of the People's Republic of China (中华人民共和国出境入境管理法释义) (2012). Beijing: Legal Press (法律出版社).

Jiang Bixin (江必新) (2015): *Comprehensive Application and Practical Guide of the Administrative Litigation Law of the People's Republic of China* (中华人民共和国行政诉讼法理解使用与实务指南). Beijing: Legal Press (法律出版社).

Jiang Jianyun (蒋剑云) (2013): "On Conflicts of Current Entry and Exit Administration Laws: An Analysis of Provisions (现行出入境管理法律冲突问题研究——以法律条文为分析对象)". In: *Journal of Fujian Police College* (福建警察学院学报) 1 (2013), pp. 66–79.

Ke Liangdong (柯良栋) (2014): *Explanations and Practical Guide to the Public Security Administration Punishments Law* (治安管理处罚法释义与实务指南). Beijing: People's Public Security University of China Press (中国人民公安大学出版社).

Ke Xiaojun (柯小军); Ou Yuwei (欧育伟) (27 February 2004): *Guangdong Police Thoroughly Investigates 'Sanfei' Foreigners, Deports 107 Individuals* (广东警方全面清查'三非'外国人遣送107人出境). URL: www.chinanews.com/n/2004-02-27/26/406899.html (visited on 18 March 2018).

Kim, Harris H. (2003): "Ethnic Enclave Economy in Urban China: the Korean Immigrants in Yanbian". In: *Ethnic and Racial Studies* 26.5 (2003), pp. 802–828.

"Korean Media Points to High Numbers of Illegally Entering, Illegal Staying and Illegally Employed Foreign Nationals in China: 'Sanfei' Foreigners Weigh on China Mind (韩媒体指出非法入境、非法滞留、非法就业在中国的外国人很多: '三非'外国人让中国伤脑筋)" (2006). In: *Global Times* (三秦都市报) 31 July (2006), p. 6.

Lan, Shanshan (2015): "State Regulation of Undocumented African Migrants in China: A Multi-Scalar Analysis". In: *Journal of Asian and African Studies* 50.3 (2015), pp. 289–304.

——— (2017 a): *Mapping the New African Diaspora in China: Race and the Cultural Politics of Belonging*. New York: Routledge.

——— (2017 b): "'China Gives and China Takes': African Traders and the Nondocumenting States". In: *Focaal – Journal of Global and Historical Anthropology* 77 (2017), pp. 50–62.

Lavener, Susan (1996): "'Be Prepared': Dealing With Labour Issues in Representative Offices". In: *China Law & Practice* 10.3 (1996), pp. 37–40.

Laws for Legal Immigration in the 27 EU Member States (2009). International Organization of Migration. URL: publications.iom.int/system/files/pdf/iml_16.pdf (visited on 5 August 2018).

Legislative Affairs Commission of the Standing Committee of the National People's Congress of the People's Republic of China, ed. (1987): *The Laws of the People's Republic of China: 1979–1982*. Beijing: Foreign Languages Press.

Li Jianguo (李建国) (2013): "On the System of Measures and Legal Remedies of Foreign Parties to Proceedings (外籍当事人的处置与救济制度研究)". In: *Policing Studies* (公安研究) 12 (2013), pp. 40–44, 57.

Li, Lianjing (2001): "Support for Anti-Corruption Campaigns in Rural China". In: *The Journal of Contemporary China* 10.29 (2001), pp. 573–586.

Li Ping (李平); Lei Jing (雷经) (2010): "Guangxi Police Strikes Hard Against Illigals and Criminals in Border Areas – 'Sanfei' Foreigners Repatriated Without Exception (广西警方重拳打击边境地区违法犯罪 '三非' 外国人一律遣送回国)". In: *Modern Life Daily* (当代生活报) 12 March (2010), p. 18.

Li Wei (李玮) (2013): "On Controlling 'Sanfei' Foreigners under the New Law (论新法下的 '三非' 外国人管控)". In: *Heihe Journal* (黑河学刊) 4 (2013), pp. 75–76.

Li Youbiao (李佑标) (2012): "On the Legal Status of Immigration Prohibition (试论阻止出入境的法律定位)". In: *Journal of Chinese People's Armed Police Forces Academy* (武警学院学报) 28.1 (2012), pp. 34–37.

Li, Zhigang; Michal Lyons; Alison Brown (2012): "China's 'Chocolate City': An Ethnic Enclave in a Changing Landscape". In: *African Diaspora* 5 (2012), pp. 51–72.

Liebman, Benjamin L. (2005): "Watchdog or Demagogue? – The Media in the Chinese Legal System". In: *Columbia Law Review* 105.1 (2005), pp. 1–157.

——— (2011): "A Return to Populist Legality? Historical Legacies and Legal Reform". In: *Mao's Invisible Hand*. Ed. by Sebastian Heilmann; Elizabeth J. Perry. Cambridge (Massachusetts): Harvard University Press, pp. 165–200.

Lin Yicong (林艺聪) (2007): "On the Application of the Administrative Licence Law on the Issuance of Visa to Foreign Nationals by Public Security Organs (公安机关颁发外国人签证使用《行政许可法》之辨)". In: *Administrative License and Government Regulation* (行政许可与政府管理). Ed. by Liu Heng (刘恒). Beijing: Peking University Press (北京大学出版社), pp. 131–136.

Liu, Alan P. L. (1971): *Communications and National Integration in Communist China*. Berkeley: University of California Press.

Liu Guixiang (刘贵祥) (2011): *Some Questions Regarding Trial Mechanisms and Law Application in Foreign Related Commercial Cases* (关于涉外商事审判机制与法律适用的几个问题). URL: www.ccmt.org.cn/showexplore.php?id=4146 (visited on 22 May 2016).

Liu, Guofu (2007): *The Right to Leave and Return and Chinese Migration Law*. Leiden: Martinus Nijhoff.

——— (2009): "Changing Chinese Migration Law: From Restriction to Relaxation". In: *International Migration & Integration* 10 (2009), pp. 311–333.

——— (2011): *Chinese Immigration Law*. Farnham: Ashgate.

Liu Guofu (刘国福) (2006): *Migration Law: A Study of the Right to Leave and Return* (移民法：出入境权研究). Beijing: China Economic Publishing House (中国经济出版社).

——— (2008): "The Latest Development of Immigration Law: On the Transformation of China's Emmigration and Immigration Administration Law (移民法的最新发展——兼论中国出入境管理法的改造和重塑)". In: *Journal of Henan Administrative Institute of Politics and Law* (河南省政法管理干部学院学报) 5 (2008), pp. 46–58.

Liu Guofu (刘国福) (2015): “China’s New Situation of International Migration, New Challenges and New Investigations (中国国籍移民的新形势、新挑战和新探索)”. In: *Journal of Shandong University (Philosophy and Social Sciences)* (山东大学学报（哲学社会科学版）) 1 (2015), pp. 45–54.

Liu Hongxing (刘红星); Teng Li (滕莉) (2013): “The Legal Nature of the Prohibition to Exit or Enter (不准出入境的法律性质探析)”. In: *Journal of Chinese People’s Armed Police Forces Academy* (武警学院学报) 29.1 (2013), pp. 47–50.

Liu Jianchang (刘建昌); Li Xinglin (李兴林) (2012): *Practical Essentials for the Investigation of Public Security Administrative Cases (Violation of Public Security, Exit–Entry and Border Administration)* (公安行政案件调查实务要领（违反治安、出入境和边防管理编）). Beijing: People’s Public Security University of China Press (中国人民公安大学出版社).

Liu Xiaosen (柳晓森) (2003): “At the Plenary Session of the Central Political and Legal Affairs Commission Liu Gan Emphasises to Adhere to ‘Yanda’ Policy and to Strengthen Public Security Administration (罗干在中央社会治安综合治理委员会全会上指出 坚持‘严打’方针 加强治安管理)”. In: *People’s Daily* (人民日报) 13 November (2003), p. 1.

Liu Xiaoyuan (刘晓源); Li Liangwan (李良万) (2017): “Reflection and Reconstruction of the Constitutive Elements of Administrative Penalties: From ‘Three Elements’ to ‘Three Stages’ (应受行政处罚行为构成要件反思与重构——从‘三要件’到‘三阶层’)”. In: *Journal of Fujian Jiangxia University* (福建江夏学院学报) 1 (2017), pp. 53–63.

Liu Xunzhi (刘训智) (2009): “Development and Evolvement of the Modern Chinese Nationality Law (近代中国国籍法的发展与演变)”. In: *Business Culture* (商业文化) 8 (2009), pp. 219–220.

Lu Hongsheng (陆洪生) (2013): “‘Yanda’ – 1983 (‘严打’·一九八三)”. In: *Cuiyuan* (翠苑) 4 (2013), pp. 87–94.

Lu Hua (卢华); Li Conghua (李从花); Zhao Han (赵菡) (2006): “Guangxi Police Launch Special Action to Clear Up ‘Sanfei’ Foreigners (西安警方展开清理‘三非’外国人专项整治行动)”. In: *Sanqin Dushibao* (三秦都市报) 25 July (2006), A05.

Lu Jing (陆晶); Zhang Chi (张驰) (2013): “Constructing a New Pattern of Enforcement Cooperation in the Empty Strucutre of Da wai guan — Taking the Beijing-Tianjin-Hebei Area as Example (大外管放空格局中新型执法合作模式的建构——以京津冀地区为例)”. In: *Journal of Chinese People’s Public Security University, Social Science Edition* (中国人民公安大学学报, 社会科学版) 4 (2013), pp. 142–149.

Luo Bin (罗斌); Xu Rui (徐瑞); Wu Hao (吴皓) (16 November 2007): *Wuhan Clears Up ‘Sanfei’ Foreigners, Two Filipino Maids Punished for the First Time* (我市清理‘三非’外国人 首次处罚两名非法菲佣). URL: www.cnhan.com/gb/content/2007-11/16/content_840937.htm (visited on 6 February 2018).

Luo Haocai (罗豪才); Zhan Zhongle (湛中乐), eds. (1999): *Administrative Law* (行政法学). Beijing: Peking University Press (北京大学出版社).

Luo Shi (罗仕) (21 July 2015): *Guangzhou Investigates on 'Sanfei' Foreigners, Will Set up Electronic Archive on House Renting* (广州清查'三非'外国人 将建立出租屋电子档案). URL: news.ycwb.com/2015-07/21/content_20429752.htm (visited on 13 February 2018).

Lyons, Michal; Alison Brown; Zhigang Li (2012): "In the Dragon's Den: African Traders in Guangzhou". In: *Journal of Ethnic and Migration Studies* 38.5 (2012), pp. 869–888.

Ma Yina (马祎娜) (2015): "China Relaxes Threshold for 'Green Card' – Which Foreign Nationals May Apply (中国放宽'绿卡'门槛 哪些外籍人士可以申办)". In: *People's Daily Overseas Editon* (人民日报海外版) 21 November (2015), p. 6.

Mahony, Tarrant (2015): *Foreign Investment Law in China: Regulation, Practice and Context*. Beijing: Tsinghua University Press (清华大学出版社).

Manion, Melanie (2004): *Corruption by Design: Building Clean Government in Mainland China and Hong Kong*. Cambridge (Massachusetts): Harvard University Press.

Mao Lei (毛磊) (22 November 2001): *Building Up a Chinese 'Green Card' System, Citizens to Apply for Passport with ID Card or Household Register: Six Major Reforms in Chinese Exit–Entry Administration* (建立中国'绿卡'制度，公民凭身份证、户口簿申领护照：我国出入境管理作出六项重大改革). URL: www.people.com.cn/GB/shizheng/3586/20011122/611143.html (visited on 13 January 2019).

——— (19 May 2004): "Attacking Offences and Crimes, Punishing Illegal Immigration: Summary on Campaigns Launched by National Public Security Authorities to Attack Offences and Crimes as well as Illegal Immigration in the Border Regions (打击违法犯罪 严惩偷渡活动——全国公安机关开展打击边境地区违法犯罪活动暨反偷渡专项行动综述)". In: *People's Daily* (人民日报) 19 May (19 May 2004), p. 14.

"Mid of May to End of August: Beijing Joins Forces to Clean Up 'Sanfei' Foreigners. Almost 200 000 Foreign Nationals Each Day (5月中旬至8月底　北京集中清理'三非'外国人　每日实有近20万外国人)" (2012). In: *People's Daily* (人民日报) 15 February (2012), p. 4.

Migrationsbericht des Bundesamtes für Migration und Flüchtlinge im Auftrag der Bundesregierung: Migrationsbericht 2015 (2016). Berlin: Bundesministerium des Innern.

Min Zheng (闵政) (2011): "Scientifically Establishing Indicators, Elaborating towards Results, Manifesting a Rule-of-Law Spirit – Interpretation of the Ministry of Public Security of the 'Opinions Concerning the Reform of the Quality Appraisal System for Law Enforcement' (科学设立指标 发挥导向作用 彰显法治精神——公安部《关于改革完善执法质量考评制度的意见》解读)". In: *China Police Daily* (人民公安报) 25 February (2011), p. 4.

Ministry of Public Security: Chinese Police Currently Launches a New Round of Special Actions Against Illegal Immigration (公安部：中国警方正开展新一轮的反偷渡专项行动) (12 November 2003). URL: mil.news.sina.com.cn/2003-11-12/162349.html (visited on 14 February 2018).

MINZNER, Carl F. (2009): "Riots and Cover-Ups: Counterproductive Control of Local Agents in China". In: *University of Pennsylvania Journal of International Law* 31 (2009), pp. 53–123.

NANTOU OFFICE OF THE PUBLIC SECURITY BUREAU OF THE CITY OF ZHONGSHAN (中山市公安局南头分局) (5 September 2017): *Measures of the Town of Nantou on Rewarding Reports of 'Sanfei' Foreigners* (南头镇举报 '三非' 外国人奖励办法). URL: www.sohu.com/a/169665817_99956686 (visited on 30 August 2018).

NI Xing (倪星) (2014): "How Local Government Campaign-Style Governance Becomes Routinised – An Analysis Based on the 'Qingwu' campaign of the Supervision Office of S City (地方政府的运动式治理是如何走向 '常规化' 的? ——基于 S 市市监局 '清无' 专项行动的分析)". In: *Journal of Public Administration* (公共行政评论) 2 (2014), pp. 70–96.

Nottebohm Case (1955) (1955): "Nottebohm Case (Liechtenstein v. Guatemala), Second Phase Judgment". In: *International Court of Justice Reports of Judgments, Advisory Opinions and Orders* 131 (1955), pp. 4–27.

NOWAK, Manfred (1993): *UN Covenant on Civil and Political Rights: CCPR Commentary*. 2nd ed. Kehl: Engel.

OHCHR WORKING GROUP ON ARBITRARY DETENTION, ed. (24 October 2002): *Report of the Working Group on Arbitrary Detention (E/CN.4/2003/8/Add. 2)*. URL: documents-dds-ny.un.org/doc/UNDOC/GEN/G02/160/28/PDF/G0216028.pdf (visited on 14 November 2017).

——— ed. (15 December 2003): *Report of the Working Group on Arbitrary Detention (E/CN.4/2004/3)*. URL: documents-dds-ny.un.org/doc/UNDOC/GEN/G03/170/72/PDF/G0317072.pdf (visited on 14 November 2017).

OPESKIN, Brian; Richard PERRUCHOUD; Jillyanne REDPATH-CROSS (2012): *Foundations of International Migration Law*. Cambridge: Cambridge University Press.

Over 900,000 Foreigners Work in Chinese Mainland in 2016 (16 April 2017). URL: chinadaily.com.cn/china/2017-04/16/content_28949481.htm (visited on 2 October 2018).

PAN Xianglong (潘向泷); QIN Zonggen (秦总根) (2011): "On the Mechanisms of Prevention and Control of Crimes Committed by Foreign Nationals in Guangzhou (广州外国人犯罪与防控机制研究)". In: *Journal of Political Science and Law* (政法学刊) 5 (2011), pp. 84–88.

PAN Xiaotian (潘笑天) (19 May 2012): "'Sanfei' Foreigners: Beijing does not Welcome You ('三非' 外国人: 北京不欢迎)". In: *People's Daily Overseas Edition* (人民日报海外版) 19 May (19 May 2012), p. 4.

PEERENBOOM, Randall (2002): *China's Long March Toward Rule of Law*. Cambridge: Cambridge University Press.

PERRUCHOUD, Richard (2012): "State Sovereignty and Freedom of Movement". In: *Foundations of International Migration Law*. Ed. by Brian OPESKIN; Richard PERRUCHOUD; Jillyanne REDPATH-CROSS. Cambridge: Cambridge University Press, pp. 123–151.

Perry, Elizabeth J. (2011): "From Mass Campaigns to Managed Campaigns: 'Constructing a New Socialist Countryside'". In: *Mao's Invisible Hand*. Ed. by Sebastian Heilmann; Elizabeth J. Perry. Cambridge (Massachusetts): Harvard University Press, pp. 30–61.

Pieke, Frank N. (2012): "Immigrant China". In: *Modern China* 38.1 (2012), pp. 40–77.

Police Station in Shenzhen Posts English Notice: Very Effective, Staff Members Say (深圳一派出所发全英文公告 工作人员：效果很好 (20 December 2013). URL: news.china.com/social/1007/20160605/22811780.html (visited on 18 March 2018).

Polizeiliche Kriminalstatistik Bundesrepublik Deutschland: Berichtsjahr 2011 (2012). Wiesbaden: Bundeskriminalamt.

Tabulation on the 2010 Population Census of the People's Republic of China (中国2010年人口普查资料) (2010). Beijing: Population Census Office of the State Council (国务院人口普查办公室).

Problem of Sanfei Foreigners Emerges in Yanbian, Taking into Custody Those Who Cover up Their Real Identify (延边三非外国人问题突出 隐瞒真实身份逃避监管) (25 May 2012). URL: www.chinanews.com/fz/2012/05-25/3914374.shtml (visited on 6 February 2018).

Public Security Bureau of the City of Jinhua (金华市公安局) (8 April 2015): *Public Security Bureau of the City of Jinhua Issues Measures on Rewarding Reports of Activities of 'Sanfei' Individuals* (金华公安颁布举报三非人员行为奖励办法). URL: www.jhga.gov.cn/news/info.aspx?i=135163 (visited on 30 August 2018).

Qiu Hongjie (邱红杰) (12 November 2003): *Ministry of Public Security: Chinese Police Currently Launches a New Round of Special Actions Against Illegal Immigration* (公安部：中国警方正开展新一轮的反偷渡专项行动). URL: news.sina.com.cn/c/2003-11-12/17101106362s.shtml (visited on 14 February 2018).

Qiu, Quanlin (17 July 2009): *Guangzhou to Increase Checks on Illegal Immigration*. URL: chinadaily.com.cn/china/2009-07/17/content_8439196.htm (visited on 18 March 2018).

Report by the Law Committee of the National People's Congress on Amendments of the 'Exit–Entry Administration Law of the People's Republic of China (Draft)' (全国人民代表大会法律委员会关于《中华人民共和国出境入境管理法（草案）》修改情况的汇报), *NPC Press Release* (24 April 2012). URL: www.npc.gov.cn/wxzl/gongbao/2012-11/08/content_1745220.htm (visited on 27 June 2017).

Report of the Foreign Affairs Committee of the National People's Congress on the Results of the Consideration of the Proposal Handed over at the 1st Session of the 10th National People's Congress (全国人大外事委员会关于第十届全国人民代表大会第一次会议主席团交付审议的代表提出的议案审议结果的报告), *NPC Foreign Affairs Committee Press Release* (16 December 2003). URL: www.npc.gov.cn/wxzl/gongbao/2004-02/12/content_5327938.htm (visited on 7 July 2015).

Report of the Foreign Affairs Committee of the National People's Congress on the Results of the Consideration of the Proposal Handed over at the 5st Session of the 10th National People's Congress (全国人大外事委员会关于第十届全国人民代表大会

第五次会议主席团交付审议的代表提出的议案审议结果的报告), *NPC Foreign Affairs Committee Press Release* (28 October 2007). URL: www.npc.gov.cn/npc/oldarchives/cwh/common/zw.jsp@hyid=0210030______&label=wxzlk&id=373811&pdmc=hywj.htm (visited on 7 July 2015).

Report of the Law Committee of the National People's Congress on the Consultation Results on the 'Law of the People's Republic of China on the Administration of the Exit and Entry of Foreign Nationals (Draft)' (全国人民代表大会法律委员会对《中华人民共和国外国人入出境管理法（草案）》审议结果的报告), *NPC Law Committee Press Release* (13 November 1985). URL: www.law-lib.com/fzdt/newshtml/20/20050720174551.htm (visited on 6 March 2015).

Report on Opinions to Handle Proposals Submitted by Deputies of the 1st Session of the 10th National People's Congress (关于第十届全国人民代表大会第一次会议代表提出议案处理意见的报告), *NPC Foreign Affairs Committee Press Release* (14 March 2003). URL: www.npc.gov.cn/wxzl/gongbao/2003-04/04/content_5312201.htm (visited on 20 February 2017).

Research Group of the National People's Congress Launches Investigation in Zhuhai on the Amendment of the Exit–Entry Administration Law (全国人大调研组到珠海开展出入境管理法修改立法调研), *NPC Standing Committee Press Release* (9 December 2011). URL: www.npc.gov.cn/huiyi/cwh/1124/2011-12/09/content_1682899.htm (visited on 6 March 2015).

Research Institute for Prosecution Theory of the Supreme People's Procuratorate (最高人民检察院检察理论研究所); Cai Yaqi (蔡雅奇) (2013): "Deportation From the Viewpoint of Theoretical Analysis and Practical Application (从理论分析与实践使用看驱逐出境)". In: *Jiancha Ribao* (检察日报) 9 January (2013), p. 3.

van Rooij, Benjamin (2002): "Implementing Chinese Environmental Law through Enforcement: The Shiwu Xiao and Shung Dabiao Campaigns". In: *Implementation of Law in the People's Republic of China*. Ed. by Jianfu Chen; Yuwen Li; Jan Michiel Otto. The Hague: Kluwer Law International, pp. 149–178.

——— (2006 a): *Regulating Land and Pollution in China: Lawmaking, Compliance, and Enforcement; Theory and Cases*. Leiden: Leiden University Press.

——— (2006 b): "Implementation of Chinese Environmental Law: Regular Enforcement and Political Campaigns". In: *Development and Change* 37.1 (2006), pp. 57–74.

——— (2009): "The Politics of Law in China: Enforcement Campaigns in the Post-Mao PRC". Working Paper.

——— (2012): "The People's Regulation: Citizens and Implementation of Law in China". In: *Columbia Journal of Asian Law* 25.2 (2012), pp. 116–179.

——— (2016): "The Campaign Enforcement Style: Chinese Practice in Context and Comparison". In: Cheltenham: Edward Elgar.

Rosenfield, Harry N. (1955): "Consular Non-Reviewability: A Case Study in Administrative Absolutism". In: *American Bar Association Journal* 41.12 (1955), pp. 1109–1112, 1181–1183.

SAINSON, Camille; Gaston CLUZEL (1910): "La Nationalité dans le Nouveau Droit Chinois". In: *Journal du Droit International Privé* 37 (1910), pp. 407–421.

SAITO, Natsu Taylor (2003): "The Enduring Effect of the Chinese Exclusion Cases: The Plenary Power Justification for On-Going Abuses of Human Rights". In: *Asian American Law Journal* 10.13 (2003), pp. 13–36.

SHANGHAI BUREAU OF HUMAN RESOURCES AND SOCIAL SECURITY (2018): *Instructions for Applying for Foreigner's Switching Employer*. URL: www.12333sh.gov.cn/200912333/2009english/resources/instructions/ep/200911/t20091109_1102213.shtml (visited on 28 March 2018).

SHEARER, Ivan; Brian OPESKIN (2012): "Nationality and Statelessness". In: *Foundations of International Migration Law*. Ed. by Brian OPESKIN; Richard PERRUCHOUD; Jillyanne REDPATH-CROSS. Cambridge: Cambridge University Press, pp. 93–122.

SIMANSKI, John; Lesley M. SAPP (2012): *Immigration Enforcement Actions: 2011*. Washington, D. C.: Department of Homeland Security Office of Immigration Statistics.

SONG, Lili (2018): "China and the International Refugee Protection Regime: Past, Present, and Potentials". In: *Refugee Survey Quarterly* 37.2 (2018), pp. 139–161.

SONG Quancheng (宋全成) (2015): "Current Situation, Remaining Issues, and Countermeasures Concerning Illegal Foreign Immigrants in China (非法外国移民在中国的现状、症结与对策)". In: *Journal of Shandong University (Philosophy and Social Sciences)* (山东大学学报（哲学社会科学版）) 1 (2015), pp. 55–63.

STIGLITZ, Joseph (2009): "Regulation and Failure". In: *New Perspectives on Regulation*. Cambridge: The Tobin Project, pp. 11–24.

STUMPF, Juliet P. (2013): "Two Profiles of Crimmigration Law: Criminal Deportation and Illegal Migration". In: *Globalisation and the Challenge to Criminology*. Ed. by Francis PAKES. London: Routledge, pp. 91–109.

SUN Chunying (孙春英) (21 December 2001): *Jia Chunying Proposes to Vigorously and Soundly Reform the Public Security Administrative Review System* (贾春旺提出积极稳妥地改革公安行政审批制度). URL: news.sohu.com/29/30/news147483029.shtml (visited on 26 February 2018).

SUN Jianbao (孙建保) (2011): "Analysis on Understanding and Application of the Term 'guo (bian) jing' in the Clause Headings of Criminal Offenses (刑法罪名中'国（边）境'的表述理解及司法适用探析)". In: *Journal of Law Application* (法律适用) 12 (2011), pp. 54–58.

SUN Zhihui (孙智慧) (2013): *The Legal System and Practice in Entry and Exit Administration* (出入境管理法律与实践). Beijing: China University of Political Science and Law Press (中国政法大学出版社).

TAN Xiaochang (谭晓畅); WEN Yangqin (温扬勤) (2006): "City-Wide Corrective Punishment Action Launched: 'Sanfei' Foreigners Will Be Repatriated (全市开展专项整治行动'三非'外国人将被遣送)". In: *Nanfang Daily* (南方日报) 22 June (2006), p. C04.

TANG Huangfeng (唐皇凤) (2007): "Normal-State Society and Campaign-Style Governance – A Study on the 'Strike Hard' Policy in Public Security Control of China's

Society (常态社会与运动式治理——中国社会治安治理中的 '严打' 政策研究)". In: *Open Times* (开放时代) 3 (2007), pp. 115–129.

Tang Xianxing (唐贤兴); Yu Yamei (余亚梅) (2009): "The Dilemma of Campaign-Style Law Enforcement and Governance in China (运动式执法与中国治理的困境)". In: *Journal of Xinjiang University (Philosophy, Humanities & Social Sciences)* (新疆大学学报（哲学、人文社会科学报）) 37.2 (2009), pp. 43–49.

Tanner, Harold M. (1999): *Strike Hard! Anti-Crime Campaigns and Chinese Criminal Justice 1979–1985*. Ithaka: Cornell University.

Tanner, Murray S. (1994): "The Erosion of Communist Party Control over Lawmaking in China". In: *The China Quarterly* 138 (1994), pp. 381–403.

——— (2000): "State Coercion and the Balance of Awe: The 1983–1986 'Stern Blows' Anti-Crime Campaign". In: *The China Journal* 44 (2000), pp. 93–125.

——— (2005): "Campaign-Style Policing in China and Its Critics". In: *Crime, Punishment, and Policing in China*. Ed. by Børge Bakken. Lanham: Rowman & Littlefield, pp. 171–188.

Tanner, Murray S.; Eric Green (2007): "Principals and Secret Agents: Central versus Local Control Over Policing and Obstacles to 'Rule of Law' in China". In: *The China Quarterly* 191 (2007), pp. 644–670.

Task Group to the 'Research Report on Foreign Nationals Management Services of the City of Guangzhou' (《广州市外国人管理服务研究报告》课题组) (2014): "Innovating Foreign Nationals Management Service Research of Guangzhou (创新广州市外国人管理服务研究)". In: *Urban Insight* (城市观察) 2 (2014), pp. 114–122.

The National Public Security Organ's Conference on Foreign Nationals Management Work Was Held in Beijing on the 15th (全国公安机关外国人管理工作会议 15 日在北京举行)*, Central People's Government Press Release* (16 January 2007). URL: www.gov.cn/gzdt/2007-01/16/content_497908.htm (visited on 15 August 2017).

Tian Hongjie (田宏杰) (2003): "Difficult Issues in Applying the Offence of Organising Illegal Border Crossing (组织他人偷越国（边）境罪法律适用疑难问题研究)". In: *Journal of Law Application* (法律适用) 7 (2003), pp. 21–26.

Transport Department of Xinjiang Uygur Autonomous Region (新疆维吾尔自治区交通运输厅) (16 December 2014): *Zulpiye Adbuqadir* (祖丽菲娅·阿布都卡德尔). URL: www.xjjt.gov.cn/article/2014-12-16/art24893.html (visited on 11 April 2018).

Trevaskes, Susan (2002): "Courts on the Campaign Path in China: Criminal Court Work in the 'Yanda 2001' Anti-Crime Campaign". In: *Asian Survey* 42.5 (2002), pp. 673–693.

——— (2003): "Yanda 2001: Form and Strategy in a Chinese Anti-Crime Campaign". In: *The Australian and New Zealand Journal of Criminology* 36.3 (2003), pp. 272–292.

UN High Commissioner for Refugees, ed. (26 February 1999): *UNHCR's Revised Guidelines on Applicable Criteria and Standards Relating to the Detention of Asylum-*

Seekers. URL: www.refworld.org/docid/3c2b3f844.html (visited on 14 November 2017).

UN Human Rights Committee, ed. (23 July 1990): *van Alphen v. the Netherlands (Communication No. 305/1988)*. URL: www.refworld.org/cases,HRC,525414304.html (visited on 14 November 2017).

Vohra, Shyla (2007): "Detention of Irregular Migrants and Asylum Seekers". In: *International Migration Law: Developing Paradigms and Key Challenges*. Ed. by Ryszard Cholewinski; Richard Perruchoud; Euan MacDonald. The Hague: T.M.C. Asser, pp. 49–70.

Wang Afang (王阿方); Zhang Yuguang (玉光); Li Zhe (李喆) (2010): "Exploration of a New Foreign Nationals Management System in Guangdong (外管工作新机制的广东探索)". In: *People's Police* (人民公安) 6 (2010), pp. 15–17.

Wang, Alex L. (2018): "Symbolic Legitimation and Chinese Environmental Reform". In: *Environmental Law* 48 (2018), pp. 699–760. URL: ssrn.com/abstract=3052010 (visited on 20 December 2019).

Wang Chunye (王春业) (4 2017): "Developing a Negative-List Mode of the Scope of Acceptance of Administrative Reconsideration Cases (行政复议受案范围负面清单模式之建构)". In: *Studies in Law and Business (ZUEL Law Journal)* (法商研究) 4 (2017).

Wang Fangyi (王芳宜) (2017): "New Regulations on Unpermitted and Unlicenced Businesses Put into Place (无证无照经营新规施行)". In: *Brilliance* (光彩) 10 (2017), pp. 14–15.

Wang, Jun; Stephen Siu Yu Lau (2008): "Forming Foreign Enclaves in Shanghai: State Action in Globalization". In: *Journal of Housing and the Built Environment* 23.2 (2008), pp. 103–118.

Wang Mei (王妹) (26 April 2012): "Ministry of Public Security: Border Provinces and Districts Will Establish Repatriation Camps for Foreign Nationals (公安部：边境省区等将建'三非'外国人遣返场所)". In: (26 April 2012). URL: news.jcrb.com/jxsw/201204/t20120426_849819.html (visited on 31 January 2018).

Wang Yanbin (王艳斌) (2011): "Study on the Problem of 'Sanfei' Vietnamese Citizens at the Chinese Border – From the Perspective of the City of Chongzuo (中国边境'三非'越南公民问题研究——以崇左市为视角)". In: *Journal of Guangxi Police Academy* (广西警官高等专科学校学报) 5 (2011), pp. 69–72.

Weaver, Matthew (10 July 2008): *China Kills Five Muslim 'Militants' in Olympic Crackdown*. URL: www.theguardian.com/world/2008/jul/10/china.religion (visited on 22 January 2018).

Wedeman, Andrew (2004): "The Intensification of Corruption in China". In: *The China Quarterly* 180 (2004), pp. 895–921.

Wei Qi (魏琪); Zhu Xudong (朱旭东) (2009): "Study of the Reform of the Chinese Exit–Entry Administration System (中国公安出入境管理体制改革研究)". In: *Journal of Chinese People's Public Security University, Social Science Edition* (中国人民公安大学学报, 社会科学版) 5 (2009), pp. 31–36.

Weissbrodt, David, ed. (2008): *The Human Rights of Non-Citizens*. Oxford: Oxford University Press.

Wong, Kam C. (2012): *Police Reform in China*. Boca Raton: CRC Press.

Wu Chu (9 November 2011): "New Lessons in International Migration Administration (国际移民管理新课题)". In: *People's Daily* (人民日报) 9 November (9 November 2011), p. 23.

Wu, Fulong; Klaire Webber (2004): "The Rise of 'Foreign Gated Communities' in Beijing: Between Economic Globalization and Local Institutions". In: *Cities* 21.3 (2004), pp. 203–213.

Wu Gaosheng (吴高盛) (2015): *Explanations and Practical Guide to the Administrative Reconsideration Law of the People's Republic of Chins* (《中华人民共和国行政复议法》释义及实用指南). Beijing: Chinese Democratic Legal System Press (中国民主法制出版社).

Wu Guangzhen (武广震); Yang Ying (杨鹰) (2011): "The Problem of Illegal Immigration, Illegal Stay, and Illegal Employment of Foreign Nationals in Liaoning Province and Prevention Measures (辽宁省外国人非法入境、非法居留、非法就业问题及防控对策)". In: *Heihe Journal* (黑河学刊) 7 (2011), pp. 36–37.

Wu Guangzhen (武广震); Zhang Jian (张剑); Yan Wanhong (闫万鸿) (2008): "The Problem of Crimes Committed by 'Sanfei' Foreigners ('三非' 外国人违法犯罪问题)". In: *China Criminal Police* (中国刑事警察) 5 (2008), pp. 16–17.

Wu Xi (吴喜) (2013): "Administration of and Countermeasures against 'Sanfei' Foreigners at the Yunnanese Part of the Chinese–Myanmarese Border Region (中缅边境地区云南段 '三非' 人员管理及应对)". In: *Journal of Yunnan Police Officer Academy* (云南警官学院学报) 5 (2013), pp. 33–37.

Wu Xingchun (吴兴春) (2013): "On the Current Situation of the Problem of 'Sanfei' Foreigners in China and Countermeasures (我国 '三非' 外国人问题的现状和对策)". In: *Journal of Yunnan Police Officer Academy* (云南警官学院学报) 3 (2013), pp. 47–52.

Xie Huaxing (谢华兴); Guan Xuanxuan (管萱萱) (2010): "Investigation Group of Provincial Public Security Department Visits Dongguan for Investigation: Check Ups of 'Sanfei' Certain (省公安厅检查组到莞检查督导 查处 '三非' 工作受肯定)". In: *Guangzhou Daily* (广州日报) 12 August (2010), DA21.

Xin Chunying (信春鹰), ed. (2014): *Interpretation of the Administrative Litigation Law of the People's Republic of China* (中华人民共和国行政诉讼法释义). Beijing: Legal Press (法律出版社).

Xing Hongfei (邢鸿飞) et al. (2016): *Administrative Law Monograph* (行政法专论). Beijing: Legal Press (法律出版社).

Xu Min (许敏) (2008): "Analysis of Governmental Measures against the 'Sanfei Problem' ('三非问题' 的政府对策分析)". In: *The South of China Today* (今日南国) 3 (2008), pp. 9, 16.

Xu Tian (徐恬) (29 May 2012): "Report 'Sanfei' Foreigners: Investigate the Truth to Receive a Reward (举报 '三非' 外国人 查证属实可获奖励)". In: *Shenzhen Economic Daily* (深圳商报) (29 May 2012).

Ying Songnian (应松年) (2012): *Tutorial on the Administrative Penalty Law)* (行政处罚法教程). Beijing: Legal Press (法律出版社).

Yong Bin (永斌); Zhi Yong (智勇) (15 August 2016): *Dalingshan: Initiating the Campaign to Clear Up 'Sanfei' Foreigners* (大岭山：打响清理 '三非' 外国人专项行动). URL: news.sun0769.com/town/ms/201608/t20160815_6812856.shtml (visited on 8 August 2017).

Yu, Frederick T. C. (1967): "Campaigns, Communications, and Development in China". In: *Communication and Change in the Developing Countries*. Ed. by Daniel Lerrer; Wilbur Schramm. Honolulu: East-West Center Press, pp. 195–215.

Yu Qun (于群); Ma Shuncheng (马顺成) (2012): *Application and Rules of Administrative Compulsory Measures of Public Security Organs* (公安行政强制的使用与规范). Beijing: People's Public Security University of China Press (中国人民公安大学出版社).

Zeng Bin (曾斌); Cheng Hua (程华) (2011): *Practical Guide and Case Analysis on the Application of the 'Administrative Compulsion Law' by Public Security Authorities* (公安机关使用《行政强制法》实务指导与案例评析). Beijing: Qunzhong (群众出版社).

Zeng Wei (曾伟); Liu Jianchang (刘建昌) (2005): "Short Discussion on Strengthening Foreign Nationals Management of Local Public Security Bureaus (浅论加强公安派出所的外国人管理)". In: *Journal of Guangxi Police Academy* (广西警官高等专科学校学报) 1 (2005), pp. 5–9.

Zhang Chunsheng (张春生) (1999): *Interpretation of the Administrative Reconsideration Law of the People's Republic of China* (中华人民共和国行政复议法释义). Legal Press (法律出版社).

Zhang Huide (张惠德) (2011): "On Foreign Nationals Management Under the Idea of Information-Guided Policing (论情报主导警务理念下的外国人管理)". In: *Journal of Chinese People's Public Security University, Social Science Edition* (中国人民公安大学学报, 社会科学版) 6 (2011), pp. 101–107.

Zhang Huide (张惠德); Liu Hongbin (刘宏斌); Zeng Fanjing (曾范敬) (2014): "Study on the Administrative Coordination Mechanisms of Foreign Nationals Management in China (在华外国人管理行政协调机制研究)". In: *The Journal of Yunnan Administration College* (云南行政学院学报) 5 (2014), pp. 105–110.

Zhang Jianguo (张建国) (2008): "Historical Development and Feature Changes of China's Institutions to Attract Talent (我国引智机构的历史沿革和变化特点)". In: *International Talent* 国际人才交流 9 (2008).

Zhang, Li (2008): "Ethnic Congregation in an Globalizing City: The Case of Guangzhou, China". In: *Cities* 25 (2008), pp. 383–395.

Zhang Moning (张墨宁) (2012): "Foreign Nationals in Beijing: Disposed of and Valued (老外在北京: 被清理与被尊重)". In: *South Reviews* (南风窗) 13 (2012), pp. 30–32.

ZHANG Rui (张睿) (2013): "Short Analysis of the Actual Foreign Population Managment of Public Security Organs: Against the Practical Background of the New 'Exit–Entry Administration Law' (浅析公安机关外国人实有人口管理——以新《出境入境管理法》为实践背景)". In: *Legal System And Society* (法制与社会) 7.3 (2013), pp. 195–196.

ZHANG Rui (张蕊) (2012): "The Flourishing Life of Beijing's 'Sanfei' Foreigners on the Eve of Control (管控前夜, '三非' 老外的京漂生活)". In: *Bai Xing Sheng Huo* (百姓生活) 6 (2012), pp. 37–39.

ZHANG Xingxiang (张兴祥) (2003): *Theory and Practice of the Chinese Administrative Licence Law* (中国行政许可法的理论和实务). Beijing: Peking University Press (北京大学出版社).

ZHANG Xuejun (张学军) (2011): "The Systematised Connections between the Republican Government and the Overseas Chinese Community (民国政府与海外华侨社会的制度化联系)". In: *Theory Horizon* (理论界) 12 (2011), pp. 66–68.

ZHANG, Yi (5 August 2016): *Health Certificate Steps Reduced for Foreigners*. URL: chinadaily.com.cn/china/2016-08/05/content_26352183.htm (visited on 12 January 2019).

ZHOU, Guanghui (2010): "Towards Good Government: Thirty Years of Administrative Reforms in China". In: *The Reform of Governance*. Ed. by Keping YU. Leiden: Brill, pp. 137–180.

ZHOU, Min; Shabnam SHENASI; Tao XU (2016): "Chinese Attitudes toward African Migrants in Guangzhou, China". In: *International Journal of Sociology* 46.2 (2016), pp. 141–161.

ZHOU Xueguang (周雪光) (2012): "The Mechanisms of Campaign-Style Governance: The Logic of Chinas National Governance System Revisited (运动型治理机制：中国国家治理的制度逻辑再思考)". In: *Open Times* (开放时代) 9 (2012), pp. 105–125.

ZHU, Guobin; Rohan PRICE (2013): "Chinese Immigration Law and Policy: A Case of 'Change Your Direction, or End Up Where You Are Heading'?" In: *Columbia Journal of Asian Law* 26.1 (2013), pp. 1–28.

ZHU Jingao (朱金高) (2015): "Restricting Exit: A New Regulation on Execution Measures on Individuals (限制出境：一种对人执行的新规)". In: *Journal of Political Science and Law* (政法论丛) 6 (2015), pp. 144–151.

ZHUANG Huining (庄会宁) (2007): "How Many 'Sanfei' Foreigners are There After All? ('三非' 外国人究竟有多少)". In: *People's Police* (人民公安) 5 (2007), p. 24.

ZHUANG Qinghong (庄庆鸿); XU Wenmiao (许文苗); XU Xiaotong (徐霄桐) (23 May 2012): "Legal Experts Note Heated Debate as Beijing Cleans Up 'Sanfei' Foreigners – Foreign Nationals Don't Enjoy 'Super-National Treatment' in China (北京清查 '三非' 外国人引来热议,法学专家称——在华外国人没有 '超国民待遇')". In: *China Youth Daily* (中国青年报) (23 May 2012), p. 3.

ZOU, Mimi (2016): *Regulating 'Illegal Work' in China*. Working Paper 6. United Nations Research Institute for Social Development.